The
Turnpike Road System
in England
1663-1840

The
Turnpike Road System in England
1663-1840

WILLIAM ALBERT

CAMBRIDGE
AT THE UNIVERSITY PRESS
1972

Published by the Syndics of the Cambridge University Press
Bentley House, 200 Euston Road, London NW1 2DB
American Branch: 32 East 57th Street, New York, N.Y.10022

© Cambridge University Press 1972

Library of Congress Catalogue Card Number: 78-163062

ISBN: 0 521 08221 8

Printed in Great Britain by
Willmer Brothers Limited, Birkenhead, England

Contents

Maps

Charts

Preface

The pioneering works on turnpike trusts in England were written at the beginning of this century by the Webbs and W. T. Jackman, and although a number of local studies have been undertaken subsequently no serious attempt has been made to reappraise their work on a national scale. Since they wrote, economic historians have become concerned with new problems, mainly those relating to the dynamics of economic development. These early studies largely ignore or fail to deal adequately with these questions. Furthermore, many original trust documents, which the authors did not have access to, have become available in local record offices throughout the country. For the above reasons it is both necessary and possible to re-examine the development and management of the turnpike road system and its significance prior to and during the Industrial Revolution. However, any attempt to present a nationwide survey must in some respects dull the rich fabric of local history, and this study is no exception. I only hope that this book may incite local historians to correct my errors and oversights and thereby extend our knowledge of the development of the turnpike trusts.

The following study covers the years from the formation of the first turnpike authority in 1663 to 1840, when the turnpike trusts began to decline in the face of railway competition. In the first chapter the roads are considered in relation to the entire transport network in the seventeenth century; the economic conditions which were instrumental in bringing about improvement are discussed, as well as the importance of transport as a factor of economic growth. Chapter 2 is concerned with the legislative development of the turnpike trust device, and Chapter 3, based on maps drawn with reference to the individual turnpike acts, provides a detailed picture of the pattern of trust development. Chapters 4 and 7 deal with methods and relative success of trust administration and repair respectively. Chapter 5 is concerned with the financing of the turnpike trusts and Chapter 6 with the relationship between trust formations and the rate of interest. The main criterion for assessing the effectiveness of the trusts is whether the facilities which they provided contributed towards lowering the cost of land transport, and this question is taken up in the final chapter. As it is felt that little new information can be added at this stage to the already voluminous literature on coaching, this subject has not been dealt with in this study.

In order to avoid confusion place names are given, where possible, in their modern form.

Norwich, 1971   W. I. A.

Acknowledgements

I owe my greatest debt of thanks to Professor A. H. John, without whose constant advice and guidance the thesis upon which this book is based could never have been written. I would also like to thank Dr R. G. Wilson who read and re-read the manuscript and made many valuable suggestions and Professor A. S. Milward whose advice and encouragement proved invaluable. The Central Research Fund of the University of London provided a generous travel grant which enabled me to visit the local record offices, and I would like to thank the staffs of those offices for their kind assistance. I am grateful to Professor S. F. C. Milsom and Anthony Rowland for their help with the legal considerations relative to turnpike securities. Carol Roberts assisted me in preparing and executing the computer work, and Paul Hardman and Stephen Greenwald helped me compile some of the data. I owe special thanks to Dr D. K. Aldcroft for his most helpful comments, to David Bailey, Roy Hay, John Ginarlis, and Shman Monet for their criticisms and advice, and to Margaret Haddon who typed the manuscript.

The author and publisher are grateful to the following for permission to reproduce copyright material: to J. M. Dent & Sons Ltd, and E. P. Dutton & Co., Ltd, for permission to quote from *A Tour through the Whole Island of Great Britain* by Daniel Defoe, introduction by D. C. Browning and G. D. H. Cole, Everyman's Library edition; to the Clarendon Press, Oxford for permission to use extracts from *The Industrial Revolution 1760–1839* by T. S. Ashton; to Harvard University Press for extracts from *American Railroads and the Transformation of the Ante-Bellum Economy* by A. Fishlow; to the Athlone Press for extracts from *Studies in the Industrial Revolution* by L. S. Pressnell; to the London School of Economics for permission to quote from *English Local Government: The Story of the King's Highway* by Sidney and Beatrice Webb; to the Gloucestershire Records Office for permission to reproduce the *Colliers Letter to the Turnpike*; and to Longmans for permission to use extracts from *Origins of the Industrial Revolution* by M. W. Flinn.

FOR MY PARENTS

Abbreviations

J. H. of C.	*Journals of the House of Commons*
B.P.P.	*British Parliamentary Papers*
Econ. Hist. Rev.	*The Economic History Review*
Beds. CRO	Bedford County Record Office
Birm. Ref. Lib.	Birmingham Reference Library
Bucks. RO	Buckinghamshire Record Office
Cambs. RO	Cambridgeshire Record Office
Fins. Lib.	Finsbury Public Library
Glouces. RO	Gloucestershire Records Office
Hal. Cent. Lib.	Halifax Central Library
H. of L. RO	House of Lords Record Office
Hunts. CRO	Huntingdonshire County Record Office
Ips. and E.Suf. RO	Ipswich and East Suffolk Record Office
Ken. Pub. Lib.	Kensington Public Library
Kent AO	Kent Archives Office
Lancs. RO	Lancashire Record Office
Leics. RO	Leicestershire Record Office
Lincs. AO	Lincolnshire Archives Office
Man. Lib. of Loc. His.	Manchester Library of Local History
Mid. CRO	Great London Council Record Office (Middlesex Records)
Norf. & Norw. RO	Norfolk and Norwich Record Office
Northam. RO	Northamptonshire Record Office
Notts. CRO	Nottingham County Record Office
Oxon. CRO	Oxfordshire County Record Office
Salop RO	Shropshire Record Office
Shef. Cent. Lib.	Sheffield Central Library
Staffs. RO	Staffordshire Record Office
War. CRO	Warwickshire County Record Office
West Rid. CRO	West Riding County Record Office (Wakefield)
Wm. Salt Lib.	William Salt Library (Stafford)
Wilts. RO	Wiltshire Record Office
Worcs. RO	Worcestershire Record Office

Introduction

In recent years studies of economic history, especially of industrial revolutions, have been greatly influenced by the problems faced by modern developing nations. Economic historians have been given increasingly to preface their studies with statements calling attention to the significance of the economic history of the industrialized countries for understanding and dealing with the problems of present day economic development. In the prologue of his recent book, Mathias points out, 'In many senses, all nations concerned with economic growth at the present time are treading the path Britain first set foot on in the eighteenth century.'[1] Supple has argued that there are many similarities between conditions in seventeenth- and eighteenth-century Britain and those in modern developing nations, and that therefore a close study of how Britain was able to achieve economic growth will prove of practical value today.[2] More broadly, Cameron has claimed that 'historical experience can be a valuable guide for both theory and policy',[3] and further, that 'There are "lessons of history" as abstract from time and place and almost as ineluctable in their import as a multiplication table.'[4] He discerns three main 'lessons'; firstly, the need for more efficient and rational use of existing capital; secondly, the need for a highly educated labour force, and therefore a modern education system; and finally, of course, the superiority of private enterprise in promoting economic development.[5] While the last observation may be seriously questioned, the first points are no doubt true and few planners would minimize their importance. However, as Rosovsky points out in commenting on Cameron's paper,[6] these 'lessons' are far too general to be of much use to countries whose real need is more rigorous and practical advice on how to achieve economic development.

It can also be argued that rather than looking to the industrialized West it would be more useful and relevant for the development economist to study the economic history of the underdeveloped nations. As Griffin has observed

---

[1] P. Mathias, *The First Industrial Nation* (London, 1969), p. 5.
[2] B. Supple 'Has the Early History of Developed Countries any Current Relevance?', *The American Economic Review*, LV, no. 2 (1965), 99-103.
[3] R. Cameron, 'Some Lessons of History for Developing Nations', *The American Economic Review*, LVII, no. 2 (1967), 312.
[4] *Ibid.* p. 312.
[5] *Ibid.* pp. 316-23.
[6] *Ibid.* pp. 333-4.

It is exceedingly improbable that one can gain an adequate understanding of present obstacles and future potential for development without examining how the underdeveloped nations came to be as they are. To classify these countries as 'traditional societies' begs the issue and implies either that the under-developed countries have no history or that it is unimportant ... it is clear that the underdeveloped countries do have a history and that it is important ...[7] It is only from an examination of the forces of history—i.e. of the historical uses of power, both political and economic—that one may obtain an insight into the origin of underdevelopment.[8]

Such an insight is an essential first step in devising an effective development policy.

One of the questions in which development economists have been particularly interested is that of the importance of social overhead capital to economic growth. This stems from the fact that all industrial revolutions have witnessed the development and expansion of those factors classified as social overhead capital, i.e. power supplies, transport, education, etc., and that experience of modern underdeveloped nations has shown that their infrastructures are generally too weak to support sustained economic development. For these, as well as other reasons,[9] decisions regarding the setting up of social overhead capital projects have become vital to those countries attempting to escape from conditions of economic backwardness.

Transport is one of the most important components of social overhead capital and one to which both developed and developing countries devote a considerable proportion of their resources.[10] Indeed, Youngson states that the vital significance of improved transport to economic development is 'one of the few general truths which it is possible to derive from economic history'.[11] What then are the 'historical lessons' which can be usefully abstracted from the British experience during the Industrial Revolution? There are a number of general economic considerations which were relevant in the eighteenth century and remain important today. For example: improved transport by decreasing costs increases the market area and, therefore, allows industry to enjoy economies of scale in production; more reliable communications ensure uninterrupted supplies of raw materials and finished goods and thus permit both continual employment of plant and equipment as well as

[7]Keith Griffin, *Underdevelopment in Spanish America, An Interpretation* (London, 1969), pp. 32-3.

[8]*Ibid.* p. 48.

[9]A. J. Youngson, *Overhead Capital; A Study in Development Economics* (Edinburgh, 1967), and A. O. Hirshman, *The Strategy of Economic Development* (New Haven, Conn., 1958), pp. 83-6.

[10]W. Owen, 'Transportation and Economic Development', *The American Economic Review*, XLIX, no. 2 (1959), 180.

[11]Youngson, *Overhead Capital*, p. 73.

releasing capital from raw materials and finished goods inventories to be used in expanding productive capacity. These conditions are, however, hardly unique to the early British experience. Furthermore, they can be more profitably studied from more recent examples, occurring within the framework of modern technology and which, because more reliable statistical material is available, lend themselves more readily to cost–benefit analysis and other sophisticated techniques employed by transport economists and planners.[12]

There are also circumstances unique to British transport history which make it difficult to see how the British example can offer much to modern-day economists. The economic and social conditions under which the English transport network was formed bears little relation to those found in present-day developing nations. By eighteenth-century standards Britain was an economically advanced country. She also enjoyed considerable physical advantages, i.e. an extensive navigable river system and coastal port network, not possessed by most developing nations today.[13] In England the various transport sectors were developed gradually and were controlled almost entirely by private enterprise. The government assumed only a minimal regulatory function. Today, however, there is a need for fairly large scale initial investment in transport and other social overhead investments before any economic expansion can occur. To quote Youngson once again[14]

In the case of the latter [the developed nations] only a moderate investment in transport, power supply, irrigation—and an investment which could proceed by modest increments—was necessary for their economic potential to begin to become realizable. In the case of present-day underdeveloped countries it is not so. There is for them a difficult threshold to cross, by means of large scale public investments, before general exploitation of resources can take place.

It is generally agreed that these projects must be carefully planned and largely government controlled. Finally, technological change has radically altered the relative importance of the different transport sectors. With the advent of the internal combustion engine the roads, virtually abandoned by long-distance traffic in mid-nineteenth-century England, have now assumed a position of central importance in most countries' transport networks. Another important new dimension has been added by the growth of air transport. For all of the above reasons planners would be better advised to seek their examples from modern experience.[15]

12See for example, R. S. P. Bonney and H. Hide, 'Road Planning in Developing Areas', *Conference on Civil Engineering Problems Overseas* (Institution of Civil Engineers, 1968), pp. 253-66.
13Youngson, *Overhead Capital*, pp. 111-12.
14*Ibid.* pp. 113-14.
15Referring to U.S. railway development Fishlow has said, 'Underdeveloped countries

But even here care must be taken for as Owen has observed modern experience of transport investment provides no simple formula for an effective transport policy.[16]

If the direct relevance to the problems of underdevelopment of many aspects of the economic history of the industrialized West may be questioned,[17] the economic historian has undoubtedly gained a great deal from the development economist. The questions asked by the latter, i.e. the importance of capital formation for economic development, the relative merits of different technologies or the relationship between demographic change and economic growth, are now being asked by the economic historian. In searching for answers to these questions in the historical record many aspects of the mechanism of early industrial development have been clarified. For example, drawing on work done by economists on the question of economic growth, Ashton in 1948[18] first discussed the significance of capital formation during the Industrial Revolution.[19] This was followed in 1960 by Rostow's *Stages of Economic Growth*, based largely on the British Industrial Revolution, which stressed, among a number of factors, the need for a rapid increase in the rate of capital formation (from about 5% to about 10% of national income) in order to achieve 'take-off' into self-sustained economic growth.[20] In attempting to test this hypothesis recent studies have suggested that in fact during the Industrial Revolution the rate of capital formation rose slightly and reached Rostow's 10% minimum only in the 1840s.[21] Other aspects of historical economic development are being similarly identified and then modified as they are examined and re-examined in the light of the current concern with developing nations.

The following study of the development of the turnpike road system in England during the Industrial Revolution owes much to work that

wracked with large and unproductive agricultural sectors, illiteracy, concentrations of wealth, frequently wasteful government intervention, can take scant hope from the efficacy of railroad investment in the United States before the Civil War.' A. Fishlow, *American Railroads and the Transformation of the Ante-Bellum Economy* (Cambridge, Mass., 1965), p. 311. Also see A. R. Prest, *Transport Economics in Developing Countries, Pricing and Financing Aspects* (London, 1969), p. 32.

[16]Owen, 'Transportation and Economic Development', p. 180.

[17]See for example, Domar's comments on Supple's paper in *The American Economic Review*, LV, no. 2 (1965), 116-17.

[18]T. S. Ashton, *The Industrial Revolution, 1760-1830* (London, 1948).

[19]For an excellent discussion of this question see M. W. Flinn, *Origins of the Industrial Revolution* (London, 1966), pp. 7-18.

[20]W. W. Rostow, *The Stages of Economic Growth* (Cambridge, 1967), p. 37. (First published 1960.)

[21]H. J. Habakkuk and P. Deane, 'The Take-off in Britain', in *The Economics of Take-off into Sustained Growth*, ed. W. W. Rostow (London, 1963), pp. 74-5. Also see other papers and the discussions in this book.

has been done in the field of development economics. This is primarily in the type of questions asked and, to a lesser extent, in the techniques employed. It does not however make any pretence of offering anything to the development economist. If there is any lesson that does emerge from this study it is that a clearer picture of historical development, while not providing a blueprint for developing nations, does serve to demonstrate the danger of too readily trying to reapply old solutions in entirely different situations.

1

The Transport System in the Late Seventeenth Century

1

In 1702, the first year of the War of Spanish Succession, William Stout of Lancaster was forced to depart from his normal trade route and to send goods overland to London. Enemy ships in the Irish Sea and the Channel had made coastal carrying unsafe.[1] This was not an unusual occurrence for threats from French privateers had caused similar disruptions in the early 1690s.[2] However, he noted that the convoys in 1702 were much better than those during the previous war and that, therefore, certain low value goods, for which speed of delivery was unimportant, could be sent by sea.[3] Stout's experiences show up many of the peculiarities of the English transport system during the seventeenth and much of the eighteenth century. Because of their relative cheapness the rivers and the sea were the main arteries of trade. Under normal conditions the carriage of goods by road was limited to short hauls (to market or the nearest water) or to longer distance carriage of relatively valuable goods such as cloth.

'Normal conditions' were probably becoming more difficult to define after the mid-seventeenth century. Far reaching economic change underlay the political and social changes taking place from 1641. The growing demands of industry and the steady rise in the volume of trade, especially from 1688, created new pressures on many traditional institutions.[4] The transport system was one of these. Although England was naturally endowed with fairly good transport facilities, including extensive stretches of navigable river and many fine harbours, they, in their relatively unimproved state, were unable to cope adequately with the mounting volume of traffic. The particular problems which plagued each transport sector were therefore beginning to be felt more acutely.

---

[1] *The Autobiography of William Stout of Lancaster 1665-1752*, ed. J. D. Marshall (Manchester, 1967), p. 138.
[2] *Ibid.* pp. 98-9, 108.
[3] *Ibid.* p. 138.
[4] These pressures led to the abolition of industrial monopolies, the relaxation of the regulation of industrial production as well as the weakening or dissolution of trading monopolies. C. Hill, *Reformation to Industrial Revolution* (London, 1967), pp. 135-43.

The basic limitation of the English river system was the limited area it served, because without improvements many extensive stretches of river remained unnavigable. It was to rectify this situation that most acts for improving river navigation were obtained. Little however could be done to control the vagaries of the weather; floods in the spring, ice in the winter and droughts in the summer contributed greatly to the unreliability of river transport. Other problems were imposed by the users of the rivers. The dumping of ballast and the destruction of river banks often hindered navigation.[5] The alternative use of rivers as a means of power was another factor inhibiting their efficiency. Weirs, dams and mills blocked many rivers making continuous navigation difficult, and the cost of river transport was increased by the tolls extracted by the owners of these various projects.[6] Further, there was no regulation of the amounts which could be demanded, and on the Thames legislation was finally needed to protect carriers.[7] Although disappearing in the eighteenth century, monopolies of river carriage and wharfage also contributed to raising the costs of carriage by limiting the facilities available.[8]

Coastal shipping encountered difficulties of a similar character to those found on the rivers. The harbours were constantly silting up and having to be dredged. The maintenance of dock facilities and the construction of new ones increased financial burdens, while tolls collected for their improvement were sometimes spent on unrelated projects.[9] Bad weather often kept ships at anchor for weeks or drove them to port seeking refuge from storms. Lack of adequate maps meant a considerable degree of uncertainty. War was perhaps the most serious threat to coastal shipping, as merchant seamen were often impressed into the Navy and enemy privateers seriously disrupted trade. Not only were entire cargoes liable to be lost, but ships frequently had to wait for long periods in port for convoys. In 1690 William Stout reported that, because of the lack of convoys, shipment from London to Liverpool could take up to six months.[10] Prices also rose during wars. The carriage of sea coal from Hull to London was 10s per chaldron during peace and 14s during time of war.[11] There were delays experienced in loading and unloading. In 1739 it took from fourteen to twenty days to load grain at York and some weeks before the ship

[5] T. S. Ashton, *An Economic History of England: the Eighteenth Century* (London, 1964), p. 73.
[6] T. S. Willan, *River Navigation in England, 1600-1750* (London, 1936), pp. 20, 47.
[7] 6 and 7 Wm. & Mary c.16.
[8] Willan, *River Navigation*, pp. 116-17.
[9] Ashton, *Economic History of England*, p. 72.
[10] *The Autobiography*, pp. 98-9.
[11] *J. H of C.* xxiii, p. 494.

could be unloaded in London.[12] Goods were also often damaged in shipment. It was claimed in 1720 that 'the clothiers in Yorkshire would rather give double the price for land carriage than have their wool brought by sea where it receives so much damage ... '.[13] William Stout commented that although coastal shipping was cheaper than land carriage '[goods are] long a-coming, and damage by rats, who eat out the corks in liquor and oyl casks, to the loss (of) some whole casks of oyle and vinigar'.[14] For the above reasons coastal shipping was both unreliable and costly.

Roads were maintained by the parishes through which they passed. This system, established in 1555, was not capable of dealing with the problems created, especially on the main routes, by the increasing volume of traffic. This was due to the incompetence of both parish administration and its surveyors, the unwillingness of the parishioners to perform their statutory duties and wide-spread ignorance of proper repair methods.[15] Because repair was ineffective the roads, like the other transport sectors, suffered from the ravages of the seasons. Daniel Bourn, writing in 1763, claimed that thirty or forty years before the roads had looked 'more like a retreat of wild beasts and reptiles, than the footsteps of man'.[16] A similarly dismal picture is given by the innumerable contemporary descriptions of the conditions of the roads during this period.[17] Coach travel, rapidly increasing in popularity during the seventeenth century, was slow, uncomfortable and often dangerous, particularly at any distance from London.[18] Goods carriage was also difficult, and in many areas only packhorses could be used.[19] As late as 1760 there was no wagon trade between Liverpool and Manchester, and wool and cotton had to be carried by packhorse between Yorkshire and Lancashire.[20] In areas where the use of wagons was practicable, the physical difficulties encountered and the relatively small quantities of goods which could be carried made transport very costly.

The transport system was thus beset by a series of problems which plagued the roads, rivers and the coast. If no one place in the country

---

[12]*J. H. of C.* xxiii, p. 494.
[13]*Journal of Commissioners for Trade and Plantations* (1720), p. 220, quoted in R. W. Unwin, 'The Aire and Calder Navigation, Part 1: The Beginning of the Navigation', *The Bradford Antiquary*, N.S. XLII (1964), 40.
[14]*The Autobiography*, p. 108.
[15]See below, p. 15.
[16]Daniel Bourne, *A Treatise upon Wheel-Carriages ...* (London, 1763), p. 9.
[17]W. T. Jackman, *The Development of Transportation in Modern England* (second edition, London, 1962), pp. 85-101.
[18]J. Crofts, *Packhorse, Waggon and Post, Land Carriage and Communications under the Tudors and Stuarts* (London, 1967), pp. 109-32.
[19]Jackman, *Development of Transportation*, pp. 141-2.

could serve as a paradigm for the effects of these problems, none escaped them completely. The transport system was therefore unable to fulfil its economic function efficiently, and this increased the difficulty of both industrial and agricultural expansion and consequently slowed down economic growth.

2

Transport serves a rather obvious economic function – to carry goods and raw materials between producers and consumers.[21] Its efficiency can be measured by the cost, in both time and money, at which this is done. The higher the cost, all else being equal, the more inefficient the service. It is important to have an efficient transport system for 'by enabling the market to be extended, [it] permits a greater degree of specialization, and therefore of productivity to be achieved'.[22] As Adam Smith wrote[23]

Good roads, canals, and navigable rivers, by diminishing the expense of carriage, put the remote parts of the country more nearly upon a level with those in the neighbourhood of the town. They are upon that account the greatest of all improvements. They encourage the cultivation of the remote, which must always be the most extensive circle of the country. They are advantageous to the town, by breaking down the monopoly of the country in its neighbourhood. They are advantageous even to that part of the country. Though they introduce some rival commodities into the old market, they open many new markets to its produce.

Although Smith discussed the extent of the market in physical terms, it can also be seen as a function of total cost. Following from his argument, a decrease in the price of any input would increase the market for that particular good. He probably was particularly concerned with transport costs because these formed such an inordinately high percentage of total costs, and also because by 1776 improvements in transport, especially the canals, had clearly shown that these costs could be reduced substantially.

In agriculture inefficient transport meant the slow spread of innovation, especially enclosure, for there would be little incentive to apply

[20] *Ibid.* pp. 142f.
[21] It serves as a consumer good itself – people travel for pleasure. It also brings consumers to producers of services. A. M. Milne and J. C. Laight, *The Economics of Inland Transport* (London, 1965), pp. 1-23.
[22] *Ibid.* pp. 19-20.
[23] Adam Smith, *An Enquiry into the Nature and Causes of the Wealth of Nations*, ed. Edwin Cannan (New York, 1937), p. 147.

new techniques if sufficient markets could not be reached to absorb increased yields.[24] The agricultural innovations in East Anglia were due to the light soil and the history of enclosures, but also to the availability of river and coastal transport and the proximity to London and Holland.[25] The problems which hampered the distribution of agricultural goods also had an adverse effect on industry, for many industries, notably textiles, depended on agriculture for their raw materials, and a high percentage of the price of these was often attributable to transport costs. Coal, another important industrial input, was severely affected by transport charges. In 1738 a three-mile land journey to the River Don increased the price of coal by 66%, and the price when finally landed in London had been raised seven times.[26] High transport costs made it necessary for industry to be located close to its source of raw material, which often proved to be at a considerable distance from its markets. Final product distribution was also affected by carriage costs, and unless adequate transport facilities were readily accessible, markets tended to remain limited, and industry consequently on a small scale. For example, neither the Staffordshire pottery industry nor the coal trade of Derbyshire was able to expand until water transport was made available and the roads improved.[27]

The unreliability of transport was another factor which hampered industrial expansion. Delays in the delivery of raw materials made it difficult to achieve continuity in the employment of labour and capital, and this inhibited the development of large-scale units of production.[28] The difficulties in reaching markets tied up capital by slowing down the turnover of finished goods' inventories, and the necessity of holding stocks of raw materials to ensure supplies further curtailed the use of capital for industrial expansion.

The problems which beset industry and agriculture as a result of the failings of the transport system also affected the organization of English society. There were quite marked regional as well as parochial distinctions, such as dress, diet and dialect, and these were caused in part by the difficulty of communication.[29] As Professor Ashton noted, 'To the southerner Lancashire must have seemed almost an uninviting as Newfoundland and its denizens scarcely less uncouth than the High-

[24]Ashton, *Economic History of England*, p. 40.

[25]A. H. John, 'The Course of Agricultural Change 1660-1760', in *Studies in the Industrial Revolution*, ed. L. S. Pressnell (London, 1960), pp. 131-2.

[26]*J. H. of C.* xxiii, p. 493.

[27]N. McKendrick, 'Josiah Wedgwood: An Eighteenth Century Entrepreneur in Salesmanship and Marketing Techniques', in *Essays in Economic History*, Vol. III, ed. E. M. Carus-Wilson (London, 1962), p. 353. A. C. Wood, 'The History of Trade and Transport on the River Trent', *Thoroton Society Transactions*, LIV (1950), 12.

[28]Ashton, *Industrial Revolution*, pp. 13-14.

[29]Ashton, *Economic History of England*, pp. 13-14.

landers of Scotland.'[30] Parochialism probably fostered insularity and a degree of reaction to change, and this was antithetical to economic growth. John Byng, writing in 1781, attested with regret to the fact that improved road transport was destroying this aspect of English life. He commented[31]

I wish with all my heart that half the turnpike roads of the kingdom were plough'd up, which have imported London manners, and depopulated the country — I meet milkmaids on the road, with the dress and looks of strand misses; and must think that every line of Goldsmith's Deserted Village contains melancholy truths.

3

Attempts were made throughout the sixteenth and seventeenth centuries to overcome the problems discussed above. The administrative machinery for dealing with the maintenance of both roads and rivers was formally established in the sixteenth century. In 1532 the responsibility for maintaining the rivers was vested in the King's Commissioners of Sewers,[32] and in 1555 the parishes were made liable for the upkeep of their own roads.[33] There were also schemes for improving particular roads or rivers. For example, special powers were granted in 1575–6 for repairing a road in the Isle of Sheppey and in 1584–5 for roads in the Weald of Kent and Sussex.[34] There were acts for improving the navigation of the River Exe in 1539[35] and the River Lea in 1571,[36] and Letters Patent were obtained in the early seventeenth century for the improvement of the rivers Avon, Tone and Lark.[37] Owing to either violent local opposition, or lack of funds, or insufficient engineering ability, projects of this kind met with limited success before the Restoration.[38]

The short-lived revival of interest in transport improvements between 1662 and 1670 saw the passage of nine river navigation acts,[39]

30 *Ibid.* p. 13.
31 *The Torrington Diaries*, ed. C. Bruyn Andrews (London, 1935), Vol. 1, p. 6.
32 S. and B. Webb, *English Local Government: Statutory Authorities for Special Purposes* (London, 1922), pp. 19-20.
33 See below, pp. 14-15.
34 See below, pp. 15-16.
35 Jackman, *Development of Transportation*, pp. 164-5.
36 *Ibid.* pp. 165-8.
37 Willan, *River Navigation*, pp. 26-7.
38 Jackman, *Development of Transportation*, pp. 182-3. The projects given above are but a sample. For a more detailed discussion see *ibid.* pp. 157-93 and Willan, *River Navigation*, pp. 1-28.
39 From this period river legislation was to be more concerned with the extension of navigation and not, as in previous years, with the repair or maintenance of existing navigation. See Jackman, *Development of Transportation*, pp. 182-3.

acts for the improvement of the harbours of Dover, Wells and Great Yarmouth and the first turnpike act.[40] During these years attempts were also made to improve the roads by strengthening the parish road repair system.[41] In 1662 and 1670[42] temporary statutes were passed which authorized the levying of rates to supplement statute duty, and in 1691 this power was given permanently.[43] In the last turbulent years of Stuart rule fears of popish plots and the constant disputes between the King and Parliament left little time for such mundane matters as transport improvement. It was not until after the Glorious Revolution and the return of domestic stability that improvement activity could begin again. Between 1695 and 1700, seven new river acts, three acts for harbour improvement and four new turnpike acts were passed.[44] Interest in these improvements continued and was substantially increased in the eighteenth century.

The initiative for transport improvement was local. Those interested got together, organized support and petitioned Parliament for the authority to undertake a particular project. Not all proceeded smoothly, for these schemes generally met with strong opposition. This was especially true with regard to attempts to extend river navigation, which of all improvements probably offered the greatest threat to established interests. Opposition came from farmers who felt that their monopoly of local markets would be broken, from landowners who thought that boatmen would destroy river banks and their lands would be flooded, and from land carriers and the owners of weirs or mills who feared for their livelihoods.[45] The most determined opposition came from those in established river ports or markets who were afraid that the opening of new facilities would divert trade. For example, the extension of the navigation of the Aire and Calder to Leeds and Wakefield was actively opposed by York, Tadcaster and other towns on the rivers Ouse and Wharfe who quite rightly feared that they would lose the profits of the wool trade.[46] Similar disputes were fought throughout the country.[47] The growing number of improvement acts in the late seventeenth and early eighteenth centuries attests to the fact that gradually the improvers were winning out over the older entrenched interests. This was due primarily to the continual growth in the volume of traffic which placed constant pressure on transport facilities. It may also have owed some-

---

[40]See below, Appendix A.
[41]See below, pp. 15-16.
[42]14 Car. II c.6 and 22 Car. II c.12.
[43]3 Wm. & Mary c.12.
[44]See below, Appendices A and B.
[45]Willan, *River Navigation*, pp. 42-7.
[46]R. W. Unwin, 'Aire and Calder Navigation, I', pp. 12-13.
[47]Jackman, *Development of Transportation*, pp. 196-206.

thing to the acts passed in the 1660s and 1690s which both helped spread the idea that better transport facilities could be obtained and at the same time showed more clearly how this could be done. Furthermore, once begun transport improvement itself tended to create conditions which made subsequent improvements more likely. For example, in 1709 an act was obtained for the improvement of the harbour at Whitehaven,[48] and in 1740, in a petition to Parliament, the harbour trustees claimed[49]

That the high Roads leading to the said Town of *Whitehaven* are very narrow, having been seldom made use of by Carts, or Wheel Carriages, till the late Years, but that, since the Improvement of the Harbour aforesaid, the Resort of Persons from other Parts of the Country has been so great, and likewise such Increase of Carts and Wheel Carriages, as well as loaden Horses, passing with Goods to and from *Whitehaven* that the said Roads are become ruinous, and almost impassable in Winter.

The more intensive use of transport facilities, often made possible by their improvement, placed additional burdens on nearby roads, rivers or coastal ports.[50] This in turn made it more likely that they too would be improved. The increasing amount of legislation devoted to the roads, rivers and harbours in the second half of the seventeenth century was the beginning of a concerted attempt to mitigate the restrictions imposed by inadequate transport facilities. The improvement of the transport system both resulted from the pressures placed on existing facilities by the quickened pace of economic activity and was a factor which made further expansion possible.

[48] 7 Anne c.9.
[49] *J. H. of C.* xxiii, p. 433.
[50] It would seem that generally the rivers and harbours were improved before the roads. For example, in Yorkshire river navigation acts were passed at the turn of the century and in the 1720s and 30s, but turnpiking did not begin until the late thirties and forties.

2

The Origins
of the Turnpike Trust

1

The first turnpike authority was established in 1663 on the New Great North Road between Wadesmill in Hertfordshire and Stilton in Huntingdonshire.[1] Although the next turnpike act was not to be passed until 1695, the principle embodied in this first act, that travellers should contribute towards road repair, became the basic concept underlying most road improvement in the succeeding two centuries. Although the early road repair legislation has been considered before,[2] the relationship between the turnpike acts and the general road repair acts has not been adequately analysed. It is essential to do this because the turnpike trust evolved from the older system of parochial administration, and this fact both influenced the character of the turnpike acts and determined in part the location of turnpike trusts prior to the 'Turnpike Mania' of the years 1751-72.

By a statute of 1555[3] the parishes were made responsible for repairing their own roads. With regard to this statute, the Webbs observed that[4]

With agriculture in revolution, and the Manorial Courts in decay, Parliament apparently set itself to construct, not so much new law as new social machinery for the administration, all over England and Wales, of what was deemed an entirely local service. The ancient common law obligation, descended from the *trinoda necessitas*, was, for the first time, definitely allocated among the several parties, and the procedure to be followed was peremptorily laid down.

The parishioners were obliged to spend four days a year working on the roads under the supervision of surveyors appointed by the parish churchwardens. In 1563[5] the number of days required was increased

---

[1] 15 Car. II c.1.
[2] The two most complete treatments of this subject appear in: (1) Sidney and Beatrice Webb, *English Local Government: The Story of the King's Highway* (London, 1913), pp. 14-61, 114-16; (2) Jackman, *Development of Transportation*, pp. 32-68.
[3] 2 & 3 Philip and Mary c.8.
[4] Webbs, *King's Highway*, p. 14.
[5] 5 Eliz. c.13.

to six, and additional powers were given to the surveyors.[6] The act was amended in 1575–6[7] and in 1587[8] the statute was made perpetual.

The system of parish road repair, created by the foregoing acts, had many weaknesses. The surveyor was responsible for organizing and directing annual road repairs, keeping the roads free from obstructions and nuisances and reporting those who failed to do their work.[9] He was not paid for his work, was liable to be fined if he refused to accept the post and could also be fined for negligence.[10] Repair methods were crude, and more effective techniques could be learned only through practical experience. Further, most surveyors served for only one year, and this lack of continuity militated against any technical advance. Individuals were forced to act as surveyors and to direct their fellow parishioners who were also compelled to perform statute duties. The latter were often as reluctant to do this work as the surveyors were to do theirs, and it is therefore not surprising that road repair was frequently carried out in a haphazard and ineffectual manner.[11] As the Webbs point out, 'In England, at least, this Statute Labour seems in the sixteenth and seventeenth centuries to have been performed with the utmost remissness. Whether there was ever a time in which this work was commonly done with any degree of conscientiousness or exactitude we may well doubt.'[12]

It may soon have become apparent that the system of parish repair needed to be strengthened, for in 1563[13] the justices of the peace were empowered to indict and present parishes that failed to maintain their roads. The offending parish was presented at the quarter-sessions, and if after a given time their roads were not put in proper repair a fine was levied and the proceeds used by the surveyor.[14] Statute labour could be supplemented in other ways. Acts of Parliament authorized justices to levy rates for the repair of certain roads,[15] fines were imposed

[6] The surveyors were authorized to dig gravel without paying for it, to cleanse ditches and to prevent rubbish being placed on the roads. They were to give an account of the conditions of the roads and present to the Highway Sessions those who refused to perform the required labour. Those appointed as surveyors were obliged to serve, and if they refused they could be fined.

[7] 18 Eliz. c.10.

[8] 29 Eliz. c.5.

[9] Webbs, *King's Highway*, pp. 15-17.

[10] *Ibid.* pp. 15-17.

[11] There are a great many references to the failures of this system. Webbs, *King's Highway*, pp. 27-50; Jackman, *Development of Transportation*, pp. 54-8; Littleton, *Proposal for Maintenance and Repair of the Highway* (1692), pp. 2-3; Daniel Defoe, *Essay on Projects* (London, 1697), p. 69; Rev. Henry Homer, *An Enquiry into the Means of Preserving and Improving the Public Roads of this Kingdom* (London, 1767), p. 20.

[12] Webbs, *King's Highway*, p. 28.

[13] 5 Eliz. c.13.

[14] Jackman, *Development of Transportation*, p. 35; Webbs, *King's Highway*, pp. 19-20, 23.

[15] 18 Eliz. c.10 (1575-6). The justices of the Isle of Sheppey were to levy a rate for the maintenance of the road from 'Myddleton' to King's Ferry. (cont.)

on individuals who refused to do their statute duty, and special rates could be levied in order to repay surveyors for funds they had expended on repair.[16] In 1654, the Commonwealth Parliament enacted an ordinance which abolished statute labour and replaced it with a system financed by parish rates.[17] The rates, which were not to exceed one shilling in the pound, were to be paid by the parishioners and the money used to hire labour and purchase materials for repairing the roads. This act does not seem to have been implemented and was nullified with the Restoration.[18] In 1662[19] the system of statute labour was revived, and the surveyors were given the power to levy a rate, not greater than sixpence in the pound, to supplement the six days statute duty.[20] This provision was to be in force for three years, and the rate had to be levied unless the parishes could prove that it was not needed. However, it does not seem that such rates were ever paid.[21] In 1670[22] the justices were again empowered to levy a highway rate, and although this act proved somewhat more successful than its predecessor,[23] it too was temporary, and expired in 1673. Only in 1691 was the power to levy rates for road repair made permanent in 3 Wm. & Mary c.12.

---

27 Eliz. c.19 (1584-5). Owners and occupiers of iron works in Sussex, Surrey and Kent had to provide one cart of 'Sinder, Gravell Stone Sande or Chalke' for repairing the roads, for every six loads of coal or ore and every ton of iron they carried on the roads between 12 October and 1 May. This was amended by 39 Eliz. c.19 (1597-8). The owners and occupiers were to pay the justices three shillings for every three loads of coal or ore and every ton of iron carried plus one load of gravel etc. for every thirty loads of coal or ore and every ten tons of iron carried. 3 Jac. I c.19 (1605-6). The hundreds of Kingston, Effingham, Copthorne, Wallington, Wotton, Reigate and Emlinbridge were to contribute towards the repair of the one and a half mile road between Nonsuch and Taleworth in Surrey.

[16]Webbs, *King's Highway*, pp. 16-17.

[17]*Ibid.* pp. 20-1. Jackman, *Development of Transportation*, pp. 52-3.

[18]Jackman, *op. cit.* p. 53. Webbs, *King's Highway*, p. 21. The parish of Radwell petitioned the Hertfordshire Quarter-Sessions in 1656, asking whether a full pound rate could be made. This suggests that some were aware of the ordinance. (*Hertford County Records. Calendar to the Sessions Books, Sessions Minute Book and other Sessions Records, 1619-1657*, Vol. V, ed. William Le Hardy (Hertford, 1928), p. 483.) In Warwickshire, the parish of Bulkington was permitted to make a rate in 1654; although the justices claimed that this was to be seen as an extraordinary case and not to serve as a precedent. (*Warwick County Records*, Vol. III, ed. S. C. Radcliffe and H. C. Johnson (Warwick, 1937), pp. 228-9.)

[19]14 Car. II c.6.

[20]The surveyors together with two substantial householders were to make this rate, and it had to be approved by the justices. See Jackman, *Development of Transportation*, pp. 59-60.

[21]Jackman, *op. cit.* pp. 60-1. Webbs, *King's Highway*, p. 22.

[22]22 Car. II c.12.

[23]It is not known to what extent this act was successful; however in Hertfordshire at least five parishes were able to levy rates under the powers of this act. (*Hertford County Records. Calendar to the Sessions Books, Sessions Minute Book and other Sessions Records, 1658-1700*, Vol. VI, ed. William Le Hardy (Hertford, 1930), pp. 218, 211, 223.)

2

The first turnpike act in 1663 was a temporary measure designed to provide funds to supplement statute labour on a section of the New Great North Road which the parishes concerned found particularly difficult to maintain. The conditions which led to the passage of this act can be traced back to the early seventeenth century.

In 1609 a bill for repairing the 'Biggleswade Highways' was read in Parliament;[24] however, the details of this bill are not recorded, and it was defeated.[25] In 1621-2, a second bill was presented for repairing the road between Biggleswade and Baldock on the Old Great North Road,[26] in the following terms:[27]

An Acte for the repaire of the great Roade and highway to London from the Northe partes of England Betweene Bigleswade & Baldocke in the Com. Bedd' & Hertf.
Whereas the great Roade and higheway leading from the Towne of Bigleswade ... to the Towne of Baldocke ... being five miles in length and the higheway for a great part from the North parts of this Realme of England towards the Cittie of London by the often and Contynuall drifts and droves of Cattell driven towards the said Cittie for the servinge thereof and by meanes of the frequent passages of Waynes Carts and Carriadges to and from the said Cittie into the north of England the same is made soe fowle, full of holes, sloughes, gulles & gutters that yt is now in the winter tyme made impassable and soe dangerous that noe Coatch Carte nor horse loaded cane almost passe that waie. That notwithstanding the villages adiacent doe bestow their daies workes appointed by the Statute, yet by reason that the most parte is a flatte and waterishe Levell & consisteth of a deepe and lough Clay and by reason of the smallnes of the said Villages adiayninge and the Length of the said waye and the want of stones & Gravel, that there is little or noe Amendemt, but the same continues still more dangerous & ympasable to the great hurte of Travellers and passangers.

It was proposed that a toll be taken 'in the said waie called Edworth hill', and that the funds be used by surveyors appointed by the Lord High Chancellor and the Lord High Treasurer. But this was defeated, 'because it was a Tax upon all Passengers, thereby savouring of a Monopoly'.[28]

The problems experienced in respect of the 'Biggleswade Highway' were not unique, for throughout the seventeenth century parishes in Hertfordshire along both the New and Old Great North Road found it

[24]*J. H. of C.* i, p. 403.
[25]*Ibid.* p. 404.
[26]F. G. Emmison, 'The Earliest Turnpike Bill (Biggleswade to Baldock Road), 1622', *Bulletin of the Institute of Historical Research,* XII (1934-5), 108-12.
[27]*Ibid.* pp. 111-12.
[28]*Ibid.* p. 108.

difficult to maintain their roads. Of the sixty-six presentments made between 1619 and 1661,[29] thirty-nine were against parishes along the New Great North Road.[30] Besides the presentment of the individual parishes on this road, the justices were also concerned with the road as a whole. In April 1631 the justices received an order from the Lords of the Privy Council charging them with keeping the main roads in the county in good repair.[31] The justices ordered that all the ditches on the roads from Theobalds to Royston and Barkway be scoured and that new ones be dug if necessary. The inhabitants of the parishes along the road were to perform twice the required statute duty,[32] and if sufficient local materials could not be found, they were to be purchased from the proceeds of a parish rate. This does not seem to have brought about the desired improvement, for in October 1631 the following order was made[33] in quarter-session:

And as divers of the said highways are 'worne and torne' by reason of the great burdens wherewith diverse people passing through the county do load their waggons and carts, it is further ordered that certain justices shall attend the Lords of the Privy Council and petition that some course may be taken *to enforce those so passing through as aforesaid with waggons excessively laden, to contribute towards the repair and amending of the said highways.* [my italics]

The problem of maintaining this road and the proposed solution preceded the first turnpike act by over thirty years. Although many parishes were finding it difficult to repair their roads, it seems that a single parish may have been directly responsible for initiating the turnpike act of 1663.

The parish of Standon, on the Great North Road between Wadesmill and Buntingford, was the most frequently presented in the county.[34] Road repair may have been particularly difficult for this parish because of the hilly terrain and the great number of malt wagons *en route* to Ware, many of which entered the main road just north of the parish.[35]

---

[29] *Hertford County Records*, Vols. v and vi, *passim*.

[30] Five presentments were of parishes on the Old Great North Road, and the others were of parishes throughout the county. Of the latter group, the majority were for roads leading into the Great North Road.

[31] *Hertford County Records*, Vol. v, pp. 141–2.

[32] This device had been used before. The parish of Amwell, on the Great North Road below Hertford, had difficulty repairing the main road, and in 1630/1 the justices ordered the parishioners to work twelve days on the roads and directed that all parishes in the Hundred of Hertford contribute one day's statute work. (*Hertford County Records*, Vol. v, p. 137.)

[33] *Ibid.* p. 151.

[34] *Hertford County Records*, Vol. v, p. 15 (1621), p. 21 (1622), p. 33 (1623/4), p. 96 (1627/8), p. 110 (1628), p. 123 (1629), p. 298 (1641), p. 354 (1644), p. 355 (1644); *Hertford County Records*, Vol. vi, p. 16 (1658), p. 60 (1661).

[35] This information was provided by Miss Pegrum of the Hertfordshire County Record Office.

Furthermore, the responsibility for repairing four miles of the Great North Road, as well as part of the road leading towards Bishop's Stortford,[36] may have over-taxed the resources of this relatively small parish.[37] In 1624, after the parish had been presented for three consecutive years, the justices ordered the parishioners to double the amount of their statute duty.[38] However, this had little effect, and the presentments continued. In a petition to the quarter-sessions in 1646,[39] the parishioners claimed that they were unable to maintain their portion of the London Road. They asked for assistance and suggested a tax on the heavy loads drawn on the road. This request, similar to that made by the justices of Hertfordshire to the Privy Council in 1631, was not granted. The parish was again presented in 1658, and two years later it appealed to Parliament for relief in repairing the roads.[40] The petition was referred to the committee drafting the Highway Act of 1662,[41] and nothing more was heard of it. Perhaps the committee felt that the highway rate prescribed in this act would resolve the parish's difficulties. This, however, does not seem to have happened, and in 1663 the inhabitants of Standon again petitioned for leave to bring in a bill for repairing the roads within the parish.[42] This petition was soon joined by two others from parishes in the counties of Cambridge and Huntingdon,[43] and they were combined into a single bill in April,[44] which became the first turnpike act in June 1663.[45]

Throughout the early seventeenth century the Hertford justices employed various measures designed to supplement statute labour in an attempt to provide assistance for the parishes responsible for repairing the main roads. Rates were levied, parishes were fined, statute duty was doubled and parishes were ordered to contribute towards the repair of particular roads.[46] None of these measures proved to be effective. The imposition of a toll on the New Great North Road had been suggested on at least three occasions prior to 1663,[47] and in view of the parishes' continued inability to maintain this important and heavily-

---

[36] Hertford County Records, Notes and Extracts from the Sessions Rolls (1581-1698), Vol. I ed. W. J. Hardy (Hertford, 1905), p. 82.
[37] Information provided by Miss Pegrum.
[38] Hertford County Records, Vol. v, p. 41.
[39] Hertford County Records, Vol. I, p. 82.
[40] J. H. of C. viii, p. 292.
[41] Ibid. p. 292.
[42] Ibid. p. 455.
[43] Ibid. p. 455 (Cambridge); p. 463 (Huntingdon).
[44] Ibid. p. 472.
[45] Journals of the House of Lords, xi, p. 533.
[46] In 1623/4, the parish of 'Anstye' (Anstey) claimed that they could not repair the London–Barkway Road. They were ordered to double their statute labour, and eleven nearby parishes were directed to assist in repairs. (Hertford County Records, Vol. v, p. 36.) See also p. 18 above.
[47] This is assuming that Standon's petition in 1660 asked for such a remedy. This does not include the Biggleswade–Baldock Bill of 1622.

travelled route, Parliament finally agreed to allow a toll to be taken. It is clear, however, that this was not an attempt to create a new system of road repair. The act was to be in force for only eleven years, and it was thirty-two years before the next turnpike act was passed. Parliament may have felt the difficulties of repairing the Great North Road to be exceptional, requiring the temporary assistance of this special measure.[48]

The first turnpike act was a modified version of the parish repair system, and it was initiated, because of the heavy local burden of repair, by parishes through which one of the country's busiest roads passed. In this sense it can be interpreted as an indication of the growing volume of internal trade and traffic. In its form the act was significantly different from the later turnpike acts. While parishes continued to perform statute duty, road improvement was partially financed by a tax on the road users. The individual parishes were still responsible for their sections of the main road, but county surveyors now supervised repair of the entire road within their respective counties. The justices were empowered to erect turnpike gates at Wadesmill, Caxton and Stilton. Nine surveyors appointed in each county were to meet and decide on the repairs needed, appoint toll-collectors and report receipts and expenditures to the justices annually. The surveyors could demand parish labour in addition to statute duty, but were required to pay for it at the 'usual county rate'. If initially funds were not sufficient, the proceeds of the tolls could be mortgaged, and the justices were also authorized to levy a rate on the parishes. However, 'Money so advanced by the said townes ... shall again by repaid with Interest ... as it doth arise out of the said Tolls.'[49] This provision was repealed in 1665. The amending act of that year[50] extended the powers of the former act for twenty-one years in Hertfordshire. In Cambridge and Huntingdon the first act, which seems never to have been enforced in these counties,[51] ceased to be in force from 1674.

The gate at Wadesmill in Hertford was set up in 1665,[52] and tolls were collected until 1680, when the justices declared, 'for the relief of the County the taking of the toll has of late been dispenced with'.[53] By the 1690s toll collection at Wadesmill had resumed,[54] and continued into the following century.

[48]Other petitions asking for assistance in repairing roads were turned down by Parliament. A bill for repairing Watling Street was defeated in 1662 (*J. H. of C.* viii, p. 439). In 1664, a bill for repairing highways in Bedford, Buckingham, Northampton and Warwick was defeated (*J. H. of C.* viii, p. 571). In 1693, a bill for levying a toll to help repair the roads in the parish of Islington was defeated (*J. H. of C.* xi, p. 45).

[49]15 Car. II c.1, art. viii.   [50]16 & 17 Car. II c.10.

[51]Jackman, *Development of Transportation*, p. 63. Webbs, *King's Highway*, p. 115.

[52]*Hertford County Records*, Vol. VI, p. 127.   [53]*Ibid.* p. 330.

[54]Tolls may have been collected in the 1680s; however, the next reference to the turnpike appears in 1693. *Ibid.* p. 462.

3

Thirty-two years elapsed between the passage of the first and the second turnpike acts. Although the reasons for this time-lag are not clear, a few possible causes can be suggested. Firstly, as the turnpike device was relatively new it may not have been widely known. Secondly, opposition, both locally and at Westminster, may have forstalled the passage of turnpike acts. The Webbs have claimed[55] that the proposed gate at Stilton caused so much local opposition that it was never erected, and even in Hertford toll collection was suspended for a time. Parliament turned down at least three turnpike bills before 1695,[56] and many others were defeated in the late seventeenth and early eighteenth centuries.[57] There were, however, other factors which eventually outweighed this opposition.

The most important was the growing volume of traffic[58] which made it increasingly difficult for parishes, especially those on main routes, to repair their roads. This problem could well have become more acute in the 1690s because of the serious disruption of coastal trade as a result of war with France and the consequent increase of overland transport.[59] Further, from 1691 the justices of the peace were empowered to levy a highway rate on parishes which did not repair their roads.[60] For these parishes a turnpike may have provided a desirable alternative, for if the Hertfordshire case is representative, tolls tended to take the place of highway rates.[61]

Thus the Highway Act of 1662 gave the surveyors the power to levy a rate on the parishes, and although this power was not used in Hertfordshire, those responsible for the first turnpike act seem to have felt that the tolls would replace highway rates. The Lords' Committee

---

[55]Webbs, *King's Highway*, p. 115.
[56]See above, p. 20.
[57]Bills presented for the repair of the following roads were defeated in Parliament: (*J. H. of C.* Index I, 1547-1714, under Highways, nos. 676-813).
    1696:(1) Roads in East Grinstead, (2) Islington Roads.
    1698:(1) Ferrington–St John's Bridge Roads.
    1699:(1) Seven Oaks–Tunbridge Road.
    1705:(1) Whitchurch–Chester Road, (2) Worcester–Birmingham Road.
    1706:(1) Cherhill–Calne Road, (2) Road from Petersfield to Butser Hill.
    1709:(1) Holmes Chapel–Newcastle-under-Lyme, (2) London–Chichester Road.
    1711:(1) Aylesbury–Bicester Road.
    1712:(1) Aylesbury–Buckingham Road.
    1714:(1) Kensington Roads, (2) Kingston–Southwark Road.
[58]Jackman, *Development of Transportation*, p. 122.
[59]See for example *The Autobiography of William Stout*, pp. 98-9, 114-15.
[60]Wm. & Mary c.12.
[61]This was not the case in Gloucestershire. In 1702, 1706 and 1710 rates were levied on the parishes along the turnpike road. (Gloucester QS Records, Q/SO-3, Glouces. RO.)

B

on the bill deleted provision which authorized a sixpenny rate[62] and substituted one permitting a refundable rate.[63] This clause was repealed in 1665, and a non-refundable rate was authorized. However, except in 1680 when toll collection was suspended, parishes on the turnpiked road were neither fined nor made to pay rates.[64] In 1671 and 1672, under the power given by 16 & 17 Car. II c.10, rates were levied on at least six Hertfordshire parishes,[65] but none of these parishes were on the Great North Road above Ware. It would seem that while tolls were collected the parishes were freed from paying both fines and rates. The power to make highway rates, given permanently to justices throughout the country in 1691[66] may therefore have revived local interest in turnpikes and have been partially responsible for the passage of new turnpike acts from 1695.

The turnpike acts passed between 1695 and 1706 were all similar[67] in that the justices were given the power to erect gates, collect tolls, appoint officials and supervise repair. But in 1706 a radically new concept was introduced. By an act of that year[68] the road from Fornhill to Stony Stratford was placed under the control of a group of thirty-two trustees, whose powers for repair, toll collection, etc., were generally the same as those enjoyed by the justices under previous acts. By 1714[69] the 'turnpike trust' had completely replaced the older 'justice trusts'.[70]

Besides provisions for local toll-exemptions or the placement of gates, the form of most turnpike trust acts followed a very similar pattern. The appointed trustees were authorized to erect gates, collect tolls, appoint surveyors and collectors, demand statute labour or its monetary equivalent, mortgage the tolls, elect new trustees, and undertake work necessary for repairing the roads. The justices served as arbitrators

---

[62]MSS Committee Minutes, 15 May 1663, H. of L. RO.

[63]See above, p. 20.

[64]*Hertford County Records*, Vol. VI, *passim*.

[65]*Ibid.* pp. 211, 218, 223, 229, 234.

[66]In Hertfordshire, in 1693, it was ordered 'this rate be forthwith levied on every person who is chargable as there is great need for raising the money'. (*Ibid.* p. 462.)

[67]9 Wm. III c.8 (1697/8), an act for repairing the roads from Birdlip and Crickley hills to Gloucester, was significantly different. By this act toll-gates could be erected only after someone had put up security, to guarantee that the road would be repaired within five years. Persons giving such security could collect tolls, levy a highway rate and demand statute labour. This act was similar in form to those for river navigations, with the justices acting as commissioners and repair being carried out by an undertaker. (See for example, 6 Geo. I c.27, The Derwent Navigation.) This act was not successful, and in 1701 (12 & 13 Wm. III c.9), the powers given to the undertakers reverted to the justices.

[68]6 Anne, c.4.

[69]Twenty new acts were passed between 1706 and 1713, and of these fourteen were for turnpike trusts.

[70]10 Geo. I c.9 (1723), which created a justice-controlled trust in Essex, was the sole exception.

between the trusts and the public. They were the authority to which appeals against the trusts could be made, they settled the amount of statute labour which the trusts could demand and apportioned fines between the parishes and the trusts when a road was indicted. The justices were also able to appoint someone to inspect the trust roads and report on any misuse of authority or funds; however, from about 1750 this specific provision was deleted from most new acts.

The change to trustee control may have come about because the justices were unable, owing to their many other commitments, to administer the turnpike roads effectively.[71] In Hertfordshire[72] and in Gloucestershire[73] the justices did little more than appoint surveyors and examine their accounts, and justices in other counties may have carried out their duties in as summary a fashion. As the number of turnpiked roads in a county increased the county's justices may well have found it more difficult to administer them. The turnpike trust provided an alternative method of administration, involving a devolution of authority to bodies whose responsibility extended only to a single road or group of roads, instead of all a county's turnpike roads.

4

In 1555, when the parish repair system was first established, wheeled vehicle traffic was light and primarily local.[74] In later years both the number of vehicles and the volume of through traffic increased. However, before 1662 there were no major innovations made in the parish repair system to take into account the greater repair demands being made on the parishes.[75] The first turnpike act was an attempt to do this. The tolls were to provide temporary assistance for the parishes along a portion of the Great North Road where heavy through traffic made repair particularly costly. Justice control and the other provisions of this and subsequent acts linked the early turnpikes closely with parish repair. This relationship was altered in 1706, and from 1714 the turnpikes became completely separate *ad hoc* authorities. The parishes remained liable if the roads were not repaired, and they continued to perform their statute duty; however, parish contributions formed, in

---

[71]Neither the Webbs (*King's Highway*, p. 116) nor Jackman (*Development of Transportation*, p. 70), attempt to explain why this change was made.

[72]*Hertford County Records*, Vol. VI, pp. 127, 139, 157, 225-6 etc. and *Hertford County Records, Calendar of the Sessions Books, Sessions Minute Books and Other Sessions Records*, Vol. VII, ed. William Le Hardy (Hertford, 1931), pp. 12, 34-5, 46, 77, etc.

[73]Gloucester QS Records, Q/SO-3, Glouces. RO.

[74]Jackman, *Development of Transportation*, pp. 43-8.

[75]This excludes the changes made in 1563 (5 Eliz. c.13), and the legislation of the Commonwealth Parliament.

most cases, but a small percentage of the trusts' total expenditure.[76] The tolls, initially devised to supplement statute labour, therefore became a replacement for it, and the turnpike trust gradually replaced the parish as the agency responsible for maintaining the main roads.

Turnpike acts were solicited by local residents concerned with improving a particular road or group of roads, who met and sometimes agreed to advance funds to cover the legal costs of obtaining an act. From about the middle of the century money for road repair was also subscribed at these meetings.[77] A petition was drawn up, usually by a local attorney, and given to the local member of Parliament who presented it in the House of Commons.[78] It was put into committee made up of interested M.P.s, and if the petitioners' allegations were found to be true the committee would recommend that a bill be drawn up. Seven days public notice was given after the bill's second reading in order to allow petitions to be presented to the committee considering the final draft. It was at this stage that contentious issues were discussed and amendments to the bill made.[79] The bill was then reported, and if passed, was engrossed and sent to the House of Lords. Here the bill was again committed and more petitions of support or opposition were heard. When the concurrence of the Lords was obtained and the Royal Assent added, the bill became law.

Among those who promoted turnpike trusts were town councils, merchants, manufacturers, farmers, landowners and gentlemen. They were often the people responsible for repairing the road in question; however, most turnpike schemes were proposed by groups who were liable for the repair of only a portion of the road they wished turnpiked. For example, the Doncaster–Saltersbrook Turnpike Bill was initiated by 'Gentlemen, Traders, Farmers and Inhabitants of Doncaster and Barnsley',[80] and in this case, as in many others, the greater part of the road lay outside the promoters' jurisdiction. Although it was not necessary to obtain the agreement of every parish along a proposed turnpike road, the promoters did attempt to enlist the widest possible

---

[76]The trust accounts submitted to Parliament in 1834 show that of the trusts' total income (less loans) of £1,523,650, only £125,819 (8·2%) was attributable to statute duty or composition in lieu of such duty (*B.P.P. 1836 (2) xlvii*, 297, p. 2).

[77]See below, pp. 100–1.

[78]O. C. Williams, *The Historical Development of Private Bill Procedure and Standing Orders in the House of Commons* (London, 1948), pp. 28–40. All the information on the passage of an act, presented in the above paragraph, was taken from this source. The example Williams uses was taken from the eighteenth-century 'Liverpool Tractate', which refers specifically to the passage of a turnpike act (*ibid.* p. 28).

[79]For an excellent example of the kind of difficulties a bill might run into see, R. W. Unwin, 'The Aire and Calder Navigation, Part II: The Navigation in the pre-canal age', *The Bradford Antiquary*, N.S. XLIII (1967), 25–32. I thank Dr R. G. Wilson for drawing my attention to this work.

[80]*J. H. of C.* xxiii, p. 568.

support.[81] They also had to give special consideration to any powerful individuals or groups who could oppose their bill. Special toll-exemptions, the long lists of trustees and clauses which state where turnpike gates could be erected were all the outcome of compromises made by the promoters in order to mollify opposition.

Attempts to placate opposition, however, were not always successful. Resistance to the new road authorities seems to have been particularly great in the early eighteenth century. In 1717, eleven petitions, from drovers, carriers, stage-coach proprietors, merchants, clothiers, landowners, and farmers, were presented against the Counters Bridge–Staines Bridge Turnpike Bill.[82] It was claimed that the landowners had allowed the road to fall into disrepair so that they could obtain a turnpike and thereby transfer repair costs to the road users.[83] It was also contended that the tolls would place a great burden upon the petitioners. This complaint was common to many petitions against turnpikes, as was the allegation that only a small section of the proposed turnpike road was in need of repair. Petitioners against the Brampton Bridge–Market Harborough Turnpike Bill (1721) stated that only five miles of the twenty-mile road were in bad repair, and that the tolls would disrupt goods carriage and increase prices.[84]

Adam Smith claimed that landowners and farmers near London petitioned against the formation of turnpikes in 'the more remoter counties' because they feared competition from these lower wage areas.[85] New turnpikes were sometimes opposed by creditors or trustees of existing trusts who feared that the new roads would offer competition and thereby decrease their revenues.[86] Similar misgivings prompted the undertakers of the Aire and Calder Navigation to oppose most vigorously the Selby–Leeds and Leeds–Tadcaster turnpike schemes in the early 1740s.[87] Another complaint was that the proposed

[81] For example, the Brampton Bridge–Market Harborough Road Bill was supported by petitions from the mayors, aldermen and burgesses of Chesterfield, Leicester, Derby and Nottingham, and a petition from the High Sheriff, justices, Grand Jury in quarter-sessions, 'Gents., Clergy and Inhabitants of the county of Northampton' (MSS Petitions, 19 December 1721. H. of L. RO).

[82] MSS Petitions, 12 June 1717, H. of L. RO.

[83] *Ibid.* The wording of many of the petitions was similar. The one referred to above came from waggoners, carriers, drovers and clothiers living near Marlborough in Wiltshire.

[84] Reasons why the Bill for amending the Highways from Brampton Bridge . . . should not pass into law, as it now stands . . . (British Museum Collection 516 m.17).

[85] Adam Smith, *Wealth of Nations*, pp. 147–8. For full quote see below, p. 114. A similar statement appears in R. K. Philip, *The Progress of Carriages, Roads and Water Conveyances* (London, nd.), p. 157. However, no petitions were discovered in the Commons' Journals which would support this claim.

[86] Webbs, *King's Highway*, pp. 127–8. See also *J. H. of C.* xxxvi, pp. 104, 228, 245, 247, 663, 777; xxxvii, p. 609; xlv, pp. 345, 375.

[87] Unwin, *Aire and Calder Navigation*, II, pp. 27–32. Also R. G. Wilson, *Gentlemen Merchants. The merchant community in Leeds, 1700–1830* (Manchester, 1971), p. 143.

turnpike would divert traffic from nearby roads, thereby ruining trade. This argument was used in 1727, against the Broadway Hill–Stonebow Bridge Turnpike Bill,[88] and in 1756, by the 'Owners and Occupiers of Oxford Street and the Owners and Occupiers of buildings in St. Giles, Bloomsbury, Holborn and Clerkenwell', who petitioned against the Islington–Paddington Turnpike Bill.[89] This particular objection suggests that the turnpike trusts were proving efficacious.

Not all those who opposed the trusts aired their grievances by petitioning Parliament. Some resorted to more violent measures, and during the first half of the eighteenth century there were turnpike riots throughout the country. The rioters, usually farmers, carriers, miners, and labourers, 'could see no advantage in improvement; they had been accustomed to slow movements and heavy jolting all their lives, and were quite contented to go in their old way, at their accustomed pace'.[90] As John James, the Bradford historian observed, 'The turnpikes were, by the lower classes, universally regarded as an obnoxious regulation, – more adopted for the convenience of the wealthy portion of the community, whose carriages could hardly pass on the old roads, than the benefit of such class.'[91] The hostility of the labouring classes may have been increased if they equated higher commodity prices with improved transport facilities, as did, Arthur Young noted, 'all sensible people'.[92] There were riots in Somerset, Gloucester and Hereford in the late 1720s and in the following two decades,[93] and a serious riot in Leeds in 1753.[94] There were also isolated cases of toll-gates being destroyed and collectors being assaulted.[95] In 1753, the trustees of the new Old Street Trust in London record there having been 'several Tumults and Disorders at the first erecting of the Temporary Barrs'.[96] Parliament was quick to react, and by 1727[97] the wilful destruction of toll-gates or river-locks was made punishable by three months imprisonment and a public whipping. Continued disturbances led to more severe penalties; from 1731,[98] seven years transportation and from 1734,[99] 'death without clergy'.

[88]*British Museum Collection 816 m. 16 no. 43*. A petition from the town of Pershore. See also *J. H. of C*. xx, p. 404.
[89]MSS Petitions, 31 March 1756, H. of L. RO.
[90]Philip, *Progress of Carriages*, p. 156.
[91]John James, *The History and Topography of Bradford* (London, 1841), p. 155.
[92]Arthur Young, *A Six Weeks Tour through the Southern Counties of England and Wales* (London, 1768), p. 260.
[93]Webbs, *King's Highway*, p. 123.
[94]*Ibid*.
[95]Jackman, *Development of Transportation*, p. 72. Webbs, *King's Highway*, p. 123.
[96]Minute Book – 12 July 1753. Fins. Lib.
[97]1 Geo. II c.19.
[98]5 Geo. III c.33.
[99]8 Geo. II c.20. This penalty was made perpetual in 1754 (27 Geo. II c.16).

The resistance to the Bristol Trust was both prolonged and violent. In 1727, immediately after the trust's formation, the Kingswood colliers destroyed the toll-gates and stopped coal shipments to the city.[100] In the same year colliers pulled down the Studley–Toghill Trust's gate at Marshfield on six occasions, and the trust's Sodbury Gate was also destroyed.[101] The Bristol Trust received the following letter from the colliers:

The Colliers Letter to the Turnpike

Kings-Wood 3 July 1727

Sir—

We are Informed that you are drawing up your Cause and Action against us, For Riot and Rebellion, and deem us liable to be Indicted for Common Rogues, and that you are Justified in so doing having an Act of Parliament of your side, but before you Insist, We desire you to take this Comparison: If a house is Wilfully Sett on Fire, whether they may be rendred Common Rogues that runs with their Weapons to put it out (Is a Question Mr. Turnpike) This is our case; a Fire may be wilfully kindled by Omission or Commission: but if both do Agree w'th long Continuance its harder to put it out. Now to your Act of Parliament, wherein you have got a full Grant to cutt Fuzz or Heath, out of any Common, to repair the Highways (Quoted in the 26th Page of your Act) Oh we shall have brave highways now you have got a full Power to cutt Fuzz and Heath to mend them, and Stand and get the countrys Money in for doing so.

Now Turnpikes are grown much in Fashion
The hardest Tax in all our Nation—
For where Wine & Women & Stock-jobbing past,
The Turnpike must help us at last—

Now Mr. Turnpike, who humbly beg y'r Favour to hear our Comparison Construed, note at the beginning of your Act, you complain of the badness of the Highways; which obldiges us to tell you how they came so bad: when you was Lord of a Manor, you Suffer'd your Tenant to hall a Thousand Load, be it more or less, of the Highways into your land, and not only so but in the Streets for this many years past, you have been throwing Straw in the Streets, where we have as much right to pass as you Mr. Turnpike & that you commonly Shovell up y't once or twice a year we are able to prove this Offence you have Committed Mr. Turnpike to the Omission, When you was a Magistrate you had an Act of Parliament well grounded with Experienced Actions and Good Authority, which you gave power to Command men qualified of good report Rank and Quallity to be Surveyors for to mend the Roads and Highways, or Elsewhere, where you did receive Complaint, or see your Self amiss; but by the Omission of your Duty, and your Carelessnes and Over sight you have lost y'r Honourable Magistracy, and brought your self under the reproach of a Turnpike, by mending the Highways with Fuzz and Heath: so that you have no more reason to Indict us for a Riot, than if we had been

100 John Latimer, *The Annals of Bristol in the Eighteenth Century* (printed for the author, 1893), pp. 155-6.
101 *J. H. of C.* xxi, pp. 157, 159.

going to Stop the Tide from over Flowing. So Mr. Turnpike, we most humbly beg you, when you Purches another Act of Parliament against the Colliers, not to put any Lattin in it; one thing more we would desire of you, that you would lay out all the Money that you have got by the Turnpike — in Catichismas, which you may have for two pence a piece, and give one to every one of those whose name are quoted between the 8th and 13 pages of your Act, and by that they may Learn to do their Duty in that State of Life unto the which it shall please God to call them

And call in this Act as a thing Clandestinely purchased as may apear in our nex Letter in particular: So we remain our Gracious King's Subjects untill Death

We Colliers in Kings-Wood[102]

The colliers and farmers continued to disrupt the working of the trust, and in 1735 all the gates were again destroyed.[103]

The Bristol Trust's act was renewed in 1748,[104] and new roads were placed under its control. In an attempt to allay discontent, coal, firewood, lime, hay, and corn in straw were exempted from tolls, and the duties on hogs, sheep and cattle were halved. But this again proved ineffectual and on 23 May 1749 farmers from Somerset and others destroyed the gate on the Ashton Road near Bedminster.[105] Two days later Gloucestershire farmers pulled down the St John's Cross Gate, a mile from Bristol. The leaders of these two incidents were gaoled and the Riot Act read, bringing threats of further riots.[106] 'Thursday, the 3rd, the people of Kingswood kept gathering and parties of them finished what the Somersetshire people had left undone, so that almost all the turnpikes and turnpike houses about the city were demolished.'[107] On the fifth, a regiment of dragoons arrived, the riots ended and the gates were reconstructed nearer the city.[108] The trust, controlled by city interests, had initially erected gates outside Bristol, thereby placing the heaviest toll-burden on the country people.[109] This, combined with the general suspicion of and hostility towards the trust,[110] seems to have provoked the riots. The Leeds Riots of 1753 were hardly less serious, but thereafter, although scattered outbreaks of violence occurred, there were no further serious disturbances until the Rebecca Riots in the late 1830s and 40s.

102The Colliers Letter to the Turnpike, D15/2 Glouces. RO. (Reproduced with the permission of the Gloucestershire Records Office.)
103Latimer, *Annals of Bristol*, pp. 155-7.
10422 Geo. II c.28.
105*Gentleman's Magazine* (August 1749), p. 376.
106*Ibid.*   107*Ibid.*
108*Ibid.* p. 377 and Latimer, *Annals of Bristol*, p. 275.
109The Trust's second act in 1730 (4 Geo. II c.22, art. 16) stipulated that gates were not to be placed closer to Bristol than Bedminster Downs and Westbury-upon-Trym.
110See above, p. 26. See also David Williams, *The Rebecca Riots, A Study in Agrarian Discontent* (Cardiff, 1955), p. 183.

In the late seventeenth and early eighteenth centuries the turnpike was new, untested and not widely known. It was therefore regarded with some suspicion both locally and at Westminster, and this may explain in part the relative success of those who, during this period, opposed the trusts. Of the forty-one road bills proposed between 1664 and 1713, sixteen (39%) were defeated.[111] But as the volume of traffic continued to rise, parishes found it increasingly difficult to maintain their roads, and the turnpike became the recognized method of obtaining assistance. As the trusts gained greater acceptance, opposition became less effective, and between 1714 and 1773 only approximately fifteen of the many bills brought forward were defeated.[112]

The turnpike trusts were always established for twenty-one years in the first instance, but when this term neared expiration the trustees petitioned for, and invariably received, a renewal of their authority for a further term. Initially conceived as a device to provide a temporary supplement for parish repair, the trusts became in effect semi-permanent replacements for it, and throughout the eighteenth century and the early nineteenth an increasing amount of mileage came under trust control.

111 *J. H. of C.* Index I, 1547-1714, under Highways.
112 *J. H. of C.* Index II, 1714-74, under Highways.

3

The Development
of the Turnpike System

1

The Webbs have stated[1]

If, during the eighteenth century, any one had taken the trouble to make a turnpike map of England, this would have shown, not a system of radiating arteries of communication, but scattered cases of turnpike administration, unconnected with each other; appearing at first as mere dots on the map, then gradually increasing in number and size so as to form continuous lines; and only by the end of the century becoming, as John Holt somewhat optimistically declared in 1794, 'so multiplied and extended as to form almost an universal plan of communication through the kingdom'.

As no one has yet taken the trouble to make such a map, their views have remained unchallenged. The following chapter is based primarily on maps drawn with reference to the individual turnpike acts and provides a significantly different picture from that presented by the Webbs. To gather the evidence for this purpose all the turnpike acts have been examined individually in order partly to separate the new acts from renewals, partly to date and locate the new acts as they were passed. In this way, it has been possible to build up a detailed picture of the pattern of turnpike development.

Before discussing the growth of the trusts, it is necessary to define more precisely what a turnpike act represented. These acts provide, as Professor Ashton has said, 'neither an index of the inception of schemes ... nor an index of performance. The Act came some time after the project had been put on foot but some time before operations began.'[2] Although the passage of an act does not in itself denote road improvement it is nevertheless significant, for it does show both the need for improvement as well as local interests disposed and able to secure legislation.[3] The remaining problem is that of inception. The conditions which created the need for a turnpike were cumulative. Traffic did not

[1] Webbs, *King's Highway*, p. 125.
[2] T. S. Ashton, *Economic Fluctuations in England 1700-1800* (Oxford, 1959), p. 90.
[3] John Ginarlis has pointed out to me that a few acts were never put into force.

increase nor the roads fall into disrepair in a single year, but rather over a number of years. The exact time of inception may not, therefore, tell us a great deal more than the date of an act's passage.

The years under discussion have been divided, by the type and volume of turnpike activity, into four periods: 1663–1750, 1751–72, 1773–91 and 1792–1839.[4] The first will be studied in some detail, for although there were relatively few acts passed in each year, the roads turnpiked were of singular importance, and the turnpike system created in these years was to serve as the basis for subsequent road improvements. The developments in this period will be dealt with in two parts: (1) the turnpiking of the main London routes; (2) the turnpiking of the roads around the provincial centres.

2

There were thirteen main routes leading from London, the turnpiking of which, along their whole lengths, was virtually completed by 1750. These were: (1) the Great North Road, (2) the road from London through Derby to Manchester, (3) the road from London through Cirencester to Gloucester and Hereford, (4) the road from London through Oxford to Gloucester and Hereford, (5) the Western Road to Bath and Bristol, (6) the road from London through Oxford to Birmingham and to Worcester, (7) the road from London through Warwick to Birmingham, (8) the London–Birmingham–Shrewsbury Road, (9) the London–Chester Road, (10) the road from London through Coventry to Manchester, (11) the London–Harwich Road, (12) the London–Dover Road, (13) the road from London to Portsmouth and Chichester.[5]

The Great North Road was the longest and one of the most heavily travelled roads in the country.[6] It was the main route to and from the northern counties and connected many important provincial centres

---

[4]There are a number of difficulties associated with dating the turnpike acts. Besides the use of the Julian Calendar before 1752, the regnal year does not correspond to the calendar year. These problems have been resolved in the following manner: Firstly, New Style dates will be used when discussing acts passed from 1700. Secondly, regnal years will be assigned single calendar years. This will avoid needless confusion and can be justified, as there was generally little parliamentary activity from July or August to November or December, and most acts received the Royal Assent in the first six months of a given year. For example, the first year of the reign of George I began on 2 August 1714; however, the first acts of this regnal year did not become law until 1715 (New Style). The regnal years and their corresponding dates are as follows:

1 Geo. I   − 1715 (regnal year from the beginning of August)
1 Geo. II − 1728 (regnal year from second week in June)
1 Geo. III − 1761 (regnal year from the third week in October).

[5]See Appendix C for the charts of main route turnpike trust growth.
[6]Jackman, *Development of Transportation*, p. 95.

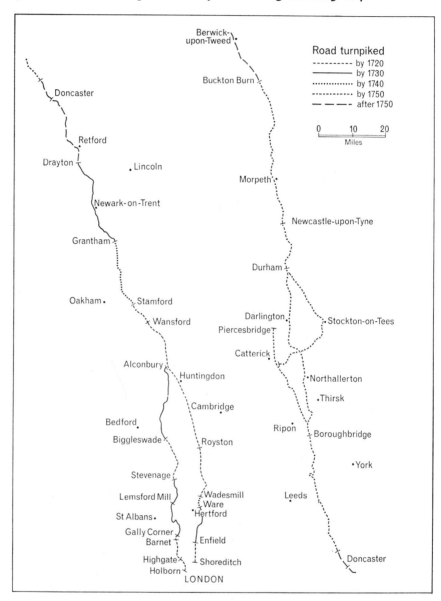

1   Great North Road

with the metropolis. It left London in two branches: one from Holborn
through Highgate, Stevenage and Biggleswade to Alconbury, and the
other from Shoreditch through Ware, Royston, and Huntingdon, joining the other branch at Alconbury, and from there continuing north to
Berwick-upon-Tweed.

There were five acts passed on this route before 1720.[7] Two were
for the road from Wadesmill (Hertfordshire) to Wansford Bridge
(Northamptonshire), and three for roads leading into London. In 1726
the road from Grantham to Little Drayton (Nottinghamshire) was turnpiked,[8] and by 1730 both branches of the road from London to Wansford
Bridge were competely turnpiked,[9] except for three miles.[10] In the 1730s
the roads from Ware to Wadesmill and from Stamford to Grantham
were turnpiked.[11]

Five new trusts were created in the 1740s,[12] four of which were in
Yorkshire, Durham and Northumberland.[13] By 1750 the entire road
had been turnpiked but for three segments: (1) Little Drayton–Doncaster (35 miles), (2) Buckton Burn–Berwick-upon-Tweed (10 miles),
(3) Barnet–Gally Corner (1 mile).

Three of the five early turnpikes (before 1720) on the Great North
Road were on roads near London, where the great volume of both local
and through traffic made it particularly difficult for the parishes to
maintain their roads. Although a turnpike offered parishes the opportunity to relieve themselves of some of their responsibility for road repair,
the new authorities did not gain immediate, widespread acceptance,
and in some areas there were significant time-lags between the turnpiking of adjoining sections of road. For example, while the road from
Shoreditch to Enfield was turnpiked in 1712, the Enfield–Ware Road
was not turnpiked until 1724, and eighteen years elapsed between the

[7]1663 (15 Car. II c.1) Wadesmill–Royston. This act included the road from Royston to
Stilton, but it does not seem it was enforced on this latter road (see above, p. 21).
1710 (9 Anne c.14) Royston–Wansford Bridge. 1711 (10 Anne c.4) Highgate–Barnet.
1712 (12 Anne c.19) Shoreditch–Enfield. 1717 (3 Geo. I c.4) Islington, Holborn, etc.–
Highgate.
[8]12 Geo. I c.16.
[9]1720 (6 Geo. I c.25) Stevenage–Biggleswade. 1725 (11 Geo. I c.20) Biggleswade–
Alconbury. 1725 (11 Geo. I c.11) Enfield–Ware. 1726 (12 Geo. I c.10) Lemsford Mill–
Stevenage. 1730 (3 Geo. II c.10) Gally Corner–Lemsford Mill.
[10]Ware–Wadesmill – 2 miles and Barnet–Gally Corner – 1 mile.
[11]1733 (6 Geo. II c.15) Ware–Wadesmill. This road was added to the Enfield–Ware Trust,
1739 (12 Geo. II c.8) Stamford–Grantham.
[12]1741 (14 Geo. II c.28) Doncaster–Boroughbridge. 1745 (18 Geo. II c.8) Boroughbridge–
Darlington–Durham. 1747 (20 Geo. II c.12) Durham–Newcastle-upon-Tyne. 1747
(20 Geo. II c.9) Newcastle-upon-Tyne–Buckton Burn. 1749 (22 Geo. II c.17) Stamford–Wansford Bridge.
[13]Besides the roads previously mentioned, the road from Boroughbridge through Catterick to Piercebridge was turnpiked in 1743 (16 Geo. II c.7), and the road from
Catterick through Yarm and Stockton-on-Tees to Durham was turnpiked in 1747
(20 Geo. II c.28).

turnpiking of the road from Highgate to Barnet (1711) and the adjoining Gally Corner–Lemsford Mill Road (1729). The initial suspicion of the turnpikes seems, however, to have abated somewhat in the 1720s, and five new trusts were created. Besides the demand for better communication with the metropolis and the desire to transfer a portion of the repair costs to the road-users, trust development was also stimulated by the example given by existing trusts and their effect on adjacent roads. For example, in the petition for the turnpike from Cory's Mill (near Stevenage) to Lemsford Mill[14] it was claimed that the traffic on the road had increased as a result of travellers attempting to avoid paying tolls on the nearby Stevenage–Bigglewade Road.

Once begun, the turnpiking of the route in the North was fairly rapid. The pattern of development in this area suggests that the first act in 1741, for the Doncaster–Boroughbridge Road, may have started a chain-reaction, for the road from Boroughbridge to Piercebridge was turnpiked in 1743, the road from Boroughbridge to Durham in 1745 and the road from Durham to Buckton Burn in 1747.

The Buckton Burn–Berwick-upon-Tweed Road was turnpiked in 1753,[15] the road from Bawtry to Little Drayton in 1766[16] and the remaining segment from Doncaster to Bawtry in 1776.[17] Defoe claimed,[18] 'From hence [Bawtry] to Doncaster is a pleasant road, and good ground, and never wants any repair.' This may explain why this road was not turnpiked before the mid-seventies.

There were six acts on the London–Manchester Road before 1720,[19] and by 1717 the road was turnpiked from Northampton to Stoke Goldington (Bedfordshire), and, but for fifteen miles, from London to Woburn (Bedfordshire). Six new acts in the 1720s[20] almost completed the turnpiking of this route. Turnpikes extended from London to Northampton, from Pitsford Bridge (five miles from Northampton) to Loughborough and from Manchester to Buxton (Derby). The Loughborough–Hartington Road was turnpiked in 1738,[21] and the road from

---

[14] *J. H. of C.* xx, p. 570.

[15] 26 Geo. II c.46.

[16] 6 Geo. III c.67.

[17] 16 Geo. III c.71.

[18] Daniel Defoe, *A Tour through the whole Island of Great Britain*, Vol. II (London, 1962), p. 181.

[19] 1706 (6 Anne c.13) Hockliffe–Woburn. 1708 (8 Anne c.9) Stoke Goldington–Northampton. 1710 (9 Anne c.34) Dunstable–Hockliffe. 1711 (10 Anne c.4) Highgate–Barnet. 1715 (1 Geo. I c.12) South Mimms–St Albans. 1717 (3 Geo. I c.4) Islington, Holborn, etc.–Highgate.

[20] 1722 (8 Geo. I c.13) Pitsford Bridge–Market Harborough. 1723 (9 Geo. I c.13) Newport Pagnell–Stoke Goldington. This road was added to the Northampton–Stoke Goldington Trust. 1723 (9 Geo. I c.11) St Albans–Dunstable. 1725 (11 Geo. I c.13) Buxton–Manchester. 1726 (12 Geo. I c.5) Market Harborough–Loughborough. 1728 (1 Geo. II c.10) Woburn–Newport Pagnell. This road was added to the Hockliffe–Woburn Trust, which by this act was placed under trustee control.

[21] 11 Geo. II c.33.

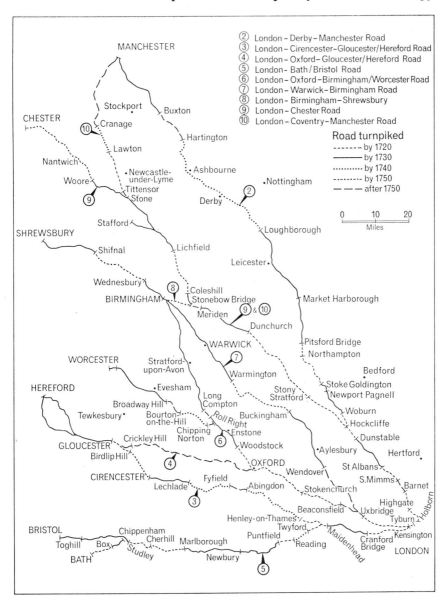

2 Roads to the north and west of London

Pitsford Bridge to Northampton in 1750.[22] By 1750, there were only two sections of the road without turnpikes: (1) Buxton–Hartington (11 miles) and (2) Barnet–South Mimms (3 miles).

The pattern of trust development on this route was similar to that on the Great North Road. Most early acts were for roads near London, the route was filled in during the 1720s and completed in the following two decades. Defoe observed,[23] 'On this road, after you are pass'd Dunstable ... you enter the deep clays, which are so surprisingly soft, that it is perfectly frightful to travellers ... From Hockley to Northampton, thence to Harborough, and Leicester, and thence to the very bank of the Trent these terrible clays continue.' This plus the heavy through traffic accounted for the rapid spread of turnpikes on this route. These factors were cited by the supporters of the Brampton Bridge–Harborough Road Act,[24] who also complained of the lack of water transport and contended that road improvement would lower the cost of carrying coal and lead and facilitate trade with other counties.

There were three acts on the main London–Gloucester Road (the route via Henley-on-Thames and Cirencester),[25] before 1720: one for the road from Gloucester to Birdlip Hill,[26] one for the road from Kensington to Cranford Bridge[27] and one for the Henley-on-Thames–Maidenhead Road.[28] In 1726, Gloucester was linked by turnpike with Hereford,[29] and a year later the roads from Cirencester to Lechlade[30] and from Cranford Bridge to Maidenhead Bridge[31] were turnpiked. The road from Lechlade to Henley was turnpiked during the 1730s, and the route was completed[32] in 1747 by an act for the road between Birdlip and Cirencester.[33]

On the Oxford route, three acts before 1720[34] connected London by turnpike with Oxford, except for nine miles between Beaconsfield and Uxbridge. Following the turnpiking of the road from Gloucester to Crickley Hill in 1723,[35] there were no further acts on this route until

[22]23 Geo. II c.8. This road was added to the Pitsford Bridge–Market Harborough Trust.
[23]Defoe, *A Tour*, Vol. II, p. 118.
[24]*B.M. Collection 516m (16)*.
[25]The preamble of 9 Geo. II. c.31 states 'to the top of Birdlip Hill (being the road to London)' and 'Crickley Hill (being the road to Oxford)'.
[26]1696/7 (9 Wm. III c.18).
[27]1717 (3 Geo. I c.14).
[28]1718 (4 Geo. I c.6).
[29]12 Geo. I c.13.
[30]13 Geo. I c.11.
[31]13 Geo. I c.31.
[32]Except for the six miles between Abingdon and Fyfield. 1733 (6 Geo. II c.16) Fyfield–St John's Bridge (Lechlade). 1736 (9 Geo. II c.14) Henley-on-Thames–Abingdon.
[33]20 Geo. II c.23.
[34]1715 (1 Geo. I c.25) Tyburn–Uxbridge. 1719 (5 Geo. I c.1) Beaconsfield–Stokenchurch. 1719 (5 Geo. I c.2) Stokenchurch–Oxford.
[35]9 Geo. I c.31.

1751, when the roads between Crickley Hill and Oxford[36] and between Uxbridge and Beaconsfield[37] were turnpiked.

The Henley route was the main road from Gloucester to London, and this may account for its earlier completion in the West. This road connected London with the cloth markets of Cirencester, Fairford, Tetbury and Minchinhampton,[38] and cheese and other produce was sent to the metropolis from Lechlade and Cricklade via the Thames.[39] The availability of water transport may explain why the road between Henley and Lechlade was turnpiked relatively later than the other sections of the road. The eastern portions of both routes also formed parts of other important trunk roads. The London–Oxford Road was on the route to Worcester and to Birmingham, and the road from Kensington to Maidenhead was part of the Western Road to Bath and Bristol. The volume of traffic on these sections was therefore probably heavier than on the western portions of the road and may have led to their being turnpiked at an early date. The supporters of the Kensington–Cranford Bridge Turnpike Act claimed that the traffic on the road had increased because people sought to avoid the gates of the Tyburn–Uxbridge Trust.[40] They also complained that this trust had been allocated one-half of the statute labour of the parishes of Fulham and Kensington, and that this made it impossible to maintain the road between Kensington and Cranford.[41]

There were five acts on the Western Road before 1720.[42] Two of these were in the West, two near Reading and one near London. By 1728, turnpike trusts extended from Bristol through Chippenham to Calne, from Bath to Chippenham and from London to Marlborough, but for five miles between Twyford and Reading.[43] This section was turnpiked in 1736,[44] and the route was completed in 1743, by an act for the eight-mile Cherhill–Marlborough Road.[45]

The Western Road connected London with Bristol, Bath and the cloth centres of the West. Describing Frome, Defoe said,[46] 'I call it an inland town, because it is particularly distinguish'd as such, being,

---

[36] 24 Geo. II c.28.

[37] 24 Geo. II c.32. This road was added to the Wendover–Buckingham Trust.

[38] Defoe, *A Tour*, Vol. I, p. 279.

[39] *Ibid.* pp. 283-4 and Vol. II, p. 131.

[40] MSS Petitions, 12 June 1717, H. of L. RO. See also, *J. H. of C.* xviii, pp. 536-7.

[41] *Ibid.*

[42] 1707 (6 Anne c.77) Cherhill–Studley Bridge. 1707 (6 Anne c.42) Bath–Kingsdown Hill (Box). 1714 (13 Anne c.28), Reading–Puntfield. 1717 (3 Geo. I c.14) Kensington–Cranford Bridge. 1718 (4 Geo. I c.6) Maidenhead Bridge–Twyford.

[43] 1726 (12 Geo. I c.8) Newbury–Marlborough. 1726 (12 Geo. I c.11) Chippenham–Kingsdown Hill (Box). 1727 (13 Geo. I c.12) Toghill–Bristol. 1727 (13 Geo. I c.13) Toghill–Studley Bridge. 1727 (13 Geo. I c.31) Cranford Bridge–Maidenhead Bridge. 1728 (1 Geo. II c.7) Puntfield–Newbury.

[44] 9 Geo. II c.31.   [45] 16 Geo. II c.10.   [46] Defoe, *A Tour*, Vol. I, p. 280.

not only no sea-port, but not near any sea-port, having no manner of communication by water, no navigable river at it, or near it. Its trade is wholly clothing, and the cloths they make, are, generally speaking, all conveyed to London.' This description could also be applied to most of the other cloth towns in the area. The lack of water transport and the consequent need to send goods by land carriage to London,[47] may have led to the early turnpiking of roads near the cloth markets of Devizes,[48] Chippenham and Calne, and probably accounts for the virtual completion of the route by 1728. Early turnpike activity near Reading[49] was due not only to the traffic from the West, but also to the great quantities of malt, meal and timber carried here for shipment to London.[50]

Sizeable portions of two of the three routes from London to Birmingham were also sections of other main roads. The main route through Coventry formed the southern part of the London–Shrewsbury Road, the London–Chester Road and the road from London to Manchester, and the route via Oxford was part of the London–Worcester Road.

By 1718, there were turnpikes on the Coventry route from London to St Albans[51] and from Dunstable to Dunchurch.[52] In Staffordshire, eight miles of the Manchester Road between Tittensor and Lawton were turnpiked in 1714.[53] In the 1720s the turnpiking of the road from London to Birmingham was completed,[54] but for ten miles between Meriden and Birmingham.[55] To the north-west, the roads from Shifnal to Shrewsbury (1726)[56] and from Birmingham to Wednesbury (1727)[57] were turnpiked. In 1729, roads were turnpiked from Lichfield through Stone to Woore and from Lichfield to Burton-on-Trent.[58] The remaining segments of the Chester Road and the Shrewsbury Road were turnpiked

[47]T. S. Willan, *English Coasting Trade 1600-1750* (Manchester, 1938), pp. 94-5.

[48]1706 (6 Anne c.26) for the road from Devizes to Shepherds' Shore on the way to the Western Road. Goods carried from Trowbridge, Bradford, Frome and Warminster passed along this road on their way to the Western Road.

[49]Besides the acts on the Western Road, in 1718 (4 Geo. I c.7) the important corn market of Basingstoke was linked by turnpike with Reading.

[50]Defoe, *A Tour*, Vol. I, p. 291.

[51]Except for the three miles between Barnet and South Mimms. 1711 (10 Anne c.4) Highgate–Barnet. 1715 (1 Geo. I c.12) South Mimms–St Albans. 1717 (3 Geo. I c.4) Islington, Holborn, etc.–Highgate.

[52]1706 (6 Anne c.4) Hockliffe–Stony Stratford. 1707 (6 Anne c.77) Old Stratford (adjoining Stony Stratford)–Dunchurch. 1710 (9 Anne c.34) Dunstable–Hockliffe.

[53]13 Anne c.31.

[54]1723 (9 Geo. I c.11) St Albans–Dunstable. 1724 (10 Geo. I c.15) Dunchurch–Meriden.

[55]And except for the road from Barnet to South Mimms.

[56]12 Geo I c.9.

[57]13 Geo. I c.14. This trust extended to 'Gibbet Lane'.

[58]2 Geo. II c.5. There is some question as to whether this trust extended to Coleshill. The renewal act in 1744 (17 Geo. II c.24) refers to the renewal of the road from Coleshill, and this road is not mentioned as being added by this act. However, Coleshill is not mentioned in the 1729 Act.

in the 1740s.[59] The road from Lawton to Cranage was turnpiked in 1731;[60] however, by 1750, thirty-four miles of the Manchester Road had still not been turnpiked.

Before 1720, the Oxford route was turnpiked, except for eight miles, from London through Oxford to Woodstock.[61] The road from Worcester to Broadway Hill (near Evesham) was turnpiked in the 1720s,[62] and by 1732 the entire road was completed to Birmingham and to Worcester,[63] except for three segments totalling fifteen miles.

The third route to Birmingham, through Buckingham and Warwick, was the slowest to develop. In the 1720s the roads from Birmingham to Warmington[64] and from Wendover to Buckingham[65] were turnpiked. The twenty-three mile Buckingham–Warmington Road was turnpiked in 1744,[66] and the route was completed in 1751, with the turnpiking of the Uxbridge–Wendover Road.[67]

Although the rates of growth of the routes differed, the pattern of their development was similar, with most early turnpikes extending from London and activity near Worcester and near, and to the north of Birmingham, in the 1720s. The London–Coventry Road was used by wagons and coaches travelling back and forth between London and Birmingham, Shrewsbury, Staffordshire, Chester, Liverpool and Manchester,[68] and goods from Birmingham as well as Gloucestershire and Worcestershire were carried on the road between Oxford and London.[69] For most of these areas the rivers and the coast provided the principal arteries of communication with London. However, the combined overland traffic was still undoubtedly considerable and contributed to the early turnpiking of these roads.

[59]Except for six miles between Coleshill and the London–Birmingham Road. Shrewsbury Road: 1745 (18 Geo. II c.19) Birmingham–Stonebow Bridge, 1748 (21 Geo. II c.25) Gibbet Lane (Wednesbury)–Shifnal. Chester Road: 1744 (17 Geo. II c.24) Coleshill, Lichfield and Woore through Nantwich to Chester.

[60]4 Geo. II c.31.

[61]1715 (1 Geo. I c.25) Tyburn–Uxbridge. 1719 (5 Geo. I c.1) Beaconsfield–Stokenchurch. 1719 (5 Geo. I c.2) Stokenchurch–Woodstock.

[62]1726 (12 Geo. I c.14) Worcester–Stonebow Bridge. 1728 (1 Geo. II c.11) Broadway Hill–Evesham–Stonebow Bridge.

[63]1726 (12 Geo. I c.6) Birmingham–Stratford-upon-Avon. 1730 (3 Geo. II c.9) Long Compton–Stratford-upon-Avon. 1730 (3 Geo. II c.21) Woodstock–Roll Right. 1731 (4 Geo. II c.23) Chipping Norton–Bourton-on-the-Hill.

[64]1726 (12 Geo I c.6).

[65]1721 (7 Geo. I stat. 1, c.24). The Tyburn–Uxbridge Road was turnpiked in 1715 (1 Geo. I c.25).

[66]17 Geo. II c.43.

[67]24 Geo. II c.32.

[68]The trustees of the Lichfield Trust, petitioning for a renewal act in 1744, asked for the addition of certain roads because of the heavy traffic between London, Manchester and Liverpool (J. H. of C. xxiv, p. 510).

[69]The report on the petition for the Stokenchurch–Enslow Bridge Trust refers to this road as part of the London–Worcester Road (J. H. of C. xix, p. 33).

Traffic to and from London was not however the sole reason for trust development along the trunk roads, once outside the metropolitan area. The supporters of the Birmingham–Banbury Turnpike Act complained not only of the heavy iron and coal traffic to London from Birmingham, but also of the great quantities of malt and barley carried along the road to Oxford.[70] The road in northern Staffordshire between Tittensor and Lawton was used by carts carrying iron-ore to the Lawton, Vale Royal and Dodington furnaces,[71] and the road from Lawton to Cranage by carts bringing iron from the Lawton furnace to the forges at Cranage.[72] The influence of the local ironmasters is evident, for on both roads the carriage of iron-ore was subject to tolls ranging from one-half to three-fourths less than the normal rate,[73] and on the Lawton–Cranage Road coal, charcoal and pig-iron enjoyed similar benefits. The heavy carriage of iron, coal and ironwares was also an important factor in the turnpiking of the roads north-west of Birmingham.[74] While through traffic may have been a contributory factor, it would seem that the formation of these trusts, and especially those in Staffordshire, was inspired primarily by local traffic conditions.

The London–Harwich Road was turnpiked from Shenfield to Harwich in 1695[75] and from Whitechapel to Shenfield in 1722.[76] Packet-boats from Holland called at Harwich,[77] and the war with France may have prompted the extensive turnpiking of this route in 1695. Besides the possible strategic considerations, there were also great quantities of agricultural goods carried on this road to the London market. 'The great road from London, thro' this whole country towards Ipswich and Harwich, is the most worn with waggons, carts, and carriages; and with infinite droves of black cattle, hogs, and sheep, of any road (that leads thro' no larger an extent of country) in England.'[78]

The first turnpike act on the London–Dover Road was passed in 1718, for the road from Southwark to Blackheath.[79] In 1725[80] the Chalk Trust[81] was ordered to pay £100 a year towards the repair of

---

[70] *J. H. of C.* xx, p. 584.
[71] 13 Anne c.31, art. 12. Also, B.C.L. Johnson, 'The Charcoal Iron Industry in the Early Eighteenth Century', *The Geographical Journal*, cxviii, part 2 (1951), 170.
[72] *Ibid.* p. 172.
[73] 13 Anne c.31, art. 12. 4 Geo. II c.3, art. 1.
[74] *J. H. of C.* xx, pp. 746, 748, 768. See below, p. 47.
[75] 7 & 8 Wm. III c.9. This justice-trust was replaced by a trustee-controlled authority in 1726 (12 Geo. I c.23).
[76] 8 Geo. I c.30.
[77] Defoe, *A Tour*, Vol. I, p. 35.
[78] *Ibid.* Vol. II, p. 121.
[79] 4 Geo. I c.5.
[80] 11 Geo. I c.25, art. 9.
[81] The Chalk Trust was formed in 1711 (10 Anne c.16) and was responsible for the road from Northfleet through Gravesend to Rochester.

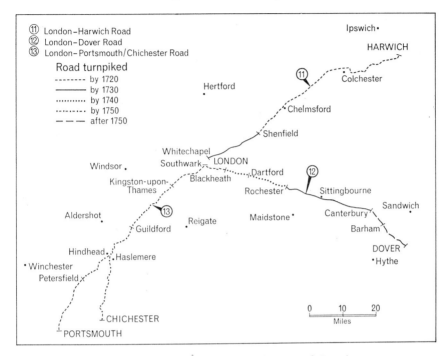

⑪ London–Harwich Road
⑫ London–Dover Road
⑬ London–Portsmouth/Chichester Road

Road turnpiked
------- by 1720
——— by 1730
·········· by 1740
··——·· by 1750
— — after 1750

3 Roads to the east and south-west of London

the road from Chatham to Boughton-under-Blean (about six miles from Canterbury). This sum seems to have proved insufficient, for in 1730 a separate trust was formed on the Rochester–Canterbury Road.[82] Besides their responsibility for this road, the trustees were also to contribute towards the repair of the four-mile road from Dover to Lydden Hill.[83] In 1738, the road from Dartford to Rochester was placed under the control of the Chalk Trust,[84] and in the same year the Blackheath–Dartford Road was added to the New Cross Trust.[85] The road from Dover to Canterbury was not turnpiked until 1753.[86]

There were two early turnpike acts on the road from London to Portsmouth and Chichester; in 1710 for the Portsmouth–Petersfield Road,[87] and in 1718 for the road from Southwark to Kingston-upon-Thames.[88] Repairing the main road near Portsmouth may have been

[82] 3 Geo. II c.15.
[83] 3 Geo. II c.15, art. 10.
[84] 11 Geo. II c.37.
[85] 11 Geo. II c.36.
[86] 26 Geo. II c.32. The road was turnpiked from Dover to Barnham Downs (about six miles from Canterbury).
[87] 9 Anne c.33.
[88] 4 Geo. I c.14.

particularly difficult when in time of war the carriage of goods into the town increased, and this may account for the act of 1710. The remaining parts of the road, from Kingston to Petersfield and from Hindhead to Chichester were turnpiked in 1749.[89]

Although the rates of growth of the main routes differed, an overall pattern of development is evident. Before 1720, most activity was near London. Eighteen (72%) of the twenty-five acts on main routes were for roads within forty miles of the metropolis.[90] In the 1720s, and

CHART I   *Main route mileage completed by 1750*

ROUTE		MILEAGE		
	total	turnpiked by:		remaining
		1730	1750	
(1) The Great North Road	387	169	354	33
(2) The London–Derby– Manchester Road	177	120	164	13
(3) The London–Cirencester– Gloucester and Hereford Road	132	83	126	6
(4) The London–Oxford–Gloucester and Hereford Road	127	78	78	49
(5) The London–Bath and Bristol Road	125·5	112·5	125·5	—
(6) The London–Oxford–Birmingham and Worcester Road	156	126	141	15
(7) The London–Warwick– Birmingham Road	110	68	90	20
(8) The London–Birmingham– Shrewsbury Road	153	122	146	7
(9) The London–Chester Road	183	131	174	9
(10) The London–Coventry– Manchester Road	189	142	152	37
(11) The London–Harwich Road	68	68	68	—
(12) The London–Dover Road	71	36	55	16
(13) The London–Portsmouth and Chichester Road	94	29	94	—
Total Mileage (less double counting)	1,563·5	897·5	1,381·5	182

especially from 1726, trusts were established all along the main routes, except the northern portion of the Great North Road. As shown in chart 1, by 1730, 897·5 miles of the total route mileage of 1,563·5 miles had been turnpiked. In the following decades most of the remaining roads came under trust control, and by 1750 only 182 miles of road had not been turnpiked.

[89] 22 Geo. II c.35.
[90] This includes roads, any part of which extended within a forty-mile radius of the city.

At the beginning of his first 'Tour', Daniel Defoe felt that it was important to draw his readers' attention to the following points:[91]

N.B. I am the more particular in my remark on this place ['Shooberry'] because in the course of my travels the reader will meet with the like in almost every place of note through the whole island, where it will be seen how this whole kingdom, as well the people, as the land, and even the sea, in every part of it, are employ'd to furnish something, and I may add, the best of every thing, to supply the city of London with provisions; I mean by provisions, corn, flesh, fish, butter, cheese, salt, fewel, timber, &C. and cloths also; with every thing necessary for building, and furniture for their own use, or for trades.

London was indeed, as Defoe claimed, the 'great center of England'.[92] The Law Courts, Parliament and the fashionable social life drew people from throughout the country, resulting in heavy passenger traffic on the roads about the metropolis. London was also the dominant financial and commercial centre of the kingdom, and the greatest entrepôt, receiving goods from home and abroad and redistributing them to all parts of the country.[93] This trade plus the growing demand for provisions from a large and increasing population, led to a great volume of goods traffic on the roads leading into the city. The pattern of early turnpike development reflects the pressure of the concentration of passenger and goods carriage on the London roads. Further, the influence of the London market pervaded throughout the country, as the volume of long-distance carriage increased in response to the growth of internal trade and buoyant conditions in the home market.[94] However, as mentioned above,[95] in areas remote from the metropolis local traffic conditions seem to have been of equal, if not greater significance. Carriage to and from provincial markets created repair problems similar to those near London, and thereby contributed to the demand for main route improvement.

The effect of the conditions cited above were not confined to the main routes. They were also felt, with varying degrees of severity, on roads leading into provincial centres and roads connecting these centres with one another. By mid-century, many important roads in the Severn and Wye valleys, the West Riding and the North had been turnpiked. The activity in these areas will be considered in the following section.

[91]Defoe, *A Tour*, Vol. I, p. 12.
[92]*Ibid.* p. 314.
[93]Willan, *English Coasting Trade*, pp. 141-3.
[94]A. H. John, 'Agricultural Productivity and Economic Growth in England, 1700-1760', *The Journal of Economic History*, xxv, no. 1 (1965), 24, 27.
[95]See above, p. 40.

3[96]

Before 1720 there was little turnpike activity in areas remote from the metropolis. Only twelve of the thirty-six new acts passed in this period were for roads more than forty miles from London. The only significant concentration of acts was in the West Country near the cloth towns of Devizes, Chippenham and Calne.[97] The development in this area may have stemmed from the war's disruption of coastal shipping which probably increased the clothiers' already heavy dependence on land transport,[98] especially since the shipping route was round Land's End and up the Channel to London. In other parts of the country there were isolated cases of turnpike development. Turnpikes were erected on short stretches of road leading into Bath (1707),[99] Gloucester (1697/8),[100] Ipswich (1711)[101] and Norwich (1695).[102] In 1698 Celia Fiennes described the state of the road near Norwich:[103]

Thence I went to Windham [Wymondham] ... mostly on a Causey the country being low and morrish and the road on the Causey was in many places full of holes, tho' its secured by a barr at which passangers pay a penny a horse in order to the mending of the ways, for all about is not to be rode on unless its a dry summer.

The busy salt route from Droitwich to Worcester was turnpiked in 1714,[104] and the important corn markets of Basingstoke and Reading were linked by turnpike in 1718.[105]

There was a boom in trust investment in the mid-twenties. Twenty-seven new acts were passed between 1725 and 1727, and over the entire decade forty-seven new trusts were created. The percentage of acts for roads within a forty mile radius of London decreased (to 32%) as turnpiking spread into the West, the Midlands and Lancashire. The main routes continued to receive the most attention, accounting for 55·3% of the legislation, though many new trusts were also established on roads leading into and connecting provincial centres.

The first 'town centred' trusts in the provinces were formed in the twenties. These trusts, responsible for groups of roads leading into

---

[96]All the new turnpike acts from 1663 to 1839 are given in Appendix B.
[97]1706 (6 Anne c.26) Devizes–Shepherds' Shore. 1707 (6 Anne c.76) Cherhill–Calne. 1714 (13 Anne c.17) Shepherds' Shore–Horsley Upright Gate.
[98]See above, p. 38.
[99]6 Anne c.42 (Bath–Kingsdown Hill).
[100]9 Wm. III c.18 (Gloucester–Birdlip Hill).
[101]10 Anne c.42 (Ipswich–Clayton).
[102]7 & 8 Wm. III c.28 (Wymondham–Attleborough).
[103]The Journeys of Celia Fiennes, Christopher Morris, ed. (London, 1947), p. 150.
[104]13 Anne c.27.
[105]4 Geo. I c.7.

CHART 2 *New turnpike acts, 1663-1839*[1]

Areas[2]		Years									Totals
		1663-1719	1720-9	1730-9	1740-50	1751-60	1761-72	1773-91	1792-1815	1816-39	
1	Home counties	13	13	4	2	9	8	3	14	7	73
2	Southern counties	6	1	3	3	24	39	5	34	19	134
3	East Anglia	2	1	2	1	4	29	5	12	5	61
4	Western counties	5	12	3	4	29	15	9	14	11	102
5	Far West	—	—	—	—	24	26	3	3	12	68
6	Northants., Cambs., Hunts. and Beds.	6	6	1	1	10	3	4	11	3	45
7	South Midlands	3	5	4	2	13	12	5	7	7	58
8	North Midlands	2	3	1	1	9	27	11	15	15	84
9	East Midlands	—	2	3	—	21	21	8	16	4	75
10	Yorkshire and Lancashire	—	3	3	13	25	19	9	30	46	148
11	Far North	—	—	—	12	16	6	3	17	10	64
	Total	37	46	24	39	184	205	65	173	139	912

[1]Appendix B lists each new turnpike act and the roads covered.
[2]The areas are defined in Appendix B and below, p. 49.

towns, allowed a town to improve its communications with its hinterland, so ensuring improved facilities for local commerce. The roads
closest to the town where often repaired first, as for example in Hereford,
where the trustees were directed to repair first the most ruinous roads
from the town's gates and bridges.[106] Also, toll-gates were frequently
placed so as not to interfere with intra-town travel.[107] In the 1720s
trusts of this kind were established on the roads leading into Bristol,[108]
Warminster,[109] Leominster,[110] Ledbury,[111] Worcester,[112] Tewkesbury[113]
and, in 1730, Hereford[114] and Bridgwater.[115] The volume of traffic on
the roads near these towns was probably considerable, for they were
all important markets,[116] and with the exception of Ledbury, Bridgwater
and Warminster, were all situated on navigable rivers in the Severn
Valley.[117] Heavy traffic to and from the river-ports did not only affect
the roads near those ports. It was claimed that the roads near Ledbury
were damaged by wagons carrying goods between the Wye and the
Severn,[118] and heavy traffic to and from the Severn was cited in the
petition for the turnpiking of the roads from Gloucester to Stone,
Berkeley, Sodbury and Dursley, in 1726.[119] The fairly extensive turnpiking in the Severn and Wye valleys suggests considerable economic
activity in this area, and more generally in the counties of Gloucester,
Worcester and Hereford.

In 1725 the improvement-minded Liverpool merchants[120] obtained
an act for the road to Prescot.[121] The desire for cheaper coal transport
was the paramount consideration both here[122] and on the road from

---

[106]3 Geo. II c.18, art. 19. Similar provisions were found in: 12 Geo. I c.14, art. 18
(Worcester Trust), 13 Geo. I c. 16 art. 22 (Warminster Trust), and 12 Geo. I c. 18,
art. 27 (Tewkesbury Trust).

[107]Webbs, *King's Highway*, pp. 127, 153.

[108]1727 (13 Geo. I c.12).   [109]1727 (13 Geo. I c.16).

[110]1729 (2 Geo II c.13).   [111]1721 (7 Geo. II c.23).

[112]1726 (12 Geo. I c.14).   [113]1726 (12 Geo. I c.18).

[114]3 Geo. II c.9. Following this trust's formation, the Leominster and Ledbury trusts
were linked to one another through Hereford, and through Gloucester to London.

[115]3 Geo. II c.34.

[116]Defoe, *A Tour*, Vol. I, pp. 268-9, 281; Vol. II, pp. 41-2, 48-9. R. B. Westerfield,
'Middlemen in English Business, particularly between 1660 and 1760', *Transactions of
the Connecticut Academy of Arts and Sciences*, Vol. XIX (1915), 150.

[117]T. S. Willan, 'The River Navigation and Trade of the Severn Valley, 1600-1750',
Econ. Hist. Rev. VIII, no. 1 (1937-8), 68–79.

[118]*J. H. of C.* XIX, p. 456. The heavy grain carriage into the town was also mentioned.

[119]*J. H. of C.* XX, pp. 644-5.

[120]T. C. Barker, 'The Beginnings of the Canal Age in the British Isles', in *Studies in the
Industrial Revolution*, ed. L. S. Pressnell (London, 1960), p. 4.

[121]12 Geo. I c.21.

[122]*J. H. of C.* XX, p. 568 and F. A. Baily, 'The Minutes of the Trustees of the Turnpike
Roads from Liverpool, St. Helens, Warrington and Ashton in Makerfield, 1726-1789',
in *Transactions of the Historical Society of Lancashire and Cheshire*, 88, Part I, p. 160.
He also says that the road was intended to facilitate both goods carriage and coach
travel to and from the port (*ibid.* p. 161).

Warrington through Wigan to Preston,[123] turnpiked in 1727. The carriage of coal to the brine-pits at Droitwich led to the Worcester–Droitwich Trust being extended to Bromsgrove in 1726,[124] and heavy iron and coal traffic accounted for the turnpiking, a year later, of the roads from Bromsgrove to Stourbridge and to Birmingham[125] and from Birmingham to Wednesbury, Bilston, Dudley and Stourbridge.[126]

For reasons which are not readily apparent there was a sharp drop in the number of trust formations in the 1730s. Only twenty-four new trusts were created, a decrease of 51% from the previous decade. However, despite the low level of activity,[127] there was a number of important roads turnpiked. In 1732 a trust was established on the road leading from Manchester through Stockport to Saltersbrook[128] (the route to Barnsley, Doncaster and Hull). Two important wool-routes were turnpiked in 1735; one from Manchester to Austerlands[129] (leading towards Huddersfield and Wakefield) and the other from Rochdale over Blackstone-Edge to Halifax and Elland.[130] In 1738, Nottingham was linked by turnpike with the Great North Road at Loughborough,[131] and a year later the roads from Worksop and from Bakewell to Chesterfield were turnpiked.[132]

In the forties the pace of turnpike development speeded up. The period was characterized by the rapid extension of turnpikes on roads in the North. Twenty-six new trusts, covering a total of approximately 610 miles, were established in Yorkshire, Lancashire and the counties to the north.

In Cumberland the harbour improvements undertaken at Whitehaven[133] has given rise to increased traffic to and from the hinterland,[134] and in 1740 the harbour trustees obtained an act for the roads leading into the port.[135] Water transport also affected, although in a different way, trust development in the West Riding. The unreliability of the

---

[123] 13 Geo. I c.10 (Warrington–Wigan). 13 Geo. I c.9 (Wigan–Preston). In both these acts coal was charged from one-half to one-third the normal toll.

[124] 12 Geo. I c.20. In the report on the renewal act in 1748 it was claimed that thirty wagons a day were employed carrying coal from Bromsgrove to the brine-pits (*J. H. of C.* xxv, p. 751).

[125] 13 Geo. I c.15.

[126] 13 Geo. I c.14.

[127] Not only did the number of acts decrease, but the total mileage turnpiked also decreased, 1720–9: approximately 967 miles. 1730–9: approximately 424 miles. This was a 56·2% drop from the 20s to the 30s.

[128] 5 Geo. II c.10.

[129] 8 Geo. II c.3.

[130] 8 Geo. II c.7.

[131] 11 Geo. II c.3.

[132] 12 Geo. II c.12.

[133] The first act for improving the harbour was obtained in 1707 (7 Anne c.9).

[134] *J. H. of C.* xxiii, p. 433.

[135] 13 Geo. II c.14.

Aire and Calder navigation coupled with its high charges prompted the merchants and manufacturers of Leeds, Halifax and Wakefield to initiate an extensive road improvement scheme. 'The turnpike promoters' professed intention was to provide an alternative system of transport completely independent of the Aire and Calder navigation centred on Selby and the River Ouse, and to a lesser extent Tadcaster and the River Wharfe.'[136] In 1741 they secured the passage of acts for the roads from Leeds to Elland,[137] Selby through Leeds to Bradford and Halifax,[138] and Weeland through Wakefield to Halifax.[139] In the same year trusts were established on the Great North Road between Doncaster and Boroughbridge,[140] on the roads from Doncaster and Rotherham towards Manchester[141] and the road from Doncaster through Wakefield to Halifax.[142]

Influenced, perhaps, by the West Riding's example[143] and affected by the exigencies of war, turnpiking spread rapidly northward in the following years. By 1745, the Great North Road had been turnpiked to Durham[144] and two years later was extended through Newcastle to Buckton Burn.[145] During this period a number of important coal routes, leading into Newcastle, Durham and Sunderland, were turnpiked.[146] Turnpike trusts were also established on the road from York to Boroughbridge[147] and from York to Tadcaster,[148] the road from Catterick towards Carlisle (to Brough-under-Stainmore)[149] and three roads leading to the port of Hull.[150]

[136] R. G. Wilson, 'Transport Dues as Indices of Economic Growth, 1775-1820', *Econ. Hist. Rev.* 2nd Series, XIX, no. 1 (1966), 111.

[137] 14 Geo. II c.25.

[138] 14 Geo. II c.32.

[139] 14 Geo. II c.23.

[140] 14 Geo. II c.28.

[141] 14 Geo. II c.31. This trust extended to Saltersbrook, joining the turnpike trust from Manchester, established in 1732 (see above, p. 47). This latter trust may have influenced the promoters of the Doncaster and Rotherham trust, for in their petition they claimed that one-half of the road to Manchester had already been repaired (*J. H. of C.* xxiii, p. 568).

[142] 14 Geo. II c.19.

[143] The first discussions, which eventually led to the passage of the Hull–Beverley Trust (1744), were begun in November 1741. (K. A. MacMahon, 'Roads and Turnpike Trusts in Eastern Yorkshire', *East Yorkshire Local History Series*, no. 18 (1964), 17.)

[144] See above, p. 33.

[145] See above, p. 33.

[146] 1747 (20 Geo. II c.13) Durham–Sunderland. 1747 (20 Geo. II c.28) Catterick–Stockton–Durham. 1748 (21 Geo. II c.27) Piercebridge–Kirkmerrington etc. 1749 (22 Geo. II c.7) Newcastle–River Wanspeck. 1749 (22 Geo. II c.9) Newcastle–North Shields.

[147] 23 Geo. II c.38.

[148] 18 Geo. II c.16.

[149] 1743 (16 Geo. II c.3) Bowes–Brough-under-Stainmore. 1744 (17 Geo. II c.22) Bowes–Middleton Tyas.

[150] 1744 (17 Geo. II c.25) Hull–Beverley. 1745 (18 Geo. II c.4) Hull–Kirk Ella. 1745 (18 Geo. II c.6) Hull–Hedon.

The years of 'Turnpike Mania' began in 1751 and continued through 1772. The period well deserves its title for more new trusts were established (389) in these twenty-two years than in either the preceding four decades or the succeeding sixty-six years. In the following section the trust development during these years will be considered briefly.

During the period 1751–60, 184 new trusts were established. Although they were spread throughout the country, there were significant concentrations in five main areas.[151] These were: (1) the West (14·7% of the total number of new acts), (2) Lancashire and Yorkshire (14·2%), (3) the Far West (13%), (4) the Southern Counties (12·5%), (5) the East Midlands (9·5%).[152]

In this period the first turnpike trusts were established in the Far West. The town-centred trust[153] was particularly popular in this area, and thirteen of the twenty-four new trusts were of this type. In the West the new trusts were concentrated near the prospering cloth centres of Frome, Trowbridge and Melksham, and to a lesser degree Cirencester and Gloucester.[154] Ten of the twenty-three trusts in the Southern Counties were in the area west of Guildford and south of Basingstoke, while only four new trusts were established in Kent. From 1753 to 1757 there was fairly extensive turnpiking in Leicestershire and in south Derbyshire, but in the last two years of the period the centre of activity in the East Midlands shifted to Nottinghamshire and central and northern Derbyshire. Five trans-Pennine routes were turnpiked in Lancashire and Yorkshire, as were roads near Harrogate and Knaresborough, and those leading from Lancaster towards Cumberland and Westmorland. There was relatively little activity in the Far North though in 1753 seven trusts were established, linking Carlisle, Penrith

[151]The counties have been assigned to the following areas:
(1) *Home Counties*: Middlesex, Hertfordshire, Essex, Buckinghamshire and eastern parts of Berkshire.
(2) *Southern Counties*: Sussex, Surrey, Kent and Hampshire.
(3) *East Anglia and Lincoln*: Norfolk, Suffolk, Lincolnshire and eastern part of Cambridgeshire.
(4) *Western Counties*: Gloucestershire, Herefordshire, Wiltshire, northern Somerset.
(5) *Far West*: Cornwall, Dorset, Devon and southern Somerset.
(6) *N.C.H.B.*: Northamptonshire, Cambridgeshire, Huntingdonshire and Bedfordshire.
(7) *South Midlands*: South of Birmingham to the borders of the other areas.
(8) *North Midlands*: North of Birmingham to the borders of the other areas.
(9) *East Midlands*: Derbyshire, Leicestershire, Nottinghamshire and Rutland.
(10) *Yorkshire and Lancashire*.
(11) *Far North*: Durham, Cumberland, Northumberland and Westmorland.
[152]The turnpike acts referred to in this section can be found in Appendix B. Also see chart 2, p. 45.
[153]See above, p. 46.
[154]The recovery in foreign trade from 1746 and export boom in 1749-50 may have contributed to trust expansion in this area; however, the depression of 1752–4 does not seem to have affected trust investment (see Ashton, *Economic Fluctuations*, pp. 76–7, 148–9).

and Kendal with one another, through the latter with Lancaster and Keighley and through Brough-under-Stainmore with the Great North Road at Catterick.

In the years 1761–72 there was a shift in the areas of trust concentration. In Yorkshire most of the new trusts were in the East Riding,[155] and only four trusts were established in Lancashire. The continuing inactivity in the West Riding woollen industry[156] may have been

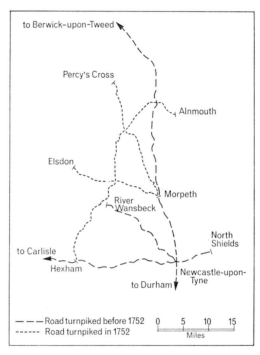

4   Morpeth-area roads

responsible for the fall in the number of new trusts in this area. Turnpike activity continued apace in the Far West (12·5% of all acts) but decreased substantially in the West (7%). In East Anglia the first extensive turnpiking took place during these years, as fifteen new trusts were formed in Norfolk and Suffolk. In the East Midlands most new trusts were in northern and central Derbyshire. Turnpiking increased considerably in the North Midlands[157] (14%), and of the twenty-eight new

[155]Ten of the fifteen new trusts in Yorkshire were in the East Riding.
[156]Wilson, 'Transport Dues', p. 113.
[157]A most unusual trust was created in this area in 1772. It was a turnpike trust for a towpath along the Severn from Coalbrookdale to Bewdley Bridge. The trustees, including Abraham and Samuel Darby, were given all the powers of trustees of road trusts, although there were special clauses dealing with the river banks and rights of passage (12 Geo. III c.109). A similar act for a tow-path from Coalbrookedale to Welsh Bridge was passed in 1809 (49 Geo. III c.121).

trusts, thirteen were within fifteen miles of the Potteries. Demands for improved transport in this area also led, in 1766, to the passage of acts for the Trent and Mersey Canal and the Staffordshire and Worcestershire Canal.[158] The Southern Counties was the area of greatest activity (18·5%), and most of the new trusts were in Kent and Sussex.

A great number of factors underlay the twenty-two-year investment boom. An increased rate of population growth, growing industrialization and urbanization, the expansion of the domestic market, the growth of exports, high agricultural prices and the greater rate of enclosure. All these factors led to a larger volume of passenger and goods traffic and, consequently, to demands for cheaper and more reliable, year-round communication. These demands gave rise to both widespread turnpiking and canal building,[159] with individuals such as Josiah Wedgwood promoting both types of improvement.[160] The continuance of low interest rates throughout most of the period undoubtedly helped to prolong the boom. However, this seems to have been a contributory rather than a central factor, for rates were low during the thirties and forties and when the 'Mania' ended in 1773.[161] The improved conditions in agriculture may have been important, for the landowners, the largest single group of trust investors, would have been better able and more willing to finance road improvement.[162]

While there were a myriad of local and national economic conditions which stimulated trust development, the pattern of this development suggests that the trusts themselves were a major influence on expansion. Except in the Far West, most of the new trusts were either near or linked with existing turnpike roads. In this way the turnpike system formed during the first half of the eighteenth century both influenced and served as the basis for subsequent development. Furthermore, many new trusts were established in interconnected groups;[163] this type of development usually took place over a short period of time. For example, of the four trusts established in the Far North in 1752, three were near Morpeth and the fourth was connected to the Newcastle–Carlisle Road, turnpiked in 1751.[164] In 1753, six interconnected trusts were created in the Carlisle–Penrith area.[165] In the East and North Midlands twenty-four of the twenty-five trusts established during the

---

158Charles Hadfield, *British Canals, an Illustrated History* (London, 1959), p. 81.
159*Ibid.* pp. 79-91.
160*Ibid.* p. 81, and see below, pp. 105-6.
161For a more detailed discussion of interest rates, see below, pp. 120-6.
162See below, pp. 113-17.
163'Interconnected groups' of trusts were trusts linked to one another.
164See map, p. 50.
165See map, p. 52.

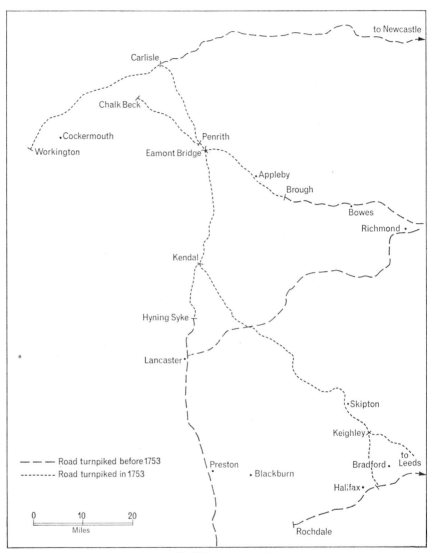

5   Carlisle-area roads

1750s were linked to at least one or other new trust, and in the East Midlands a fairly extensive network of interconnected turnpike roads was formed during these years.[166] In 1769 and 1770, five trusts were created on roads leading into Norwich, and five others were set up on adjoining roads.[167] Similar patterns of development in other parts of the country suggest that the demonstration effect was of considerable importance during the mania period.

[166]See map, p. 53.
[167]See map. p. 55.

Only four new trusts were formed in 1773, and, although there was a modest recovery in 1777, the period 1773–91 was one of little activity. Sixty-four trusts were created, a decrease of 14·2 trusts per year from the previous period. The impetus of the preceding years had been lost, and the rising interest rates from the late seventies may have helped to forestall a revival. Furthermore, it could be argued that

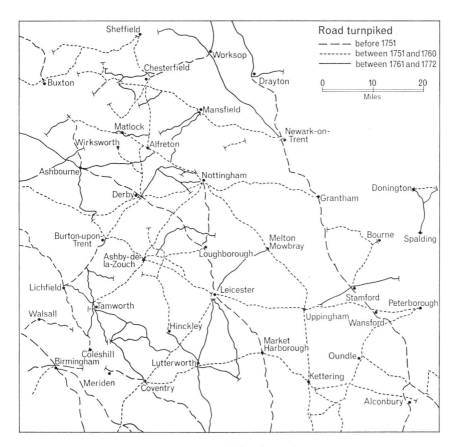

6   Eastern Midlands roads

the specific transport problems for which trusts were established had largely been met by the early seventies. As in the preceding period, most trusts were established near existing turnpikes and there were no major concentrations of new trusts during these years. Activity was greatest in the North and East Midlands (29·7%), Lancashire and Yorkshire (14%) and in the West (14%).

The number of new turnpike acts rose sharply during the speculative boom of the early nineties, reached a peak in 1793 and fell in 1794,

C

after the boom had collapsed. During the remaining years of the war the fluctuations in the level of trust formations corresponded (with a one-year lag) with the movements in building and in canal investment.[168] A short-lived recovery in 1797 was followed by three years of inactivity, a revival of interest from 1801 to 1803 and a modest boom during the years of renewed speculative activity between 1809 and 1812. The seemingly increased speculative nature of trust formations from the 1790s is underlined by the greater number of 'disinterested' investors which appear on the trusts' lists in this period.[169]

Trust formations during the war years owed much to outbreaks of speculative investment, but may also be seen as a response to the great increase, from about 1794, in the cost of land transport.[170] The demands of war seem to have been important in determining the location of some of the new trusts. For example, fourteen of these trusts were in the Durham and Northumberland coalfields, and fifteen were in Kent, where roads were turnpiked near the ports of Dover, Hythe, Margate, Ramsgate, Folkestone and Deal. In London, five important trusts were set up,[171] three of which were near the docks. There was also considerable activity in the expanding and prosperous cotton-textile areas. In Lancashire an extensive network of turnpikes (comprising fourteen trusts) was formed, linking together Bury, Bolton, Rochdale, Blackburn, Manchester and numerous other towns and in Derbyshire four interconnected trusts were established near Glossop.

The level of trust formations was fairly low during the immediate post-war years but recovered briefly in 1818, a year of high exports and

---

[168]See Ashton, *Economic Fluctuations*, pp. 102-3, 170-3, and H. A. Shannon, 'Bricks — A Trade Index, 1785–1849', in *Essays in Economic History*, Vol. III, ed. E. M. Carus-Wilson (London, 1962), p. 200.

[169]See below, pp. 118-19.

[170]See below, pp. 185-6.

[171]These were significantly different from the ordinary trusts. Owing to the high property values and the necessity of purchasing and pulling down houses in order to widen the roads, the trustees were authorized to pay 5% on loans (which were to be in the form of shares) while work was in progress and from 10% to 12% after the work had been completed. The clerk of the Commercial, East India Docks Trust, testifying before a committee in 1833, contended that this trust was a form of private speculation, similar to a canal company. 'The only Distinction between it [sic the Trust] and a Joint-Stock Company is that it is not perpetual.' (*B.P.P. 1833 (703) xv. 409*, pp. 40-3) By 1821 trusts of this type had issued shares to the following amounts (from *B.P.P. 1821 (747) iv, 343*, pp. 152-3):

(1) Commercial, East India Docks Trust (42 Geo. III c.101) 4¼ miles. Debt–£169,050. Average Annual Income – £12,593.

(2) Dover Street Trust (51 Geo. III c.220) ½ mile. Debt–£34,400. Average Annual Income – £1,537.

(3) Kentish Town–Upper Holloway Trust (51 Geo. III c.156) 1 mile. Debt–£16,000. Average Annual Income – £712.

(4) Poplar–Greenwich Ferry Trust (52 Geo. III c.148) 2½ miles. Debt–£25,800. Average Annual Income – £450.

(5) Highbury–Shoreditch Trust (52 Geo. III c.154) – no data.

industrial prosperity.[172] Thereafter, there was little activity until the speculative boom of the mid-twenties (1824–26), when fifty-nine new trusts were created, twenty-four of which were in Lancashire and Yorkshire. Over the entire period these counties accounted for 32 % of the new acts, the North and East Midlands for 22 % and the Southern Counties for 13 %. The trusts formed during this period were primarily on roads leading either to existing trusts or to growing urban areas.

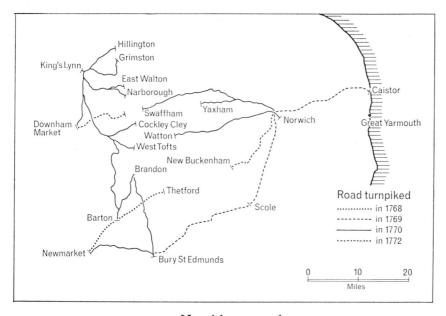

7   Norwich-area roads

These trusts also seemed to have been particularly small. For example in 1839 the mile-per-trust ratio in Yorkshire was 14·3, while the trusts established between 1816 and 1839 averaged only 6·4 miles. In Lancashire the figures were 11·4 miles-per-trust and 8·7 miles-per-trust respectively and in Sussex, 13·7 miles and 7·8 miles. The proliferation of many small trusts during these years accounts in part for the growing concern of parliamentary committees with the apparent inefficiency of the small trusts[173] and their poor financial condition. This concern was justified, as regards the late trusts, for most of them proved to be financially untenable.[174]

172A. D. Gayer, W. W. Rostow, A. J. Schwartz, *The Growth and Fluctuations of the British Economy 1790–1850* (Oxford, 1953), Vol. 1, pp. 145–7, 151–9.
173See below, p. 64.
174See below, pp. 66–8.

4

The picture of trust development which emerges from a detailed investigation of the individual turnpike acts does not lend support to the Webbs' picture of trust expansion.[175] They completely ignored the importance of turnpike growth during the first half of the eighteenth century, and, by suggesting that the main arterial routes did not come under complete trust control until the beginning of the nineteenth century, they seriously underestimated the significance of trust development during the period 1751–72. By 1750 many of the main London routes were almost completely turnpiked[176] as were a number of important inter-provincial roads in the Severn and Wye valleys, the West Riding and the North, and the turnpiking of both and London and the major inter-provincial arterial routes was virtually completed by the mid-seventies. There were, however, certain areas where trust development occurred at a later date. For example, in Lancashire many of the intra-county roads were turnpiked in the period 1789–1810. This relatively late growth was probably due to the fact that the cotton-textile industry did not begin to expand rapidly before 1780. Although there were a number of notable exceptions, both during and after the war turnpikes were generally established on short stretches of local road, rather than on arterial roads.

The Webbs claimed that turnpike development was 'scattered' and 'unconnected'.[177] This is true to the extent that the trusts were not set up one after another on continuous sections of road. However, it is misleading to imply, as the Webbs do, that there was therefore no coherent pattern to trust development. That such a pattern did emerge is borne out by the early turnpiking of the main London routes as well as the markedly interrelated nature of trust expansion throughout the country.[178]

[175]Webbs, *King's Highway*, pp. 125, 192–4.
[176]The outstanding exception to this was the London–Exeter Road.
[177]Webbs, *King's Highway*, p. 125.
[178]In the 1720s, 47% of the new trusts were linked to established trusts, in the thirties 75%, and the percentage rose to 82·5% in the forties. These figures do not include trusts established in the same year on adjoining roads.

4
Trust Administration

1

John Loudon McAdam, the most articulate critic of turnpike trusts, claimed that a sound administrative structure was the key to both well repaired roads and balanced finances. In this sense the following examination of the organization of trust management forms the basis for the subsequent examination of finance and repair.

The chapter is in three sections. The first deals with the trustees, their powers and how they controlled the trusts. Nineteenth-century attempts to reform the trust system will also be considered. The second section concerns the trusts' higher officials: the clerk, treasurer and surveyor, and the role they played in trust management. The collection of tolls, by the trusts' collectors and the later toll-farmers, will be dealt with in the final section. The main emphasis of all the sections will be on the structure of management, how it functioned and the way in which it changed through time.

Each turnpike act contained the names of those who were to serve as trustees. They included men of local importance, promoters of the legislation, town officials, local landowners, justices of the peace, and members of parliament. The extreme length of these lists coupled with the few trustees needed for a quorum suggests that most names were included simply to facilitate the passage of the act through Parliament, and once it had passed to serve as an assurance of the trusts' creditworthiness. The indifferent participation at most meetings confirms that only a few of those named were actively concerned. The inclusion of justices as trustees was the natural continuation of their authority respecting local road repair and a means of exercising a degree of supervision over the trusts. When in the nineteenth century there was growing public disquiet with the way in which some trustees were carrying out their duties, possibly in an attempt to reassert outside control, the justices were empowered to act as full members of the trusts within their respective jurisdictions.[1] The problems of control, and of who was best able to manage the turnpike trusts, were also reflected in the qualifications required of the trustees.

[1] 3 Geo. IV c.126 art. 61.

All those who held public office were obliged to fulfil a property qualification.[2] As the Webbs have noted,[3] 'Running like a red thread through all local institutions of the eighteenth century was the assumption that the ownership of property carried with it, not only a necessary qualification for, but even a positive right to carry on, the work of government.' Qualifications were not, however, demanded of trustees until 1726,[4] and from then until the late 1740s only in certain trusts. A frequent prerequisite was that a trustee had to be in possession of estates yielding £100 per year or heir to those of £300 per year.[5] The act of 1773 extended trustee qualifications to all trusts and made it mandatory for a trustee to have estates worth £40 a year, be heir to ones of £80, or to have personal property valued at £800.[6] The last qualification was peculiar to the new statutory authorities, such as the turnpike trusts and the various bodies of improvement commissioners, which were established during the eighteenth century.[7] In 1822 the trustees' qualifications were altered. The required estate values were increased to £100 and £200 respectively, and except within ten miles of London, personal property qualification was no longer considered.[8] Eleven years later James McAdam ascribed this change to: 'the Circumstance of the Landed Interest not being sufficiently attended to at Turnpike Meetings and that other Parties, in Towns particularly, possessing considerable personal wealth, frequently attend those Meetings, not having that personal interest in the Road which Landed Proprietors must naturally possess'.[9] McAdam's reasons may be seriously questioned for merchants surely had an interest in ensuring that the roads were well maintained. His comments do however lend support to the Webbs' view that contemporaries equated landed wealth with the right and the responsibility to govern.

Although restrictions were imposed on trustees, the trend was to increase their powers. The early acts listed the tolls to be collected and empowered the trustees to set up gates, mortgage the tolls, appoint officers, and elect new members.[10] During this period the justices of the peace exercised a degree of control over the trustees. The quarter-sessions could end tolls before the statutory twenty-one years if the roads were repaired and all debts repaid, and they were authorized to

[2]S. and B. Webb, *English Local Government: Statutory Authorities for Special Purposes* (London, 1922), pp. 386-9, 467.
[3]*Ibid.* p. 386.
[4]13 Geo. I c.10 and 13 Geo. I c.32.
[5]For example, 8 Geo. II c.3 art. 25 (1734) Manchester–Saddleworth.
[6]13 Geo. II c.84.
[7]Webbs, *Statutory Authorities*, pp. 472-3.
[8]3 Geo. IV c.126, art. 62 and 63.
[9]*B.P.P. 1833 (703) xv. 409*, p. 96.
[10]These were broadly the powers given in early acts, although they did vary.

appoint someone to check for the misapplication of funds or the abuse of trust powers.[11] The latter provision began to be deleted from local acts in the 1740s and 50s and the trustees were thereafter freed from direct outside supervision.[12] Meanwhile their powers were being continually augumented. By 1750, in many trusts, power was being given to erect weighing engines,[13] set up side gates, lease the tolls, buy land and divert the road, compound for both tolls and statute duty, contract for road repair, and lessen the tolls.[14] In 1773, with two exceptions, these powers were extended to all trusts.[15]

The trustees, therefore, from the mid-1770s had extensive and virtually unchecked administrative and financial powers. The Act of 1822,[16] the second consolidating the laws relating to turnpike trusts, did little to alter significantly the powers vested in the trustees. It did require that an audited account be sent annually to the clerk of the peace,[17] and this provided useful information as to the financial condition of the trusts although it could not check their supposed extravagances. Parliament seems to have been more concerned with protecting the creditors of the turnpikes than with effectively supervising the

---

11 The justices were further empowered to compel payment to the trust's treasurer of sums they found due. There has been no record found of this clause being applied.

12 The justices continued to serve as mediators of disputes between the trust and the public and settled the amount of statute labour due to the trust.

13 The power to erect weighing engines was given as early as the 1720s (1 Geo. II st. 2. c.3 arts. 7 and 8 – 1728, Maidenhead–Twyford and Henley Trust). It was extended to all trusts by 14 Geo. II c.42.

14 *Side-gates*: The setting of these gates was to protect against the avoidance of the main gates. The power to erect these gates was given early in the southern counties: Middlesex (3 Geo. I c.4 – 1717), Berks. (4 Geo. I c.6 Pri. – 1718), Wilts., Berks., and Southampton (4 Geo. I c.7 – 1718). However, this clause was not generally included in all local acts until the 1750s.
Buying land and diverting roads: Like the above clause, this was found in early acts. Beds. and Herts. (9 Geo. I c.11 – 1723). However, this clause was not generally included in local acts until the 1740s. The trustees were empowered to buy land for the roads. If the owners and the trustees could not agree on a price a jury was to be empanelled and their verdict on the price was to be final. The trustees were then authorized to sell the old land and use the proceeds for the new road.
Compounding for tolls: In some acts the trustees were empowered to take a lump sum from those passing through the gates. However, this seems to have been a fairly common practice even if no specific provision was included in the local act.
Compounding for statute duty: See below, p. 166.
Contracting road repairs: See below, pp. 152-7.
Lessening the tolls: Clauses empowering the trustees to lower tolls were included in most acts from the 1740s. The trustees could, with the consent of a proportion (usually two-thirds) of the creditors, lower the tolls and subsequently raise them to the level given in the act.

15 13 Geo. III c.84. The powers of compulsory purchase were not included in this act. However, they were included in most local acts. The power to contract repairs was also not given in 1773; however, this practice was fairly widespread by the 1770s. See below, pp. 152-7.

16 3 Geo. IV c.126.

17 *Ibid.* arts. 78-80.

manner in which the trustees carried out their duties. This was implicit in many of the nineteenth-century reports,[18] and is reflected in the local and the general acts which gave the creditors first claim on the toll-receipts[19] and which exempted trusts from fines following road-indictment if this would 'endanger[ing] the securities of the creditors who have advanced their money upon the credit of the tolls'.[20] Given this attitude, it may have been felt that a too severe restraint on the trusts would have jeopardized the invested funds.

The trustees were given their powers for twenty-one years, and when this period expired they sought and were invariably given acts continuing their authority. Despite the fact that no trust was ever refused a renewal, some trustees were unsure of their position. They therefore felt it was necessary when petitioning for a renewal act to claim that either parts of the road were still not repaired, which was often true, or that money was owed to creditors. Parliament, on the other hand, seems to have recognized the virtual permanence of the trusts, at least by 1820, and found it necessary to remind the trustees[21]

to remove a mistaken notion, founded perhaps on obsolete practice or opinions, that the existence of some debt is absolutely necessary for establishing a claim before Parliament for the renewal of such Acts. On the contrary an extinction of debt must be taken as strong proof of good management, and therefore as an additional reason for entrusting the maintenance of the roads to the same hands.[22]

The expense of obtaining a renewal act was a heavy burden on the finances of the trusts. The average cost of the 128 renewal acts examined in 1833 was £436 3s, and Mr Irish, the compiler of these figures, estimated that a quarter of the current trust debt was due to the high cost of the continuance acts.[23] The 1820 Committee had recommended lowering the expense of obtaining these acts,[24] and in 1826-7 a Select Committee on Turnpike Trust Renewal Bills was formed to deal with the question. They resolved that because the turnpike trusts were serving the public interests they should be exempted from all Private Bill

---

[18] See below, p. 72.

[19] B.P.P. 1840 (256) xxvii. 1, p. 9.

[20] 3 Geo. IV c.126, art. 110.

[21] B.P.P. 1820 (301) ii. 301, p. 5.

[22] This reminder doesn't seem to have been completely successful for in 1832 Charles Tyrell, an M.P., received a letter in which it was claimed that the Little Yarmouth-Blythburgh Trust had sufficient funds to pay off their debts, but that they had lowered the tolls and paid high interest rates in order to retain a debt. This had been done, it was contended, so that the act could be renewed. Letter 19 January 1832, S1/1/82.1 Ips. & E. Suf. RO.

[23] B.P.P. 1833 (703) xv. 409, pp. 55-7.

[24] B.P.P. 1820 (301) ii. 301, p. 5.

charges.[25] But no immediate action was taken on the committee's recommendations, and the problem was not resolved until the passage of the first of the Turnpike Renewal Acts in 1831.[26] These acts, passed annually, did away with the costly renewals by extending the life of all trusts from one year to the next.

The time and place of the first meeting of the trust was prescribed in each local act, which also gave the number of trustees necessary for a quorum.[27] While some acts required a minimum number of meetings[28] the trustees were free to hold as many as they desired. Four meetings a year were made compulsory by the act of 1773[29] although the second consolidating act, being more realistic as to the nature of trustees' participation, required only one annual general meeting.[30] This last act also made it possible for three trustees to constitute a quorum, unless the local act gave a specific number needed.[31]

It was necessary to allow but a few trustees to constitute a quorum for, as the minutes show, meetings were usually badly attended. Despite generally indifferent participation there was relatively higher attendance at the initial meetings possibly due to a greater interest in the policy decisions made at these meetings, i.e. the setting of gates, appointment of officers, leasing of tolls or employment of collectors, and the borrowing of funds. In all trusts there was a pattern of decreasing attendance, but the inactivity of the trustees of the smaller provincial trusts seems most pronounced. These trusts generally had but few meetings, most of which were not well attended, and the paucity of minutes suggests that many were administered by only a few members. While there was a tendency for decreasing attendance in both the larger provincial trusts and those in London, the frequency of meetings was higher and the trustees' participation better in these than in the smaller trusts.[32]

25B.P.P. 1826-7 (383) vi. 1, pp. 1-2. They said that the renewed bill for a turnpike was of a particular character distinct from the first bill, which although 'Public' was still in the domain of private interests. The renewal acts were needed to overcome the 21 year clause, inserted as a Public benefit, although it was actually a detriment to the trusts. It was this character of the renewal bills which warranted their exemption from the Private Bill charges.

261 & 2 Wm. IV c.6.

27The number of trustees listed in the local acts was anywhere from 30 to 500. The number necessary for a quorum was usually from 5 to 7.

28This condition was found only occasionally before 1750. 18 Geo. II c.32 − 1745 (Birmingham–Edgehill Trust), required two general meetings per year. 20 Geo. II c.6 − 1747 (Reading–Puntfield Trust) required monthly meetings.

2913 Geo. II c.84 art. 50. Meetings were not to begin before 10 a.m. or end later than 2 p.m.

303 Geo. IV c.126 art. 69.

313 Geo. IV c.126 art. 67. This clause also provided that each meeting should elect a Chairman who was to have the tie-breaking vote; he was also able to vote in the first instance and therefore in effect had two votes.

32C.A.A. Clarke, 'The Turnpike Trusts of Islington and Marylebone 1700-1825' (unpublished M. A. thesis, University of London, 1955), pp. 58-9. He says that in the first

This better attendance allowed for a degree of bureaucratic control not usually found among the smaller trusts. The New Cross Trust was divided into five administrative districts each under a committee responsible to the general meeting,[33] and similar procedural methods were employed by many London trusts and certain of the larger provincial trusts.[34] However, the more sophisticated organizational structure did not mean necessarily greater efficiency, and was in many cases simply a consequence of the greater mileage or higher traffic density on certain roads.

The larger trusts as well as the smaller trusts were easily mismanaged. According to McAdam, before his arrival the Bristol Trust's roads were badly repaired, the finances chaotic and the administration ineffectual.[35] He did not claim, as he hardly could have, that the trustees had been dishonest, but rather that their control had been weak and authority and funds had fallen to the 'lowest order of society',[36] i.e. the surveyor, clerk and treasurer. His criticism of weak management was valid generally, for many commissioners had neither the ability nor the inclination to administer their trusts effectively. The minutes or rather the scarcity of minutes of the smaller trusts confirm that here especially the trustees gave but cursory attention to their duties. While it is clear that there was a great need for improved management, this is not to say that all trusts were being badly managed. On the contrary, the generally improved condition of the roads afforded by the turnpikes,[37] indicates that although administrative procedure may have been crude and wasteful, nonetheless, it was reasonably effective. The 'distressed' finances of the trusts was cited as another indication of the trustees' inability, but as will be suggested[38] the financial condition of many trusts was better than the aggregate figures seem to indicate.

As a consequence of the limited interest taken in trust management, control of many trusts soon passed into the hands of a few commissioners, especially in the small provincial trusts. The trustee control of these bodies was also frequently interlocking – the same trustees managing more than one turnpike road. In the 1820s many of the

---

year there were 20 meetings with an average attendance of 24 (1721), and by 1741 the meetings drew but 9. The minutes of the Old Street Trust show high attendance (15-40 trustees) for the first few years and fairly good attendance thereafter. (Minute Book, July 1753-July 1778. Fins. Lib.)

[33] Minutes, T9/A1/1 Kent AO. 23 February 1748.

[34] See below, pp. 148-50.

[35] John Loudon McAdam, *Observations on the Management of Trusts for the Care of Turnpike Roads* (London, 1825), pp. 6-10.

[36] *Ibid.* p. 9.

[37] See below, pp. 139-42.

[38] See below, p. 88.

turnpikes centred on Leeds were run by the same trustees,[39] and to the north near Harrogate a similar grouping existed, four trusts in this area being run by the same commissioners.[40] Other trusts in the West Riding connected by interlocking trustee control were found near Knaresborough[41] and Wakefield.[42] Indeed, in most parts of the country, except in London and in the larger provincial trusts, a degree of this overlapping trustee control was evident.[43]

The trust groupings were analogous to the larger provincial trusts in that they exerted control over a fairly wide area. Unlike the latter, however, they were initiated in segments and not as single radial

[39] The names given below are of those trustees who signed the trust minutes or who appeared in other trust documents. Only those who served on more than one trust have been listed.
Leeds–Dewsbury Trust, Minute Book 1816-33, box 29 West Rid. CRO. (Edward Hague, Thomas Todd, John Halliday.)
Dewsbury–Gomersal Trust, Minute Book 1826-55, box 49 West Rid. CRO. (Edward Hague, Thomas Todd, John Halliday, William Gomersal.)
Holmelane End–Heckmondwycke Trust, Interest Ledger 1826-39, box 4 West Rid. CRO. (William Gomersal, Emmanual Emmet, Joshua Taylor.)
Leeds–Whitehall Trust, Road Book 1825-53, box 23, West Rid. CRO. (Emmanual Emmet, Joshua Taylor.)
Leeds–Wakefield Trust, Minute Book 1794-1821, box 45 West Rid. CRO. (Joseph Oates, Richard Kempley, Thomas Becket, John Blayds, Christopher Oates.)
Leeds–Harrogate Trust, Minute Book 1801-19, box 57 West Rid. CRO. (Joseph Oates.)
Leeds–Holmefield Lane End Trust, Minute Book 1817-38, box 52 West Rid. CRO. (Joseph Oates, Richard Kempley, Thomas Beckett, Sir John Beckett, Christopher Beckett, William Beckett, John Blayds.)
Leeds–Selby Trust, Mortgage Ledger 1751-1872, box 60 West Rid. CRO. (John Blayds, Christopher Beckett, John Beckett.)
Leeds–Otley Trust, Minute Book 1821-74, box 31 West Rid. CRO. (John Blayds, Christopher Beckett, William Beckett.)
[40] Kirkby Hill Moor–Ripon Trust, Minute Book 1752-1814, box 27 West Rid. CRO. (In the 1750s and 60s, Gregory Rhodes, William Richardson, A. Dawson, John Lister.)
Harrogate–Hutton Moor Trust, Minute Book 1752-1814, box 27 West Rid. CRO. (Gregory Rhodes, William Richardson, John Lister, A. Dawson, G. Norton.)
Ripon–Pateley Bridge Trust, Minute Book 1756-1815, box 27, West Rid. CRO. (Gregory Rhodes, William Richardson, A. Dawson.)
Harrogate–Boroughbridge Trust, Minute Book 1752-1870, box 27 West Rid. CRO. (Gregory Rhodes, William Richardson, G. Norton, John List, Thomas Lamplugh.)
[41] Knaresborough–Pateley Bridge Trust, Minute Book 1759-1881, box 27 West. Rid. CRO. (In the 1760s and 70s, Edward Norton, Thomas Lamplugh, Sir John Ingilby, Thomas Collins.)
Knaresborough–Wetherby Trust, Minute Book 1775-1870, box 27 West Rid. CRO. (Thomas Collins, Thomas Lamplugh, Edward Norton.)
[42] Doncaster–Tadcaster Trust, Minute Book 1741-1835, box 54 West Rid. CRO. (In the 1740s and 50s, Henry Browne, Sir Rowland Winn, G. Dalston, R. Frank.)
Redhouse–Wakefield Trust, Minutes 1741-1830, box 54 West Rid. CRO. (Henry Brown, G. Dalston, R. Frank.)
Wakefield–Weeland Trust, Minutes 1741-1826, box 54 West Rid. CRO. (Henry Browne, G. Dalston, R. Frank.)
[43] Mr G. Hollis, clerk of the Winchester–Popham Trust, stated that the nine trusts leading out of Winchester were run by virtually the same trustees (*B.P.P. 1833 (703) xv. 409*, p. 154). Sir James McAdam, testifying before the same committee, claimed that five or six trusts near Stamford in Lincolnshire were run by the same trustees (*ibid.* p. 81).

complexes.[44] The groups of interconnected trusts afforded a degree of unified control in certain areas, and afforded also in many instances a reflection of the dominant interests in an area. In Staffordshire those engaged in the potteries controlled at least two trusts,[45] and in Leeds, the woollen interests[46] were the guiding force behind a number of trusts. A relatively closer community of interests in many provincial districts distinguished the extent of trustees' control in these areas from that in the metropolis. In London the great diversity of interests in a limited area gave rise to a large number of independently managed trusts. These trusts had a low mile-per-trust ratio,[47] and before the Metropolis Road Act of 1826, there was little interlocking trustee control.

Although the trustees were often attacked for their administrative shortcomings, it was on the small scale of trust operations rather than upon the trustees themselves that the bulk of the criticism fell. Perhaps this was due in part to the attention of Parliament being closely focused on the London trusts, where fragmentary control was the most evident. Indeed, except for Essex, the entire south east had a lower mile-per-trust ratio than most other parts of the country.[48] It also may have owed something to the fact that many of the trusts created in the early nineteenth century were small and, partly because they were new, many were also in a bad financial condition.[49]

John Loudon McAdam in evidence before a Parliamentary Committee in 1819 contended that the London roads were the worst in the country.[50] This was due, he said, to the heavy traffic and the bad materials used in repairing the road.[51] The smallness of the trusts did not allow for the large-scale effort needed to overcome these problems, and in many cases the trustees were opposed to 'scientific', i.e. his, repair techniques.[52] He claimed that the only way to effect improvement was to consolidate the London trusts.[53] The Committee accepted McAdam's opinions and reiterated them as their resolutions. Because of the defective state of the roads and injudicious management they

[44]See above, pp. 44, 46.
[45]Burslem–Newcastle-under-Lyme Trust, Minute Book 1776-83, 88/2/41 Wm. Salt Lib.; Newcastle-under-Lyme–Blyth Marsh Trust, General Statements of Accounts 1823-45, 53/31 Wm. Salt Lib.
[46]R. G. Wilson, 'Transport Dues', p. 111.
[47]Before the Metropolis Road Act of 1826, the trusts in Middlesex had a mile-per-trust ratio of 7·9, the lowest in the country (B.P.P. 1821 (747) iv. 343).
[48]Ibid.
[49]See below, pp. 90-1.
[50]B.P.P. 1819 (509) v. 339, p. 19.
[51]Ibid. pp. 26-7.
[52]Ibid.
[53]Ibid. p. 29.

suggested the unification of all trusts within ten miles of London.[54] They felt that this would not only improve the London roads, but also serve as a model for the rest of the country. It was not, however, McAdam's influence alone which led to attempts to reform the trusts in London. There were other important factors which underlined this move.

The population of London had almost doubled between 1780 and 1820[55] and the coaching age was at its height in the early decades of the nineteenth century. This led to a great increase in the number and variety of vehicles on the city's roads.[56] This in turn multiplied the repair problems faced by the London trusts as well as the inconveniences suffered by the road users. A major source of inconvenience was the great number of toll houses, toll gates and side bars in and around the city. By 1827, there were 56 toll houses, 47 gates and 44 bars on the roads controlled by the Metropolis Roads Commission.[57] 'XY', writing in *The Times* in 1816,[58] voiced what was probably a widely felt grievance when he complained bitterly of the stops which had to be made almost every mile to pay a toll or show a ticket to 'men placed in a situation unfavourable to civilized manners, and who might be usefully employed in mending the roads, which they now obstruct in the most disagreeable manner'. He urged that 'one general management' of the trusts in London would 'introduce improvements hitherto unthought of'. An outstanding example of the beneficial nature of such trust unification was provided two years later by the consolidation of the North Wales portion of the Holyhead Road.

This trust's success was cited by yet another select committee which met in 1820 and reiterated the proposal for the consolidation of the London trusts.[59] Their reasons were essentially the same as those of the 1819 Committee – a great deal of expense and inconvenience would be saved and the new unified trust would 'hold forth an example that cannot fail of being rapidly imitated in all parts of the country'.[60] However, the London trusts were clearly unwilling to serve as an example for anyone, as is shown by their firm opposition in that year (1820) to a bill which proposed to consolidate seventeen trusts con-

[54]*Ibid.* p. 6.
[55]B. R. Mitchell and P. Deane, *Abstract of British Historical Statistics* (Cambridge, 1962), p. 19 and P. Deane and W. A. Cole, *British Economic Growth, 1688-1959* (2nd edition, Cambridge, 1967), p. 118.
[56]T. C. Barker and M. Robbins, *A History of London Transport, Passenger Travel and the Development of the Metropolis* (London, 1963), Vol. I, pp. 2-6.
[57]First Report of the Commissioners of the Metropolis Turnpike Roads, *B.P.P. 1826-27 (339) vii. 23*, p. 31.
[58]*The Times*, 8 February 1816, p. 4b.
[59]*B.P.P. 1820 (301) ii. 301*, p. 3.
[60]*Ibid.*

trolling $277\frac{1}{4}$ miles of road both north and south of the Thames.[61] A committee of London trusts was formed, petitions against the bill were submitted and it never received a second reading.[62] This committee was reactivated a year later to fight another attempt to consolidate the trusts. The committee argued that the roads were in good repair, under authorized administration, that the bill impugned the honesty of the trustees and would take control from those who best knew the local problems.[63] Even though the trusts organized a highly successful petition campaign, getting 116 petitions submitted against the bill,[64] it was defeated by only a single vote.[65]

This narrow defeat must have encouraged the reformers for they continued to agitate. In 1825 they succeeded in getting a select committee to look into the question of the London trusts.[66] This committee was headed by Lord Lowther, an outspoken proponent of consolidation, and J. L. McAdam was once again the chief witness. It is therefore not surprising that the committee's findings simply provided more detailed confirmation of what previous committee's had found. It was claimed that the roads were badly repaired, materials were unsuitable, administration lax, the financial position chaotic, and that the great number of toll-gates hindered the free flow of traffic.[67] They concluded[68]

that a consolidation of all the trusts adjoining London is the only effectual method of introducing a proper and uniform system of management in the roads, economy in the funds, and of relieving the public from the present inconvenient situations and obnoxious multiplicity of turnpike gates, with which the inhabitants are now faced in every direction.

These conclusions were essentially restatements of McAdam's testimony, and while it is difficult to question his opinion on the physical state of the roads there is some doubt as to whether the London trusts were in as adverse a financial condition as McAdam suggested.

A rough idea of the financial condition of the London trusts can be gained by examining the accounts submitted by the trusts to Parliament in 1821.[69] For the county of Middlesex, in which most of the London trusts were found, the accounts show twenty trusts controlling 158 miles of road with mortgage debts of £296,625, arrears of interest of £6,182,

---

[61]*B.P.P. Public Bills 1820 i*, pp. 305-22.
[62]Harrow TT Minutes – 26 June 1820, LA/HW/TP 17 Mid. CRO.
[63]*Ibid.* 19 March 1821.
[64]*J. H. of C.* lxxvi, pp. 183, 198, 203, 207, 216, 311, 321, 354, 356, 368-9.
[65]S. and B. Webb, *King's Highway*, p. 177.
[66]*B.P.P. 1825 (355) v. 167.*
[67]*Ibid.* pp. 3-8.
[68]Quoted in Jackman, *Development of Transportation*, p. 282.
[69]*B.P.P. 1821 (747) iv. 343.*

and income and expenditure (both averaged over three years) of £95,475 and £86,050 respectively.[70]

The very high level of mortgage debt would seem to confirm the view that the London trusts were in financial peril. However, a closer examination of the data shows that this was not true.

A breakdown of the Middlesex accounts is given in column 1 of chart 3. This data does not, however, present a true picture of conditions prevailing in London, for a disproportionate share of both the debt and arrears of interest are attributable to three small trusts. The Commercial, East India Docks Trust, formed in 1802,[71] had a mortgage debt of £169,050 (57% of the county total), arrears of interest of £3,380 (71% of the country total), while controlling only $4\frac{1}{4}$ miles of road. The other two trusts, the Archway–Kentish Town Trust (1811)[72] and the Poplar–Greenwich Ferry Trust (1812),[73] were responsible for a total of $3\frac{1}{2}$ miles of road and had debts of £42,438. As mentioned above,[74] these trusts were 'proprietory trusts' which issued shares and were therefore significantly different from the ordinary trusts. The special nature of these trusts and the fact that they were relatively new accounts for their high debts and makes it desirable to exclude them from our calculations. This is consistent with the contemporary view on this question, for none of these trusts was included in any of the proposed bills for consolidating the London trusts.

The omission of the above three trusts (column 2, chart 3) provides a much more representative picture of conditions in London. Interest charges accounted for a small, manageable percentage of expenditure and compared extremely favourably with the average for all trusts (column 3). Only in Essex did the trusts pay out a smaller proportion of their funds in interest charges. The arrears of interest were negligible, and twelve of the seventeen trusts had no arrears at all. Finally, the income and expenditure per mile of the London trusts was higher than in any other part of the country and almost ten times the national average, while the debt per mile was only double that average.[75] This meant that the London trusts were able to spend the greatest part of their funds directly for road repair.[76]

The preceding analysis suggests that although the trustees in London may not have been using the most up-to-date repair techniques, and

[70]Mistakes in the 1821 data were corrected in 1833, *B.P.P. 1833 (703) xv. 409.*
[71]42 Geo. III c.101.
[72]51 Geo. III c.156.
[73]52 Geo. III c.149.
[74]See above, p. 54n.
[75]*B.P.P. 1833 (703) xv. 409*, pp. 168-9.
[76]For a full explanation of the relevance of the trusts' accounts see below, pp. 88-90.

while the multiplicity of toll gates and toll bars was a real and pressing inconvenience, nevertheless they managed their financial affairs extremely well. These findings raise some doubts as to the validity of McAdam's damning criticisms of the trusts and also put the protests against consolidation into proper perspective. They suggest that the trustees who fought against the consolidation bills were not all inefficient

CHART 3   *1821 Accounts*[1]

	Middlesex trusts	Middlesex trusts (A)[2]	All counties
1. Number of trusts	20	17	956
2. Total mileage	158	150	18,244
3. Debt/mile[3]	£1,877	£545·5	£245·6
4. Arrears of interest/mile	£ 39·1	£ 8·5	£ 28·7
5. Income/mile[4]	£ 604·3	£547·8	£ 57·6
6. Expenditure/mile	£ 544·6	£537·4	£ 54·8
7. % of expenditure for interest payments[5]	17·7%	5%	22·4%
8. % of expenditure available for repair expenses[6]	72·3%	85·0%	67·6%

Notes

[1]Data from *B.P.P. 1821 (747) iv*, and corrections in *B.P.P. 1833 (703) xv*, pp. 168–9.

[2]This column excludes three trusts: Commercial and East India Docks Roads, the Archway Trust, and the Poplar–Greenwich Ferry Trust.

[3]Debt includes floating debt and mortgage debts.

[4]Income and expenditure are averaged over three years.

[5]This is calculated by assuming that the trusts paid their interest obligations in full every year at a rate of 5%. In fact, as the arrears of interest show, they did not do this, so we are probably overstating the actual amount paid out in interest. Also some trusts were able to pay lower rates of interest.

[6]This figure is arrived at by taking the average amount spent by all trusts between 1834 and 1838 on administrative expenses (8·5%, see below, p. 88) adding 1·5% as an allowance for legal costs (from 1831 all trusts had their authority renewed each year by a general act (1 & 2 Wm. IV c.6) and therefore legal expenses were somewhat lower in the 1830s than in the early 1820s), adding this total to the amount paid out as interest and subtracting this figure from 100%.

and incompetent men seeking to retain control of a lucrative local concession, but rather men who may have felt, with some justification, that they were doing a good job.

Following the 1825 Committee report the third attempt to consolidate the London trusts was made. The bill introduced for this purpose differed substantially from previous ones in that it covered only about 133 miles of turnpike road run by fourteen trusts all north of the Thames instead of 277 miles of road both north and south of the river encompassed by the 1820 bill.[77] The 1826 bill did not include, as had former consolidation bills, the large and influential New Cross

[77]7 Geo. IV c.142.

Trust (40 miles), Southwark–Highgate Trust (61 miles) and Whitechapel–Shenfield Trust (34 miles). This had the effect of considerably weakening opposition, for evidence suggests that these trusts, especially the New Cross Trust, had been most active in organizing campaigns against the 1820 and 1821 bills.[78] In 1826, the amount of opposition was sharply reduced. The committee of London trusts was not formed, as had been done before, and less than thirty dissenting petitions were presented.[79]

Critics claimed that this was due to the omission of the afore-mentioned trusts from the bill and to the fact that it was rushed through Parliament. Writing in *The Times* in November 1826, the trustees of the Brentford Trust pointed out[80]

Under the plea that the session was nearly at an end, and the public interest were suffering, those who solicited, or as it is technically called in modern language, 'worked the bill' used the greatest activity to forward it through its different stages. It was read a first time when there were hardly more than ten members present, and almost as soon as the usual forms would admit, a second time in nearly as thin a house. When, as the trustees learnt what was going forward, they solicited to be heard, that the calumnies which had been heaped upon them might be refuted, the only favour they could obtain was, that the bill should be sent to a committee upstairs; but they were informed . . . that it was too late to say anything against the principle of the bill, as that had been established by the second reading.

Despite determined opposition, the Metropolis Roads Commission came into existence in July 1826.[81] It was hoped at the time that it would solve the problems of the London roads as well as providing a model which would be adopted by trusts throughout the country. For while schemes had been proposed for strengthening the road authorities, from 1819 the Parliamentary committees relied almost entirely on trust unification as a solution. J. L. McAdam in the 1819 Report, while paying particular attention to the London roads, also claimed that local consolidations were desirable throughout the country.[82] He said

[78] In a letter from the New Cross Trust to the Harrow Trust (Harrow Trust, Minutes – 27 July 1822, LA/HW/TP 17 Mid. CRO) the trust was thanked for the successful defeat of the Metropolis Road Bill, and the New Cross trustees desired that a permanent committee be set up to look after the trusts' interests. The New Cross Trustees were active in trying to promote a working together of the London trusts. As early as 1809 they had tried to form a committee of London trusts to see if any improvement in their condition could be made. (Kilburn Trust, Minutes – 1 June 1809, LA/HW/TP 3 Mid. CRO.)

[79] *J. H. of C.* lxxxi, pp. 223, 231, 234, 271, 296. Also *Index to the House of Lords Journals, 1820–1833*, p. 395.

[80] *The Times*, 15 November 1826, p. 3e.

[81] 7 Geo. IV c.142.

[82] *B.P.P. 1819 (509) v. 339*, p. 29.

that unification would reduce administrative costs,[83] allow the purchase of repair materials on a more favourable basis,[84] and provide the funds necessary for the employment of a knowledgeable 'General Surveyor'.[85] McAdam also said that there would be initial opposition from local interests, but thought that once the advantage of consolidation became evident the idea would spread and be employed.[86] Until 1839, the various committees repeated these suggestions, in only slightly altered form, as their resolutions.[87]

The success of the Metropolis Roads Commission was cited in 1833 by a House of Lords select committee as evidence that local trust consolidations were the only answer for the difficulties facing the turnpike system.[88] However, as with previous committees which had made similar recommendations since 1819, no scheme as to how these consolidations could be carried out was offered. The first attempt to do this came two years later in a bill to consolidate all the trusts in England.[89] The bill proposed that a central board of commissioners be set up with the power to compel local trusts to consolidate. These trusts were to elect boards to manage the affairs of the new unified trust, but the central committee was to have control over appointments, salaries, all items of expense over £100, and any other aspect of management. These quite radical proposals were clearly modelled on the administrative provisions of the 1834 Poor Law Amendment Act, which provided for a central board with fairly wide powers over unions of local poor law authorities.[90] Indeed, as the Webbs have observed,[91] Edwin Chadwick, the author of this act, and John McAdam held many similar views on the need for more professional administrators and for more central control of local government. However, forced unification and the extreme degree of centralization advocated in the 1835 bill went far beyond anything McAdam had ever proposed. He seems to have supported voluntary consolidation and favoured only a limited form of supervision, mainly in the form of a central audit of trust accounts.[92]

[83] Ibid. p. 30.
[84] Ibid. p. 27. He made this observation with particular reference to the London Trusts.
[85] Ibid. p. 28. The need to have a professional surveyor was one of his major tenets. He states that Lord Chichester had consolidated nine Sussex trusts for the purpose of hiring a general surveyor, although the trusts remained financially separate (ibid. p. 29).
[86] Ibid. p. 30.
[87] B.P.P. 1820 (301) ii. 301, p. 3. B.P.P. 1821 (747) iv. 343, p. 3. (They advocated the consolidation of London trusts.) B.P.P. 1825 (355) v. 167, pp. 5-6. B.P.P. 1826-27 (383) vi. 1, p. 3. B.P.P. 1833 (703) xv. 409, p. iii. B.P.P. 1836 (547) xix. 335, p. iv.
[88] B.P.P. 1833 (703) xv. 409, p. 3.
[89] B.P.P. (Public Bills) 1835 iv, pp. 539-45.
[90] S. E. Finer, The Life and Times of Edwin Chadwick (London, 1952), pp. 88-92.
[91] Webbs, King's Highway, p. 174.
[92] B.P.P. 1819 (509) v. 339, p. 29.

The 1835 Bill was dropped,[93] and in the following year a similar bill was defeated after 157 petitions had been presented against it,[94] but the proposals contained in these bills continued to be put forward. In 1836 a select committee recommended the formation of a central board in London to control the finances and management of the trusts,[95] and in 1839 another select committee presented a detailed scheme for the formation of local trust unions.[96]

The committee resolved that trust unions should be formed with maximum radii of fifteen miles, and that the present trustees elect members to a new united board.[97] Further, they recommended that the annual Turnpike Renewal Acts should cease.[98] The trusts were being perpetuated by these acts, and if they were no longer passed consolidation could be easily forced as the trusts' statutory terms expired.[99] To protect the creditors the funds of the trusts were to remain separate until an equitable settlement could be arranged.[100]

In 1840 yet another committee was appointed to enquire into the state of the roads. Consolidation was again the main theme, but the proposals were distinctive. The committee suggested that the government pay off the trusts' creditors by raising money on the security of the tolls 'and it appears to us that the holders of these bonds will not have any cause of complaint when it is considered that a permanent security will be given in the place of one which is now temporary and dependent on the periodical renewal of acts of parliament'.[101] Essentially this idea was not new, but was significant in that it did not, as in previous proposals,[102] call for the virtual nationalization of the turnpike trusts. Because of the differing financial conditions of the trusts the committee was 'of opinion that no general measure of consolidation can be carried into effect, with advantage to the public, till some provision is made for securing to the creditors the fair value of their present claim'.[103] The government was to serve as the vehicle for securing these claims while management of the roads remained in local hands. The turnpike trusts and the parish roads were to be divided into

---

[93]*J. H. of C.* xc, p. 489.

[94]*B.P.P. (Public Bills) 1836 vi*, pp. 427-40. *Index to J. H. of C., 1820-1837.*

[95]*B.P.P. 1836 (547) xix. 335*, p. iii.

[96]*B.P.P. 1839 (295) ix. 369*, p. iv. A bill presented in the same year for creating trust unions was defeated.*B.P.P. (Public Bills) 1839 v*, pp. 501-16, and *J.H. of C.* xciv, p.403.

[97]*B.P.P. 1839 (295) ix. 369*, p. iv.

[98]*Ibid.*

[99]*Ibid.* This suggestion was made by Sir James McAdam (*ibid.* p. 40).

[100]*Ibid.* pp. iv-v.

[101]*B.P.P. 1840 (256) xxvii. I*, p. 11.

[102]Webbs, *King's Highway*, pp. 187-9. They give a splendid summary of the various 'irresponsible' nationalization proposals.

[103]*B.P.P. 1840 (256) xxvii. I*, p. 11.

districts and sub-districts and placed under the same control.[104] The sub-district boards were to consist of parochial way-wardens and local magistrates, and the district boards of all the county magistrates within the district plus the chairman and vice-chairman of the sub-district boards.[105] In effect, the proposal was an attempt to remove the trustees and place the authority for all road repair with the justices of the peace.

The various parliamentary committees were unsuccessful in their attempts to promote trust reform through consolidation. It was not until 1849 that a rather weak act, 'to facilitate the Union of Turnpike Trusts' was passed,[106] and this simply provided a framework within which the trusts could, if they wished, consolidate with one another. This act was too limited and came too late to help the turnpike trusts.

The more concerted efforts from the early 1830s to improve the turnpike system were part of a more widespread movement of reform undertaken by the Whig government, the most notable achievements of which were the New Poor Law (1834), the Municipal Corporations Act (1835)[107] and the reorganization of the parish road system.[108] Trust reform was, however, undoubtedly low on the list of government priorities and was probably pushed even lower as active opposition to any form of centralized control increased after the passage of the Poor Law Amendment Act. The Whigs saw their parliamentary majority steadily eroded from the early 1830s, and with the growing unrest throughout the country from 1836, they may have felt it was impolitic to weaken their support in local areas by another unpopular measure. The strong opposition to trust reform arose both because of the fear of centralized government control and because solvent trusts did not want to unite with trusts in financial distress.[109] Parliament was concerned with reform but seems to have been unable to reconcile its concern with its desire not to compromise the trusts' creditors. This remained a major obstacle to reform. All the above factors combined to ensure that the London experiment was not attempted in other parts of the country.

2

The clerk, treasurer and surveyor were appointed or employed to implement trust policies, and their authority depended on the interest

[104]*Ibid.* p. 12.
[105]*Ibid.*
[106]12 & 13 Vic. c.46.
[107]Asa Briggs, *The Age of Improvement* (London, 1959), p. 225.
[108]5 & 6 Wm. IV c.50.
[109]*B.P.P. 1839 (295) ix. 369*, p. iv.

shown by the trustees. The officers of the large trusts were, for the most part, only employees carrying out the trustees' orders. In the trusts run by only a few commissioners the officials often became more than agents and in some cases became the effective controllers of the trust. The policies pursued by the trusts owed much of their success or failure to these men, who in the early trusts were usually local men serving part-time and with no special qualifications for their posts. By the nineteenth century the situation had altered somewhat, and many trusts were staffed by officials more knowledgeable in their tasks, i.e. professional surveyors, solicitor-clerks, and local bankers as treasurers.

The clerk was a salaried, but part-time, employee hired to deal with the trusts' paperwork. Although his duties varied in each trust, they were for the most part similar. He took minutes at the meetings and was responsible for placing advertisements, handling correspondence and carrying out other miscellaneous duties. As he was often a local solicitor he also handled legal work for the trusts. The only significant limitation imposed upon this office was that stipulated in the Act of 1822, by which the offices of clerk and treasurer could not be held concurrently by the same person or by partners.[110]

In most trusts the clerk was the least important higher official. Except for legal matters, his tasks were fairly routine. Because many smaller trusts left day-to-day management to the officers, the clerk's authority may have been greater in these than in the larger ones, whose trustees supervised management more closely. It is difficult to judge the importance of the clerk's post itself from the trust documents, but when combined with the office of treasurer it often proved decidedly influential. The Duke of Norfolk effectively controlled at least three trusts in the Sheffield area by having his agents as clerk and treasurer,[111] and control of trusts through picked officers was probably practised in other parts of the country as well. The clause in the Act of 1822 was recognition of the authority inherent in the control of these two posts.

Besides the clerk's influential position, the post also offered considerable pecuniary advantages. In 1833[112] it was estimated that one-fourth of the total trust debt was attributable to the cost of renewal acts, and this, plus the amounts paid for the acts initiating trusts, was ample

[110] 3 Geo. IV c.126, art. 71.

[111] Glossop–Marple Bridge Trust, General Accounts 1833, Arundel Castle MSS D36, Shef. Cent. Lib. (Norfolk's agent, Matthew Ellison, was treasurer and his brother Thomas was the clerk). Chapel-en-le-Frith–Entreclough Bridge Trust, *B.P.P. 1839 (447) xliv. 299*, pp. 24–5 (Matthew Ellison–Treasurer and Thomas Ellison–clerk). Sheffield–Glossop Trust, Mr Hall's Report on the Turnpike Road from Sheffield to Glossop, 29 August 1823, p. 4, CPG-14(11) Shef. Cent. Lib. He states that the road was managed by Michael and Thomas Ellison.

[112] *B.P.P. 1833 (703) xv. 409*, p. 57.

incentive for holding the office. As K. A. McMahon has pointed out,[113] 'by the early years of the nineteenth century, to more than one local attorney, a turnpike trust virtually represented a personal vested interest', and in many cases this interest extended to more than a single trust.

In London clerks usually worked exclusively for one trust, and by the nineteenth century they seem to have been full-time employees.[114] In the provinces, however, many clerks served more than a single trust. In the West Riding, William Stephenson of Holmfirth and Samuel Hailstone of Bradford were clerks to eight and six trusts respectively, and in the same county two clerks held posts with five trusts each, seven with three trusts and sixteen with two trusts.[115] A similar pattern of office holding was to be found in many other counties. Interlocking officers in the provincial trusts is further evidence of the trust groupings in these areas.

The treasurer, by virtue of his duties, was an important and influential official. He received and held funds, made disbursements and kept the trust accounts. It was incumbent on the trustees to appoint a person of good repute for two reasons: first, because the treasurer's authority was easily misused, and second because a reputable treasurer was more likely to assure and encourage investment in the trust. A trustee was usually appointed to the post and a bond required for his performance.[116] He was paid a small salary and in some trusts received only a gratuity for his services.

By controlling trust funds and generally being himself a trustee, the treasurer was in an excellent position to influence trust policies. As with the clerk, he was able to do this mainly in those trusts whose commissioners showed little interest in management. Without more detailed research into the trust documents it is difficult to isolate those instances in which the treasurer guided specific decisions. The case of the Duke of Norfolk's agents in Sheffield was a clear example,[117] and the treasurer of the Northampton–Harborough road frequently had to make decisions for it was difficult to get five trustees to meet every

---

[113]K. A. McMahon, 'Roads and Turnpike Trusts in E. Yorkshire', p. 61.
[114]Register of Returns 1820, MR/UT Mid. CRO.
[115]B.P.P. 1839 (447) xliv. 299, pp. 124-5.
[116]This was a requirement in some local acts and in 1773 was made mandatory for all trusts (13 Geo. III c. 84 art. 65).
[117]In a memorial dated 29 August 1823, Mr Hall, the Duke of Devonshire's agent, accused Norfolk's agents, Matthew and Thomas Ellison, of managing the road against the interests of Devonshire. They had ceased repairing a segment of road by Devonshire's land and refused to resume repairs. Also that they had overdrawn the trust account without the knowledge of Mr Hall (Mr Hall's Report, CPG 14-(11) Shef. Cent. Lib.).

four months.[118] With many of the smaller trusts in the hands of but three or four trustees, the treasurer's office was invested with considerable influence.

The treasurer frequently lent money, as did the other trustees, on the credit of the tolls. He also advanced sums on a short-term basis to cover deficit balances. These short-term loans were of great importance to the trust, and it was this feature of the treasurer's position which may have contributed to the increasing number of banker–treasurers being appointed in the nineteenth century.

In the eighteenth century the treasurers were mainly local gentlemen or solicitors, who may also have served concurrently as clerk or surveyor.[119] By the nineteenth century, however, many treasurer's posts were held by bankers.[120] Dr Pressnell has observed[121] that by being named as a trustee 'the banker was offered useful reinforcement of his creditworthiness by official recognition that he was a man of substance – albeit moderate – and respectability'. Conversely, by appointing a banker as treasurer the trust benefited from the banker's respectability, which offered an assurance to investors. The bankers were also useful in providing funds, although it seems not all of them were willing lenders.

George Grote, of Grote, Prescott and Co., was appointed treasurer to the Marylebone–Finchley Road Trust in 1826.[122] When, in 1829, the trust requested a £1,000 loan the bankers replied that they could not comply as the money market was too uncertain.[123] The trust asked them to reconsider, and when they still refused Grote was asked to resign.[124] Richard Parrott, another banker, more willing to advance the £1,000, was appointed treasurer.[125] Although he agreed only on a 'temporary' loan, it was not repaid, and in 1830 he advanced a further £1,000.[126] Not all bankers were hesitant to serve as treasurers or to lend money. In 1817, Thomas Blayds of Beckett, Blayds and Co., the Leeds bankers, was appointed treasurer to the Leeds–Holmefield Lane End Trust.[127] Of the £10,400 first loan, the Becketts advanced £1,000 and John

118*Rusticum et Commerciale*, Vol. II, pp. 184-5.
119The Chalk Trust had a surveyor–treasurer from at least 1725/6 to 1742/3, when a surveyor was hired. Quarter-Session Records. A/SB 1725/6-1742/3, Kent AO.
120L. S. Pressnell, *Country Banking in the Industrial Revolution* (Oxford, 1956), p. 270. 'By 1834 . . . at least 419 out of the 1,039 trusts employed private bankers directly as treasurers.'
121*Ibid.* p. 373.
122Minutes – 22 May 1826, LA/HW/TP 18, Mid. CRO.
123*Ibid.* 12 May 1829.
124*Ibid.* 16 June 1829.
125*Ibid.*
126*Ibid.* 20 July 1830.
127Minutes – 1817, box 52 West Rid. CRO.

Blayds £200.[128] By 1824, after a second loan and funding of arrears, these sums had increased to £1,900 and £360 respectively.[129] By 1837 these bankers were serving as treasurers with fifteen trusts in the Leeds area.[130]

The Bradford bank of Peckover, Harris and Co. (later Harris and Co.) was treasurer to the Wibsey Low Moor–Huddersfield Trust.[131] They subscribed £300 in 1823,[132] and in the following years provided, although reluctantly, sizeable overdrafts. In 1825 the trust was £3,000 overdrawn, and the bank notified them that no further bills would be paid.[133] However, they continued to provide short-term loans, and in 1830 they carried a £2,285 overdraft.[134] Treasurers were frequently called upon to make short-term advances to their trusts,[135] and this made it advantageous for a trust to appoint a banker–treasurer.

During the early nineteenth century there was a growing tendency to appoint banker–treasurers. The benefits accruing to the trusts from a banker's good name, his resources and his financial connections, were clearly ample incentive for his appointment. But equally the toll receipts must also have proved a useful source of deposits for the banker and this explains his willingness to act on behalf of several trusts, despite the occasional claims made upon him. Thus the interrelation of provincial trust administrations, through similar clerks or trustees, was reinforced by bankers. Beckett, Blayds and Co. with their extensive interests are an excellent example. The Bradford bank of C. H. and A. Harris and Co. served as treasurer to the Shipley–Bramley Trust, and Charles and Arthur Harris were treasurers to seven other trusts in the Bradford area.[136] In the East Riding, George Liddell, of the Beverley bank of Pease and Liddell, was the treasurer of eight trusts, and other Beverley bank, Bower, Hutton and Co., served as treasurers to three trusts.[137] The Gurneys were the treasurers of six Norfolk

---

[128]Mortgage Ledger 1817–72 (Sir John Beckett – £400, Christopher Beckett – £200, Thomas Beckett – £200, William Beckett – £200), box 52, West Rid. CRO.

[129]Ibid.

[130]B.P.P. 1839 (447) xliv. 299, pp. 124–5. Thomas Blayds – eight trusts, William Beckett – two trusts, Christopher Beckett – two trusts, Beckett, Blayds and Co. – three trusts.

[131]Minutes of Meeting – 7 February 1823, HAS.-A, Hal. Cent. Lib.

[132]Subscription List, February 1823. (£1,500 was subscribed by the Yorkshire Joint-Stock Bank Co., HAS-A, Hal. Cent. Lib.)

[133]Letter, 25 November 1825, HAS-A, Hal. Cent. Lib.

[134]Letter, 14 September 1830, HAS-A, Hal. Cent. Lib.

[135]Pressnell, Country Banking, pp. 385–9.

[136]B.P.P. 1839 (447) xliv. 299, pp. 124–5. Other bankers in Yorkshire involved in turnpike trusts included: (1) Leatham and Co.–two trusts, William Leatham–four trusts, Edward Tew (Leatham's partner)–one trust; (2) J. T. Patchett, manager of the Halifax–Huddersfield Banking Co.–five trusts; (3) Christopher Rawson (Halifax banker)–four trusts.

[137]Ibid. pp. 124–5.

trusts,[138] and in Derbyshire the banks Crofton and Co. and Arkwright and Co. were active in trust affairs.[139] Robert Barlow, a Bolton banker, served as treasurer to ten trusts, and Edward Loyd, of the Manchester bank of Jones, Loyd and Co., was treasurer to nine trusts.[140]

The surveyor was probably the most important of the trust's officers. He was employed to supervise road repair, under the direction of the trustees. But as many trustees knew little about repair methods or paid insufficient attention to their duties, the surveyor was frequently left with the responsibility for both repair and expenditure. Although the extent of the surveyor's authority varied from trust to trust, even under the most watchful of trustees a dishonest or ignorant surveyor could create problems. McAdam observed[141] that both ill-repaired roads and the unsound financial state of many trusts was due to surveyors who were indigent or knew nothing of proper methods of repair. The funds entrusted to them were consequently either embezzled or ineffectually used. The surveyors' importance stemmed not only from the trustees' disinterest, but also from the wide powers and duties given this office by acts of parliament.

In the early trusts the quarter-sessions appointed surveyors who met and decided on the repair needed.[142] They were empowered to take funds directly from the collectors,[143] and in some trusts to appoint the collectors[144] and mortgage tolls.[145] They were allowed to dig gravel or other materials from any common or private lands, paying only for damages. Furthermore, they were authorized to demand labour for road repair, in addition to statute labour from within a radius of four miles, provided the work was not more than two days per week, and not during 'Harvest or Seed' time. Labourers were to be paid the 'usual county' wage, but disputes could be adjudged by the justices. It would seem that even though they themselves were forced to serve,[146] the surveyors had almost total control of these early trusts.

With the passage of the first 'trustee-trust' in 1706[147] the surveyor's powers began to be radically altered. His control of the collectors and the tolls was transferred to the trustees, and although he continued to

---

[138]*Ibid.* pp. 70-1.
[139]*Ibid.* pp. 24-5. Crofton and Co. — nine trusts, Gilbert Crofton — three trusts, Arkwright and Co. — four trusts, Charles Arkwright — three trusts.
[140]*Ibid.* pp. 58-9.
[141]McAdam, *Observations on the Management of Trusts*, pp. 9-18, 30-1. *B.P.P. 1810-11 (240) iii. 855*, p. 31. *B.P.P. 1819 (509) v. 339*, pp. 20-1.
[142]For example, the Bath Trust (6 Anne c.42 art. 2).
[143]For example, Reigate–Crawley Trust (8 & 9 Wm. III c.15, art. 3).
[144]This was more prevalent on the early trusts, e.g. see 15 Car. II c.1, art. 1.
[145]This was to be done under the justices' order, see 9 Wm. III c.18, art. 5.
[146]In all these acts a £5 fine was levied on those who did not serve when appointed.
[147]Fornhill–Stony Stratford Trust (6 Anne c.4).

supervise statute labour, the authority to demand labour was rescinded. This may have been because the more 'private' nature of the new trusts made this power inappropriate, for it was still included in a late justice-trust in Essex in 1724.[148] Gravel could still be dug without payment, but by 1715 'reasonable satisfaction' was being demanded for materials taken from private lands. As the Webbs point out,[149] 'the Surveyor appointed by the new road authority is gradually invested with nearly all the powers of the Parish Surveyor of Highways appointed from among the inhabitants'.

The Act of 1773 did not significantly alter the surveyor's powers. He was required to give a bond for his performance,[150] but this had been previously demanded in many local acts. Jobbery was made a bit more difficult. The surveyor could make contracts for material carriage and could have an interest in that contract if he was given 'a License in writing ... from the said Trustees'.[151] To clear up any doubts as to his authority the act stated

That the Surveyors of every Turnpike Road ... may, with the Approbation of the Trustees ... apply any Part of the Tolls and Statute Duty arising to, from or in respect of every such Turnpike Road in the Execution of all and every the said Powers, (etc) ... contained in the said Act or Acts ... for the Amendment and Preservation of the Highways, and shall and may execute and enforce the same ... as the Surveyor of any Parish, Township or Place can or may do or apply the same, by virtue of or under such Act or Acts of Parliament.

The powers granted in local acts from 1773 were summarized and extended to all trusts in 1822. By that time the surveyors had been invested with a few new powers[152] and also with broader authority both for obtaining materials[153] and suppressing nuisances.[154] Because of the extensive powers given to the surveyors and their principal role in trust administration it was incumbent on the trustees to appoint an honest and knowledgeable person. As John Scott observed[155]

There are many cases in which it will be highly necessary for trustees to exercise impartial judgement; but in none perhaps so much as in the choice of officers, particularly surveyors. The post of surveyor is indeed a post of such

[148]Harlow–Woodford Trust (10 Geo. I c.9).
[149]Webbs, *King's Highway*, p. 117.
[150]13 Geo. III c.84 art. 65.
[151]*Ibid.* art. 36.
[152]*Ibid.* art. 70.
[153]3 Geo. IV. c.126. They were empowered to enter lands and stake out roads (art. 83). They could impound 'beasts' found straying on the road and demand five shillings for their return (art. 122).
[154]3 Geo. IV c.126 arts. 97–9.
[155]Quoted in J. Bateman, *The General Turnpike Road Act* (London, 1822), p. 81.

consequence to a road, that the ideas of integrity and capability are alone ideas that should be annexed to the man who offers himself as a candidate for it.

However, before the nineteenth century those employed were rarely knowledgeable and often dishonest.

There were few 'professional' road surveyors in the eighteenth century, nor was repair technique much advanced from that employed by the parish surveyors. The trustees, therefore, had little to choose from when hiring a surveyor, and men of widely diverse occupations were employed. James McAdam's list of those who had served before him on six trusts to which he was general surveyor[156] were, except for the first, fairly typical of those engaged throughout the country. They included a Lloyd's Coffee House underwriter, many 'old infirm men', a carpenter, a coal merchant, a baker and a publican. There was the occasional gifted surveyor, such as John Metcalf, but in this period the surveyors' skills were, for the most part, barely adequate for their tasks. Dishonesty was also not uncommon, and some surveyors supplemented their salaries by jobbery[157] or by presenting false bills.[158]

'Surveyors are elected because they can measure; they might as well be elected because they can sing; but they are more commonly elected because they want a situation.'[159] This caustic observation was made by J. L. McAdam in 1810, and his continued complaints about 'unknowledgeable' surveyors might suggest that the nineteenth-century surveyor was no more capable than his eighteenth-century counterpart. This does not seem to have been true. As the number of turnpike trusts increased in the second half of the eighteenth century a new type of surveyor appeared to meet the growing demands for skilled supervision. While their methods may not have been as advanced as McAdam's, the new professionals offered a more considered approach to road repair than did the part-time amateur.

In Kent, the Collis family were actively engaged as professional surveyors. James Collis was appointed surveyor of the Tonbridge–Maidstone Trust in 1765,[160] a James Collis was surveyor of the New Cross Trust in 1797[161] and Thomas Collis was engaged by the Chalk Trust in 1817.[162] In 1819 William Horne, a stage and mail coach proprietor, praised 'Mr Collis's' improvement of the Dover Road

[156]B.P.P. 1819 (509) v. 339, p. 35.
[157]See below, p. 156.
[158]Robert Mitchell, surveyor of the Colnbrook Trust, was dismissed in 1728/9, after it had been discovered that he had not paid all his bills. (Minutes–4 January 1728/9 and 10 April 1729. T. P. Col. 1 Mid. CRO.) Also see Clarke, 'Turnpike Trusts', pp. 68–9.
[159]B.P.P. 1810–1811 (240) iii. 855, p. 31.
[160]Minutes, 22 May 1765, T2/1, Kent AO.
[161]Minutes, 27 May 1797, T9/A1/3, Kent AO.
[162]Report from Thomas Collis on the condition of the roads (1817), T7/A3, Kent AO.

and stated that Collis had started work on the Brighton Road.[163] In 1837 John and Thomas Collis were surveyors of five trusts in north-east Kent, and William Collis was the surveyor of six trusts in the Canterbury area and earned a total annual income of £290.[164] Professional surveyors could also be found in many other parts of the country.[165]

The McAdams were undoubtedly the most famous of the professionals. In 1819 John Loudon and his sons James and William worked for twenty-five trusts.[166] By 1837 fifty-eight trusts, mainly in the southern parts of the country, employed a member of the family.[167] In the 1790s John Hare of Kimberley was the superintendent surveyor of six trusts in Norfolk and Suffolk,[168] and in 1837 Garret Taylor Knott earned £360 as surveyor to nine trusts in these two counties.[169] J. H. Maher was the surveyor of four Norfolk trusts and one trust in Lincolnshire (£325 per year), George Cave was the surveyor of nine trusts in the counties of Northampton, Oxford, Warwick and Buckingham (£410 per year) and J. A. Stokes was employed by eleven trusts in the counties of Gloucestershire, Warwickshire and Worcestershire (£787 per year). In Sussex, William Kenchin (£205 per year), Richard Barret (£199 per year) and Jesse Heath (£100 per year) were surveyors to eight, seven and five trusts respectively, while Thomas Thurston was employed by seven trusts in Kent (£182 per year). Matthew Frost (Derbyshire, £239 per year), Liddle Elliot (Staffordshire, £367 per year), Lynch S. Cotton (Cheshire) and William Parsons (Leicestershire, £455 per year) were surveyors of six trusts each, and Charles Bailey (Bedfordshire), and Aaron Blandford (Hampshire) were each employed by five trusts.

In the nineteenth century there were still some fraudulent surveyors[170]

---

[163]B.P.P. 1819 (509) v. 339, p. 14.

[164]B.P.P. 1839 (447) xliv. 299, pp. 52-3.

[165]It has been assumed that surveyors employed by five or more trusts were professionals.

[166]R. H. Spiro Jr, 'John Loudon McAdam, Colossus of Roads' (unpublished Ph.D. thesis, University of Edinburgh, 1950), p. 479.

[167]B.P.P. 1839 (447) xliv. 299. Sir James McAdam: (Bucks.–2 trusts), (Cambs.–4), (Berks.–4), (Essex–6), (Middx.–5), (Kent–5), (Surrey–4), (Oxon.–2), (Lincs.–1), (Hants.–3), (Herts.–7). Loudon McAdam: (Glos.–1), (Notts.–2), (Mon.–1). Christopher McAdam: (Devon–3), (Cornwall–3). William McAdam: (Hants.–1), (Somerset–2). J. L. McAdam: (Glos.–1).

[168]Yoxford–Aldeburgh Trust, Minutes – 1 May 1792, EH:50/5/4B Ips. & E. Suf. RO; Little Yarmouth Trust, Minute–18 April 1796, EH:50/5/3B1 Ips. & E. Suf. RO; Ipswich–South Town Trust, Minutes–20 May 1785, EH:50/5/2B1 Ips.& E. Suf. RO; Norwich–North Walsham Trust, Minutes–21 January 1797; Thetford Trust, Minutes –19 April 1792; Norwich–Swaffham Trust, Minutes–17 April 1770. (The last three documents are from the Norfolk County Council's Archives in the Norf. & Norw. RO.)

[169]B.P.P. 1839 (447) xliv. 299. All references in this paragraph, except footnote 168, were taken from this report.

[170]For example, William Peacock, surveyor of the New Cross Trust, embezzled money from the trust and absconded. (Minutes–27 November 1815, T9/A2/1 Kent AO.)

and many employing outmoded techniques; but despite the dishonest and the inefficient, the number of professionals was increasing. The trustees, who before could only hope for at the most an honest and diligent employee, were now able to hire surveyors better versed in their trade.[171] The employment of full-time, professional surveyors, as well as the increasing number of banker–treasurers, suggests that trust administration was gradually assuming a more professional character in the nineteenth century. The Webbs record similar developments taking place at this time in the staffing of other local authorities.[172]

3

The collection of tolls was one of the trustees' most troublesome duties. The problems stemmed from both the methods of collection and the complicated procedure governing the levying of tolls. Each local act contained a schedule of tolls, and provisions for making discriminatory charges were added by the numerous general acts. Limits on weights carried, the number of horses permitted in draught and the breadth of wheels were imposed by acts in the seventeenth and eighteenth centuries,[173] and in 1740 the trusts were allowed to erect weighing engines to enforce the weight restrictions.[174] From the passage of the first 'Broad Wheel Act' in 1753,[175] regulations, toll concessions and extra charges became increasingly intricate and difficult to interpret.[176] An attempt was made in 1773 to clear up the muddle of charges.[177] The act's first twenty-eight clauses were devoted to defining all the cases in which extra charges could be demanded. However, as with the thirteen amending acts passed between 1773 and 1822,[178] the provisions probably succeeded only in creating greater confusion. The situation was not appreciably simplified by the 1822 Act, which had forty-one clauses dealing with tolls and extra charges.[179] The profusion of acts and regulations made it difficult for the trustees to know exactly what they could demand or the travellers what they were required to pay.

---

[171]For a discussion of the advances made in repair techniques, see below, pp. 142-8.
[172]Webbs, *Statutory Authorities*, pp. 453-7.
[173]See below, pp. 181-2.
[174]14 Geo. II c.42.
[175]26 Geo. II c.30.
[176]See below, pp. 82-3.
[177]13 Geo. III c.84.
[178]Fifteen amending acts were passed, thirteen concerned tolls and extra charges. (14 Geo. II c.14); (14 Geo. II c.57); (14 Geo. II c.82); (16 Geo. III c.39); (16 Geo. III c.44); (17 Geo. III c.16); (18 Geo. III c.28); (18 Geo. III c.63); (25 Geo. III c.57); (52 Geo. III c.145); (53 Geo. III c.82); (55 Geo. III c.119); (57 Geo. III c.37).
[179]3 Geo. IV c.124.

Besides the many different charges there were also concessions granted to certain road users, and these added to the general ambiguity surrounding the collection of tolls. Most acts allowed toll-free passage to the royal family, the military, the Post, carriages during elections, local churchgoers on Sundays, funerals, and to carts with agricultural implements, manure or goods not going to market. By 1822 the exemptions were 'much more numerous than those of the old general turnpike acts, but nearly the same as have been contained in most of the local acts lately passed'.[180] Many trusts also had their own special exemptions dictated by the demands of local interests. Carts carrying ore to the Lawton, Vale Royal, and Dodington furnaces were granted one-fourth tolls,[181] and from Lawton to the forges at Cranage only one-third of the normal toll was taken on 'Pit coals, Charcoal, Iron-stone, or Pig metal'.[182] The carriage of coals was given lower tolls on many of the early trusts in Yorkshire and Lancashire,[183] and similar clauses granting special concessions were found in acts throughout the country.[184] These local concessions while decreasing the trusts' revenue did not create as much confusion as did the many general exemptions and the multitude of extra charges.

The trustees also had to cope with travellers attempting to bypass their gates, and the minutes record frequent cases of toll evasion. William Rawley, Lord Stafford's agent, commenting in 1758 (?) on 'the temper of the people about Wakefield' said that it[185]

is what it always was bad, very bad. One Comfort they have that as many as please can go round by Okenshaw (a long and very bad way) and come in at Agbridge turnpike. Some actually do this ... There are some who ride thro' the Calder at Sunset to save their penny, such sordid dogs dwell in this Country.

The avoidance of tolls was not limited to the public. Isaac Hutch, a trustee of the Wadhurst–West Farleigh Trust, was cited for passing a gate without paying,[186] and the Tonbridge–Maidstone Trust[187] demanded £50 from W. Master Esq., for he had passed a gate toll-free

---

[180]Bateman, *General Turnpike Road Act*, p. 24n.

[181]13 Anne c.31.

[182]4 Geo. II c.3.

[183]See above, p.p. 33 and 46-7.

[184]The Low Moor Ironworks was able to secure toll-free passage on the Wibsey Low Moor Trust in 1823, by offering free 'dross' for road repair and by the partner's substantial financial contribution of £2,000 (copy of Resolution 1823, HAS-98 Hal. Cent. Lib.). Their exemption was partially rescinded by an act in 1830, and completely removed by another amending act in 1838 (letter 7 December 1837, HAS-89, Hal. Cent. Lib.). See also MacMahon, 'Roads and Turnpike Trusts in E. Yorkshire', p. 51.

[185]Undated letter to the clerk of the Sheffield–Wakefield Trust, Tibbitt's Collection, 363-42 Shef. Cent. Lib.

[186]Minutes – 23 April 1777, T5/1 Kent AO.

[187]Minutes – 18 April 1788, T2/1 Kent AO.

for thirty years. Although the trusts were given ample authority for preventing toll evasion it was difficult to check effectively all the ingenious methods employed.

The trustees appointed gatekeepers, responsible for interpreting the complex regulations and collecting the toll dues. They had to measure wheels, weigh wagons, determine who was eligible for exemptions and impose fines. 'The varying rates of charge, the exemptions and the compositions, the validity of tickets for return journeys or other gates, and many other complications of the toll made it impossible to devise any effective check on their receipts.'[188] Despite the difficulty in controlling the gatekeepers some trusts did employ inspectors to check on the collectors,[189] and the trusts' minutes record endless cases of collectors being replaced for withholding funds.

Besides defrauding the trusts, the gatekeepers also often fleeced the innocent traveller. In 1818 a committee of the New Cross Trust reported that the collectors on their road and the other turnpikes on the Dover Road were defrauding the trusts and overcharging the travellers.[190] The witnesses to the Parliamentary Commission in 1796[191] contended that collectors frequently did not weigh vehicles, but accepted 'gifts' instead. When charged that 'It is notorious that they [the collectors] are the most uncivil class of His Majesty's subjects', Lewis Levy replied, 'I believe that they are more sinned against than sinning; there are very few men that take money from the pockets of the people that are not complained against.'[192] Despite Levy's claim, numerous examples of collectors' dishonesty and rudeness[193] generally support the validity of contemporary complaints against the 'pikemen'.

The collectors throughout the country came from the same general occupations. Cordwainers were hired in Warwickshire[194] and Suffolk,[195] and in Kent, the New Cross Trust[196] in 1818 appointed two

---

188Webbs, *King's Highway*, p. 138.
189Rochester–Maidstone Trust, Minutes – 9 July 1730, T12/1 Kent AO. (The trust hired a man to tally the number of vehicles passing a gate, and when his account did not agree with the gatekeeper's the keeper was fired.) Doncaster–Saltersbrook Trust, Minutes–August 1771, Goodchild Collection. (Thomas Gibson, a labourer, was hired to spy on two gates at which the trustees suspected the toll collectors were withholding funds. The gates were let for the first time in the same year.)
190Minutes – 5 September 1818, T9/A2/2 Kent AO.
191*B.P.P. 1796 (May) F.S. x*, p. 752.
192*B.P.P. 1825 (355) v. 167*, p. 32.
193The cases of gatekeepers' rudeness are endless. The best collection of examples is in: Mark Searle, *Turnpikes and Tollbars* (London, 1930). On 1 March 1809 Joshua Norton asked the gatekeeper at the Hyde-Ashford gate the way to Ashford and was immediately 'severely beaten to the ground by blows from a stick'. He made his enquiry at 3 a.m., and this may explain the collector's violent reaction. (Misc. MSS. T21/Z1 Kent AO.)
194Bromsgrove–Stratford Trust, Minutes – 27 July 1762, CR 446/1 War. CRO.
195Little Yarmouth Trust, Minutes – 18 April 1796, EH:50/5/3B1 Ips. & E. Suf. RO.
196New Cross Trust, Minutes – 30 September 1818, T9/A2/2, Kent AO.

sawyers, a ropemaker, a bookseller, a pursemaker, a tailor, a warehouse-man, and a collector of stamp duties. Lewis Levy, probably the largest employer of gatekeepers, hired gentlemen's servants and others recommended to him.[197] Women were frequently hired as collectors. The Ludlow Trust appointed Mary Lock in 1751,[198] the Wrotham Heath Trust employed a female collector in 1771,[199] and of the six gate-keepers employed in 1787 by the Wadhurst–West Farleigh Trust three were women.[200] When the Chalk Trust's collector died in 1800 his widow was appointed in his place.[201]

Although the conditions of their employment varied, the gatekeepers seem to have been fairly well treated by the trusts. Except in London, the collectors were usually paid from five to seven shillings per week.[202] In the 1750s the London trusts were paying from nine to twelve shillings,[203] and by 1800 the Kilburn Trust offered fourteen shillings per week.[204] By the 1820s the collectors at Hyde Park Gate received ten shillings per day,[205] and weighers for the New Cross Trust were being paid seven shillings and sixpence per day.[206] While the collectors' wages in the provinces were fairly low, the perquisites may have offset this to some extent. Gatekeepers were given rent-free houses and often supplied with candles and fuel. The Liverpool–Prescot Trust con-structed extra rooms to accommodate their gatekeepers' families[207] and the Bedfont–Bagshot Trust[208] and the New Cross Trust[209] supplied blankets and mattresses, the latter also providing bedsteads in each gatehouse.

The collector's post lent itself to misuse, and with the advent of the weighing machine the opportunities for fraud probably increased. Except for replacing the gatekeepers, there was little the trusts could do to control them effectively, and consequently many trusts resorted to

---

[197]*B.P.P. 1825 (355) v. 167*, p. 32.
[198]Ludlow 1st Trust, Order Book – 27 November 1751, SRO 356/23/307 Salop RO.
[199]Accounts – 1771, U442 058 Kent AO.
[200]Minutes and Accounts – 1787, T5/1 Kent AO.
[201]Minutes – 17 July 1800, T7/A1 Kent AO.
[202]Bromsgrove–Stratford Trust, Minutes – 1776 (6s/wk), CR 446/2. War. CRO; Tren-than Trust, Accounts – 1773 (6s/wk), 272/32 Wm. Salt Lib.; Wrotham Heath Trust, Accounts – 1769(7s/wk), U442 058 Kent AO; Wadhurst–West Farleigh Trust, Minutes and Accounts – 1766 (5s/wk), T5/1 Kent AO.
[203]*J. H. of C.* xxix, p. 647.
[204]Minutes – 11 December 1797 (at principle gates), LA/HW/TP 3 Mid. CRO.
[205]*B.P.P. 1825 (355) v. 167*, p. 31.
[206]Minutes – 30 September 1818, T9/A2/2 Kent AO.
[207]Baily, 'Minutes of the Trustees of the Turnpike Roads', p. 197. In 1805, John West-brook, the Chalk Trust collector, complained that his toll house was damp and un-healthy. Two months later the trust ordered a new room built. (Minutes–10 April 1805, T7/A1 Kent AO.)
[208]Minutes, 29 August 1728, T.P.Bed.1 Mid. CRO.
[209]Minutes, 25 August 1804 and 26 January 1818, T9/A2/2, Kent AO.

leasing the proceeds of their gates. By 'farming the tolls' they were assured of a steady income and freed from the expense and uncertainties of collection.

The lessees of the toll gates contracted to pay the trusts a fixed sum, usually in instalments, in return for the right to the proceeds from the gates. Although gates had been leased as early as 1702,[210] it was not until 1773 that a formal procedure was laid down for auctioning the tolls.[211] The trusts were required to advertise the toll auction one month in advance and to include in the notice the net amount of the previous year's proceeds. The tolls were to 'be put up at the Sum they were let for or produced in the preceding year', and there was to be a three-minute interval after every bid. If no one placed a further bid the 'last Bidder shall be the Farmer or Renter of the said Tolls'. He was to provide sureties and pay the trust in monthly or quarterly instalments. In 1822 the procedure was slightly altered.[212] The clerk or treasurer were allowed to bid for the trust, toll leases could not be made for more than three years and if the tolls were not let at the auction private tenders could be accepted, providing that the amount was not less than realized in the preceding year.

Before the late eighteenth century the lessees were usually local men who came from the same occupational groups as did the trusts' gate-keepers. The Rochester–Maidstone Trust let two of their gates in 1730, one to a saddler and the other to a widow.[213] When in 1735 they did not bid for the tolls, they were appointed as collectors at their respective gates.[214] They renewed their leases in the following year, and the trust's three gates were let to individual toll-farmers until at least 1749.[215] Trusts frequently let their gates separately and this indicates that many farmers operated on a small scale and probably did their own collecting.

By the nineteenth century, although there were still many small lessees, professional toll-farmers were becoming more common. Thomas Brown, a butter factor from Hunslet, James Kippax of Huddersfield

210 Gloucester–Birdlip and Crickley Hill Trust. In 1702 and again in 1710 the justices let the gates. (Gloucester QS Records, Q/SO-3, Glouces. RO.)

211 13 Geo. III c.84 art. 31.

212 3 Geo. IV. c.126, arts. 55-8.

213 Minutes – 6 August and 31 December 1730, T12/1 Kent AO. (Women lessees were found in other parts of the county. Mary Deighton, a widow, leased the Grimston bar from 1817 to 1825 and Mary Millwin farmed the tolls of the Hull Bridge Bar in 1822. MacMahon, 'Roads and Turnpike Trusts in E. Yorkshire', p. 54.)

214 Minutes – April 1735, T12/1 Kent AO. (The Chalk Trust's collector in 1718/19, Wm. Goodwin, became the lessee of the tolls in 1720. He also supervised repair and statute labour. Q/SB 1718/19 and 1720, Kent AO.)

215 Minutes to 1749, T12/1 Kent AO. The saddler, Richard Drivor, leased the Standing Gate until 1749, Mary Waters leased the Maidstone Gate until 1739 when it was leased by William Athdowns, a labourer from Boxley.

D

and John Ward, a Bradford woolstapler, leased tolls in the East and West Ridings,[216] and the bidders for the Wibsey Low Moor Trust's gates in 1839 included fourteen men who claimed toll-farming as their occupation.[217] The largest lessee in this area was Joshua Bower (1773–1855), a Hunslet glass manufacturer and colliery owner. He leased many gates in Yorkshire, and it was claimed[218] that he had 'at one time nearly all the tolls between Leeds and London, some in Hants, Dorset and Wilts besides numerous others in various parts of the country'.

Lewis Levy (1786–1856)[219] was undoubtedly the greatest and most famous toll-farmer in the entire country. He was the principal partner of a group of toll renters in the London area.[220] As early as 1812 he was leasing the tolls of the Eastern District of the Bedfont–Bagshot Trust,[221] and thirteen years later claimed to be renting three-fourths of the tolls in London.[222] In 1839 he declared[223] that, although he had previously farmed from £400,000 to £500,000 of tolls, he was then taking only about a fourth of that amount. Not all toll-farmers, however, had the extensive interests or enjoyed such good fortune as did Levy[224] and Bower.

John Bryant leased the Harrow and Hastings gates from 1831 to 1833.[225] Each time he calculated his receipts he was £4–£5 behind the rent he was paying, and he was eventually forced to declare bankruptcy. These gates were taken by Stephen Stevens in 1835, and he was able to realize a profit from them until 1837.[226] Stevens leased thirty-one different gates in the Wealdon district between 1829 and 1839. His profits were only modest before 1833, but from then until 1836 he made over £100 per year from the ten gates he controlled. He ran into considerable difficulty in the following years, however, and the final entry in his account book records a £1,636 loss from the eight gates he had farmed between 1837 and 1839.

[216]MacMahon, 'Roads and Turnpike Trusts in E. Yorkshire', p. 54, records their interests in the East Riding. They bid for the tolls on the Wibsey Low Moor Trust in 1839. (HAS 59. Hal. Cent. Lib.) Kippax took the Rochdale–Halifax Trust's bars in 1838. (HAS-110 Hal. Cent. Lib.)

[217]List of Bidders (HAS-59, Hal. Cent. Lib.).

[218]R. V. Taylor, *Biographia Leodiensis* (Leeds, 1865), p. 456. Taylor claims that Bower left an estate of £100,000. In fact he left only £14,000 (Probate Registry, Probate of Will, October 1855).

[219]Dates provided by Dr V. D. Lipman.

[220]The London trusts' records show Levy associated with at least four others in farming tolls: Elisha Ambler, George Brown, William Wotton and John Wooton.

[221]Minutes 4 August 1812, T.P. Bed. 5 Mid. CRO.

[222]B.P.P. 1825 (355) v. 167, p. 30.

[223]B.P.P. 1839 (295) ix. 369, p. 13.

[224]Levy's estate was probated at £250,000 (Probate Registry, Probate of Will, January 1857).

[225]Account Book 1831–33, Q/CI–122, Kent AO.

[226]Account Book 1829–39, Q/CI–219, Kent AO

Toll-farming solved many of the trusts' collection problems but also posed new ones. The trusts continued to supply and maintain the gatehouses, but they no longer had to pay or supervise the collectors.[227] Toll evasions became less of an immediate problem although the trustees had to be concerned lest decreasing proceeds lowered the tolls' rental value. The letting of the gates, while freeing the trustees from the effects of the collectors' fraudulent practices, did not protect the road users, who, it was claimed, were continually overcharged by the farmers.[228] The lessees were also notorious for their collusion at toll auctions. Robert Pitcher, a Lambeth gatekeeper, claimed[229] that the renters' profits must have been considerable because the London toll auctions had been rigged for thirty years, and the trustees powerless to prevent it. Jackman[230] presents the case of a 'typical' toll auction at which the trustees were helpless dupes in the hands of the devious toll-farmers, and the Webbs[231] concur that there was 'a series of elaborate combinations and private "knock outs" among the toll farmers'. However, the trustees could hardly have been unaware of attempts at collusion, and if the sums offered were too low they could have collected the tolls themselves as they frequently did. Also, if combinations were widespread, steady or decreasing incomes would be excepted, and this was not the case[232] until the railways began affecting toll revenues in the thirties and forties. There undoubtedly were combinations among the toll-farmers, but without further evidence it is impossible to gauge the extent of such practices, the profits they realized or how much the trusts lost by leasing their gates. If Stevens's accounts are at all indicative, the lessees offered the trusts a valuable service, for their profits were low and the risks considerable.

4

The effectiveness of the turnpike trusts can be evaluated in a number of ways. As will be suggested,[233] from the standpoint of road repair and lowering of transport costs it can be claimed that generally the trustees carried out their duties successfully. Another criterion for as-

[227]Levy said that the trusts reserved the right to discharge collectors (*B.P.P. 1825 (355) v. 167*, p. 32).
[228]*B.P.P. 1836 (547) xix. 335*, p. 117.
[229]*Ibid.* p. 115.
[230]Jackman, *Development of Transportation*, pp. 682-3.
[231]Webbs, *King's Highway*, p. 139.
[232]R. G. Wilson, 'Transport Dues', p. 119. He argues that the frequent down-turns in turnpike revenue were not due to the farmer's chicanery, but to the periodic trade depressions.
[233]See below, pp. 140-2, 186-7.

sessing the trustees' performance is the manner in which they controlled their finances. This includes not only the management of the mortgage debt, but also the percentage of funds allocated to road repair.

The Webbs have claimed 'The most defective side of turnpike administration was that of finance',[234] and 'The most serious of all financial defects was ... the deficit into which many bodies of Trustees fell.'[235] The question to be considered is how many trusts were hampered by an adverse financial condition and whether the number of such trusts increased during the nineteenth century.

Dr Pressnell has pointed out[236] that a mortgage debt is not in itself *a priori* grounds for assuming a trust was in an unsound financial position. Unlike the canals and the railways, the turnpike trusts were unable to finance initial improvements by issuing shares. In this sense, the mortgage debt represented the trusts' capital rather than a debt *per se*. If the trustees were conscientiously paying interest and this payment did not account for a disproportionate share of their income, it can be said that the trustees were handling this aspect of their finances reasonably well.

Successful management of the morgage debt did not, however, necessarily mean that a trust was being well administered. The percentage of income devoted to direct repair expenditure must also be considered. This provides a fair indication of the trustees' attention to the maintenance of their roads, although it is not a measure of the effectiveness of their repair techniques. From 1834 to 1838 inclusive (when sufficient national data first became available), the trusts spent 67% of their incomes on repair,[237] 20% on interest payments[238] and 8·5% on administration.[239] These figures suggest that on aggregate the trusts were devoting a fairly high percentage of their toll income to road repair. The breakdown of these figures, presented below, allows for a detailed, quantitative appraisal of the success or failure of the trusts in effectively managing their debts and allocating their resources.

The data used was taken from the trusts' accounts returned to Parlia-

234Webbs, *King's Highway*, p. 135.

235*Ibid.* p. 141.

236Pressnell, *Country Banking*, pp. 367-8.

237*B.P.P. 1840 (256) xxvii.1*, p. 9. 'Repair' included manual labour, team labour, carriage of materials, materials for surface repairs, land purchased, damage done in obtaining materials, incidental expenses, tradesmens' bills and the estimated value of statute labour performed. The first four accounted for £36/mile, while the remaining improvements absorbed £9/mile. If repair is taken as a percentage of expenditure (income excluded loans and statute labour) it was 69·5%.

238*Ibid.*

239*Ibid.* Administrative charges include the salaries of treasurers, clerks, surveyors and law charges. This tends to overstate the administrative expenditure for surveyors' salaries are more properly included as a repair expense. 4·5% was the balance of income over expenditure.

ment in 1821 and 1837.[240] In the former, the first country-wide survey undertaken, each trust was required to list its mileage, mortgage debt, annual income and expenditure (both averaged over three years), number of trustees, balance of accounts and amount of sinking funds. These accounts show the degree of trust indebtedness, but provide no information as to the way in which the trusts allocated their funds. The 1837 Return, one of a number of standardized returns submitted from 1833, contains thirty-eight categories for income, expenditure, debts and assets. This return allows not only for an appraisal of trust debt, but also shows in great detail how the trusts spent their funds.

In order to judge whether a trust was in a favourable financial position it has been necessary to set up a number of criteria. As these must be more or less arbitrary, the picture which they present must be viewed as an approximate one. Nonetheless, a comparison of the figures for the two years does give a general indication of long-term trends.

The maximum percentage of income which the well-run trust could have paid as interest has been set as 20%. This takes into account trusts recently formed or those engaged on major construction projects, both of which have temporarily low income and high debts. The well-managed trust must also have had less than three years' arrears of interest. Given that interest payments were relatively low, this sum could have been liquidated with comparative ease within a few years. The minimum amount which should have been devoted to repair has been set at 55%–65%. This takes into account expenses such as legal costs or debt repayments which are more properly amortized over a number of years. The 1821 Return has been considered from the standpoint of mortgage debt and arrears, while the later return has been judged with reference to all the above points. Because of this, the analyses of the earlier return probably understates the number of trusts in an adverse financial position.

A comparison of the aggregate figures for the two years does not reveal a significant change. In 1821, 60·4% of the trusts, responsible for 57·5% of the trust mileage were, by the above criteria, in a bad financial condition. By 1837 the percentages had dropped to 59·3% and 52·4% respectively. The most one can conclude from these results is that during the twenties and thirties the overall financial condition of the trusts probably did not deteriorate and may have improved very marginally.

If the question of the trusts' administrative efficiency is approached solely from the point of view of the road users, whose primary concern

[240]These reports and the calculations made are discussed in Appendix D.

was the amount of money the trustees spent on repairing the roads,[241] the picture is somewhat brighter. In 1837 57% of the trusts controlling 62·7% of the mileage were devoting 55% or more of their expenditure towards road repair. This suggests that those who used the turnpike roads may have benefited at the expense of the trusts' creditors.[242]

A brief consideration of the counties in which a high percentage of the trusts or trust mileage suffered from adverse finances may cast some light on the factors underlying their financial problems. In eight of the sixteen worst counties,[243] a high proportion of the trusts were formed after 1790, and the majority of these 'new' trusts seem to have been faced by financial difficulties. For example, in Yorkshire forty-one of the forty-three new trusts were in a bad financial position. The 'new' trusts were often speculative, and because of high initial expenses the trustees were generally unable to liquidate the debts readily. While these trusts seem to have contributed to the picture of financial distress in the northern counties (except Nottingham and Shropshire) and in Kent and Sussex, in the South-west there were but few trusts formed in the later period. The key to the problems in this area seems to have been the low traffic density and the consequent inadequate incomes. These two factors can, however, provide only a partial explanation, for some counties had many 'new' trusts, low incomes per mile and a high proportion of trusts in a favourable financial position.

Another factor which must be considered is the size of the trusts. From the parliamentary commissions' desire for trust consolidation it may be inferred that larger trusts were more efficient; however, of the ninety-two 'large' trusts (those controlling more than forty miles of road), forty-five were in an adverse financial position.[244] Although differences in terrain and income-per-mile must be taken into account, this figure suggests that large size did not in itself necessarily lead to more efficient management. Professor Pollard, referring to industry in the period, has said[245]

It is by no means certain that larger size was always considered desirable or could even theoretically be defended as being superior. On the contrary organization theory itself suggests that while there may be technical, financial or marketing advantages in growth, management difficulties tend to work in the opposite direction, towards a lower optimum size.

[241]This is subject to the proviso regarding the effectiveness of repair technique, cited above, p. 88.
[242]This subject is discussed in greater detail below.
[243]Sussex, Kent, Yorkshire, Lancashire, Cheshire, Derbyshire, Northumberland, and Westmorland. (See Appendix E.)
[244]See below, Appendix F.
[245]S. Pollard, *The Genesis of Modern Management. A Study of the Industrial Revolution in Great Britain* (London, 1965), p. 10.

This statement could also be applied to the turnpike trusts for although the general level of administrative competence seems to have been rising in the nineteenth century, the practice of large-scale management was still in its infancy, and the ideas of J. L. McAdam, the leading exponent of administrative reform, were slow to gain acceptance.[246] It could be argued that more consolidations would have encouraged the spread of better management techniques, but this must remain conjectural. Also, it must be remembered the Metropolis Roads Commission worked so well partly because the trusts taken over were in a relatively good financial condition,[247] the roads were in reasonable repair,[248] and the most debt-laden trusts in London were not included in the consolidation. In other parts of the country conditions were not so favourable. Many small trusts had low incomes and very large debts, and their position became more desperate from the mid-1830s when the competition from the railways began to be felt with devastating effect.[249] In 1837, the trusts collected £1,510,000 in tolls,[250] and by 1849 receipts had fallen by 26·5% to £1,097,482. The magnitude of the problem had been completely altered, and it is unlikely that trust consolidation could have provided any more than the most marginal benefit to the turnpike system. Taking all the above factors into account, the failure of a consolidation movement to develop may not have been as disastrous as the Webbs have implied.[251]

Both the parliamentary reports and the Webbs' studies have tended to stress the failures and inadequacies of the turnpike trusts. Their observations, based primarily on singling out the malpractices of certain trusts as being representative of the entire system and on a misunderstanding of the significance of the mortgage debts, has perpetuated the impression that the turnpike system as a whole was incompetently administered. This is not an entirely fair picture. Judged by present-day standards the trusts may seem to have been badly run, but in the early years of the nineteenth century modern administrative techniques were in their infancy, and during this period the turnpike trusts do not seem to have lagged behind other local statutory authorities in adopting new ideas.[252] The trustees were able to take advantage of the advances made in banking and civil engineering,[253] which allowed trust administration to be placed on a more professional footing. The contracting of toll

[246]See below, p. 148.
[247]See above, pp. 67-8.
[248]First Report of the Commissioners of the Metropolis Turnpike Roads, *B.P.P. 1826-27* (*339*) *vii. 23*, pp. 16-29 – James McAdam's report on the condition of the trusts' roads.
[249]*B.P.P. 1839 (295) ix. 369*, pp. iii-iv.
[250]*B.P.P. 1872 (5) xviii*, p. 4.
[251]Webbs, *King's Highway*, pp. 179-80.
[252]Webbs, *Statutory Authorities*, pp. 453-7.
[253]See below, pp. 142-8.

collection and road repair, while open to many abuses, also seems to have proved beneficial.[254] Finally, although the analysis of accounts presented above does lend support to the Webbs' claims it also modifies these claims somewhat by showing that a substantial number of trusts and much of the trust mileage was being managed with a fair degree of competence, and that a fairly high proportion of trust funds was going directly for road repair.

[254]See below, pp. 152-7.

5

The Financing of the Turnpike System

1

The great majority of trust income was derived from the tolls granted by local acts. The trustees often mortgaged these tolls in order to cover the costs of obtaining the acts or to provide funds for initial road improvements. Besides these first loans, over the years it was frequently necessary to solicit further sums for new road projects, to secure renewal acts or to repay former loans. As a result of their need for money in advance of, and often in addition to, toll receipts, the trusts became an important sector for local investment, and as they grew in number and spread throughout the country so their importance increased. The turnpikes not only afforded an opportunity for the employment of local savings, but also provided valuable social overheads for the entire economy. In this chapter the nature and sources of trust investment will be considered, and it is hoped that this will add to our understanding of this important aspect of the Industrial Revolution.

The turnpikes, unlike the canals or railways, were not permitted to raise capital by issuing shares. The trusts were not granted this authority because of their particular nature and functions. They were originally envisaged as a temporary device, supplementary to the system of parish road repair. They were created primarily to maintain existing facilities, not to construct new ones and were therefore not faced with the heavy fixed capital expenditure entailed in canal or railway construction. Furthermore, the use of shares creates private ownership and implies profits. Both were precluded by the fact that the trusts operated upon the 'King's Highway'. However, the trusts did require capital for putting roads in repair, sometimes for constructing new roads, for setting up gates and building toll-houses. To cover these expenses and those incurred in obtaining the act, funds were borrowed, and in later years additional loans were often necessary to finance further improvements, the addition of new roads or the cost of renewal acts.

The trusts could raise long-term capital through the use of bonds, annuities or mortgages, instruments used in a subsidiary capacity by the canals and railways.[1] Bonds were secured on the tolls, the trustees adding their personal surety for the loan. This extra guarantee was desirable for investors, but not for the trustees, and bonds were employed only when all other means of raising funds had failed. They were most frequently used by trusts whose adverse financial position deterred investors from investing in the other securities. The Sheffield–Glossop Trust was one of these. The trust was unable to pay interest on the £18,650 originally subscribed,[2] and when in the 1820s additional funds were required, bonds had to be offered. By using bonds and having the Dukes of Devonshire and Norfolk and the Earl of Surrey as joint-sureties, the trust was able to raise £34,500.[3] The trusts could circumvent the usury laws by selling annuities; however, while popular in government finance, they were rarely used by the trusts.[4] Both annuities and bonds were therefore of marginal importance in trust finance, and seem to have been used only under special circumstances.

The principal method of raising long-term capital was to mortgage the tolls. The local acts sometimes set the maximum rate of interest payable, as well as a limit on the amount that could be borrowed. The latter restriction was seldom prescribed, and most trusts were free to raise unlimited funds on mortgage. The loans were secured against the tolls, and each mortgagee was assigned 'such proportion of the tolls arising and to arise on the said turnpike road, and the toll gates and toll houses erected or to be erected for collecting the same, as the sum of _____ doth or shall bare to the whole sum now or hereafter to become due and owing on the security thereof'.[5] The mortgages were to be valid until the trust's statutory term expired. However, an outstanding debt assured that a trust would be able to secure a renewal act.[6] Thus, the mortgage debt, by guaranteeing a trust's perpetuation, ensured the continuation of its own security.

The money borrowed on mortgage was not to be considered permanent capital, in the sense of share capital, but rather a loan. This is consistent both with the nature of mortgages and with the concept of trusts as temporary authorities. The toll-mortgage had many characteristics which differentiated it from an ordinary mortgage of land, and the

[1] G. H. Evans, *British Corporation Finance, 1775-1850. A Study of Preference Shares* (Baltimore, 1936), pp. 45-53.
[2] Trust Accounts, 1827-39, CPG-2 Shef. Cent. Lib.
[3] *Ibid.* This trust was singled out in 1833 as having the largest debt relative to toll receipts (*B.P.P. 1833 (703) xv. 409*, p. 33).
[4] They were also seldom used by the canal companies. Evans, *British Corporation Finance*, p. 51.
[5] 3 Geo. IV c.126 art. 81. The mortgages issued prior to 1823 were generally similar, although the wording may have varied.
[6] See above, p. 60.

trusts were, in fact, not temporary. As their terms expired trusts sought and were invariably granted acts renewing their powers for an additional twenty-one years. Since a toll-mortage matured only when a trust ceased to operate, the mortgage debt was 'virtually' as permanent as the trust. There were, however, legal considerations which qualified a toll-mortgage's permanence.

The absence, in most toll-mortgages, of a stated date of maturity meant that there could be neither default nor ejectment at this stage. However, a breach of condition could result in foreclosure, and 'A default of payment of a half-year's interest on the appointed day, will be sufficient breach of condition to enable the mortgagee to foreclose.'[7] The mortgagees could take possession of the gates and recover the interest due as well as their principal and the collection expenses.[8] While they were able to foreclose if interest was not paid, it is unclear whether they could institute ejectment only to recover their principal.

The Barrowstowness Canal Act (1783) contained the following provision:

That so long as the said Interest (or Annuity) shall continue to be regularly paid ... (as stipulated) ... or within Three months of the respective Times hereby appointed for the Payment of the same; it shall not be in the Power of the said A.B. .... to enter upon Possession of the said Tolls, Rates, Duties, and Premises, or to commence and carry on any Action or Suit for attaining the same.[9]

This is, in effect, a restatement of the principle of ejectment due to breach of condition. Although this clause was not found in the turnpike acts, if it was a generally accepted principle of law its inclusion may have been considered redundant. The absence of any clause which defined the grounds for ejectment suggests that this may have been the case. Without a more detailed study of the relevant legal aspects this can be proposed only as a tentative conclusion.[10]

The canal mortgage affords an interesting comparison with the turnpike security. As with trust mortgages, those issued by canals had, before the 1790s, no date of maturity,[11] and similar questions arise

---

[7] R. H. Coote, *A Treatise on the Law of Mortgage* (London, 1821), p. 518. This is with particular reference to land mortgages.

[8] 13 Geo. III c.84, arts. 52-3 and 3 Geo. IV c.126, arts. 47-9.

[9] Evans, *British Corporation Finance*, p. 46.

[10] None of the many works on turnpike trusts deals with this question. Furthermore, it is not covered in any work on legal history or in Evans, *British Corporation Finance*, or A. B. DuBois, *The English Business Company after the Bubble Act, 1720-1800* (New York, 1938).

[11] Evans, *British Corporation Finance*, p. 47. He adds that there was nothing preventing a solicitor from appending a date of maturity.

regarding the recovery of principal.[12] This point was partially clarified in 1794. 'In a canal act of that year it was provided that every mortgage made under that statute should be redeemable by the company upon six calendar months' notice, and also that each should be payable by the company upon like notice from the mortgagee.'[13] An identical clause was included in the act for the Yarmouth Bridge–South Town Trust in 1775,[14] but although this provision became more common in canal acts from the mid-nineties,[15] it was not generally found in turnpike acts either before or after this period.

If a breach of condition occurred a single mortgagee could initiate an action of ejectment.[16] However, 'such a person ... shall not apply the tolls ... received by him ... to his ... exclusive use and benefit, but to and for the use and benefit of all the mortgagees ... *pari passu*, and in proportion to the several sums which may be due to them as such mortgagees.'[17] The mortgage debt was in effect a single loan; the individual mortgages represented a proportion of it, and each mortgagee had equal rights against the tolls regardless of the date of his mortgage.[18] This was advantageous for the trust for it permitted them to borrow at any time, without the necessity of having to create second or third mortgages.[19] It also improved the marketability of the securities, for the new lenders would have had equal status with the original investors.

The toll-mortgage was a specialized, and in many ways, a unique security. Although many of the relevant legal considerations are unclear a few tentative observations may be made as to the affect the toll-mortgage had upon the trusts' financial administration.

While the toll-mortgage was, under certain conditions, advantageous, if interest was not paid regularly it could become a potential liability. Upon default of interest payment a single mortgagee, regardless of his percentage holding of the total debt, could foreclose. A creditor of the Halifax–Sheffield Trust brought an ejectment to recover four years arrears of interest on a £100 mortgage.[20] At that time (c. 1800), the trust's total mortgage debt was £3,600. With arrears outstanding, creditors, by threatening to foreclose, could force the trustees to raise the

---

[12]*Ibid.* pp. 46-8.

[13]*Ibid.* p. 47.

[14]15 Geo. III c.67.

[15]Evans, *British Corporation Finance*, p. 47.

[16]J. Bateman, *The General Turnpike Road Act*, p. 63n.

[17]3 Geo. IV c.126, sec. 49.

[18]In the sense of creating a single loan with equal rights for the mortgagees, the toll-mortgage was similar to the modern debenture.

[19]The issuing of priority mortgages was sometimes necessary if a trust found itself in a difficult financial position and in need of attracting secondary investors. See below, pp. 109–10.

[20]*Doe ex dem Banks v. Booth*, 2 Bos and P (P.C.) 219. 21 June 1800.

interest rate. In practice, although the mortgagees often agitated for higher interest rates, they rarely resorted to taking over the gates.[21] The difficulties entailed in such a procedure, plus the trustees' active opposition, may have succeeded in deterring most creditors from this course of action.

Although the toll-mortgage was not clearly defined until the later decades of the eighteenth century,[22] the singular characteristics of trust borrowing had, by the 1750s, given rise to a mortgage similar in form to that described above. The rights and obligations of both creditors and trustees were circumscribed by the toll-mortgage. A realization of its special features is therefore essential to an understanding of the dynamics of trust finance.

2

Before the second half of the eighteenth century the financing of turnpike trusts seems to have been undertaken in a somewhat piecemeal fashion. Capital was seldom raised through subscription, but rather by loans solicited after the trust was established. The few surviving trust records of this period indicate that this was a fairly common practice. The Bedfont–Bagshot trustees, at their first meeting in 1728, directed the clerk to borrow £1,000 at the 'cheapest' interest,[23] and the £400 required by the Chalk Trust was obtained after the trust was formed in 1718/19.[24] The Rochester–Maidstone Trust borrowed £400 in 1728 to cover the cost of its act and the erection of toll gates,[25] and in the following year £200 was borrowed for road repairs.[26] The Kensington, Fulham, Chelsea Trust did not borrow money until after a report had been received concerning the road repairs needed,[27] and the Fulham Field Trust did not consider soliciting loans until their second meeting.[28] The treasurer of the Redhouse (Doncaster)–Wakefield Trust made the first loan (£100) to the trust in 1743, two years after

---

[21]There were few turnpikes in the possession of creditors relative to the great number of trusts which had arrears of interest. (*B.P.P. 1840 (280) xxvii. 15.*)

[22]13 Geo. III c.84 contained the first clauses dealing with the trustees' and creditors' rights and obligations.

[23]Minutes – 3 May 1728, T.P. Bed. 1 Mid. CRO.

[24]Quarter-Sessions Records, Q/SB 1719 Kent AO.

[25]Minutes – 22 June 1728, T12/1 Kent AO.

[26]Minutes – 31 July 1729, T12/1 Kent AO.

[27]Minutes – 13 June 1726, MS58/7001 Ken. Pub. Lib. The first meeting was held on 26 May 1726.

[28]Minutes – 14 June 1731, MS58/7039 Ken. Pub. Lib. The solicitor presented his bill for the act at this meeting, and the trustees made the following order: 'Ordered that a Method for raising money for the payment there of the [solicitor's bill] and for repairing the said road be taken into Consideration on the next Board day.'

the first meeting.[29] The trustees of the Wakefield–Weeland Trust decided to borrow £1,000 at their first meeting in 1741,[30] and the clerks of both the Harrogate–Boroughbridge and Knaresborough–Green Hammerton trusts were ordered to advertise for loans at their respective trusts' first meetings.[31] The Gloucester–Hereford Trust,[32] the Colnbrook Trust,[33] the Marylebone and Islington Trusts,[34] the Liverpool–Prescot Trust,[35] the New Cross Trust,[36] and the Old Street Trust[37] all seem to have raised their initial capital after they were established.

It seems that during this period the trusts' financial support was narrowly based. They were able to raise needed capital from relatively few individuals, mostly local gentlemen or landowners, who were often also trustees. For example, although the amount of the Colnbrook Trust's mortgage debt varied and changed hands, it was held by a single creditor from 1728 to 1825.[38] Adrian Moore, the chairman of the Bedfont–Bagshot Trust, was the trust's only creditor from 1728 to 1743/4.[39] In that year the debt was taken up by five of his fellow trustees.[40] Henry Guise Esq. advanced the £2,000 needed by the Gloucester–Hereford Trust in 1730,[41] and the £800 lent by Lady Northton to the Chappel-on-the-Heath Trust in 1731, remained the trust's only debt until 1743.[42] The Rochester–Maidstone Trust borrowed £1,000 from a trustee in 1729,[43] and at his death two years later another trustee took up the loan until it was repaid in 1738/9.[44] Jonathan Bush held £1,900 of the £2,000 mortgage debt of the Henley Bridge–Magdalen Bridge Trust,[45] and Baldwin Duppa was the sole creditor of the Chalk Trust from 1721 until the loan was repaid three

[29]Minutes – 19 May 1743 (the first meeting was on 27 April 1741), box 54 West Rid. CRO.

[30]Minutes – 22 April 1741, box 54 West Rid. CRO.

[31]Harrogate–Boroughbridge Trust, Minutes – 28 April 1752, box 27 West Rid. CRO; Knaresborough–Green Hammerton Trust, Minutes – 11 May 1752, box 27 West Rid. CRO.

[32]Minutes – 1 July 1726, D204/2/2 Glouces. RO.

[33]Minutes – 4 November 1728, T.P. Col.1 Mid. CRO.

[34]Clarke, 'The Turnpike Trusts of Islington and Marylebone', p. 96.

[35]Baily, 'Minutes of the Trustees of the Turnpike Roads', p. 188.

[36]Minutes – 20 May 1718 (£172 was borrowed to obtain the act [Minutes – 19 April 1718] but it is not made clear when this was borrowed), T9/A1/14 Kent AO.

[37]Minutes – 3 July 1753.

[38]Minute Book 1728-84, T.P. Col. 1 and Account Book 1823-41, T.P. Col. 3 Mid. CRO.

[39]Minute Book 1728-57, T.P. Bed. 1 Mid. CRO.

[40]Minutes – 16 January 1743-4, T.P. Bed. 1 Mid. CRO.

[41]Minutes – 22 September 1730, D204/2/2 Glouces. RO. He may have lent the money earlier, for in 1747, when the trust sought renewal, it was stated in the report that £2,000 had been borrowed after the act was passed. (*J. H. of C.* xxv, p. 351.)

[42]Account Book 1731-67, D621/X4 Glouces. RO.

[43]Minute Book – 31 July 1729, T12/1 Kent AO.

[44]Minutes – 22 June 1738, T12/1 Kent AO.

[45]*J. H. of C.* xxvii, pp. 58-9, 122, 123.

years later.[46] Robert Isaacson Esq., a trustee, was the Woburn Trust's only creditor from 1728 to 1740,[47] and Sir Ralph Asheton, Bart., was the sole investor in the Blackstone Edge Trust from 1735 to 1767.[48]

Although the capital required by trusts in and around the metropolis was probably greater than in most other parts of the country, the London trusts also depended on a few investors. The Highgate–Hampstead Trust raised £7,000 initial capital from four investors in 1718 and 1719,[49] four trustees advanced £3,700 to the New Cross Trust in 1718[50] and the total mortgage debt of the Fulham, Chelsea, Kensington Trust was held by two creditors in 1726/7.[51] John Ewer, the Fulham Field Trust's treasurer, was the trust's sole creditor from 1731 until 1736, when he declared bankruptcy.[52] From 1736 to 1764 the entire mortgage debt was held by K. Gould, a trustee.[53] Some London trusts relied heavily on short-term financing. They paid their workmen with negotiable, interest bearing bills of credit called 'turnpike bills' or 'check notes', which were issued in small denominations and repaid in sequence as funds became available,[54] a method not unlike that used by government departments in times of war. The Kensington Trust, with a £2,000 mortgage debt, had £7,400 of these bills outstanding in 1732,[55] and the Islington Trust had £9,935 in 1742.[56] While floating debts were carried by trusts throughout the country, the large-scale use of bills of credit seems to have been peculiar to the London area.

After initial borrowing the trusts frequently found themselves in need of additional funds, either to cover heavy repair expenditure or to repay primary lenders. The secondary investors were generally similar, as regards their position, to the initial lenders. When Leonard Bartholomew died in 1731, the £1,000 mortgage debt of the Rochester–Maidstone Trust was taken up by Roger Twisden, a trustee.[57] £400 was repaid six years later, and the remaining £600 was advanced by Sir Christopher Powell, another trustee.[58] J. Rogers, the Colnbrook

---

[46]Quarter-Session Records, Q/SB-1723 Kent AO.

[47]Mortgages and a letter dated 31 March 1740, from the executors of Mrs Isaacson (CH. 16/5A Beds. CRO).

[48]Accounts 1735-90, HAS – 52, Hal. Cent. Lib.

[49]*J. H. of C.* xxii, p. 250.

[50]Minutes – 1718 accounts, T9/A1/14 Kent AO.

[51]MSS Accounts of Trust for Roads in Fulham, Chelsea and Kensington, 2 May 1732; H. of L. RO.

[52]Minutes – 30 August 1731. MS 58/7039 Ken. Pub. Lib. Ewer was elected treasurer after he had made the loan, 6 September 1731.

[53]Minutes – 4 November 1749, MS 58/7039 and Minutes – 10 November 1764, MSS 58/7040 Ken. Pub. Lib.

[54]*J. H. of C.* xxii, p. 250. *J. H. of C.* xxix, p. 650 and Clarke, 'Turnpike Trusts', pp. 101-7.

[55]MSS Accounts, 2 May 1732, H. of L. RO.

[56]Clarke, 'Turnpike Trusts', p. 104.

[57]Minutes – January, 1737/8, T12/1 Kent AO.

[58]Minutes – 5 January 1737/8, T12/1 Kent AO.

Trust's sole creditor was repaid his £2,500 in 1738,[59] and the mortgage was transferred to Thomas Eyre, a trustee, who held it until his death in 1778.[60] The chairman of the Bedfont–Bagshot Trust lent £1,000 in 1728, £1,000 in 1729, £500 in 1731 and £200 ten years later.[61] In 1719, the New Cross Trust issued a £369 mortgage to William Moore, a Deptford bricklayer, probably as payment for his services.[62] In the same year William Juson took over this security and lent a further £300, possibly to pay off mortgages held by two Deptford carpenters.[63] Subsequently Juson advanced £1,000 in 1746 and £331 in 1748.[64] Bartholomew Wood made three loans, totalling £3,200, to the same trust between 1747 and 1753.[65] Robert Isaacson lent £200 to the Woburn Trust in 1728, added £800 more in the following year, and by 1740 was owed £1,300.[66] Sir Ralph Asheton advanced £500 to the Blackstone Edge Trust in 1735, and by 1767 he had made ten further loans, totalling £5,500.[67] In order to protect his initial investment of £450, K. Gould lent the Fulham Field Trust an additional £150 in 1750, to cover the cost of a renewal act.[68]

The great majority of extant documents suggests that during the first half of the eighteenth century trust finance was based on relatively large individual loans and a select group of both primary and secondary investors.

3

From about 1750 the financing of turnpike trusts began to assume a new character. While post-enactment borrowing continued, the soliciting of subscriptions, prior to a trust's formation, became increasingly common. By the late sixties the use of subscriptions was firmly established to the virtual exclusion of the former method. This is reflected in the trust documents and was given official recognition by a new clause, dealing with the enforcement of subscriptions, which began to be inserted in local acts. The clause, as stated in the Act of 1773, provided

[59]Minutes – 5 December 1738, T.P.Col. 1 Mid. CRO.
[60]Minutes – 13 March 1775, T.P. Col. 1 Mid. CRO, and Mortgage, 1738, T.P. Col. 8/3, Mid. CRO.
[61]Minutes – 1 June 1728, 13 January 1728/9, 27 April 1731, and 5 October 1741, T.P. Bed. 1, Mid. CRO.
[62]Mortgages 1719, T9/F6 Kent AO.
[63]*Ibid.* and *J. H. of C.* xxix, p. 661 and Minutes – 18 October 1718 (order to prepare mortgages), T9/A1/14 Kent AO.
[64]*J. H. of C.* xxix, p. 661.
[65]*Ibid.*
[66]Letter, 31 March 1740, CH. 16/5A Beds. CRO.
[67]Register of Securities, 1735-1872, HAS 52, Hal. Cent. Lib.
[68]Minutes – 16 June 1750, MS 58/7039 Ken. Pub. Lib.

That if any Person or Persons shall agree to advance any Sum or Sums of Money, to be employed in the making or repairing a Turnpike Road or Highway intended to be made a Turnpike, and shall subscribe his ... Name ... every such Person shall be liable to pay every Sum or Sums of Money so subscribed ... and in Default of Payment thereof within Twenty one Days after the same shall become payable ... it shall and may be lawful for every such Treasurer or other Person to sue for and recover the same, in any of His Majesty's Courts or Record.[69]

The initial financing of the Lincoln Heath–Peterborough Trust serves as an example of the subscription procedure. The following agreement was signed by the proposed trust's supporters in September, 1755:[70]

We whose Names are here under written do hereby promise to advance and lend at an Interest not under four p. cent the sums against each of our names towards procuring an act of Parliament for and amending the Road from Lincoln Heath ... upon credit of the tolls to be taken upon the said Road upon condition that no part of the sum ... shall be called until the sum of six thousand pounds be subscribed.

Forty-four subscribers agreed to advance a total of £6,200. A few lent fairly large amounts, although no loan was for more than £500, and the majority were for fifty or a hundred pounds. Dividing the total subscription into fractional sums gave increased opportunity to the small investor, and thereby broadened the basis of the trusts' financial support.

Although local gentlemen and landowners continued to dominate as initial investors in most trusts, merchants, manufacturers, artisans, shopkeepers, and others now began to take a more active interest in trust investment.[71] The subscription list of the Hitchin–Bedford Trust[72] (1757) included besides the 'Gents' and 'Esqs.', a tanner, four maltsters, a baker and two drapers. A mercer and a goldsmith were among the subscribers to the Leicester–Narborough Trust in 1753,[73] and two innkeepers, a weaver, a hosier, a shoemaker and a miller were among the ninety-nine subscribers to the Sedbergh Trust in 1765.[74] A clerk, two victuallers, a fellmonger and two millers provided £350 of the £1,300 subscribed for the Dunchurch–Southam Trust in 1794.[75]

---

[69]13 Geo. III c.84 art. 35.
[70]Subscription List 1755, ASW 10/57/3 Lincs. AO.
[71]While investors' occupations are often stated in the trust documents in many cases only names are given. To discover the occupations of many trusts' investors would require very detailed local research and as this was impracticable much information on trust investors has not been used.
[72]Register of Securities 1757-60, X46/6 Beds. CRO.
[73]Securities Book 1754-1877 T/X/4/1 Leics. RO.
[74]Register of Mortgages 1765, box 71 West Rid. CRO.
[75]Mortgage Ledger 1797-1872, CR/560/59 War. CRO.

Four innkeepers, a surgeon, a baker, a carrier and a labourer were among the seventy-six initial subscribers of the Chapel-en-le-Frith–Entreclough Bridge Trust in 1793,[76] and the subscription list of the Sheffield–Glossop Trust included two victuallers, a hairdresser and three carpenters.[77] Among the original investors of the Oldham–Ripponden Trust (1795), were two labourers, five innkeepers, a brewer, two mercers, a hatter, a butcher and a stonemason.[78] A horse dealer, a hatter, four innkeepers and a shopkeeper invested in the Banbury–Barcheston Trust (1804),[79] a maltster, a brewer and a grocer in the Deal–Sandwich Trust in 1798,[80] and the Little Yarmouth Trust (1798) received loans from a glazier, two carpenters, a currier and a brick-layer.[81]

Although this type of investor appeared on many subscription lists, his loans usually formed a small proportion of the total amount sub-scribed. The greatest part of the subscription capital was advanced by the groups which stood to profit most from improved roads – land-owners, merchants and manufacturers. In order to secure their loans it was incumbent upon those who most actively desired a turnpike – the promoters – to convince these people of the advantages which the turn-pike would afford. The following is an excellent example of the type of arguments used to attract the landowners' investment.

In September 1766 the promoters of the proposed Boston–Wainfleet Trust advertised that on the twenty-fifth of that month a meeting would be held, 'at which time and Place all persons interested are desired to attend by themselves or agents'.[82] John Bourne, agent of the Croft and Holbreck Estates, upon seeing this notice wrote the following letter to the proprietor, William Drake:[83]

Upon seeing the above Advertisement in the Publick Papers, I have thought it necessary to transmit a copy of it to you as your Estates at Croft adjoins Wainfleet thro' w'ch Place the Road in Question goes & has no other Road to the South but this intended Turnpike w'ch is from Croft the direct Road to London by w'ch the Cattle fed on your Estate always goe. Tis my opinion when it is executed 'twile be of Utility & Benefit to your Estate.

Drake replied that if the turnpike would prove of benefit to his tenants he would be ready to forward it 'as farr as lies in my power'.[84] After

[76]Securities, Arundel Castle MSS D.58 Shef. Cent. Lib.
[77]List of Subscribers 1818, CPG-8(6) Shef. Cent. Lib.
[78]Mortgage Ledger 1795, box 46 West. Rid. CRO.
[79]Mortgage Ledger 1802, CR580/53 War. CRO.
[80]Security Ledger 1798-1871, T11/F3 Kent AO.
[81]Minutes – 11 June 1798. EH: 50/5/3B1. Ips. & E. Suf. RO.
[82]Letter from J. Bourne to William Drake Esq., 14 September 1766, TYR. 4/1/48 Lincs. AO.
[83]*Ibid.*   [84]*Ibid.*, note appended to the letter.

the meeting Bourne again wrote to Drake and told him that although some tenants were apprehensive that the tolls would be a heavy tax, nonetheless, he felt that the turnpike would be advantageous. He offered the following reasons:

That as Boston is a Sea Port of no small Consideration to which Place the Road is proposed from Wainfleet, which is within One Mile of your Estate a very valuable Intercourse will be established.

That Sheep may always be sent to Smithfield Market w'ch sometimes are greatly impeded by bad Roads in the Spring ... That Wolle may at all Times be sent either to Southern or Northern Markets for that Article which can now only be effected in the Summer.

On these Considerations was the Estate my own I should prefer the Completion of a Turnpike to the Present very uncertain State of the Road on which the Permanence of Business so much depends on Seasons.[85]

This admirable array of possible advantages seems to have convinced Drake of the 'Utility and Benefit' of the road, and he subsequently advanced £500 to the trust.[86]

Landowners, tenant farmers, country gentlemen, yeomen farmers and members of the landed aristocracy were the most important of the trusts' investors. They appeared in considerable numbers on most subscription lists, and rarely was their contribution overshadowed by that of other groups. It must be stressed that it is often difficult to distinguish tenant farmers from owner occupiers, and that although the title 'Esq.' or 'Gent.' usually denoted a landowner, it did sometimes include merchants, manufacturers or attorneys for whom ownership of land was a subsidiary interest.[87]

For the larger landed proprietor the turnpike, like enclosure, was 'a highly profitable investment in financial terms'.[88] Improved roads, by enhancing an area's competitive position, may have contributed to higher rental values. The Sleaford–Tattershall Trust greatly increased the rental value of lands around Billinghay in Lincolnshire,[89] and that turnpikes enhanced property values is also suggested by an advertisement for the sale of an estate in Worcestershire which cited as one of the estate's advantages the fact that 'the proposed new road from Pershore direct to Birmingham (it cuts across country and by-passes Worcester) will pass near ... (and) ... an excellent turnpike road to Worcester is now being widened'.[90] Arthur Young's comment on this

[85] Letter from J. Bourne to William Drake, 1 October 1766, TYR. 4/1/49 Lincs. AO.

[86] *Ibid.*

[87] I thank Dr R. G. Wilson for this point.

[88] J. D. Chambers and G. E. Mingay, *The Agricultural Revolution. 1750-1880* (London, 1966), p. 84.

[89] David Grigg, *The Agricultural Revolution in South Lincolnshire* (Cambridge, 1966), p. 44.

[90] J. M. Martin, 'Some Social and Economic Changes in Rural Worcestershire, Stafford-

point is also instructive:[91] 'I found all the sensible people attributed the dearness of their county to the turnpike roads; and reason speaks the truth of their opinions ... but make a turnpike road through their county and all cheapness vanishes at once.' Increasing prices in local markets implies rising rental values.

Better communication was also a vital complement to enclosure, affording wider markets for the increasingly productive agricultural areas. The easier accessibility to these markets, lower transport costs and the opportunity to shift the burden of repair to the road users, recommended the turnpike to the small proprietor and the tenant farmer, as well as the larger landowner. If they were not initially party to a particular turnpike scheme, the promoters soon sought to enlist their financial support. Their efforts were, for the most part, highly successful.

Twenty-nine of the sixty-two subscribers of the Banbury–Barcheston Trust were yeomen, and twenty were 'Gents.' and squires.[92] Landed interests accounted for £1,800 of the £2,000 loaned to the Alcester–Wootton Trust (1814),[93] £1,400 of the £1,800 subscribed to the Arrow–Pothooks' End Trust (1826)[94] and £800 of the £1,300 advanced to the Dunchurch–Southam Trust (1797).[95] In Suffolk, the Ipswich–Helmingham[96] and Little Yarmouth[97] trusts were supported primarily by farmers and gentry, and in Kent, the Charing Trust (1766) was financed entirely by yeomen and 'Gents'.[98] Even in the more industrialized areas the landed interests' loans were of major importance. All but £950 of the £4,000 subscribed to the Worksop–Attercliffe Trust came from farmers, gentry and nobility.[99] The Marple Bridge–Glossop Trust (1804),[100] the Chapel-en-le-Frith–Entreclough Bridge Trust (1793)[101] and the Wibsey Low Moor Trust (1823),[102] all received much of their initial capital from local farmers and landowners.

To some trust ventures the support and investment of the larger

shire and Warwickshire 1785-1825' (unpublished Master of Commerce thesis, University of Birmingham, 1959), p. 140.

[91] Arthur Young, *A Six Weeks Tour through the Southern Counties of England and Wales* (London, 1768), p. 260.

[92] Mortgage Ledger 1802, CR580/53 War. CRO.

[93] Security Ledger 1814, CR446/9 War. CRO.

[94] Security Ledger 1826-59, CR446/11 War. CRO.

[95] Mortgage Ledger 1797-1872, CR560/59 War. CRO.

[96] Mortgages 1812-83, EH:50/5/1A1 Ips. & E. Suf. RO.

[97] Minutes — 11 June 1798, EH:50/5/3B1 Ips. & E. Suf. RO.

[98] Security Ledger 1766-1869, U442 057 Kent AO.

[99] Mortgage Ledger, 1767, box 24 West Rid. CRO.

[100] Securities D.46, Shef. Cent. Lib.

[101] Securities, 1793-1834, D.58, Shef. Cent. Lib.

[102] List of Subscribers 1823, HAS — A. Hal. Cent. Lib.

landed proprietors was of particular importance. The Dukes of Norfolk and Devonshire lent the £772 needed to obtain the Sheffield–Glossop Turnpike Act (1818), and of the £18,625 subscribed, they advanced £6,000 and £4,000 respectively.[103] By 1839 the Dukes had lent a further £19,400 and their total loans at that time accounted for £30,172 of the £74,734 debt. They were also joint-sureties, with the Earl of Surrey, for bonds totalling £34,500.[104] The former Duke of Norfolk had been an original subscriber of the Worksop–Attercliffe Trust in 1764 (£400),[105] the Balby–Worksop Trust in 1765 (£200)[106] and in 1767 he lent £1,200 to the Sheffield–Wakefield Trust.[107] Devonshire also advanced money to this road (£600), made a token £100 contribution to the Oakmore Trust (1762),[108] near his copper works at Whiston, and by 1828 he had loaned £4,800 to the Sheffield–Chapel-en-le-Frith Trust.[109] In Warwickshire, Lord Beauchamp loaned £1,500 of the £2,000 subscribed to the Evesham–Alcester Trust (1778/9).[110] The Marquis of Hertford became a major investor of this trust in 1818–19, advancing £1,600,[111] and he also lent half of the £2,000 subscribed to the Alcester–Wootton Trust (1814).[112] The Earl of Guildford expended £200 in obtaining the act for the Drayton–Edgehill Trust (1753),[113] and in 1754 the Duchess of Argyll and the Earl of Dartmoor advanced £100 and £200 respectively.[114] Guildford also loaned £100 to the Great Kingston Trust in 1773.[115]

Although, on a country-wide basis, their investment in turnpikes seems to have been less than that of the landed interests, nevertheless, merchants and manufacturers were actively concerned in the promotion of various schemes for transport improvement. In 1764 Josiah Wedgwood, in association with other pottery manufacturers, supported the Burslem–Newcastle-under-Lyme Trust, to which he loaned £150.[116] He was also one of the principal promoters of the Trent

[103]Accounts 1827-39, CPG-2 and Treasurer's Accounts 1818-19, D.67 (both in Shef. Cent. Lib.).
[104]Accounts 1827-39, CPG-2.
[105]Mortgage Ledger 1767, box 24 West Rid. CRO.
[106]Minute book 1858-74 (containing list of lenders 1765-1816), box 15, West Rid. CRO.
[107]List of Lenders 1767, Tib. Col. 364-24 Shef. Cent. Lib.
[108]Account Book 1762-84, O239M box 4 Staffs. RO.
[109]List of Mortgages, 1828, Beauchief Muniments 85-4 Shef. Cent. Lib.
[110]Security Ledger 1778-1825, CR446/21 War. CRO.
[111]Ibid.
[112]Security Ledger 1814, CR 446/9 War. CRO.
[113]Minutes – 5 June 1753, CR 580/57 War. CRO.
[114]Minutes, 1754, CR 580/57 War. CRO.
[115]An assignment of a mortgage of the Great Kingston Trust, issued in 1770, U471-T134 Kent AO.
[116]Minutes – 3 August 1836, 88/2/41 Wm. Salt Lib. The following was recorded at that date: 'That a fresh security be executed to Josiah Wedgwood Esq. for the sum of £150 in lieu of one dated 1764 the expense of such security to be paid by Mr. Wedgwood.'

and Mersey Canal.[117] Edward Knight was a major investor in the Second Ludlow Trust, which ran by his ironworks at Bringwood to the river-port of Bewdley. He loaned £500 to the trust in 1756 and £950 more by 1760.[118] The partners of the Low Moor Iron Company subscribed £2,000 to the Wibsey Low Moor Trust in 1823[119] and £1,000 to the Leeds–Whitehall Trust two years later.[120] However, in both latter cases a far greater amount of the initial capital seems to have been supplied by local landowners.

At the end of the eighteenth century Samuel Oldknow was involved in a number of transport improvement schemes in the vicinity of Marple and Mellor. He supported at least four turnpikes in this area and was also a chief promoter of the Peak Forest Canal.[121] In 1797 he agreed with William Egerton, an estate owner at Goyt, and Thomas Beard, a New Mills landowner, to a plan for a turnpike from Marple through Mellor to Hayfield and New Mills.[122] It was his intention to have the road to his mill at Mellor included and also to have £1,000 secured to him for the £3,000 he claimed he had expended on repairing the road. This shows that desire to transfer the repair burden was, indeed, a relevant consideration.[123] However, when the trust was formed the road was not included. In 1798 he agreed with Beard to solicit subscriptions for a turnpike from Marple to Stockport;[124] he also invested £100 in the Chapel-en-le-Frith–Entreclough Bridge Trust in 1802,[125] and advanced the same amount to the Glossop–Marple Bridge Trust in 1805.[126] The former trust received only minor financial support from those concerned in cotton manufacture[127] and, although they were more important in financing the Glossop Trust, their loans were equalled by those of farmers and yeomen.[128]

The textile interests actively supported the Oldham–Standage Trust to which twenty-two clothiers, eight merchants and a cotton manufacturer loaned £4,925 of the £7,125 subscribed.[129] Three cotton

---

[117]List of subscribers to the Trent and Mersey Canal, 1765, D1798 Wm. Salt Lib.
[118]Order Book and Accounts – 15 June 1756, June 1757 – £250, August 1758 – £500 and March 1759 – £200, SRO 356/23/312 Salop RO.
[119]List of subscribers 1823, HAS. A. Hal. Cent. Lib. In 1833 (?) the ironworks offered to lend £2,000 for a diversion from Bailiff Bridge to Upper Wike, 'on the condition that there be no Bar between This place and Bradford, and That none of our own Labourers be received as Workmen on the Road' (HAS 90 Hal. Cent. Lib.).
[120]Record Ledger 1825, box 23 West Rid. CRO.
[121]George Unwin, *Samuel Oldknow and the Arkwrights* (Manchester, 1924), pp. 223-7.
[122]*Ibid.* p. 229.   [123]*Ibid.* p. 230.   [124]*Ibid.* p. 230.
[125]Securities, D58 Shef. Cent. Lib.
[126]Securities, D46 Shef. Cent. Lib.
[127]Cotton interests – £278, farmers – £741, others – £986.(D58 Shef. Cent. Lib. extant mortgages only.)
[128]Textile interests – £505, farmers – £575. (D46 Shef. Cent. Lib. extant mortgages only.)
[129]Mortgage Ledger 1797-1839, box 63 West Rid. CRO.

spinners, two merchants, a cotton manufacturer and six calico printers advanced £800 of the £1,300 subscribed to the Clitheroe–Blackburn Trust (1823).[130] The majority of the initial capital required by the Oldham–Ripponden Trust was provided by clothiers, woollen manufacturers, cotton manufacturers and merchants from Manchester, Halifax, Oldham and Saddleworth.[131] In the eighteenth century the Leeds merchants were the principal promoters of and investors in the many turnpike trusts centred on their city.[132] The Leeds–Holmefield Lane End Trust, formed in 1817, received considerable support from local merchants and manufacturers[133] as did the Sheffield–Glossop Trust[134] and the New Mills,[135] Barnsley–Shepley Lane Head,[136] and Greenfield–Shepley Lane Head[137] trusts.

In other parts of the country the merchants and manufacturers gave the trusts only marginal financial support. The Little Yarmouth Trust[138] could claim only two merchant-subscribers. In Kent, two wine merchants, a shipbuilder and a timber merchant subscribed about 13% of the Deal–Sandwich Trust's initial capital,[139] and two merchant-fellmongers and a deal merchant provided 7% of the Canterbury–Sandwich Trust subscription.[140] There exist, however, few subscription lists of trusts in areas where the merchant or manufacturer's involvement in trust promotion would have conceivably been the greatest, i.e. London, Bristol, Manchester, Liverpool and Birmingham, and this makes it difficult to assess adequately their financial contribution.[141]

Besides the manufacturing and merchant interests, there were other groups which gave financial backing to turnpike schemes. Local charities,[142] friendly societies, widows and spinsters, clergymen and municipal bodies were all frequent, albeit marginal contributors. From the 1790s country bankers were providing a degree of financial support to the trusts. The loans made by the Becketts, John Blayds and Peckover,

---

[130]Mortgage Book 1823-71, TTB-2, Lancs. RO.
[131]Mortgage Ledger, 1795, box 46 West Rid. CRO.
[132]R. G. Wilson, *Gentlemen Merchants*, p. 147.
[133]Security and Interest Ledger 1817-72, box 52 West Rid. CRO. (Benjamin Gott, woollen manufacturer and merchant, was a subscriber to this trust.)
[134]List of subscribers 1818, CPG 8(6). Shef. Cent. Lib.
[135]Subscription List n.d. (1823 ?) box 1 West Rid. CRO.
[136]Subscription List 1823, box 3 West Rid. CRO.
[137]Subscription List 1822, box 3 West Rid. CRO.
[138]Minutes — 11 June 1798, EH:50/5/3B1 Ips. & E. Suf. RO.
[139]Security Ledger 1798-1825, T11/F3 Kent AO.
[140]Security Ledger 1802-68, T4/2 Kent AO.
[141]Furthermore, it is not always possible to identify the lenders' occupations. See above, p. 101n.
[142]It was claimed in 1840 that charities had £62,959 3s 2d invested in the turnpikes. (*B.P.P. 1840 (256) xxvii.1*, p. 9.)

Harris and Co.[143] are cases in point. The Yorkshire Joint Stock Bank subscribed £1,500 to the Wibsey Low Moor Trust in 1823,[144] and Timothy Cobb, of Cobb and Co., lent funds to the Banbury–Barcheston Trust (1802).[145] Peter Fector subscribed £500 to the Canterbury–Borham Trust in 1799,[146] and in the following year he and John Fector advanced £300 to the Deal–Sandwich Trust.[147] John Boorman, a Margate banker and linen draper, also loaned money to this trust.[148] Generally, however, the bankers' loans were for relatively small sums and were advanced as personal rather than bank loans.[149] The banker, in his capacity as trust treasurer, was more important as a source of short-term funds than as a long-term investor.[150]

4

It was often necessary for a trust to borrow money in addition to that raised on subscription. After the subscribed loan had been exhausted and if current income was not sufficient to allow completion of the road works, the trustees would be obliged to solicit further loans. The demands of initial subscribers for the return of their money, the expense of obtaining a renewal act and the costs of repairing new roads, were but a few of the circumstances which would have made further borrowing necessary. Threatened with the loss of their subscriptions or the possibility that no interest would be paid, the original investors were often persuaded to advance the additional funds required.[151]

The Marylebone–Finchley Road Trust, established in 1826, had by 1832 accumulated a mortgage debt of £30,210.[152] Finding themselves in financial difficulty and in need of £1,500 to cover a £1,250 floating debt,[153] the trustees sent the following letter to the creditors:

that the Trustees are at this time Wholly without funds to meet the currrent demands, and that unless the sum required be raised, the Road must be neglected, that it will get out of repair, that the traffic will diminish and that the Mortgagees will in all probability lose the money they have advanced.[154]

143See above, pp. 75–6.
144List of Subscribers 1823, HAS. A. Hal. Cent. Lib.
145Mortgage Ledger 1802, CR580/53 War. CRO.
146Journal no. 2 1799–1802, T6/1 Kent AO.
147Security Ledger 1798–1871, T11/F3 Kent AO.
148Ibid.
149Pressnell, Country Banking, p. 381.
150Ibid. pp. 381 and 385. See above, pp. 75–6.
151See above, p. 100.
152Minutes — 1 October 1832, LA/HW/TP.19 Mid. CRO.
153Ibid. 8 August 1832.
154Ibid. 8 August 1832.

Within a month the required amount had been raised.[155] A somewhat similar argument was employed by the trustees of the Leeds–Whitehall Trust. In a circular sent to the subscribers in 1831, it was said that work on the road had commenced, 'but owing to the sudden reverse in the Commercial State of the Country ... the subscriptions were not paid when called for, and workmen were compelled to abandon the undertaking'.[156] £23,000 was needed to complete the half-finished road, and the subscribers were given three alternative courses of action: (1) to abandon the project and lose their money; (2) to advance money on a new subscription; or (3) to give priority in interest payments to new lenders. The particular course followed by this trust's subscribers is not known; however, when other trusts encountered difficulties in attracting new investors, either the second or the third procedure was employed.

There were forty-two subscribers to the Leeds–Holmefield End Trust in 1817, and when in 1819 the trust was in need of additional capital, all but fifteen of the original investors offered further loans.[157] £2,200 was subscribed to the Rotherham–Swinton Trust in 1808, and two years later half the subscribers lent the trust £750.[158] Other trusts received continued financial assistance from individual investors. Lord Beauchamp provided £800 of the £1,480 borrowed by the Evesham–Alcester Trust between 1779 and 1787,[159] and the Dukes of Norfolk and Devonshire made substantial annual loans to the Sheffield–Glossop Trust.[160]

The subscribers were sometimes unwilling to lend additional funds, and if the trust was in an adverse financial position, the trustees may have been obliged to offer inducements to encourage new investors. There were two methods employed to stimulate new loans; granting preference to secondary investors with regard to payment of interest and principal, and issuing bonds secured by the trustees. The former procedure required the consent of the creditors but presumably they were generally more willing to give their permission than to increase their investment. The Barnby–Rotherham Trust raised £2,600 on a secondary preference loan in 1828, and the following note was appended to the list of creditors:[161]

and whereas, as an inducement to the same several persons to advance and lend the said several sums respectively it was agreed between them and the

155*Ibid.* 7 November 1832.
156Circular letter 11 April 1831, box 23 West Rid. CRO.
157Security and Interest Ledger 1817–72, box 52 West Rid. CRO.
158Subscription List 1809, box 80 West Rid. CRO.
159Security Ledger 1778–1825 CR 446/21 War. CRO.
160Accounts 1827–39, CPG-2 Shef. Cent. Lib.
161Secondary Subscription List 1828, box 16 West Rid. CRO.

said Trustees under the said Act that priority should be given to the same several principal sums over the said principal sums hereby secured and the Interest thereof respectively.

The Wakefield–Denby Dale,[162] Leeds–Tong Lane End,[163] and Bury–Haslingden–Blackburn[164] trusts, also gave preference mortgages to their secondary investors. The Blackburn–Colne Trust's secondary loans were secured on personal bonds which were given preference over the subscribers' loans,[165] and a similar procedure was employed by the Sheffield–Glossop Trust.[166] The use of bonds and preference mortgages was most evident in the nineteenth century. This suggests that besides trusts whose large debt and/or arrears necessitated such inducements, existing turnpikes were becoming a relatively less attractive investment.

Although, as secondary lenders, the landed interests continued to provide the greatest proportion of requisite capital, merchants, manufacturers, tradesmen and others assumed a somewhat more prominent role as secondary investors than they had as initial subscribers.

The Barnby–Rotherham Trust was initially financed almost entirely by landowners. However, they advanced only £430 (16%) of the £2,600 second loan.[167] The other lenders were: a maltster (£500), a gardener and a park-keeper (£700), a local charity (£340) and a widow and a spinster (£300). In 1826, 74% of the Arrow–Pothooks' End Trust's subscription capital was provided by the landed interests.[168] Between 1827 and 1829 an additional £1,700 was borrowed: £700 from the Exchequer Loan Commission, £500 from the trust's surveyor, £300 from a yeoman and £100 from a labourer.[169] £1,550 (68%) of the £2,300 subscribed to the Norwich–Swaffham Trust came from landowners and gentry and £500 (22%) from a Norwich staymaker.[170] Between 1771 and 1773 an additional £2,900 was borrowed, and £750 of this came from Richard and John Gurney, and other Norwich merchants.[171] £2,500 was advanced to the Deal–Sandwich Trust by secondary lenders, and £1,156 (40·5%) came from tradesmen, merchants, a labourer and a Deal pilot.[172]

The Rev. George Wigan of Old Swinford was the sole investor of

162Minutes – 11 March 1830, Goodchild Collection.
163Security Book 1829-68, box 7 West Rid. CRO.
164Accounts Book 1820-40, TTA-6 Lancs. RO.
165Schedule of Act (7-8 Geo. IV), DDBd 57/1/1 Lancs. RO.
166Accounts 1827-39, CPG 2 Shef. Cent. Lib.
167Secondary Subscription List 1828, box 16 West Rid. CRO.
168Security Ledger 1826-59, CR 446/11 War. CRO.
169*Ibid.*
170Entries of Securities, 1770-75, Norf. and Norw. RO.
171*Ibid.*
172Security Ledger 1798-1871, T11/F3 Kent AO.

the Stourbridge Trust from 1753 to 1767, during which time he advanced £3,000.[173] Of the additional £1,500 borrowed between 1768 and 1782, George Wigan loaned £500, two local gentlemen £800, and an ironmonger, a baker and a local charity £320.[174] The Evesham–Alcester Trust, supported at the onset entirely by the landed interests, also received the majority (80%) of its secondary loans from this group, the remaining 20% being supplied by tradesmen and a surgeon.[175] Sir Ralph Asheton, the Blackstone Edge Trust's only creditor between 1735 and 1767, loaned the trust £5,500.[176] In 1773, J. John and Robert Royds, London and Halifax merchants, and George Lloyd Esq. took over this loan and advanced an additional £1,000 apiece.[177] The Harrogate–Boroughbridge Trust received £1,300 from a linen weaver and a linen draper and £1,000 from two gentlemen, in 1753–4.[178] £1,500 of the £2,100 raised on a second loan in 1771 came from merchants and tradesmen.[179] John Smith, a plumber and glazier of Preston, loaned £2,000 to the Preston–Wigan (North of Yarrow) Trust in 1823, and he advanced a further £500 in 1826.[180] A Preston grocer also loaned £500 to this trust in 1834.[181]

Besides loans from the public, from 1817 the trusts began to receive financial assistance from the government. The Exchequer Bill Loan Commission, established in that year,[182] was authorized to issue £1,750,000 of Exchequer Bills from the Consolidated Fund as loans to help further public works in order to afford 'Employment for the labouring Classes of the Community'. In 1826[183] the sum was raised to £3,500,000. Those who borrowed from the Commission had to meet fairly stringent conditions. The project for which the funds were needed had to be approved, and the trustees were often required to give their personal bonds. The Exchequer loan was to have priority over other loans and therefore the creditors had to give their consent. A sinking fund was to be created and the principal repaid at a given rate, generally 5%, annually.[184] Trusts with revenues which would have made re-

---

[173]Record Book 1753-1819, 899:31 BA 3762/4(iv) Worces. RO.
[174]*Ibid.*
[175]Security Ledger 1773-1825 CR446/21 War. CRO.
[176]See above, p. 99.
[177]*Ibid.*
[178]Order Book (including mortgages), 1752-1870, box 14 West Rid. CRO.
[179]*Ibid.*
[180]Mortgages 1823 and 1826, DDL502 and 504, Lancs. RO.
[181]Mortgage, 1834, DDL506, Lancs. RO.
[182]57 Geo. III c.34. Also see M. W. Flinn, 'The Poor Employment Act of 1817', *Econ. Hist.Rev.* 2nd ser. XIV, no. 1 (1961), 82-92.
[183]3 Geo. IV c.86.
[184]*B.P.P. 1833 (703) xv. 409.* Appendix no. 1, 'An Account of Turnpike Trusts indebted to the Exchequer Loan Bill Loan Commission', pp. 202-9 and Appendix no. 2, 'An Account of the Turnpike Trusts', pp. 210-15.

payment difficult were permitted to take a special toll, the proceeds of which were to be kept separate and applied to repayment of the loan.[185] The interest demanded was usually 5%, but in 1826 the rate was reduced to 4% on all previous loans on which there were no arrears outstanding.[186]

Because of the strict conditions demanded by the Commission, the trusts sought their assistance only when funds could not be raised from other sources. The Bedfont–Bagshot Trust needed £5,000 in 1826, to repair a bridge.[187] After an attempt to borrow this sum had failed, the clerk was ordered to apply to the Commissioners.[188] The trustees were reluctant, however, to give their personal security for the loan. 'That it is desirable to avoid giving personal security and that therefore it will be better either to apply to the Exchequer Loan Commission for a smaller sum or to renew the Act, so that it shall have a duration equal to the repayment of the £5,000.'[189] The Commission subsequently agreed to a £4,000 loan, at 5% interest and with a 12·5% sinking fund.[190]

The Wibsey Low Moor Trust requested £12,000 from the Commission in August 1833.[191] They wanted £8,000 to liquidate their debts and £4,000 to complete an extension of the road. Although the Commissioners declined to advance the £8,000, they offered to lend the money needed for the extension.[192] The trust refused this offer, claiming that the sum was inconsequential and could be raised from private sources at a lower rate.[193] However, they were unable to borrow the money, and in December they again applied to the Commission.[194] They were offered £5,000 which was to be repaid at 5% annually and carry 5% interest. The Commission required a personal bond from the trustees, the assent of four-fifths of the creditors and a guarantee that the projected works would be finished by December 1836.[195] The trustees agreed to these conditions and the loan was made.

By 1833, 109 trusts in England and Wales had borrowed £401,850 from the Commission and £210,053 remained due.[196] Less than 10% of the trusts received funds from the Commissioners, and in 1833 the

[185]57 Geo. III c.34, sec. 27.

[186]3 Geo. IV c.86, sec. 11.

[187]Minutes (Western District) – 13 March 1826, T.P. Bed. 6 Mid. CRO.

[188]Ibid. 29 May 1826.

[189]Ibid. 19 June 1826.

[190]Ibid. 28 August 1826.

[191]Letter to Commission, 13 August 1833, HAS-104, Hal. Cent. Lib.

[192]Letter to the trust, 20 August 1833, HAS-104.

[193]Letter to the Commission, 24 December 1833, HAS-104.

[194]Ibid.

[195]Letter to the trust, 24 November 1834, HAS-104.

[196]B.P.P. 1833 (703) xv. 409. Appendix no. 1, pp. 208-9.

loans accounted for only 2·97% of the trusts' total bonded debt. However, despite this small aggregate percentage, to certain trusts, especially those on the Holyhead Road,[197] the Commission's loans were of great importance.

5

Turnpike trusts received financial support from a wide variety of social and economic groups within the local community, for with few exceptions trust investment was of a local nature. Although the trusts drew loans from a fairly limited area, the investors came from the extremes of position and wealth; from the rich and powerful Dukes of Norfolk and Devonshire to the lowly labourer, and from Parliament to the village tradesmen and craftsmen. While trust investment was therefore democratic, it is clear that the greatest proportion of capital invested came from the landed classes – farmers, gentry and landowners. This is not particularly surprising for, although the manufacturing sector of the economy was growing rapidly, industrial and urban areas were still small islands in a vast agricultural sea. Furthermore, as Professor Flinn has pointed out: 'Since wealth in surplus to normal consumption requirements was highly concentrated in the landed classes, if more capital was to be made available for economic expansion it was from this class above all that it would come.'[198] Besides controlling the requisite wealth, the landed interests also had much to gain by supporting the turnpike trusts.

The variety of improvements undertaken throughout the eighteenth century bear witness to the concern of landowners with increasing the values of their holdings and farmers with raising the productivity of their lands, thereby to enhance their competitive position. The valuable economies afforded by the turnpikes, i.e. lower transport costs, a reduction of the road repair burden and easier accessibility to markets, made the turnpikes one of the more desirable improvement investments.

The trusts, in certain instances, seem to have created external economies which gave one area an advantage over another. For example, Adam Smith claimed[199]

197 *Ibid.* Appendix no. 1, p. 208. Six trusts on the Holyhead Road borrowed a total of £31,000.
198 M. W. Flinn, *The Origins of the Industrial Revolution* (London, 1966), p. 47. This must be considerably qualified for a recent study of canal investment has shown that canals and river navigations did not receive the bulk of their financial support from the landed classes but from the rising urban middle classes – merchants, manufacturers, traders, and professional men. J. R. Ward, 'Investment in Canals and House Building in England, 1760–1815' (unpublished D.Phil. thesis, Oxford, 1970), pp. 225–34.
199 Adam Smith, *Wealth of Nations*, p. 142, See above p. 25.

It is not more than fifty years ago, that some of the counties in the neighborhood of London petitioned against the extension of the turnpikes into the more remoter counties. These remoter counties, they pretended, from the cheapness of labour, would be able to sell their grass and corn cheaper in the London market than themselves, and would thereby reduce their rents, and ruin their cultivation.

A similar complaint was voiced in 1763, by the steward of the Duke of Kingston's Buckinghamshire estates, who said[200]

The lands in Hanslop are let very dear, as not worth so much as formerly, by reason of the Improvements made at a greater distance from London, and the Turnpikes opening a convenience of the London Markets; the tenants are all grown poor, the Lands not duly stockt, and the Duke has thereupon under consideration a considerable abatement of their Rents.

These fears, whether substantive or imagined, may have acted as a stimulus to local turnpiking. By securing a turnpike the promoters may have sought to mitigate any comparative disadvantage engendered by road improvement in other areas, while at the same time realizing economies similar to those achieved in these areas. This embraces two concepts; firstly, that investment which gave rise to a disequilibrium promoted additional investment to redress the imbalance, and secondly, that the 'demonstration effect' was a pertinent consideration. While there is no evidence of these factors being operative over long distances, the pattern of turnpike development suggests that they did have some relevance locally.

There were, however, a number of alternative investment opportunities which competed for the landed interests' capital. Disregarding the external economies generated by road improvement, the return on turnpike mortgages still compared favourably with the yields realized on land purchase or the Funds.[201] Canals offered both valuable economies and in certain cases extremely high returns. However, there is no evidence that they competed for funds with the turnpikes. The prosperous years of the early 1790s witnessed both the 'Canal Mania' and a sharp rise in the number of new turnpike acts, and this suggests that there was ample capital to finance both forms of transport improvement.[202]

Chambers and Mingay have observed that[203] 'Enclosure was ... by far the most profitable use of capital in connection with land, and perhaps more profitable than many riskier commercial or industrial

---

[200]G. E. Mingay, *English Landed Society in the Eighteenth Century* (London, 1963), p. 196.
[201]Chambers and Mingay, *Agricultural Revolution*, p. 84. They say that the gross yield on land purchase was from 5% to 6%.
[202]See below, pp. 126, 129.
[203]Chambers and Mingay, *Agricultural Revolution*, p. 84.

ventures.' Investment in enclosure enhanced the prospects for subsequent investment in turnpikes, as a greater volume of agricultural goods traffic exerted pressure on the existing transport facilities. The order in which these improvements were instituted was frequently reversed, and the turnpike then became a factor making enclosure more feasible. However, there were many factors which governed the timing of both enclosures and turnpikes, and to imply direct causality would be misleading. As Dr H. G. Hunt has remarked 'They [enclosures and turnpikes] were both part of a much larger expansion of the economy in which the stimuli came from many directions.'[204]

The county of Leicester serves as an interesting, although not necessarily representative, area for studying the relationship between enclosures and turnpikes. Dr Hunt[205] holds that in this county parliamentary enclosures generally preceded turnpike development. This does not, however, seem to have been the case. The parliamentary enclosures were heavily concentrated in the 1760s (46) and the 1770s (42), with a decrease in activity in the eighties (16) and a slight resurgence in the nineties (23).[206] By 1738 turnpikes connected Leicester with Market Harborough and Northampton to the south and through Loughborough with Derby and Nottingham to the north.[207] There was considerable activity in the 1750s as roads were turnpiked from Leicester in three directions: through Ashby-de-la-Zouch to Burton-on-Trent,[208] through Narborough to Coventry[209] and through Uppingham to Peterborough,[210] Melton Mowbray was linked to Nottingham and Uppingham,[211] Ashby-de-la-Zouch with Tamworth,[212] Loughborough and Hinckley,[213] Lutterworth with Market Harborough and Coventry,[214] and Market Harborough with Kettering.[215] By 1765 Leicester was connected by turnpike to Melton Mowbray,[216] Welford,[217] and Lutterworth,[218] and there were three turnpikes from Lutterworth: to Daventry, [219] to Hinckley[220] and to Welford.[221] In this county the turnpikes came, for the most part, before parliamentary enclosure. Furthermore, the great majority of enclosures in the sixties and seventies were within one to three miles

[204]H. G. Hunt, 'The Chronology of Parliamentary Enclosure in Leicestershire', *Econ. Hist. Rev.* 2nd series, x, no. 2 (1957-8), 272.
[205]*Ibid.* pp. 271-2.
[206]*Ibid.* p. 266.
[207]12 Geo. I c.5, Market Harborough–Loughborough, 1726. 11 Geo. II c.3, Nottingham–Cotes Bridge, 1738. 8 Geo. I c.13, Church Brampton–Market Harborough, 1722. 11 Geo. II c.33, Derby–Loughborough, 1738.
[208]26 Geo. II c.10 1753.
[209]27 Geo. II c.22 1754.
[210]27 Geo. II c.10 1754.
[211]27 Geo. II c.19 1754.
[212]33 Geo. II c.41 1760.
[213]33 Geo. II c.46 1760.
[214]28 Geo. II c.40 1755.
[215]25 Geo. II c.57 1752.
[216]4 Geo. III c.84 1764.
[217]5 Geo. III c.78 1765.
[218]4 Geo. III c.84 1764.
[219]5 Geo. III c.105 1765.
[220]2 Geo. III c.39 1762.
[221]*Ibid.*

of an existing turnpike.[222] In other parts of the country the pattern may have been somewhat similar, for the sharp increase in turnpike activity in the 1750s preceded the subsequent increase in enclosures in the 1760s and 1770s.

The first half of the eighteenth century witnessed considerable investment in agricultural 'improvements',[223] and the decline in agricultural prices during the 1730s and 1740s further stimulated this investment, as farmers and landowners sought to reduce factor costs to meet the falling prices.[224] However, turnpike investment fell off sharply in the 1730s and, although there was some recovery in the forties, turnpike activity did not increase substantially until 1750.[225] During the 'depression' period the landowners were often forced to assume financial responsibilities which in more prosperous times were borne by their tenants. 'The landlord's expenses for repairs and new construction of farm buildings, fences, gates, embankments and cottages were generally heavy during the difficult years.'[226] Dr Mingay concluded that this expenditure 'was closely bound up with the problem of attracting new tenants and keeping old ones during the depression period'.[227] Concessions on land tax were also granted,[228] and in some areas the heavy arrears of rents during this period further increased the demands on the landowners' capital.[229] Although the effects of low prices were felt with varying degrees of severity in different parts of the country, the sluggishness of turnpike activity suggests either a decrease in the surplus capital of the landed interests or that their funds were being used for other, more immediately pressing projects.

The decline in the overall level of trust investment in the thirties and forties must be explained in light of the considerable domestic economic expansion which took place during these years.[230] Falling agricultural prices, while adversely affecting many of those in agriculture, also led to a rise in real income and consequently an increased

---

[222]See Appendix G. This was computed by superimposing the turnpikes on a map of the enclosures. This map was made up from the list of enclosures in H. G. Hunt, 'The Parliamentary Enclosure Movement in Leicestershire, 1730-1842' (unpublished University of London Ph.D. thesis, 1955), pp. 306-11.

[223]A. H. John, 'Agricultural Productivity and Economic Growth in England, 1700-1760', *Journal of Economic History*, xxv, no. 1 (1965), 21.

[224]Chambers and Mingay, *Agricultural Revolution*, pp. 39-40.

[225]See above, pp. 47-9.

[226]G. E. Mingay, 'The Agricultural Depression, 1730-1750', in *Essays in Economic History*, Vol. ii, ed. E. M. Carus-Wilson (1962), p. 317.

[227]*Ibid.* p. 317.

[228]*Ibid.* pp. 317-18.

[229]*Ibid.* pp. 311-14 and Chambers and Mingay, *Agricultural Revolution*, p. 40.

[230]A. H. John, 'Aspects of English Economic Growth in the First Half of the Eighteenth Century', in *Essays in Economic History*, Vol. ii, ed. E. M. Carus-Wilson (1962), pp. 360-73.

demand for industrial goods.[231] Professor John has argued that during these years 'the terms of trade between manufactures and primary products turned in favour of the former'.[232] This resulted in greater 'affluence especially in the growing industrial centres' and 'encouraged the savings necessary for capital formation'.[233] Turnpike development during these years was heavily concentrated in the northern industrial areas,[234] and this lends support to the view that non-agricultural investors were taking a more active part in financing road improvements. However, capital provided by landed interests was also important in the financing of turnpikes near growing urban and industrial centres. Landed proprietors may have been getting relatively higher rents near these centres and therefore may have been more willing and better able to support trust ventures than those at a greater distance from these markets.

Conditions in agriculture began to improve in the late forties and the general upward trend in agricultural prices from 1750 brought increased prosperity to both farmer and landowner. Rents began to rise in the 1760s[235] and by 1790 the incomes of the landed classes had risen appreciably.[236] Besides enjoying rising rental values, the landowners were relieved of having to undertake certain farm improvements, arrears of rents decreased and the burden of the land tax was gradually shifted to the tenant.[237] This left the landed proprietors with increased surplus capital and although some was expended in conspicuous consumption or used to speculate in the Funds, the majority of landowners employed their profits productively.[238] The rise in the number of enclosures in the sixties and seventies bears witness to this, and the sharp increase in the number of turnpike acts in 1750, and the continued high level of activity in the following two decades, may also owe much to the prosperity in agriculture.

There were, however, a great many factors which influenced the passage of a turnpike act, i.e. the volume of traffic, the rate of interest, the influence of existing turnpikes, and the demonstration effect[239]

---

[231]*Ibid.* pp. 365-71.
[232]*Ibid.* p. 371.
[233]A. H. John, 'Agricultural Productivity', p. 31.
[234]See above, p. 47.
[235]Chambers and Mingay, *Agricultural Revolution*, p. 112.
[236]Mingay, *English Landed Society*, p. 52.
[237]*Ibid.* pp. 56-7.
[238]*Ibid.* p. 72.
[239]H. G. Hunt, 'The Chronology', p. 271. He claims that this was also a relevant consideration in enclosure. 'Considerable weight must be given to the psychological influence of enclosure on neighbouring proprietors of open fields and common rights; when an enclosure proved successful it would tend to overcome much conservatism and inertia in adjoining parishes and encourage the landowners there to take similar action.'

E

(exemplified by the passage, over a short period of time, of a number of acts in the same area). To assign central importance to any one factor is therefore to simplify a complex question.

Although the landed interests seem to have been the single most important source of trust capital, loans from other groups were also significant. Merchants and manufacturers, concerned with lowering transport costs and opening reliable, year-round communications, lent their support to many trust schemes. However, although in the fore-front of promotion, their financial contributions do not seem to have been always commensurate with their concern. For example, Josiah Wedgwood, a principal promoter of the Burslem–Lawton–Newcastle-under-Lyme Trust, advanced but £150 to that trust,[240] and Samuel Oldknow made only £100 token loans to two trusts near his mill at Mellor.[241] Manufacturers' and merchants' loans were often more important in aggregate, but even in industrial regions their investment was frequently equalled or overshadowed by that of the farmers or gentry.

Some of the capital invested in turnpikes came from people who, unlike landowners, farmers, merchants and manufacturers, probably did not consider themselves directly affected by improved roads. They advanced money because the turnpikes offered a relatively secure investment with a fairly good return. Local charities, members of the clergy, widows and spinsters, surgeons, shopkeepers, craftsmen and labourers fall within this category. Although it is difficult to gauge the extent of their contribution, in certain instances their relatively more 'disinterested' investment accounted for a significant proportion of trust capital. 28% of the capital subscribed to the Arrow–Pothooks' End Trust[242] came from these groups, as did 38% of the Dunchurch–Southam Trust's capital[243] and 28% of the Little Yarmouth–Blythburgh Trust's capital.[244] Their assistance as secondary lenders was also often quite substantial. The number of small investors, in both primary and secondary capacities, seems to have increased towards the end of the eighteenth century, and this suggests rising middle-class savings. The importance of this source of funds has often been underestimated, but it is clear that it became increasingly important for the trusts.[245] The speculative character of trust investment from the 1790s may owe much to the ample pools of savings available at the local level, and the eager-

---

[240]See above, p. 105.
[241]See above, p. 106.
[242]Security Ledger 1826-59, CR446/11 War. CRO.
[243]Mortgage Ledger 1797-1872, CR580/59 War. CRO.
[244]Minutes – 11 June 1798, E.H.: 50/5/3B1 Ips. & E. Suf. RO.
[245]This is supported by Ward's work on the sources of canal investment although his findings suggest that the financial support of the urban middle classes was relatively far more important for the canals than for the turnpike trusts. See above, p. 113n.

ness of the small saver to realize a return on his idle balances. The turn-pikes were able to mobilize effectively these local savings, which may not have been made available for more risky direct investment in industry or commerce, and apply them towards the development of a form of social overhead capital essential for industrial and commercial expansion. In this sense the turnpike trusts acted as 'conduits' connecting the 'reservoirs of savings' with the 'wheels of industry'.[246]

Professor Pollard has written:[247] 'until the canal (or the railway) monies freed hoards of merchants, landlords and others for industrial development, capitalists could not really tap much of the savings of the British economy'. However, the turnpike trusts did tap some of these savings and made them available to 'capitalists' in the form of an improved transport system.

[246]M. M. Postan, 'Recent Trends in the Accumulation of Capital', *Econ. Hist. Rev.* Vol. VI, no. 1 (1935), 2. Referring to the Industrial Revolution, he says 'The reservoirs of savings were full enough, but the conduits to connect them with the wheels of industry were few and meagre.'

[247]S. Pollard, 'Investment, Consumption and the Industrial Revolution', *Econ. Hist. Rev.* 2nd ser. Vol. XI, no. 2 (1958), 221-2.

6

The Rate of Interest
and the Turnpike Trusts

1

In his influential work, *The Industrial Revolution 1760–1830*, Ashton first put forward his thesis about the relationship between the rate of interest and early economic growth in Britain. He argued:[1] 'The lower the rate at which capital could be obtained – the smaller the advantage forgone in locking it up in a fixed form – the further would capital works be extended', and 'If we seek – it would be wrong to do so – for a single reason why the pace of economic development quickened about the middle of the eighteenth century, it is to this [lower interest rates] we must look.' Subsequently he modified his views somewhat by noting that those in industry might not be affected by slight changes in the rate of interest in so far as this reflected an alteration in the real rate (the profitability of investment); although they would be influenced to the extent that the change represented a change in the money rate (the difficulty in obtaining funds).[2] Flinn has put this point most lucidly:[3] 'In general he [the businessman] was interested not so much in the actual level of the rate at any one point in time so much as in the difference between this rate and the marginal productivity of capital at the moment.'

While the relevance of interest rates to industry is therefore uncertain[4] it is generally accepted that for such things as public utility investments the prevailing level of rates was of the utmost importance.[5] Ashton has argued that for projects 'concerned with buildings and means of communication (where a long time must elapse between the beginning of an enterprise and the return of profits) it [the rate of interest] is of the greatest consequence'.[6] He has also pointed out that when interest rates were high the supply of loanable funds was inter-

[1] T. S. Ashton, *The Industrial Revolution*, pp. 10-11.
[2] T. S. Ashton, *An Economic History*, pp. 27-8.
[3] Flinn, *Origins of the Industrial Revolution*, p. 50.
[4] L. S. Pressnell, 'The Rate of Interest in the 18th Century', in *Studies in the Industrial Revolution*, ed. L. S. Pressnell (London, 1960), p. 195.
[5] Flinn, *Origins of the Industrial Revolution*, pp. 50-1, and see below, p. 121.
[6] T. S. Ashton, *Economic Fluctuations*, p. 86.

rupted and investment therefore likely to be curtailed.[7] In supporting and considerably expanding Ashton's thesis, Pressnell has added that the entire 'structure of rates', both long-term and short-term rates, must be considered.[8] He pointed out that when short-term rates were near or above long-term rates[9] investors tended to move to the short end of the market thereby reducing the funds available to long-term borrowers. 'The rise and fall in public utility investment, for example, appears to fit broadly into a framework of a widening and a narrowing respectively of the "normal" spread between interest rates.'[10] Pressnell concludes, 'It seems safe to say that the rate of interest entered into a significant proportion of decisions to undertake economic activity.'[11]

In this chapter the above proposition will be considered with respect to investment in turnpike trusts. Also, by examining the movements in the rates of interest offered to the trusts' creditors it will be possible to gauge the extent to which financial trends in London were indicative of conditions in the provinces. It is important to establish this, for Ashton and Pressnell use London rates as a guide to economic activity throughout the country[12] suggesting by this that there was a national capital market, and if changes in these rates were not being quickly registered in provincial markets their case is substantially weakened.

2

The number of turnpike acts passed annually provides the only measure of the level of trust investment. There are, however, problems associated with using figures derived in this way. Firstly, they include both acts for creating new trusts and those for renewing or amending the powers of existing trusts. Acts for new trusts represent an investment which could possibly have been postponed. Renewal acts could not however have been as easily delayed. As a trust's statutory term neared expiration the trustees were forced to seek a renewal act both to protect their creditors and to prolong their own authority.[13] Some renewal acts placed additional roads under the trustees' jurisdiction; but the majority of such acts were obtained primarily to fulfil the parliamentary

---

[7]*Ibid.* p. 87.
[8]Pressnell, 'The Rate of Interest', pp. 204-10.
[9]Short-term rates are taken to be the discount on Navy Bills and the yield on East India Bonds while the long-term rates are reflected in the yield on Consols or on Bank of England stock. See Pressnell, 'The Rate of Interest', pp. 179-80.
[10]*Ibid.* p. 208.
[11]*Ibid.* p. 210.
[12]Ashton, *An Economic History*, p. 27. Also see below, pp. 126-7.
[13]See above, pp. 60-1.

requirement. For the above reasons the gross number of turnpike acts does not give a realistic picture of the level of trust investment.[14] In the following analysis trust investment will be measured by the number of new acts passed in each year.

The amount of capital invested varied considerably from one trust to another. Consequently, it is difficult to gauge the magnitude of yearly investment by looking only at the number of new acts passed. The amount of road mileage turnpiked annually would serve as a useful supplement. However, while it is possible to calculate the total trust mileage added in each year, mileage in itself is of little value unless the differences in terrain and road use are also considered. For example, a twenty-mile trust in East Anglia was less costly than a road of similar length over the Pennines or through the Midland clays, and trusts in or near London were more expensive to maintain than those in less heavily travelled areas. Not only do these factors defy measurement, but the trustees were also not obliged to undertake immediate repair of an entire road. The initial investment may not therefore have been commensurate with either mileage, terrain or traffic density.

A direct yearly correlation of trust investment and the rate of interest is difficult because of the lag between the time of local inception and the passage of an act. However, this lag may not have been of long duration. In 1726, after a report that the roads leading into Bristol were in disrepair, the city council allocated £100 for their maintenance.[15] This soon proved inadequate and the council petitioned Parliament for a turnpike which was granted in the following year.[16] The promoters of the Wibsey Low Moor–Huddersfield Trust held their first meeting in October 1822.[17] By February funds had been subscribed, and the trust commenced operations late in 1823.[18] It appears from the Commons Journals that there was generally less than a year between the presentation of a petition and the passage of an act. Therefore, for the purpose of correlation, the rates of interest will be brought forward by one year. For example, the numbers of new acts in 1746 will be compared with the interest rates in 1745.[19] Although this is still

[14]The following table demonstrates the increasing distortion engendered by the use of the gross number of acts:

Decade	Total Acts	Index	New Acts	Index
1720-29	59	100	48	100
1730-39	60	101·6	26	54·2
1740-49	102	172·9	37	77·1

[15]John Latimer, *The Annals of Bristol in the 18th Century* (Bristol, 1893), pp. 155-6.
[16]13 Geo. II c.12.
[17]Draft of first agreement, October 1822, HAS – A. Hal. Cent. Lib.
[18]List of subscribers, February 1823, HAS – A. Hal. Cent. Lib.
[19]The interest rates in the graphs below, are taken from Pressnell, 'The Rate of Interest', pp. 211-14. The author wishes to thank L. S. Pressnell and the publishers (The Athlone Press) for permission to use this material.

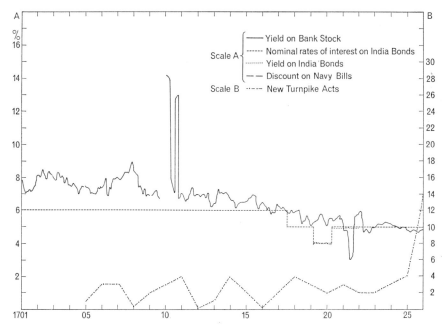

CHART 4 *New turnpike acts and interest rates, 1701–26*
(*Scale A rates are advanced by one year; e.g. 1719 rates are shown in 1720.*)

an approximation, it should give a somewhat better picture of the prevailing monetary conditions at the time when promoters first thought to
obtain a turnpike.

The fairly high level of trust investment in the 1720s came at a
time when the long-term rate of interest in London was declining.[20]
As the trusts were offering the maximum rate on loans[21] it would seem
that the cost of borrowing was of less importance than the easy credit
conditions which the low rates suggest. Rates were extremely low
throughout the 1730s; nonetheless the number of new trusts created
dropped sharply. During these years the short-term rates were near to
or higher than the long rates, and this may have reduced the amount
of funds available for long-term investment. However, relatively similar
financial conditions during the 1720s did not perceptibly deter the
formation of trusts.

Despite the persistence of low rates in the 1740s, turnpike investment, while greater than in the preceding decade, remained at a fairly
low level. This may have been due in part to the continuing difficulties
in agriculture and economic conditions generally unfavourable to long-

[20] All rates referred to are London rates.
[21] See below, p. 128.

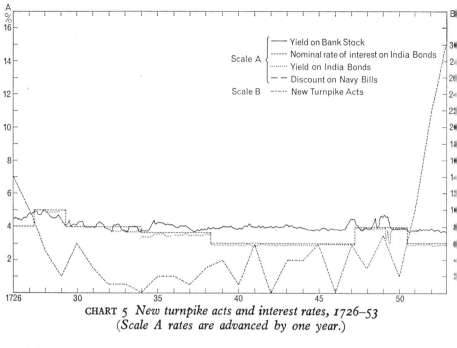

CHART 5 *New turnpike acts and interest rates, 1726–53*
(Scale A rates are advanced by one year.)

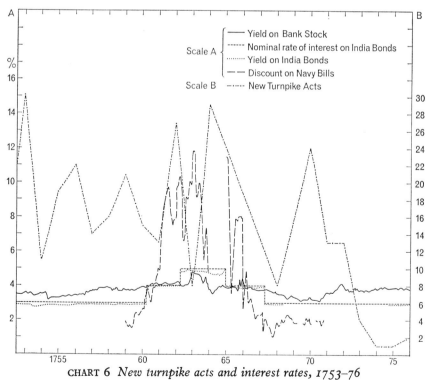

CHART 6 *New turnpike acts and interest rates, 1753–76*
(Scale A rates are advanced by one year.)

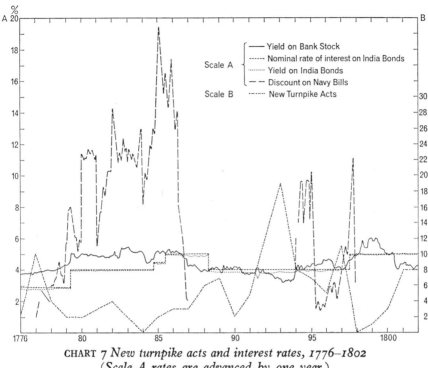

CHART 7 *New turnpike acts and interest rates, 1776–1802*
(Scale A rates are advanced by one year.)

term investment.[22] The 'Turnpike Mania' began in the 1750s. 186 new trusts were formed in these years. This is forty more than had been created during the first half of the century. While the low interest rates undoubtedly facilitated this investment, low rates during the two previous decades had not provoked similar development. In the fifties many new trusts were either close to one another or adjoining existing turnpikes, and this suggests an inter-influence not uncommon to investment booms. The improving conditions in agriculture may also have helped to create a favourable climate for the rapid extension of the turnpike system.

During the first half of the 1760s turnpike investment does not seem to have been checked either by the gradual rise in long-term rates or the sharp increase in short-term rates. The high rates may have been responsible for the drop in the number of acts in 1763; however activity increased in the following two years, while the prevailing short-term rates continued to be higher than the long rates. By 1773 the number of new acts passed had fallen off considerably. This trend continued until the early nineties. It is interesting to note that when

[22]Ashton, *Economic Fluctuations*, p. 95.

in 1777 rates began to rise, the level of trust investment had been low for over four years.

During the eighteenth century there were but few years of extensive turnpike development which were not also years of low interest rates. If, as Professor Ashton suggests, the cost of borrowing was vital in determining the level of trust investment, one would expect sympathy between the movement of rates and investment at or near the major turning points. However, such sympathy is not evident before the 1790s. Rates were low for over twenty years before the 'Turnpike Mania' of the fifties and sixties and the boom ended well before rates began to rise in the late 1770s. There also seems to be little correlation between the relative movement of short- and long-term rates and the level of trust investment. While low rates undoubtedly facilitated trust investment, and although continued low rates helped to prolong the investment booms, other factors (i.e. the improving conditions in agriculture from 1750, the demonstration effect, the influence of existing turnpikes, and the impetus of the investment boom) had an equal, if not greater influence on trust formation. It was not until after 1790 that the rates seem to have exercised a direct influence. In the nineteenth century trust investment assumed a clearly speculative nature, not evident in the preceding years.[23]

3

The many trust records examined have yielded a great deal of information regarding the rates of interest paid by turnpike trusts throughout the country, and as Dr Pressnell has suggested, they cast 'much valuable light on the financial structure of eighteenth century England'.[24] He has stated that the numerous turnpike trust records 'are the most instructive, possibly, of local movements in the supply of money'.[25] Initial trust capital was raised primarily within local markets as were the subsequent loans which were frequently needed. Furthermore, income could not be readily increased, the rate of interest was limited to 5% and repayment was generally prolonged. Although these factors contributed to making trust rates indicative of the movement in local rates, there were extra-market conditions which qualified the representative nature of the rates.

In the early decades of the eighteenth century the turnpike trust was still a relatively recent innovation and high rates may therefore have been needed to attract investors. Also, during this period the virtual

23The periods of active turnpike investment (the early nineties, 1809–12, and 1824–6) were times of widespread speculative investment.
24L. S. Pressnell, *Country Banking*, p. 554.
25*Ibid.* p. 554.

permanence of trusts had not yet been established, and consequently interest rates may have tended to rise as statutory terms neared expiration. The trustees of the Hockliffe–Woburn Trust sought a renewal act in 1743,[26] and claimed that existing loans carried at 5% could be reduced to 4%. In the 1730s at least three other trusts were able to lower their rates soon after renewal acts had been secured.[27] Trusts having high debts or heavy arrears of interest may have had to offer the maximum rate as an inducement to new investors,[28] while trusts with similarly unsound finances were frequently obliged to reduce the rates paid to their creditors.[29]

Taking the above factors into consideration, when the trusts had to raise funds externally the rates paid were probably a fair indication of prevailing local rates. If, however, additional borrowing was not necessary, the propensity of a trust to adjust its rates depended to a large extent upon the sensitivity of trustees and creditors to changing conditions. Some investors, for example, could not readily take advantage of higher returns available elsewhere. Local craftsmen, shopkeepers, labourers, widows and spinsters[30] were more concerned with the security offered and the steady income derived than with capital gain, and it is therefore unlikely that they would have brought pressure on the trustees to increase rates and would also have been in a difficult position to resist a fall. The majority of trust investors, local gentry and landowners, were, in general, better able to realize alternative investment opportunities. However, many of these individuals advanced funds to the trusts for the convenience and the direct benefits[31] provided by the improved roads, rather than simply as a speculative investment. Among this group of investors there may therefore have been some reluctance about forcing the trustees to raise rates. In so far as the trustees were drawn from this group and were themselves creditors, the same considerations would apply to them in forcing changes of interest rates. The debt structure of the individual trust must also be taken into account. If a large percentage of the bonded debt was in the hands of few creditors they could more easily and effectively demand higher rates than if the debt was held in small amounts by a large number of creditors.

---

[26]*J. H. of C.* xxiv, p. 355.   [27]See below, p. 128.
[28]The secondary preference loan was another method used to attract investors.
[29]The Leeds–Holmfield Lane End Trust paid 3% (1831-9) because of lack of funds (Security Ledger 1817-72, box 52 West Rid. CRO).
    The Bawtrey–Tinsley Trust issued 4% securities in place of those bearing 5%. It was claimed that because of financial difficulties the higher rate could not be paid. (Minutes – 22 November 1826, box 35 West Rid. CRO.)
[30]Widows and spinsters represented by solicitors were in a better position to take advantage of higher rates offered in other fields.
[31]See above, pp. 102-3.

The earliest recorded rate discovered was that paid by the Gloucester Trust. This justice-trust, formed in 1697–8, borrowed £300 at 6% in 1701,[32] and continued to pay the same rate until 1712, at which time the records cease. In Kent the Chalk Trust, also controlled by justices, paid 6% in 1718/19,[33] a year after the legal rate had been reduced to 5%. In the following year the rate dropped to 5% and remained at this level until 1735. Before the mid-thirties, 5% was the most common rate paid throughout the country.[34]

During the middle and late thirties some trusts were able either to reduce their rates or to borrow below 5%. Three such trusts cited in the appendix were granted renewal acts shortly before they lowered their rates, and this may in part explain the reductions.[35] The Kensington Trust was able to lower its rate only after short-term bills of credit were issued to the mortgagees in place of the slower maturing securities.[36] Access to a special source for loans may account for the $4\frac{1}{2}$% paid by the Blackstone Edge Trust, whose sole creditor until 1773 was Sir Ralph Asheton.[37]

Throughout the first four decades of the eighteenth century provincial trust rates showed little response to the steady fall in London rates. This suggests either a lack of sympathy between financial trends in the metropolis and those in the provinces or that trust rates were somehow not representative of local conditions. The latter may well have been the case, for even the trusts in the London area were unable to reduce their rates before the mid-thirties. An element of risk, arising perhaps from the idea that the turnpikes were temporary authorities, may have been attributed to trust investment, and this would have helped sustain the high rates.

Although there were some rate reductions in the 1740s, lower rates were more widespread in the 1750s,[38] reflecting in part the success of Pelham's conversion. During the 1750s there seems to have been increased sensitivity to the financial trends in the London market. This was especially evident with regard to the rates paid by the newly

[32] Gloucestershire Quarter-Sessions Records, Q/SO-3 Glouces. RO.

[33] Kent Quarter-Sessions Records, Q/SB-1718/19 – 1735 Kent AO.

[34] The interest rates paid by the trusts are given in Appendix H. See below, pp. 256-70.

[35] Great North Road Trust, 9 Geo. II c.9 (1736). Rochester–Maidstone Trust, 9 Geo. II c.7 (1736). New Cross Trust, 11 Geo. II c.18 (1738).

[36] 'The Board taking into consideration the State of this and the large Debt now carrying an Interest of 5 p Cent and no person having as yet proposed lending money at the rate of 4 p Cent.

Resolved that this Trust will accept and receive such Monies as shall be offered at $4\frac{1}{2}$ p Cent in order to discharge their Debts now bearing 5 p Cent.'

The mortgagee immediately offered to turn in his 5% mortgage (£1,000) for bills of credit at the new rate. (Minutes – July 1733, MS 58/7001 Ken. Pub. Lib.)

[37] Register of Mortgages 1735-1872, HAS – 52 Hal. Cent. Lib.

[38] This was due, in part, to the greater amount of material found for trusts after 1750.

formed trusts. This sympathy is not, however surprising, for London rates had been low for over two decades and a similar trend in the provinces was to be expected. The more pertinent issue is whether the provincial rates were responsive to changes in the London rates. The rate reductions made in the forties and fifties were a much protracted reaction to the long trend of low rates and not a response to any short-term movements. This indicates that the financial links between London and the provinces were still, at best, somewhat remote.

From 1760 to 1764 both long and short-term London rates were higher than they had been in the preceding decades. This was reflected by the high rates paid by a large number of trusts and the upward adjustment of trust rates in the sensitive areas of London, Kent, Birmingham and Manchester. The picture was not, however, uniform, for some trusts were able to maintain low rates while others did not raise their rates until those in London had begun to decline. Pressnell has cited the rates paid by the Droitwich Trust as an example of the responsiveness of provincial rates to London trends.[39] But when in 1764 this trust was able to borrow at 4%, most other trusts were either increasing their rates or continuing to pay 5%. Furthermore, none of the trusts, with the exception of two in Kent and one in Oxford, responded to the improved conditions of the later sixties.

In the early seventies, although low rates were being paid by some trusts, only in Kent was there any response to the continued low level of London rates. The more stringent conditions of the American War period were, however, felt throughout the country. Trusts which had not increased their rates did so in the early eighties, and by 1785 there were but few trusts offering less than 5%. Only the Droitwich and the Bedfont–Bagshot trusts were able to take advantage of the improved conditions from 1786, and only the former trust the low rates of the early nineties.[40] Other trust rates showed little or no downward movement before the 1820s. An increasing number of investment opportunities, especially the canals in the early 1790s, and the growing public concern with turnpike trusts' financial difficulties may have helped keep the trust rates at their high level during these years.

It will be recalled that Pressnell's argument is that there was a close sympathy between the movements of London and provincial interest rates and that therefore the connection between the financial market in London and those in the provinces was close enough 'for London rates to indicate broad monetary trends in the country as a

[39]Pressnell, *Country Banking*, pp. 554-6.
[40]The Kilburn Trust attempted to lower its rate in 1792; however, they were unable to find loans at less than 5%. (Minutes – 5 October 1792, 14 January 1793, 15 July 1793, LA/HW/TP 2 Mid. CRO.)

whole, at any rate at the margins of economic activity'.[41] However, the movements in trust rates indicate that before about 1775 the financial links between provincial markets and the metropolis with regard to long-term rates were not as close as he has implied. These findings support those of Dickson who, in his definitive study of early British government finance, has concluded that the fall in the yields of the Funds in London during the first half of the eighteenth century 'was, as contemporaries argued, due to special causes, specifically to an increase in the savings seeking gilt-edged investments just at the time when the bonds available for purchase were diminishing in amount'.[42] Growing public confidence in the stability of the government, a steady reduction in both the funded and unfunded debt between 1720 and 1740, and an increasing demand for securities combined to raise the price of the Funds.[43] Also during this period the greatest part of the public debt was held by people living in and around London.[44] There were relatively few provincial investors,[45] and the holdings of the landed interests, the largest group of trust investors, was not very extensive.[46] Therefore, although London did have financial links with the provinces through the London banks and the insurance companies, the special conditions in this market and its fairly distinct group of investors meant that conditions in London were probably not very representative of those in other parts of the country, at least before the third quarter of the eighteenth century. The closer adjustment of trust rates to London from this period suggests that local capital markets were being brought into closer touch with London. The growth of country banking, which became widespread during the wars of 1793–1815, was instrumental in bringing this about. The country banks formed a vital institutional link which helped to break down the autonomy of local markets and thereby create a greater degree of national financial unity.

4

To sum up the argument briefly. The argument of both Ashton and Pressnell is that the prevailing rates of interest were of vital significance for those contemplating investment, especially investment in public utilities. This argument in turn hinges on their belief that the yields of the Funds were indicative of financial conditions throughout the country. Examined with regard to investment in turnpike trusts both

[41]Pressnell, 'Rate of Interest', p. 179.
[42]P. G. M. Dickson, *The Financial Revolution in England. A Study in the Development of Public Credit 1688-1756* (London, 1967), p. 483.
[43]*Ibid.* pp. 481-2.   [44]*Ibid.* pp. 301-3, 452-3.
[45]*Ibid.* pp. 297-8.   [46]*Ibid.* p. 302.

these points have been found wanting. Firstly, if as Pressnell argues trust rates can be taken as representative of local rates of interest, then before the third quarter of the eighteenth century London rates were at best an indifferent guide to provincial financial conditions. Although the rates offered by the trusts did respond to London trends, the response was often delayed to such an extent as to suggest no more than the vaguest connection between London and provincial capital markets. Secondly, the level of trust investment before the 1790s, as measured by the annual number of new acts, did not seem to have been influenced markedly by changes in the rates of interest. This may, of course, be because the number of new acts is not a very good guide to the magnitude of trust investment,[47] which is probably better measured by the amount of money the trusts spent on their roads. However, it would seem that trust expenditure was governed more by local economic conditions than by movements in the rates of interest. For example, because of the slow expansion of the woollen industry in Yorkshire many trusts in the Leeds area were in a bad financial position until after the American war.[48] Consequently the trusts were unable to spend much on road repairs and little new investment took place. From 1783 toll receipts began to rise as conditions in the woollen industry improved. The trusts were then able to carry out needed repairs despite the fairly high interest rates of the period.[49]

[47]See above, p. 122.
[48]R. G. Wilson, 'Transport Dues', pp. 112-13.
[49]Ibid. p. 113.

7

Trust Road Repair

The turnpike trusts were established so that the roads could be better repaired; but most trustees had probably less first-hand knowledge of repairing roads than did the parish authorities whom they superseded. Furthermore, there was neither an adequate technology upon which they could draw nor experienced road builders to whom they could turn. Consequently the trustees were obliged to adopt methods used by the parish surveyors and to improvise. Through experiment and experience some changes were made in techniques, although by the end of the eighteenth century the technology of road repair had advanced but little. The major innovations were not to come until the following century with the advent of McAdam and Telford. In this chapter both the repair procedures employed and the developments in repair theory will be discussed. This is essential for they not only influenced one another but influenced the effectiveness of the turnpike trusts. Other aspects of repair will also be considered: administration, the rise of contracting and the wages and conditions of the road labourers.

1

Before discussing the trusts' repair methods it is necessary to describe briefly the leading concepts which lay behind repair policy during the eighteenth century. These concepts and the legislation which they fostered influenced the trustees' attitude towards road repair, and the negative emphasis of these concepts may have been instrumental in impeding the advance of repair technology.

Throughout the seventeenth and eighteenth centuries the question of how best to maintain well-repaired roads centred less on the repair techniques to be used than on the type of restrictions which should be imposed on the road users. The trustees in their petitions to Parliament frequently complained that the heavy weights drawn and the narrow wheels used were not only the main cause of impassable roads, but also contributed to the continuance of high debts.[1] Despite the protests of

[1] See for example *J. H. of C.* xxi, pp. 614, 661, and xxxiv, pp. 238, 247, 267.

both carriers and tradesmen,[2] who claimed that the restrictions on wagons were increasing the price of land carriage, Parliament ceaselessly pursued a policy of restriction.

In 1621 four-wheeled wagons and carriages weighing more than a ton were prohibited on the roads.[3] By an act of 1662[4] the maximum weight wagons could carry was set at 20 cwt in winter and 30 cwt in summer. There were to be no more than seven horses in draft, and the fellies of wheels were to be not less than 4½ inches wide. This act expired in the following year, and the five acts passed between 1662 and 1719 were concerned solely with limiting the draft power of wagons.[5] In 1719 a wheel restriction was once again imposed, setting the minimum felly width at 2½ inches.[6] There was no further legislation until 1741,[7] when wagons were exempted from the wheel provision during the summer months. However, a new restriction was immediately added. Wagons could now carry no more than 60 cwt, and to enforce this the trustees were empowered to erect weighing engines and charge 20s for every hundredweight over the prescribed limit.

Weighing engines were intended to protect the roads from the effects of heavy weights; however, they proved only marginally successful. The machines were difficult to operate, for the compound lever platform scale was not widely used, and vehicles had to be hoisted off the ground by means of chains attached to a steel yard.[8] Weighing was both inconvenient and expensive for the road users, and many of those testifying before the Parliamentary Committee in 1796 contended that a 50% increase in toll charges would be preferable.[9] They also claimed that the machines were inaccurate and the collectors fraudulent.[10] Thomas Hollis, a Hammersmith brickmaker, informed the committee that he often made a 'present' to the man on the Uxbridge Road weighing engine,[11] and the evidence of other witnesses attests to the prevalence of this practice. Furthermore, the engines were often leased, and to save themselves work the lessees compounded for passage in lieu of weighing.[12] The weighing engines thereby became, in many cases, simply an extra source of income,[13] and in 1796 the committee recommended that the trustees be not permitted to lease the machines 'as

[2]See for example *J. H. of C.* xxvii, pp. 152, 156, 166, 169.

[3]Jackman, *Development of Transportation*, p. 52.

[4]14 Car. II c.6.

[5]1670 (22 Car. II c.12), 1695/6 (7 Wm. III c.29), 1708 (6 Anne c.29), 1711 (9 Anne c.18), 1715 (1 Geo. I c.11).

[6]5 Geo. I c.12.   [7]14 Geo. II c.42.

[8]McMahon, 'Roads and Turnpike Trusts in E. Yorkshire', p. 50.

[9]*B.P.P. 1796 F.S. x*, pp. 751-4.

[10]*Ibid.* pp. 751-4.   [11]*Ibid.* p. 752.   [12]*Ibid.* pp. 752-4.

[13]The Knaresborough–Skipton Trust erected a weighing engine in 1791. It was claimed that this was necessary to protect the roads and so that interest payments could be met. (Minutes – 26 November 1791, box 27 West Rid. CRO.)

weighing engines are intended to prevent excessive weights, and not to encrease the revenues of the turnpikes'.[14] Nonetheless, the 'evils of compounding' continued, and caused the Committee of 1833 to suggest that the engines should be abolished.[15]

The second phase of the campaign to restrict road use was directed against the narrow wheel. The first 'Broad Wheel Act' in 1753[16] made it mandatory for all wagons travelling on the turnpike roads and being drawn by more than five horses, to have wheels with fellies of no less than nine inches. Vehicles with such wheels could be drawn by up to eight horses and carry unlimited weight. Further to encourage their use, an act in 1755[17] granted three years toll-free passage to wagons having nine-inch wheels. Another act in 1757[18] prescribed half-tolls on broad wheeled wagons within 100 miles of London, while one-half more was demanded for those with narrow wheeled wagons. From 1765[19] nine-inch wheels were no longer exempt from weighing unless the axles were of different lengths so that the wagon rolled a sixteen-inch path. In an attempt to consolidate the growing body of legislation all previous acts were repealed and replaced by a single act in 1767.[20] A second consolidating act in 1773[21] contained twenty-eight clauses dealing with wheels, weights, carriage construction and the number of draft animals permitted.

The parliamentary reports in the late 1790s and the early nineteenth century were concerned almost exclusively with the question of weighing engines, carriage construction and the relative merits of conical and cylindrical wheels. It was to one of these committees (1810) that John Loudon McAdam first presented his ideas on road repair. He pointed out that the committees had concentrated their attention on carriage construction as the main solution for badly repaired roads; however, 'the nature of the roads on which the carriages were to travel has not been so minutely attended to'.[22] He claimed that the bad state of the roads was due to the misapplication of materials and defective road formation. This, he said, could be remedied by 'the introduction of a better system of making the surface of roads, and the application of scientific principles'.[23] Although others had written on road repair, McAdam was the first explicitly to deny the effectiveness of regulation and suggest instead a well thought out system of repair. His testimony marked an important turning point, and although the 'Great Wheel Controversy' continued, from 1810 both Parliament and the trusts

[14]B.P.P. 1796 (April) F.S. x, p. 748.
[15]B.P.P. 1833 (703) xv. 409, p. iv.
[16]26 Geo. II c.30.   [17]28 Geo. II c.17.   [18]30 Geo. II c.28.
[19]5 Geo. III c.38.   [20]7 Geo. III c.40.   [21]13 Geo. III c.84.
[22]B.P.P. 1810–1811 (240) iii. 855, p. 27.
[23]Ibid.

began to pay greater attention to the more germane problems of repair and administration.

With both Parliament and the weight of contemporary opinion supporting a policy of regulation,[24] it is not surprising that the trustees' ideas about repair remained conservative. Despite the improvements made in repair methods by some of the more enlightened trusts, the general level of repair technology at the end of the century was essentially the same as it had been in the 1720s. Vehicle restrictions were, for the most part, ineffective. The act's complexities made them difficult to enforce, and collectors freely accepted bribes for the passage of both overweight vehicles and narrow wheels. Furthermore, as regulation was widely accepted as a panacea for the trusts' repair problems, it may have helped to forestall a significant reappraisal of repair procedures, and thereby have retarded the development and introduction of more effective repair techniques.

But although vehicle regulation dominated the writings of most eighteenth-century critics, methods of road repair also received some attention. The majority of procedures suggested were, however, either unoriginal or if original, were not effective. The basic ideas on repair were put forward by Thomas Procter in 1607.[25] He observed that the main cause of bad roads was that water was allowed to stand on the road surface.[26] To remedy this he suggested that the ditches near the roads be cleansed and the centre of the road made higher than the sides so that the water could drain away. The roads should be constructed on a foundation of rammed-down soil bound with timber and stones and then covered with gravel, sand or rubbish.[27] Thomas Mace, writing in 1675,[28] and William Mather in his book, *Published for the Use and Instruction of Young Surveyors* (1696),[29] reiterated Procter's proposals with only minor alterations.

Except for R. Phillips, who advocated the use of the concave road,[30] most eighteenth-century writers accepted the desirability of the convex road form.[31] They also generally agreed that roads should be both wide and straight. The question of road surfacing was not however given

[24]See for example, Daniel Bourn, *A Treatise upon Wheel-Carriages*, pp. 2-8, Henry Homer, *Enquiry into the Means of Preserving and Improving*, p. 83, John Scott, *Digests of the General Highway and Turnpike Laws* (London, 1778), pp. 340-2.
[25]Thomas Procter, *A Profitable Worke to this Whole Kingdom* (London, 1607).
[26]*Ibid.* p. 6.
[27]*Ibid.* pp. 9-12.
[28]Thomas Mace, *Profit, Conveniency and Pleasure to the Whole Nation* (London, 1675).
[29]William Mather, *Of Repairing and Mending the Highways* (London, 1696).
[30]R. Phillips, *A Dissertation Concerning the Present State of the High Roads in England* (London, 1736/7), pp. 25-31.
[31]Daniel Defoe, *An Essay upon Projects* (London, 1697), p. 91. Homer, *Enquiry into the Means of Preserving and Improving*, p. 30. Bourn, *Treatise upon Wheel-Carriages*, pp. 47-8. Scott, *Digests of the General Highway*, p. 226.

equal consideration. The Rev. Henry Homer said that the materials used should be suited or adapted to the surface upon which they were placed.[32] Most writers were similarly vague on this point. John Scott contended that flints, pebbles, sand and broken stone should not be used and that cast (cleaned) gravel or ballast was preferable.[33] The materials, he said, should be spread evenly over the road surface so that vehicles did not come in contact with road's foundation.[34] This was the nearest anyone came to discussing the preparation and placement of materials. Not surprisingly, the injudicious use of road materials proved to be one of the major weaknesses of trust repair.

The extent of the advances made in repair theory can be gauged by comparing the procedures advocated by Thomas Proctor in 1607 with those suggested by John Scott 166 years later. Both men accepted the desirability of the convex road form and the need for prepared foundations. Scott showed a greater concern with the kinds of materials suitable for road surfacing and with the construction of trunks or arches to carry watercourses under the roads.[35] These differences were hardly significant. Trust repair practices generally reflected the slow advance of repair theory. As will be shown, despite certain innovations the trusts' repair procedures differed little from those expounded by Thomas Proctor at the beginning of the seventeenth century.

It would be difficult to reconstruct an accurate picture of the trusts' repair methods, for the trustees rarely made sufficiently detailed repair orders.[36] At times the instructions were so vague that nothing can be learned. For example, in 1729 the trustees of the Colnbrook Trust ordered 'that the Surveyor lay out any Sum not exceeding one hundred pounds in repairing the road where most ruinous'.[37] The surveyor of the Bedfont–Bagshot Trust was simply to provide teams and 'put the roads in good Repair'.[38] In other cases directions were much more specific. In 1730 the contractors to the Harborough–Loughborough Trust were instructed 'to make the Said Road seven and Half wide at the top of the Said Road and an Inch and half in Every yard Descending with Sufficient Ditches to Carry of the Water'.[39] In the following year they ordered that another road be constructed in a similar manner also 'that the Coat of Gravell Sufficient to be Laid on the Said road should be Eighteen inches thick in the Thinest part'.[40] While surveyors were

32Homer, *An Enquiry*, p. 40.
33Scott, *Digests*, pp. 334-5.
34*Ibid.* p. 337.
35*Ibid.* pp. 227-8.
36Repair directives did become more detailed in the nineteenth century.
37Minutes – 6 September 1729, T.P.Col.1 Mid. CRO.
38Minutes – 15 May 1728, T.P.Bed.1 Mid. CRO.
39Minutes – 30 September 1730, T/MB/1/1 Leics. RO.
40*Ibid.* 6 December 1731.

often ordered to carry out particular repair, i.e. road widening, ditching etc., detailed procedural directives, similar to those of the Harborough–Loughborough trustees, were seldom made. The trust accounts and minutes therefore give at best only a general indication of how the roads were repaired.

There are three main features of road repair which must be considered: foundations, road form and surfacing. The last of these was frequently referred to in the minutes and seems to have been the trustees' primary concern. Although the first two received far less attention in the trust minutes, they may have been more closely attended to than the documents suggest.

It would seem that few trusts constructed their roads upon elaborate foundations. The main type of foundation used was that made of faggots or bavins placed below the road surface. The Kensington, Fulham, Chelsea Trust purchased 36,257 bavins in 1726,[41] and during the next four years an additional 38,000 were used on the road.[42] Defoe observed that in some places north of Royston the road materials available were of poor quality and the ground of such heavy clay that the trustees were obliged to put down 'timber and green faggots'.[43] This is confirmed by the minutes of the Great North Road Trust in Huntingdon which in 1729 record 'that fifteen dozen wood be bought to amend the road between Wabridge Gate and Alconbury Town'.[44] In Gloucestershire, the surveyor of the Gloucester–Birdlip and Crickley Hill Trust was instructed to lay down faggots where there were 'Quick Sands' or springs in the road.[45] John Metcalf, who worked on many roads in Yorkshire, Lancashire, Derbyshire and Cheshire, made stone foundations under some of his roads, and in boggy places he laid heather and ling, covering them with a layer of gravel.[46] The practice of putting down faggots or brush may also have been used in other areas where the ground was soft or where surface materials sank easily into the underlying clay.

The trusts' roads were formed in a variety of shapes, most of which were dictated by the need to provide for efficient drainage. The 'Ploughman's Road' was horizontal, raised above the nearby land and had deep ditches on either side.[47] Phillips claimed that by the application of large quantities of materials such roads in London were

[41] MSS Accounts of Trust for Roads in Fulham, Chelsea and Kensington, 2 May 1732, H. of L. RO.
[42] Ibid.
[43] Defoe, A Tour, Vol. II, p. 122.
[44] Minutes – 29 March 1731, Hunts. CRO.
[45] Minutes – 1 July 1763, D204/3/1 Glouces. RO.
[46] Jackman, Development of Transportation, p. 268.
[47] Scott, Digests, p. 319.

sometimes five to eight feet above their original level.[48] The 'Angular Road' was constructed on a diagonal slant in order to allow water to drain off one side.[49] The road advocated by Phillips, the concave road, was so built to permit water to course down the centre, clearing away loose soil and leaving a hard foundation.[50] In 1717 the Islington Trust made some of their roads in this form, but soon gave it up as impractical.[51] The Whitechapel Trust and the Watton Trust built their roads in a series of hills and valleys, resembling waves.[52] Water collected in the depressions and was then let off into nearby ditches. The road form most frequently recommended was the convex road.[53] Although there is little in the trust documents to support their claim, the Webbs contend that there had developed 'by the end of the century, something like a consensus of opinion, among the more intelligent Trustees and Surveyors, in favour of a moderately convex surface'.[54]

Although construction of foundations and attention to road form were an important part of the repair procedures of certain trusts, most trust repair was concerned primarily with placement of large quantities of materials upon the road. The majority of repair orders dealt with the acquisition of materials, and carting and material costs generally comprised the greatest proportion of repair expenditure. However there were but few directives made which stipulated how the materials were to be applied. For example, the surveyor of the Colnbrook Trust was directed in 1730 to 'provide Ten Ton of pebbles to be used in the way within the Town of Colnbrook and that he caused the holes in the pavement of the said Town to be also Amended'.[55] Nothing was said on how he was to apply the materials. This was characteristic of the orders given to surveyors of many other trusts. The instance of the Harborough–Loughborough Trust was the only one from during the eighteenth century in which the repair directives were made in detail. This suggests that on many roads the placement of materials may have been as haphazard as some critics have claimed.

Trust repair methods were criticized not only for the ill-considered placement of materials, but also for the kinds of materials used and for the failure adequately to prepare the materials before putting them on the roads. This failure on the part of the trustees of the Harrow Trust occasioned the following complaint, in 1816, from the Vestry of Paddington:[56]

[48]Phillips, *Dissertation*, p. 2.   [49]Scott, *Digests*, p. 320.
[50]Phillips, *Dissertation*, pp. 25-31.   [51]Clarke, 'Turnpike Trusts', pp. 250-1.
[52]Scott, *Digests*, p. 322.   [53]See above, p. 135.
[54]Webbs, *King's Highway*, p. 133.
[55]Minutes — 1 June 1730, T.P. Col.1 Mid. CRO.
[56]Harrow Trust, Minutes — 5 January 1816, LA/HW/TP 16 Mid. CRO.

that the present dangerous state of the Road is principally occasioned by a large quantity of Gravel mixed with clay which has lately been laid upon it, and that many men are actually employed at this time in adding to the nuisance by laying more of the like mixture upon the Road.

Despite this complaint and others like it some trusts did realize the desirability of using prepared materials. Screened gravel was being used in London in the 1730s,[57] and in Leicestershire in the 1750s.[58] From 1750 the New Cross Trust was using sifted gravel,[59] and in 1789 the Kilburn Trust ordered that all gravel 'be well sifted and clean from Dirt and Loom'.[60] The kind of materials used on a road depended primarily on what was locally available. Although gravel seems to have been the most popular, pebbles, flints, broken stones, chalk, sand and copper slag were also used.

Besides road construction and maintenance, the trusts also succeeded in bring about a considerable number of related improvements. In some areas roads were widened and straightened.[61] Ditches were dug or cleansed to facilitate drainage, and arches and drains were constructed to allow water-courses, which had at one time flooded the roads, to run under them. In London the roads were watered in the summer to keep down the dust, and during the winter when major repair work ceased, men were employed to fill ruts and drain water from the roads. The trusts erected mile-stones, fences were put up on some roads and trees and hedges were cut back on others.

It is difficult to assess the effectiveness of the trusts' repair techniques in the eighteenth century because of the diverse and questionable nature of contemporary opinion. Jackman has stated:[62]

A road which would be good for one section where the roads were generally bad, might be very bad in another section where, as a general thing, the roads were in good condition. Further, a road might appear very good, and fully equal to the necessities, to a man whose range of observation had been very limited; whereas the same road might appear very bad to a traveller who had seen the wider horizon, especially the roads of France.

Opinion was influenced by the time of year in which a journey was made and by the weather, for in the winter months or after a heavy rain the condition of the roads tended naturally to deteriorate. Furthermore, as the century progressed standards of judgement changed, and this adds

[57]Colnbrook Trust, Minutes – 26 July 1731, T.P. Col.1. Mid. CRO.
[58]Leicester–Hinckley Trust, Minutes – 1 November 1756, T/X/4/2 Leics. RO.
[59]Accounts, 1739-54, 1765-72, T9/F1/1 and T9/F1/2 Kent AO.
[60]Minutes – 19 October 1789, LA/HW/TP 2 Mid. CRO.
[61]Webbs, *King's Highway*, pp. 133-4.
[62]Jackman, *Development of Transportation*, p. 86.

to the problem of evaluation. Despite these factors, contemporary accounts do reveal a good deal about the effects of trust repair.

Daniel Defoe, a writer well aware of road conditions and one of the first to write about the turnpike trusts, found that by the 1720s the roads placed under trust control had been substantially improved. About the trusts, he wrote[63]

it must be acknowledg'd that they are very great things, and very great things are done by them; and 'tis worth recording, for the honour of the present age, that this work has been begun, and is in an extraordinary manner carry'd on, and perhaps may, in a great measure be completed within our memory.

Defoe's detailed descriptions of turnpike roads show that the trusts were better able to repair the roads than were the parishes. His observations are of particular importance for they were made at a time when there were still relatively few trusts, and the difference between trust and parish repair, especially on the main routes, could therefore be clearly seen.

R. Phillips, writing in 1737, claimed that in London trust repair had succeeded only in making the roads worse than they had been.[64] While his claims were probably somewhat exaggerated, the heavy traffic, the clay soil and the scarcity of gravel did make the London roads particularly difficult to repair.[65] It must be remembered, however, that Phillips decried the effectiveness of all repair techniques save his own, and this may have biased his views.

Arthur Young was one of the turnpike trusts' most outspoken critics. However, despite his oft-quoted vitriolic comments, he found most trust roads on his Northern Tour to be well-repaired.[66] His observations on the state of the roads suggests that in his mind road improvement and turnpike trusts were synonymous. A few quotes may serve to illustrate this point.

In the line from Dereham, 30 miles to Harleston, the direction is diagonally across all the Norwich roads, yet *I found the road as good as a turnpike.*[67] [my italics]
The roads of a county [Hertford] so near the Metropolis, can scarcely be bad : six great leading turnpikes passing through so small a district, would alone

[63]Defoe, *A Tour*, Vol. II, pp. 120-1.
[64]Phillips, *Dissertation*, preface.
[65]Jackman, *Development of Transportation*, p. 99.
[66]Edwin Gay, 'Arthur Young on English Roads', *The Quarterly Journal of Economics*, XLI (1927), 545-51. He has quantified Young's comments on the roads travelled on his Northern Tour. He found that of the 940 miles of turnpike road, Young claimed 490 miles to be good, 210 miles middling and 240 miles bad (p. 551).
[67]Arthur Young, *General View of the Agriculture of the County of Norfolk* (London, 1804), p. 489.

give this character, but *there are many cross-roads nearly as good as turn-pikes.*[68] [my italics]

The road [Tetford-Oxford] called by a vile prostitution of language a turn-pike, but christened, I apprehend, by people who know not what a road is.[69]

Edwin Gay had said[70] that Young expected the turnpike roads to be well-repaired, and that 'The frustration of a travellers' normal expectation is in part responsible for the vigour of his condemnation.'

The most informative and complete study of the condition of the roads was that made by W. T. Jackman. His excellent compilation of agricultural reports and 'travels' confirms that the turnpike trusts brought about considerable improvements.[71] Better roads were associated with the turnpikes to such a great degree that Jackman found it necessary to point out: 'Turnpikes were not always good roads, however.'[72] The evidence of the increasing rate of travel also supports the view that trust repair was proving beneficial.[73] Furthermore, while the effects of competition and greater wagon capacities must be considered, the fall in land carriage rates in the late 1750s and early 60s and their relative stability during the following period of rising prices and increasing economic activity, suggests that the trusts' repairs were effective enough to offset the cost (i.e. tolls) to the carriers.[74] Although the changes in coach fares are more difficult to interpret, the same conclusion would seem to apply.[75]

In 1813 Richard Edgeworth declared that there were but twenty miles of well-repaired road in England,[76] and the Parliamentary Committee in 1819 contended that the state of the turnpikes in England and Wales was generally defective.[77] But these qualitative opinions could well have been based on much higher standards, which in fact were the product of continuous road improvement over the decades. It was during this period, and primarily through the works and influence of J. L. McAdam and Thomas Telford, that scientific repair techniques were developed and a more rigorous conception of the 'well-repaired road' was formed. 'What were then the best-kept turnpikes, once thought something like perfection come now to be deemed only

---

[68]Arthur Young, *General View of the Agriculture of the County of Hertfordshire* (London, 1804), p. 221.

[69]Arthur Young, *A Six Weeks Tour through the Southern Counties*, p. 90.

[70]Gay, 'Arthur Young', pp. 550-1.

[71]Jackman, *Development of Transportation*, pp. 85-101, 285-302.

[72]*Ibid.* p. 91, n.1.

[73]*Ibid.* pp. 335-9.

[74]See below, pp. 179-84.

[75]Jackman, *Development of Transportation*, pp. 341-6.

[76]Richard Edgeworth, *An Essay on the Construction of Roads and Carriages* (London, 1813), p. vii.

[77]*B.P.P. 1819 (509) v. 339*, p. 4.

passable, whilst the condition of the worser sort of roads is again felt to be an intolerable public nuisance.'[78] Although many trusts were not using the more advanced techniques, the evidence presented above suggests that a large number of trusts were able, nonetheless, to discharge their repair obligations with considerable success.

In the late eighteenth and early nineteenth centuries, due largely to the interest shown by the Post Office and the Board of Agriculture,[79] increased attention was given to the condition of the roads and the ways by which they could be improved. The Board of Agriculture, established in 1793, became concerned with the question of roads through its investigations of agricultural improvements. Many of the Reports were critical of the way in which the roads were being repaired and some measure of reform was urged. In 1806 Sir John Sinclair, Bart., chairman of the Board, headed a committee which was to report on the use of broad wheels and 'other matters relating to the Preservation of the Turnpike Roads and Highways'. This committee was the first of many established between 1806 and 1840 to investigate the affairs of the turnpike trusts and the parish roads. The two reports made by this committee and the reports of the 1808 Committee were concerned primarily with wheels, weights and carriage construction; road repair was but a secondary consideration. A third committee was set up in 1810, and it was to this committee that J. L. McAdam first submitted his proposals for road repair.

In his memorandum[80] McAdam first dismissed the widely-held theory that the roads could be improved by restrictions, and claimed instead that more effective repair methods were needed. The main aim of his repair policy was the construction of a smooth, elastic road surface formed upon a dry sub-soil. Cleaned materials were to be broken into small uniform pieces and laid on the road in two layers, the first layer being consolidated before the second was applied. He also suggested that materials formerly placed on the roads might be taken up, broken and re-used. The roads were to be as flat as possible, allowing for a slight fall from the centre of one inch in the yard. The building of foundations he considered both too expensive and unnecessary, for he said that a properly consolidated road surface formed upon a well-drained sub-soil could support any weight.[81]

[78]Webbs, *King's Highway*, p. 165.
[79]*Ibid.* pp. 167, 170.
[80]*B.P.P. 1810–1811 (240) iii. 855*, pp. 27-32.
[81]*B.P.P. 1819 (509) v. 339*, pp. 23-6.

His repair theory incorporated the established ideas about convexity, but, unlike others, he was more explicit as to the degree of convexity required. This was important, for although many trusts made their roads in the convex form this was often done by simply piling great quantities of materials in the centre of the road thereby making travel hazardous. His idea of using cleaned material was not new but his insistence on small, uniform size was. By using materials prepared in this way road surfaces were made smooth and travel therefore easier. His conception of a consolidated, elastic road surface to serve as an impenetrable covering over a dry sub-soil was both novel and important. This solved the problem of roads becoming seas of mud as the materials were forced down into the sodden sub-soil, and also helped to prevent the roads being broken up by freezing in the winter months.

In 1816 McAdam was appointed general-surveyor to the Bristol Trust. Here he was first able to put his repair theories into practice. It was during this period that he turned his attention to the problems of trust administration.[82] He found that the Bristol Trust was being poorly managed. There was 'A large increasing debt, obscure and perplexed accounts, dilapidated funds, speculation, fraud and ignorance among the inferior officers, ineffectual control and misdirected authority among the higher'.[83] He reformed administrative procedure by hiring capable and honest surveyors and by instituting an elaborate series of checks on all aspects of repair and expenditure.[84] From his experience in Bristol he concluded that faulty administrative organization was the underlying cause of badly repaired roads. Thereafter he directed his labours equally 'towards the introduction of a wise and well-regulated system of management for the roads as towards their mechanical construction'.[85]

McAdam's repair methods were successful because he was able clearly to distinguish the fundamental problems of road repair and offer simple and comprehensive methods to deal with them. His techniques recommended themselves to the trusts by not only being effective, but proving, in many instances, cheaper than former methods, which depended primarily on frequent and costly increments of materials. Under his system the care taken in preparing the materials reduced the costs of both materials and carting. Furthermore, because of this insistence on material preparation, his repairs tended to be labour intensive, and his techniques were therefore welcome in the period of falling wages after

82 R. H. Spiro, 'John Loudon McAdam, Colossus of Roads' (unpublished Ph.D. thesis, University of Edinburgh, 1950), p. 236.

83 J. L. McAdam, *Observations on the Management of Trusts for the Care of Turnpike Roads* (London, 1825), p. 10.

84 *Ibid.* pp. 11-13.

85 J. L. McAdam, *Remarks on the Present System of Roadmaking* (7th edition, London, 1823), p. vi.

1815.[86] He claimed that in Bristol he had reduced costs by reversing the ratio of man to horse (i.e. carting) hours from 1 : 4 to 4 : 1.[87] When James McAdam was made surveyor of the Epsom Trust in 1818, repair costs for the three previous years had averaged £2,372; materials and carting accounting for 58·9 %.[88] In his first year as surveyor the repair expense was reduced to £1,929 and materials and carting to 16·9 %.

McAdam's policies proved highly successful in Bristol. In 1816 he was approached by the nearby Bath Trust,[89] and in the following year he served as an advisor to nine trusts in East Sussex.[90] His fame as a road-maker spread, and by 1819 he and his sons were acting as advisors or superintendent-surveyors to thirty-four trusts.[91] Four years later, 147 trusts were employing either a member of his family or his policies.[92] Surveyors were frequently urged to adopt McAdam's techniques. The trustees of the Huddersfield–Wibsey Low Moor Trust ordered their surveyors to repair the roads in accordance with McAdam's principles,[93] and in the East Riding the surveyor of the White Cross Trust was instructed 'to follow "Mr McAdam's Book on the Repair of Highways" and produce it at every meeting of the trustees'.[94]

His ideas on repair and administration gained wide acceptance not only because they were effective, but also because they were actively propagated. The family's work on numerous turnpike roads played an important part in this as did the encouragement McAdam received from the Post Office and the Board of Agriculture. In 1818 Lord Chichester, the Postmaster-General, appointed McAdam general-surveyor to nine Sussex trusts,[95] and in the following year the Post Office endorsed McAdam's claim for compensation from Parliament for his work on the roads.[96] The support given by the Board of Agriculture

[86]*B.P.P. 1819 (509) v. 339*, p. 4. The committee concluded that McAdam's system was successful, inexpensive and had increased the employment of the poor. Spiro ('John Loudon McAdam' p. 231) claims that McAdam's system was not cheaper; however, the evidence presented in the 1819 Report indicates that the repair expense of the Bristol Trust did decrease. 1816 – £15,685; 1817 – £14,387; 1818 – £13,470. (*B.P.P. 1819 (509) v. 339*, p. 31.)

[87]Spiro, 'John Loudon McAdam', pp. 475-6.

[88]*B.P.P. 1819 (509) v. 339*, p. 35.

[89]*B.P.P. 1820 (301) ii. 301*, p. 16. McAdam was not engaged by the Bath Trust. Benjamin Wingrove, a trustee, was able to secure the post for himself. McAdam replaced Wingrove as surveyor in 1826. (Spiro, 'John Loudon McAdam', pp. 285-7.)

[90]*B.P.P. 1820 (301) ii. 301*, p. 16.

[91]Spiro, 'John Loudon McAdam', Appendix E, p. 479.

[92]*Ibid.* pp. 480-3.

[93]Letter, 19 June 1823, HAS – A. Hal. Cent. Lib. The letter concerns the printing of circulars giving notice of the trust's intention of farming repairs. The writer says that it will not be necessary to mention forming the road on McAdam's plan, as he will incorporate his plan in the contracts.

[94]McMahon, 'Roads and Turnpike Trusts in E. Yorkshire', p. 56. This order was made in 1820.

[95]*B.P.P. 1819 (509) v. 339*, p. 20.

[96]*B.P.P. 1820 (301) ii. 301*, pp. 13-14.

was, however, of greater significance. McAdam's theories were first brought to the public's attention by Sir John Sinclair in the 1810 Committee Report,[97] and in 1819 McAdam's second book, *A Practical Essay on the Scientific Repair and Preservation of Public Roads*, was printed and distributed by the Board. His policies were also publicized by his frequent and influential appearances before various parliamentary committees, and by his books. His first book, *Remarks on the Present System of Roadmaking . . .*, published in 1816, had gone through nine editions by 1827.[98]

The other important influential road-maker of the period was the Scottish engineer Thomas Telford. He first began building roads in Shropshire, where he was appointed county surveyor in 1786.[99] From 1802 to 1828, as surveyor to the Commissioners of Highland Roads, he supervised the construction of almost a thousand miles of road as well as numerous bridges, harbour installations and canals.[100] It was for these later projects, undertaken in Scotland and elsewhere, rather than road building, that Telford was most famous.

In 1810 a committee was set up to investigate complaints made by the Post Office and Irish M.P.s that the Holyhead Road was in ruinous condition.[101] The committee engaged Telford to make a complete survey of the road and report on the improvements needed. He submitted his report in the following year, but it was not until 1815 that any action was taken. In that year the Holyhead Road Commission was formed, and Telford was appointed to supervise the work.[102] He was charged with constructing the difficult section of road through North Wales, and was also directed to make improvements on the southern portion of the road below Shrewsbury. He applied his considerable engineering skills to the construction, and by 1818 much of the work on the Welsh roads was completed.[103] With the active support of the Commission's chairman, Sir Henry Parnell, Telford was also able to introduce needed administrative reforms. To ensure that the road from Shrewsbury to Holyhead would be properly maintained, the six Welsh trusts were consolidated and their roads placed under the direct control of the Commission.[104] Similar consolidations proved impracticable

[97]Spiro, 'John Loudon McAdam', pp. 199–200.
[98]*Ibid.* pp. 272–3. There had also been an American edition, and the book had been translated into German.
[99]Sir Alexander Gibb, *The Story of Telford: the Rise of Civil Engineering* (London, 1935), pp. 23–5.
[100]Webbs, *King's Highway*, p. 183.
[101]Jackman, *Development of Transportation*, p. 272.
[102]*Ibid.* p. 273.
[103]Mervyn Hughes, 'Telford, Parnell and the Great Irish Road', *Journal of Transport History*, VI, no. 4 (1964), 202.
[104]*Ibid.* pp. 202–4.

on the English portion of the road, nonetheless Telford was able to bring about a substantial number of improvements on the road from London to Shrewsbury.

Telford's repair methods differed from those employed by McAdam. The latter favoured an elastic road surface constructed upon natural sub-soil, while Telford advocated roads formed on built up stone foundations.[105] He was also more concerned than McAdam with the engineering problems associated with road building, such as reducing gradients, drainage and widening and straightening roads. The relative advantage of this aspect of Telford's system was clearly demonstrated in the controversy over the repairing of the Whetstone and St Albans trusts, the southernmost portions of the Holyhead Road.

Telford, as general-surveyor of the Holyhead Road Commission, suggested various improvements to these trusts, including plans for reducing the gradients on two particularly steep hills.[106] He supervised the construction of two sections of road for the St Albans Trust;[107] but the Whetstone Trust was unable to agree with the Commission on the terms under which the latter would take over repairs.[108] The trust did, however, accept Telford's proposals, and hired James McAdam to implement them.[109] At this time (1823) James McAdam was also being employed by the St Albans Trust and was responsible for maintaining the roads which Telford had constructed.[110] It seems that repair work on these trusts' roads was poorly executed, for in the annual Commission Report Telford was critical of both the trusts' repair methods and administration.[111] In 1828 a committee, led by Sir Henry Parnell, reported on the condition of the trusts. It was found that the roads were in an 'extremely bad state',[112] and Parnell was convinced he knew the reason. 'In my opinion, the main cause of these roads being in an imperfect state, is Mr McAdam's being the surveyor of

[105]Jackman, *Development of Transportation*, p. 270, n.3.

[106]*B.P.P. 1828 (546) iv. 255*, pp. 20-1, and H. C. F. Lansberry, 'James McAdam and the St Albans Turnpike Trust', *Journal of Transport History*, VII, no. 2 (1965), 121-3.

[107]Lansberry, 'James McAdam', pp. 121-3.

[108]*B.P.P. 1828 (546) iv. 255*, pp. 21, 24, 47-8. (The Commission wanted to take over part of the road, repair it and then return control to the trustees. The trustees were willing to have the Commission repair the roads; however, they did not want to resume their control over it once the Commission had carried out the repairs.)

[109]*Ibid.* p. 21.

[110]Sir Henry Parnell had recommended McAdam to both the trusts (*ibid.* p. 22).

[111]*B.P.P. 1824 (305) ix. 293*, pp. 9-10 (Telford was critical of the repairs and the materials used by both trusts). *B.P.P. 1825 (492) xv. 63*, p. 6 (Telford claimed that the St Albans Trust was much improved). *B.P.P. 1826 (129) xi, 47*, pp. 5-6 (Telford contended that both roads were being improved, but he disapproved of the materials used by the Whetstone Trust). *B.P.P. 1826-1827 (412) vii. 81*, pp. 5-6 (Telford was critical of both trusts' repairs). *B.P.P. 1828 (476) ix. 227*, pp. 8-9 (Telford continued to be critical of both trusts; however, he claimed that parts of the St Albans Trust were well repaired).

[112]*B.P.P. 1828 (546) iv. 255*, p. 3.

them.'[113] In the committee's resolutions he broadened his criticism substantially:[114]

The Committee hope, that the experiment which has now been tried on these Roads, of the principle of weak elastic Roads, having an appearance of smoothness on the surface produced by constant raking and scraping, will at last open the eyes of the Public, and turn the attention of all Road Trustees to secure strength and hardness as the essential qualities of a good Road.

However if, as it was claimed, the roads were constructed upon a wet clay sub-soil and covered with earth, sand and gravel, this would not reflect on the senior McAdam's system, but rather on his son's lack of control and attention to the repair work.[115] It was the difficulty and expense of obtaining proper materials[116] coupled with James' failings as an engineer which led to the roads being badly repaired, not the inherent weakness of his father's system. The trustees of the Whetstone Trust professed themselves satisfied with his work, except for the repairs on Barnet Hill.[117] When Parnell asked George Byng, a trustee, 'Then in point of fact Mr McAdam was not equal to his work?' Byng replied, 'He was not a good engineer.'[118]

From the standpoint of sound engineering practice Telford's methods were far superior to McAdam's, but they were also very much more expensive.[119] It was probably for this reason that his system was used primarily on roads which received direct financial assistance from the government (i.e. the Holyhead Road, the Glasgow–Carlisle Road, the Highland Roads). McAdam's system was more popular not only because of its greater simplicity and relatively lower cost, but also because it was more vigorously promulgated. Telford did not possess McAdam's single-minded devotion to spreading his ideas. McAdam wrote three books describing his principles of repair and administration, while the first book on Telford's repair techniques did not appear until 1834,[120] the

---

[113]*Ibid.* p. 22.   [114]*Ibid.* p. 4.

[115]Lansberry, 'James McAdam', p. 121. ('The McAdams' zeal to see that every trust was provided with a professional assistant, preferably a McAdam, outpaced their ability to ensure the detailed supervision of the road'.)

[116]*Ibid.*   [117]*B.P.P. 1828 (546) iv. 255,* p. 45.

[118]*Ibid.* p. 24.

[119]Spiro, 'John Loudon McAdam', pp. 391-2. Gibb, *Story of Telford,* pp. 175-6. Telford's biographer contends that McAdam's roads could not have withstood modern traffic, but concedes that Telford's roads were perhaps beyond the requirements of the time.

[120]Sir Henry Parnell, *A Treatise on Roads* (second edition, London, 1838). This book contains not only an exposition of Telford's principles, but also a prolonged attack on the 'un-scientific' and ineffective nature of McAdam's techniques (especially Chapter II). Parnell mentions Benjamin Wingrove, 'an eminent and practical road surveyor' (p. 79), as an exponent of Telford's repair methods (also p. 143). This 'eminent and practical road surveyor' was discharged from the Bath Trust in 1826 for spending too much money on repair. He was replaced by J. L. McAdam (H. Spiro, Jr., 'John

year of his death. His labours were divided among a great many projects, and this possibly precluded on his part a popularization campaign comparable to that of McAdam and his sons.

Through their work both Telford and McAdam helped to advance the level of repair technology. The new techniques were not adopted by every trust, and those who did use them often did so incorrectly. Indeed, the McAdams sometimes met with failure.[121] However, the nineteenth-century roads were able to accommodate a greatly expanded volume of traffic,[122] while permitting increased rates of travel.[123] This suggests that road repair was being carried out with a greater degree of technical competence.

3

Road repair policy was formulated by the trustees in their general meetings. They decided what sections of the road would be repaired, how much was to be spent on improvements and occasionally they stipulated how the work was to be done. They were advised as to the condition of the roads and the repairs required by committees to whom this responsibility was delegated or by the surveyor. After ascertaining what needed to be done, they either directed the surveyor to undertake the work or made contracts for the repairs. In the former case, the surveyor was supervised by either the general meeting, a committee of trustees or the treasurer. If the road repair was contracted, the surveyor acted as overseer – reporting to the trustees on the contractor's work. While the surveyor was placed in charge of directing labour and procuring materials, wages and prices were set or approved by the trustees.

The above is a composite picture of repair administration drawn from the numerous trust documents examined. In practice, however, individual trust procedures varied considerably.

The Colnbrook Trust, established in 1727,[124] was responsible for the fourteen miles of the Western Road between Cranford Bridge and Maidenhead Bridge. It would seem that the two surveyors, appointed at the first meeting (1 June 1727), were working under explicit orders from the trustees, for in 1728 one of the surveyors was dismissed after

Loudon McAdam in Somerset and Dorset', *Notes and Queri es for Somerset and Dorset* XXVII, Part cclxii, no. 64 (1956), 88-9).
[121]Spiro, 'John Loudon McAdam in Somerset', p. 89.
[122]Jackman, *Development of Transportation*, pp. 306-12.
[123]*Ibid.* pp. 335-9, appendix 5, pp. 683-701.
[124]13 Geo. I c.31.

having employed labourers on the road without the trustees' consent.[125]
The following order was made at the same meeting:[126]

That no new work be done on the said Road between this and the next Meeting save only that not exceeding Six men be Employed at the discretion of Mr. Goodwin the Surveyor to drain and level the said Road And if there shall be occasion of mending holes That he apply to Mr. Bofouth(?) a Trustee and Treasurer for his consent and directions therein.

From 1728 the treasurer was placed in direct control of all repair work, and from time to time certain trustees were appointed to view the roads and make reports to the general meeting.[127] It appears from the entries in the minutes that while the trustees paid fairly close attention to road repair during the thirties, their vigilance decreased in the following decades.[128]

At their general meetings, the trustees of the Huntingdonshire section of the Great North Road Trust decided how much was to be spent on repairs.[129] The direction of repairs was left to a committee, which ordered the purchase of materials, set labourers' wages and detailed the repairs to be undertaken. This committee must have exercised a fairly strict control over their surveyors, for in 1739 a trustee asked Mr Hastings, the surveyor, 'to take usual winter care of all the road whereof he is Surveyor and *he refusing to do anything therein without a particular order for that purpose*' (my italics).[130] The committee immediately issued the requisite order. The direction of repair by committee was a fairly common procedure employed by trusts throughout the country.[131]

The trustees of many of the smaller provincial trusts exercised but little control over road repair. Although specific improvements were ordered and directives were made for buying materials or paying labourers, the paucity of detailed instructions in the minutes suggests

[125]Minutes – 4 November 1728, T.P. Col.1 Mid. CRO. He was dismissed after it had been found that he had not paid his labourers' bills (*ibid*. 4 January 1728/9).
[126]*Ibid*. 4 November 1728.
[127]*Ibid*. 4 November 1728, 1 June 1730, 12 October 1730 and 30 March 1730.
[128]The repair orders made during the 1730s were fairly detailed, while those made in later years were more general. This may indicate only that the minutes were less complete in the later period.
[129]Minute Book 1725-45 (typed transcript), Hunts. CRO.
[130]*Ibid*. 2 December 1739.
[131]Committees directed the repair of the following trusts: the Bedfont–Bagshot Trust – (Minutes – 3 June 1728, T.P. Bed. 1 Mid. CRO). Kensington, Fulham, Chelsea Trust – (*J. H. of C.* xxix. p. 650). Liverpool–Prescot Trust – (Baily, 'Minutes of the Trustees of the Turnpike Roads', pp. 166-7; special committees were set up, but the trust was run by the general meeting). New Cross Trust – (Minutes – 31 March 1718, T9/A1/14 Kent AO). Rochester-Maidstone Trust – (Minutes – 22 July 1728, T12/1 Kent AO). Old Street Trust (Minutes – 3 July 1753, Fins. Lib.).

F

that the surveyors were invested with considerable authority for repairing the roads. The trustees did examine the surveyors' accounts, occasionally a trustee or a committee was appointed to inspect the roads and sometimes a surveyor was dismissed for negligence or fraud; however the great number of adjourned meetings in the minute books of many smaller trusts indicates that in general the trustees' supervision of repair was minimal.[132]

While some trustees supervised repair work more closely than others, relatively few trusts maintained a consistent degree of control over repairs. For example, detailed repair directives were issued by the Harborough–Loughborough Trust from 1726 to the early 1730s, at which time most of the contract work seems to have been completed.[133] Although the trustees continued to concern themselves with repair, the minutes indicate that from this period many of the repair decisions were deferred to the surveyor. A similar situation developed on the Colnbrook[134] and the Northampton–Harborough Trusts. In 1764 the surveyor of the latter claimed that he and the treasurer were obliged to make many repair decisions as it was difficult to get the five trustees necessary for the quarterly meetings.[135] For the first few years after their inception most trusts held frequent, well-attended meetings at which an active interest was taken in road repair. However in later years the number of meetings and the attendance usually declined, and annual or bi-annual meetings became the rule. As a result, day-to-day repair work was left to the surveyor, supervised by either the treasurer or one or two interested trustees.

It would seem that generally the trustees of the larger trusts and those in urban areas paid more attention to the direction of road repair than did the trustees of the smaller provincial trusts. Also the former trusts' administrative structures were frequently more complex.[136] This did not necessarily mean, however, that these trusts were better able to repair their roads. Numerous orders and declarations in the trust minutes and detailed surveyors' reports and accounts, while giving the impression of a well organized administration, sometimes only obscured what was in fact an ineffectual and inefficient one.

The Kensington, Chelsea, Fulham Trust was a perfect example of

---

132For example, after the Drayton–Edgehill Trust's first meeting, the trustees met only to appoint new trustees or to let the tolls (Minute Book 1753-1822 CR 580/57 War. CRO). The minute books of the Stratford–Bromsgrove Trust suggest a similar situation (Minute Books 1754-67 and 1767-1806 CR 446/1 and CR 446/2 War. CRO).
133Order Book 1726-64, T/MB/1/1 Leics. RO.
134See above, p. 149.
135*Rusticum et Commerciale*, Vol. II, pp. 184-5. A letter from Stephen Mills, Surveyor of the Northampton to Harborough Trust.
136See above, pp. 61-2.

this. The trust's organizational structure was highly elaborate.[137] Meetings were held monthly and general meetings quarterly. The surveyor had to present an annual estimate to the trustees and submit a report at each monthly meeting. His duties were clearly defined, down to the type of gravel he was to use. He was authorized to carry out emergency repairs and to remove dangerous 'nuisances' from the roads. This implies that most repair orders were made at the meetings. Despite this seemingly efficient system, between 1731 and 1765 three parliamentary committees found that this trust was being mismanaged.[138] The report in 1765 criticized the trust's repair methods and suggested that some alteration should be made in the trust's 'execution'. Further, they recommended that a section of the trust's road, near Knightsbridge, should be taken over by the Commissioners for Paving the Westminster Streets.

There were complaints throughout the nineteenth century about the trustees' lax administrative procedures;[139] but the first concerted attempt at reform did not come until 1816, with the publication of McAdam's *Remarks on the Present System of Roadmaking*. In 1810, when he first presented his 'Observations on the Highways of the Kingdom',[140] his sole concern was with repair techniques. However, his experience as surveyor of the Bristol Trust convinced him that the trusts' administrative weakness was the underlying cause of both badly repaired roads and high debts.[141] The trusts' funds had, he said 'fallen into the hands of the lowest order of society under the vague control of the deliberative body of the Trustees'.[142] He proposed a comprehensive series of reforms to remedy these problems.

His main complaint was that the surveyors hired were unknowledgeable, often fraudulent and drawn from 'the lowest orders of society'.[143] He wanted the trusts to be staffed by competent professionals. A general surveyor, a gentleman of education, talent and station, should be hired to supervise repair and the purchase of materials[144] under the direction of a strong and efficient executive department.[145] He should have under him sub-surveyors chosen from the yeomanry, given a proper education and paid liberally for their services.[146] The sub-surveyors were to submit accounts in duplicate, one for the general

---

137*J. H. of C.* xxix, pp. 648-50.
138*J. H. of C.* xxi, pp. 837-8; xxix, p. 648; xxx, p. 429.
139Webbs, *King's Highway*, pp. 130-2.
140*B.P.P. 1810-1811 (240) iii. 855*, pp. 27-32.
141McAdam, *Remarks*, p. 21.
142McAdam, *Observations*, p. 9.
143*Ibid.* p. 36.
144*Ibid.* p. 37.
145*Ibid.* p. 30.
146*Ibid.* p. 37.

surveyor and one for the treasurer.[147] He suggested that trusts combine to hire a general surveyor[148] and favoured the consolidation of the London trusts, for he believed this would reduce administrative expense and allow for large-scale material buying.[149] He also felt that the bad state of trust finances called for public accounts and a degree of parliamentary supervision.[150]

McAdam's ideas on trust administration, as those on repair, were widely publicized. The Webbs have claimed:[151] 'it was rather in the art of road administration than in road technology that McAdam so greatly served his day and generation'. He himself contended that many trusts had adopted his repair techniques without instituting his suggested administrative reforms.[152] It would be difficult to assess the validity of his claim without a very detailed study of individual trusts' administrative procedures; however the increasing number of full-time surveyors and banker–treasurers employed by the trusts, indicate that at least his demands for professionalism in trust administration were being met.[153] Furthermore, it appears that trust minutes were more detailed in the nineteenth century, and this suggests that the trustees, influenced perhaps by McAdam, were giving more attention to the direction of repair. However, as in the preceding period, the effectiveness of the trusts' repair policies cannot be measured by the number of minute book entries.

4

Contracting is an aspect of repair administration which merits special consideration for it has been generally misunderstood. The Webbs have contended that the trustees' failings as administrators led them to

fall back on the common administrative expedient of that period, that of 'farming' ... As applied to the turnpike roads, this meant that some local farmer or jobbing craftsman would undertake, for a lump sum, to keep a given stretch of highway in repair. According to the ablest contemporary road administrator, this practice proved as ruinous to the roads as it had to the workhouse and the prison.[154]

[147]McAdam, *Remarks*, p. 19.
[148]*B.P.P. 1819 (509) v. 339*, p. 29.
[149]*Ibid.* and *B.P.P. 1825 (355) v. 167*, pp. 71-2.
[150]*B.P.P. 1819 (509) v. 399*, pp. 29-30.
[151]Webbs, *King's Highway*, p. 173.
[152]McAdam, *Remarks*, p. ii.
[153]See above, pp. 91-2.
[154]Webbs, *King's Highway*, p. 132.

This is an over-simplification. While contracts were often made for initial road construction, subsequent repairs and road maintenance were usually left to the trust surveyors. The farming of an entire road was rare, and other types of contracting, especially for materials, were far more common.

The greatest repair expenses were those for materials and carting.[155] The trust minutes indicate that the search for and purchase of materials was one of the trustees' major preoccupations. Labourers had to be employed to extract and prepare the materials and carters hired to haul them. As supplies near the roads became depleted new sources had to be found and purchased. Faced with the problems of organizing and supervising this activity, many trustees found it easier to make contracts for the supply of materials. While this practice does not seem to have been widely employed in the early years, the trust documents show that by the second half of the eighteenth century it had become a common practice, and in 1773 a provision was included in the General Act defining how these contracts were to be made.[156] The surveyors were permitted to contract for materials, ten days' notice was required and they were to have no interest in any contracts made.

The following notice, although more elaborate than most, generally typifies the form of material contracts:[157]

TO GRAVEL DIGGERS,
and others

CONTRACTS FOR GRAVEL
for the years 1839 and 1840

THE COMMITTEE OF THE TRUSTEES OF THE BAGSHOT ROAD will receive TENDERS for the supply of GRAVEL, to be delivered on the said Road, as specified in the accompanying Schedule.

The Gravel to be delivered thoroughly sifted with half-inch sieves, freed and cleansed from all clay, hoggin, sand, earth, or other matters, to the satisfaction of the Committee of Trustees and the Sub-Surveyor; and the said Sub-Surveyor shall be at liberty, if the gravel delivered shall not be so properly cleansed, to cause the same to be re-sifted when in the depots, charging the Contractor or Contractors with the expense thereof, and paying for such quantity of gravel only, as shall remain after being so re-sifted with the said half-inch sieves.

The Contractor or Contractors to cause the heaps he or they shall deliver at the various depots, to be properly trimmed up, ready for admeasurement,

155In 1837 the trusts spent about 40·6% of total repair expenditure on these two items (*B.P.P. 1839 (447) xliv. 299*).
15613 Geo. III c.84 art. 36.
157Bedfont–Bagshot Trust. Misc. Documents Mid. CRO.

at his or their own expense, and to find all Tools, Tackle, Sieves, Pumps, Carts, and every requisite for the due performance of the said work.

The whole of the Gravel required, to be delivered in depots, on or before the last day of September, in each of the years, 1839 and 1840, agreeably to the annexed Schedule, under the forfeiture of Five Pounds per week, for every week after the time specified, which fine will be extracted and deducted from the amounts of the respective contracts.

Sealed Tenders for the above, addressed to the Committee of Trustees, to be delivered at the Wheat Sheaf Inn, Virginia Water, before 10 o'clock, on Monday the 19th of March, 1838, when persons delivering Tenders must attend.

By the nineteenth century, especially in the urban areas, most trusts were contracting for their materials. This proved convenient for the trustees, and if the contractors operated on a sufficiently large scale economies may have been realized and passed on to the trusts in lower prices. However, although some contractors worked for more than one trust, there is no evidence of the development of large contracting firms. With the exception of those who supplied materials by canal,[158] most contractors seem to have been local farmers or tradesmen who worked in a limited area.

Although some trusts contracted repairs in the early eighteenth century, only in later years did this practice become widely accepted. The Gloucester Trust contracted repairs in 1706,[159] and in the 1720s the toll-collectors of the Chalk Trust were paid for repair work.[160] In 1726 the Harborough–Loughborough Trust made a contract with William Webb and Tillman Bobart for the repair of a 1,500 yard portion of road, as a sample of their methods.[161] Their repairs proved to be too expensive and they were not re-hired.[162] In 1730 the repair of the road from Oadby to Leicester was contracted by Samuel Pawley and the trust's surveyor, William Bousher.[163] They were hired to 'Ditch and Make Ready to gravell Two hundred yards of the Road'. Presumably, their work was found satisfactory, for in 1732 they repaired the road from Oadby to Glen.[164] During these years the trust's surveyor was employed repairing and maintaining other parts of the road. The combination of contracts and surveyor's work was characteristic of many trusts' repair policies. The Liverpool–Prescot Trust contracted the repair

[158]New Cross Trust, Minutes – 20 February 1815, T9/A2/1 Kent AO. Mr Wildgoose supplied flints to this trust via the Grand Surrey Canal. He also supplied the Surrey Trust (New Cross Trust, Minutes – 26 December 1814).
[159]Glouces. QS Records, Mich-Sess. 1706, Q/SO-3 Glouces. RO.
[160]Kent QS Records, Q/SB 1720-28 Kent AO.
[161]Minutes – 30 August 1727, T/MB/1/1 Leics. RO.
[162]*Rusticum et Commerciale*, Vol. II, p. 183.
[163]Minutes – 7 September 1730, T/MB/1/1 Leics. RO.
[164]*Ibid.* 3 April 1732.

of portions of its roads in 1727, 1754 and the 1780s,[165] and in the 1750s at least five Yorkshire trusts contracted repairs.[166] In 1751 John Metcalf began a career during which he was to construct, under contract, segments of road for many trusts in the West Riding, Lancashire, Derbyshire and Cheshire.[167]

The practice of repair contracting seems to have become fairly widespread by the late eighteenth century. As in the earlier period contract work was usually combined with surveyor-directed repairs. In 1782 the Kilburn Trust contracted parts of its road,[168] and in 1821 the Harrow Trust made contracts for the gravelling of the road between the mile-posts.[169] The New Cross Trust, which does not seem to have entered into many contracts, in 1805 paid out £253 for work contracted on the roads near Bexley Heath and Bromley Hill.[170] The Wibsey Low Moor Trust contracted its entire road in 1823,[171] although in later years the surveyor became increasingly active. The trustees of the Marylebone–Finchley Road Trust, initially opposed to contracting repairs,[172] in 1826 entered into a contract with Samuel Scarfe for repairing a three mile portion of the road.[173] Until the early 1830s all the major road construction work was done on contract, the surveyor being responsible for supervision and road maintenance.[174]

The most serious criticism levelled against the practice of contracting was that it occasioned jobbery. The local acts prohibited the trustees from deriving any profit from their positions and a similar restriction was imposed on the surveyors. These provisions do not, however, seem to have acted as an effective deterrent. In 1732 the majority of materials (gravel and bavins) used by the Kensington, Fulham, Chelsea Trust were purchased from four trustees,[175] and in 1765 the chief gravel contractor, Mr Scott, was an acting trustee.[176] At the same time the trust's carpentry work was being done by Mr Spencer whose partner was a

[165]Baily, 'Minutes of the Trustees of the Turnpike Roads', Part I, pp. 174-5, Part II, pp. 41, 70, 72-3. All these contracts proved unsatisfactory.
[166]Wakefield–Redhouse Trust, Minutes 1758, box 54 West Rid. CRO; Harrogate–Boroughbridge Trust, Minutes – 3 March 1753, box 27 West Rid. CRO; Kirkby Hill–Ripon Trust, Account Book 1752-1814, box 27 West Rid. CRO; Keighley–Kirby-in-Kendal Trust, Minutes – 5 July 1753, box 22 West Rid. CRO.
[167]John Metcalf, *The Life of John Metcalf, commonly called Blind Jack of Knaresborough* (York, 1795), pp. 124-45.
[168]Minutes – 13 August 1782, LA/HW/TP2 Mid. CRO. They seem to have let sections of the road to different contractors (*ibid.* 26 July 1784).
[169]Minutes – 12 March 1821, LA/HW/TP 17 Mid. CRO.
[170]Abstracts of Annual Accounts 1805, T9/F2/1 Kent AO.
[171]Circular for contracting, 8 September 1823, HAS – 77, Hal. Cent. Lib.
[172]Minutes – 12 June 1826, LA/HW/TP 18 Mid. CRO.
[173]*Ibid.* 26 December 1826.
[174]*Ibid.*
[175]MSS Report on Trusts . . . 2 May 1732, H. of L. RO.
[176]*J. H. of C.* xxx, p. 429.

trustee.[177] In 1754 the surveyor of the Liverpool–Prescot Trust contracted repairs,[178] and in 1780 Mr Chorley, a trustee, became the main contractor.[179] In 1730 the repairs of sections of the Harborough–Loughborough Trust roads were contracted by their surveyor.[180]

In the 1760s and early seventies, Mr Chippendale and Ralph Richardson, both trustees, contracted the repairs of the Knaresborough–Pateley Bridge, the Harrogate–Hutton Moor and the Kirkby Hill–Ripon trusts.[181] The repairs of the two later trusts and those of the Ripon–Pateley Bridge Trust were contracted in the 1790s by Harrison, Ferry and Co.[182] Both men were trustees and Charles Harrison was the treasurer of the Kirkby Hill–Ripon Trust.[183] The treasurer of the Kippings Cross Trust, Mr Twort, contracted carts to the trust in the early 1780s.[184] Other carters were paid 2s 6d per day; he received 3s 6d. In the 1820s the partners of the Low Moor Iron Works were trustees of at least three trusts to which they contracted furnace dross.[185] William Wilimot, surveyor of both the Warwick–Paddlebrook and Chipping Campden trusts,[186] contracted the repairs on both trusts' roads.

It would seem that jobbery was a fairly widespread phenomenon,[187] though it was not necessarily associated with extra profits. The trustee who contracted the repairs of the Liverpool–Prescot Trust was paid £600, while the previous contractor had received £1,100,[188] and Clarke[189] notes that the jobbery practised on the Islington and Marylebone trusts did not result in higher prices.

Both repair and material contracting became increasingly popular

---

[177]*Ibid.*
[178]Baily, 'Minutes of the Trustees of the Turnpike Roads', Part II, p. 41.
[179]*Ibid.* p. 70.
[180]Minutes — 7 September 1730 and 3 April 1732. T/MB/1/1 Leics. RO. Also see, *Rusticum et Commerciale*, Vol. II, p. 183.
[181]Harrogate–Hutton Moor Trust, Account Book 1752-1814, box 27; Kirkby Hill–Ripon Trust, Account Book 1752-1814, box 27; Knaresborough–Pateley Bridge Trust, Account Book 1759-1839, box 27 (all documents in West Rid. CRO).
[182]*Ibid.* and Ripon–Pateley Bridge Trust, Minute Book 1756-1815, box 27 West Rid. CRO.
[183]*Ibid.*
[184]Account Book 1765-1811, T1/3 Kent AO.
[185]Wibsey Low Moor–Huddersfield Trust, Bills for Repairs . . . , HAS — 91 Hal. Cent. Lib.; Leeds–Collingham Trust, Account Book 1827-66, box 56 West Rid. CRO; Huddersfield–Bradford Trust, Receipt for furnace dross — 10 January to 11 June 1828, HAS — 93 Hal. Cent. Lib.
[186]Warwick–Paddlebrook Trust, Order Book — 11 May 1826, CR 446/34; Chipping Campden Trust, Minutes — 19 August 1824, CR 446/39 (documents in War. CRO).
[187]See Webbs, *King's Highway*, p. 132 and Peter L. Payne, 'The Bermondsey, Rotherhithe and Deptford Turnpike 1776-1810', *Journal of Transport History*, II, No. 3 (1956), 140.
[188]Baily, 'Minutes of the Trustees of the Turnpike Roads', p. 70.
[189]Clarke, 'Turnpike Trusts', p. 67.

because of the advantages which they offered to the trustees.[190] The most important of these was that the trustees were relieved of the detailed organization and supervision of repair work or material procurement. It was easier for them, through their surveyors, to check material deliveries or completed repairs than to supervise these activities through their various stages. The trusts may also have benefited from the contractors' greater knowledge or resources, but this, however, is doubtful, given the small scale of most contractors' operations and the generally low level of technical competence. With the exception of the material contractors on the canals, the paviors hired by the trusts in the cities, and the gifted John Metcalf, contractors do not seem to have had any special qualifications for their jobs.

The Webbs claimed that the trustees' inactivity and lack of administrative ability caused them to farm out the repair of their roads.[191] While this may have been true, in relatively few cases was an entire road farmed. Furthermore, both Telford[192] and McAdam[193] made use of material and repair contracts, and they can hardly be accused of either 'inactivity' or 'lack of administrative ability'.

5

The labourers employed on the roads were not, as the canal or railway navvies, a clearly distinct group of workers. Most road labourers were local men employed on a semi-permanent basis or hired casually. When not working on the roads they were employed in agriculture or, if in an urban area, they may have found work on other building projects. Women and children also worked on the roads. In 1762 the Chappel-on-the-Hill Trust paid two girls and a boy for picking pebbles,[194] and in the 1790s women and children were being employed by the Canterbury–Dover Trust to pick gravel at 6d per load.[195]

Some trusts demanded that only able-bodied labourers be hired. The trustees of the Great North Road Trust required 'for ye future that ... Surveyor ... do not employ any Labourers, but such as are strong abble bodied men, and who are willing to do their work and not allow above 10d per day and give ye preference to ye parishes upon ye

[190]See Pollard, *The Genesis*, pp. 38–47, for a discussion of subcontracting in industry.
[191]Webbs, *King's Highway*, pp. 131-2.
[192]*Life of Thomas Telford Civil Engineer written by Himself*, ed. John Rickman (London, 1838), pp. 166, 210.
[193]McAdam, *Observations*, pp. 18–19 and *B.P.P. 1828 (311) ix. 23*, pp. 12–13 (Second Report of ... The Metropolis Turnpike Roads). All materials, implements for repair and repair work were contracted.
[194]Account Book 1731-67, D621/X4 Glouces. RO.
[195]Journal – February 1799, T6/1 Kent AO.

road'.[196] In 1728, the Bedfont–Bagshot Trust ordered that no 'old man past Labour be hired for the roads'.[197] The following extract from the minutes of the Droitwich Trust gives some idea of what was considered to be 'old' and 'past Labour'; 'in the future no Person be employed as a Labourer on any of the Roads that is more than Thirty years of Age'.[198]

In the nineteenth century hiring practices altered radically. Trusts, primarily those in the southern counties, began to employ pauper labour, a practice initiated by the parishes.[199] The use of paupers on the trust roads was advocated by J. L. McAdam.[200] In 1810, he contended that 'women or men past hard labour' should be employed breaking stone.[201] He claimed 'a woman *sitting* will break more limestone for a road than two strong labourers on their feet with long hammers in a given time'.[202] He had success in using women, children and older labourers in Bristol,[203] and pauper labour was employed by other trusts which adopted his system.[204] In 1816 the New Cross Trust, in need of a hundred additional labourers for the works on Shotter's Hill, employed men on the parish lists.[205] James McAdam, testifying before a parliamentary committee in 1824, stated that pauper labour was being used by many trusts in Essex, Sussex, Lincolnshire, Hampshire and the Home Counties.[206] 'I have a great number of instances of men with no less than ten children, and the wife, being wholly employed upon the turnpike roads.'[207] One such case was that of an ex-convict his family who were put to work on the Fulham Road. 'His sons and himself lift the road, the smaller boys pick the stones and the wife and the girls rake the roads and keep it in order afterwards.'[208] Labourers' children were taken at nine or ten years of age and put to work, with women, breaking stones with small

[196]Minutes – 23 March 1741/2 Hunts. CRO.
[197]Minutes – 11 November 1728, T.P. Bed.1, Mid. CRO.
[198]Minutes – 5 September 1785, b705:584, BA 704/1 Worcs. RO.
[199]Webbs, *King's Highway*, p. 198.
[200]*B.P.P. 1819 (509) v. 339*, pp. 30-1. McAdam claimed (*ibid.* p. 30) 'I have always found that in every place where improvement of the roads has been commenced, under advice given by me, it has been desired very much by the inhabitants that the people unemployed (not, perhaps, paupers that generally receive parish relief, but those people who come to ask for relief because they can not get work) should be employed on the road; and it has been very much my wish to gratify that desire by giving them work.'
[201]*B.P.P. 1810-1811 (240) iii. 855*, p. 31.
[202]*Ibid.* p. 32.
[203]*B.P.P. 1819 (509) v. 339*, p. 31.
[204]*B.P.P. 1824 (392) vi. 401*, p. 11 (Select Committee on Labourers' Wages), and *B.P.P. (509) v. 339*, pp. 30-1.
[205]Minutes – 18 December 1816, T9/A2/1 Kent AO.
[206]*B.P.P. 1824 (392) vi. 401*, p. 11.
[207]*Ibid.* p. 11.
[208]*Ibid.* p. 11.

hammers.[209] It would seem that the use of unfree labour and the ruthless exploitation of children was not restricted to the 'dark satanic mills'.

The main objections to employing paupers were that they did as little work as possible and that the work they did was often badly done. James McAdam claimed 'we consider the paupers sent to us by the parishes the worst description of labourers we receive.'[210] In order to overcome their aversion to hard work, piece or 'task' rates were introduced.[211] This, James McAdam said, 'had instilled a spirit of more activity and industry into the operations, as far as the roads are concerned, and that we get very much more labour done for the money'.[212] If the labourers refused to work for piece rates, as many did, they were returned to the parish.[213]

With reference to the parochial system, the Webbs concluded that[214] 'The employment of pauper labour on the roads was as ineffective a device for keeping the highways in good repair as it was for providing for the destitute.' Besides the general inefficiency of pauper labour, workers could not be dismissed if they were idle, 'work had often to be done at the season when it was least effective, because it was then that the labourers needed relief', and 'the distribution of the unemployed [did not] bear any relation to that of the highways requiring repair'.[215] The trusts were able, however, to circumvent many of these difficulties. They hired only the labourers they required, those who did not work were dismissed and the payment of piece rates enabled the trusts to squeeze the maximum amount of work out of their labourers. Furthermore, according to McAdam,[216] most road repair work was undertaken between October and April, a peak period of unemployment. The trusts, by providing employment during these months, thereby helped to relieve the parish poor rates.[217] The conditions under which the paupers laboured were probably not very different from those experienced today by convicts put to work in chain gangs on the roads in the southern United States. For the above reasons it would seem that pauper labour may have been somewhat more effective on the turnpike trusts than on the parish roads. While this labour may not

209 *Ibid.* p. 13.
210 *Ibid.* p. 12.
211 *B.P.P. 1819 (509) v. 339*, pp. 30-1.
212 *B.P.P. 1824 (392) vi. 401*, p. 13.
213 *Ibid.* p. 12.
214 Webbs, *King's Highway*, p. 200.
215 *Ibid.* pp. 199-200.
216 *B.P.P. 1824 (392) vi. 401*, p. 15.
217 *Ibid.* p. 13. *B.P.P. 1819 (509) v. 339*, p. 4. The committee claimed that McAdam's system had increased the employment of the poor

have been as efficient as labour hired on the open market, it seems to have been adequate for the requirements of McAdam's system.

A comprehensive survey of trust labourers' wages has been precluded by the paucity of continuous wage data. Few wage books or vouchers have been uncovered, and most account books show only the total amounts paid for 'day labour'. There are occasional references to wage rates in the trust minutes, and these together with the wage accounts of three trusts provide the basis for the following discussion. The very incomplete nature of the data must necessarily qualify any subsequent conclusions.

The wage-data for the London area consists of references in the minute and account books of the New Cross and Kilburn trusts and the wage books of the Fulham Field Trust[218] (merged with Kensington, Fulham, Chelsea Trust in 1767) for the years 1753–7, 1771–8 and 1787–99.

The Kilburn Trust paid its labourers 1s 4d per day in 1743,[219] and the same rate was offered in 1781.[220] From 1753 to 1755 the Fulham Field Trust paid 1s 4d per day in the winter and 1s 6d in the summer. The seasonal differential was deleted in 1755, and 1s 6d was paid until 1780. The same rate was being offered in 1772 by the New Cross Trust.[221] The Kilburn Trust's labourers petitioned for higher wages in 1795, and their rates were increased to 9s per week.[222] In 1801, wages were again advanced, and the following order was made:[223] 'That in the future and until further orders to the contrary the Labourers to be employed on the Road be paid ten shillings p. week, in consideration of the dearness of Provisions at the present time.' The Kensington Trust increased wages to 1s 8d in 1780, and from 1785 to 1799 paid 1s 8d in the winter and 2s in the summer. In 1800, the advanced price of provisions and the difficulty in finding labourers forced the New Cross Trust to raise wages to 14s per week.[224]

Throughout the eighteenth century road labourers' wages in the metropolis were lower than those received by labourers in the building trades. Gilboy's wage figures show general labourers in Westminster earning 1s 8d

[218]'Surveyors accounts of Cash paid to Labourers 1753-1757', MS 58/9873 Ken. Pub. Lib. 'Accounts of Cash Paid to Labourers 1771-1778', MS 58/9374 Ken. Pub. Lib. 'Weekly accounts of Cash Paid to Labourers 1787-1799', MS 58/9375 Ken. Pub. Lib.

[219]Surveyor's Accounts 1743-72, LA/HW/TP1 Mid. CRO.

[220]Account Ledger 1772-1825, LA/HW/TP5 Mid. CRO.

[221]Account Book 1765-72, T9/F1/2 Kent AO.

[222]Minutes – 29 June 1795, LA/HW/TP2 – Mid. CRO.

[223]Minutes – 12 January 1801, LA/HW/TP3 Mid. CRO.

[224]Minutes – 25 October 1800, T9/A1/3 Kent AO. Carting costs on the Canterbury-Dover Trust rose from 7s per day in 1798 to 10s per day in 1801. Gravel-picking rates also increased from 8d and 6d per load in 1798 to 1s and 8d per load in 1801. The latter rate was paid to women and children (Journal 1799-1802, T6/1 Kent AO).

per day from 1700 to 1787 and craftsmen's labourers being paid some-what more.[225] In Southwark, bricklayers' labourers received 2s from 1727 to 1790 and 2s 2d to 1794,[226] while labourers in Greenwich were paid 1s 8d from 1700 to 1770 and 2s to the end of the century.[227] There is a similar trend in the movement of wages for both these labourers and those who worked on the roads; however, if Gilboy's wages represent 'average London rates among the labourers in a "middling" position', the road labourers must have been in a lower category. This suggests that road work, a job requiring few skills, provided employment for both the unskilled London labourers and those coming from the lower wage rural areas. Referring in 1824 to the London road labourer, James McAdam said:[229] 'I should state that the labourers generally in London are of the very worst class, and, with the exception of the Irish labourers, are generally gentleman's grooms and men who have run away from the country and left their families.'

The wage data for the West Riding come from various minute book references and from two series of wage accounts and vouchers of the Rotherham–Wentworth Trust (1767–72)[230] and the Sheffield–Wakefield Trust (1761–76).[231]

The Wakefield–Weeland Trust paid its labourers 10d per day in 1741,[232] and 9d per day was offered, in 1742, by the Doncaster–Tadcaster Trust.[233] In 1752, the Knaresborough–Green Hammerton Trust paid 1s per day to labourers who agreed to work for an entire season and 10d to those hired on a casual basis.[234] The wages paid by the Rotherham and Sheffield trusts varied considerably. In any one pay period the range could extend from 4d to 1s 6d per day, with as many as nine different rates being paid.[235] To overcome the difficulties of evaluating this wide range of wage rates, figures have been calculated for the number of labourers receiving each wage (November 1761–June 1764) and for the number of days worked at each rate (August 1767–December 1776). Only those rates most frequently paid will be cited here, for these probably represent the average wage of the adult

---

225E. Gilboy, *Wages in Eighteenth-Century England* (Cambridge, Mass. 1934), pp. 8-9.
226*Ibid.* pp. 260-1.
227*Ibid.* p. 47.
228*Ibid.* p. 19.
229*B.P.P. 1824 (392) vi. 401*, p. 14.
230'An Account of the Labº employed under the Direction of Saint. Wroe', WWM A1286 Shef. Cent. Lib.
231Vouchers and Accounts, T.C.406-11, T.C.364-5, T.C.450-2 Shef. Cent. Lib.
232Minutes – 7 May 1741, box 54 West Rid. CRO.
233Minutes – 30 March 1742, box 54 West Rid. CRO.
234Minutes – 21 May 1752, box 27 West Rid. CRO. One week's pay was to be left with the Treasurer as a surety.
235For example, from January to June 1764 labourers were employed at 6d, 8d, 9d, 10d, 1s, 1s 1d, 1s 2d, 1s 3d, and 1s 4d.

male labourer. From November 1761 to June 1764 1s 2d was the rate most frequently paid.[236] From 1767 to 1769 1s 2d, 1s 3d and 1s 4d were the dominant rates, the latter two being paid somewhat more often.[237] By 1770 few labourers were receiving 1s 2d,[238] and from 1771 to 1776 most workers were being offered either 1s 3d or 1s 4d.[239]

Gilboy found that the general labourer in the industrial districts of the West Riding received 1s per day from 1702 to 1756, and that by 1740 this rate was also being paid in the lower-wage area around Knaresborough and Ripon.[240] The figures for turnpike labourers' wages do not agree with her findings, for even the 1s rate paid in 1752 contained a 2d per day incentive bonus, the normal rate being 10d. The small sample of trust wage rates may explain this discrepancy. There is another factor which may account for the difference. Work on buildings and bridges entailed the employment of masons and carpenters and, if London rates are indicative, craftsmen's labourers tended to receive a somewhat higher wage than the general labourer. Also general labourers on building projects were paid more than road labourers. If Gilboy's wages for general labourers in the West Riding were taken primarily from bridge and building accounts, this may explain the lower level of trust wages.[241] While the wages in the Sheffield–Rotherham area were slightly higher than the median wages for industrial districts, the movement of wages was similar to that of general labourers' wages in the West Riding, North Riding and Lancashire.[242]

[236] *Sheffield–Wakefield Trust*

		Labourers paid at		per day	
	1s	1s 1d	1s 2d	1s 3d	1s 4d	other rates
Nov. 1761–Jan. 1762	7	3	19	—	—	5
Feb. 1762–Aug. 1762	2	5	12	1	—	4
Dec. 1762–Sept. 1763	15	—	17	13	—	14
Sept. 1763–Jan. 1764	2	2	13	—	—	12
Jan. 1764–June 1764	9	3	14	6	4	20

[237] *Rotherham–Wentworth Trust*

		Days worked at		per day	
	1s	1s 1d	1s 2d	1s 3d	1s 4d	other rates
Aug. 1767–Feb. 1768	2	—	85	28	169½	73½
1769	57	57½	319	639	314½	72

Sheffield–Wakefield Trust

		Days worked at		per day	
	1s	1s 1d	1s 2d	1s 3d	1s 4d	other rates
1768	23	31	429½	712½	472½	93
1769	4	—	444½	720	714	177½

[238] Rotherham–Wentworth Trust – 1s 2d paid for 82½ days of 978½ days. Sheffield–Wakefield Trust – 1s 2d paid for 47 days of 1,853 days.

[239] There was one period when this was not true. From 3 October to 26 December 1772, the Rotherham–Wentworth Trust paid 1s 2d for 200 of the 578 days worked.

[240] Gilboy, *Wages in Eighteenth-Century England*, p. 177.

[241] She states (*ibid.* p. 176) that the rates for the West Riding are scattered and few. She mentions (n.2 p. 176) five bridge accounts which were included in the series for Ripon. Furthermore, although the justices did repair roads, their primary responsibility was for county bridges and buildings.

[242] Gilboy, *Wages*, pp. 160, 176, 180.

Wage accounts (1767–75)[243] of three farms near the Rotherham–Wentworth and Sheffield–Wakefield trusts, provide data for a comparison of the wages of agricultural workers and road labourers. These farms were not only close to the roads but the overseer, Saintforth Wroe, was also the surveyor for both trusts. The same labourers worked on both trusts' roads, but the names of those employed as farm labourers rarely appeared in the road accounts.[244] From 1767 to 1775 the farm workers were paid 10d and 1s;[245] four to five pence per day less than the road labourers. The considerable difference in the money wage may have been offset to some extent by the perquisites enjoyed by the farm worker.[246] Although the difference in wage rates is greater than that indicated by Gilboy's figures, she found that, except for mowing and during the harvest, the general labourer was paid a slightly higher money wage than the agricultural worker.[247]

Near Wentworth, farm and road work was carried out by two mutually exclusive groups of labourers; however it would seem that in other areas these two employments were combined.[248] This is suggested by the differential wage rates paid in 1752 by the Knaresborough–Green Hammerton Trust,[249] and in 1730 by the Harborough–Loughborough Trust:[250]

Ordered that the Labourers now Imployed [sic] upon the road be allowed Six Shillings p week from the time (June 1st) till Michalmas next and Each man to be paid five Shillings p Week and to have the remainder of his Money paid him upon Michalmas day next provided they Continue the said work till Michalmas Next and if Any of them Desent the Said to have five shillings p week for the Said Worke and no more unless Leave is given them for two or three days in their own Harvest if any to get.

By paying a higher wage to labourers who agreed to work for an entire season, the trusts were attempting to ensure having an adequate work force during the harvest period, when agricultural wages rose. In

243 Wage Accounts, WWM-A1502-05 Shef. Cent. Lib.
244 A comparison of the names on the wage accounts of the farms and the trusts shows that in 1768 none of the farm labourers worked on the roads. In 1769 only three farm labourers did road work.
245 Street Farm — 10d and 1s per day.
  Wentworth — 10d per day.
  Tankerley — 10d per day.
246 Young found that in this area (Ecclesfield and Wentworth House) labourers received 1s and board in 1768 (Gilboy, *Wages*, p. 173).
247 *Ibid.* pp. 52, 80–2, 148–50, 173–5, 259–61, 265–8, 277–9, 280–2.
248 Gilboy, *Wages*, pp. 159, 221.
249 See above, p. 161.
250 Minutes — 1 June 1730, T/MB/1/1 Leics. RO.

Gloucestershire, the Marshfield Trust paid labourers 1s per day from October to March and 1s 2d per day from April to October,[251] and the Stokenchurch Trust (Oxon.) paid an additional 6d per day during the harvest.[252] In 1807 the Kilburn Trust offered its labourers 6d per week more during the hay harvest,[253] and the Kensington Trust paid higher wages during the summer months.[254]

Wages were forced up during the war years by the scarcity of labour, coupled with an increasing demand for agricultural workers and the demand for labour created by the canal mania of the early nineties.[255] By the first decade of the century road labourers in the area of the metropolis were earning from 1s 8d to 2s 2d per day,[256] and in 1810 the Old Street Trust increased labourers' wages from 16s to 18s per week.[257] In Staffordshire, the Cheadle Trust offered 1s 6d in 1793 and 2s 1d in 1808.[258] The Skipton–Colne Trust raised wages from 2s in 1807 to 2s 6d in 1810.[259] The Innings Lane Trust, near Kidderminster, paid 1s 5d in 1807, 1s 6d and 1s 7d in the next two years, and 1s 6d from 1809 to 1813.[260]

There are few wage figures for the immediate post-war years. A comparison of rates paid in the 1820s reveals that the highest wages (2s to 2s 6d per day) were being offered in Lancashire and the West Riding.[261] In the counties to the south, with the exception of London, wages were considerably lower. The Bedfont–Bagshot Trust paid its 'Mile-Men' 12s per week during the 1820s,[262] but the general labourer was paid only 10s.[263] The nearby Hampton–Staines Trust paid 1s 8d

[251] Wage Account 1769-70, D 1610 Glouces. RO.

[252] Minutes – 11 January 1768, Ch.S1 Oxon. CRO. 'that Holiday pay to the Ten Labourers employed by him last Harvest an additional pay of Six pence a day for the Harvest Month ammounting to the Sum of five pounds Eighteen Shillings and sixpence.'

[253] Minutes – 9 July 1807, LA/HW/TP 3 Mid. CRO.

[254] See above, p. 160.

[255] E. L. Jones, 'The Agricultural Labour Market in England, 1739-1872', Econ.Hist.Rev. 2nd ser. XVII, no. 2 (1964), 323-4.

[256] See above, p. 160.

[257] Minutes – 5 September 1810.

[258] Huntley and Wetley Rocks District, Account Book 1762-1830 (1808 rate), D239M box 5 Staffs. RO; Dilhorne District, Account Book 1790-1805, D236M box 7 Staffs. RO. In the same area, 1s 4d per day had been paid in the 1770s (Ipstones Trust, Account Book 1770-1806, 52/31 Wm. Salt Lib.).

[259] Wage Receipts 1807 & 1810, TTL 12-33 Lancs. RO.

[260] Account Journals 1798-1871, 705:585, BA705/1 Worcs. RO.

[261] Sheffield–Wakefield Trust, Receipts 1820 (2s/day), WC1255 Shef. Cent. Lib.; Glossop–Sheffield Trust, Receipts 1826 (2s 4d–2s 8d/day), CPG-8, Shef. Cent. Lib.; Dore Trust, Wage Accounts 1817-18 (2s 2d–2s 6d/day), MB362 Shef. Cent. Lib.

[262] Minutes – 12 April 1815, T.P.Bed.5 Mid. CRO. Also B.P.P. 1833 (703) xv. 409, pp. 78-9. Mile-Men were labourers put in charge of keeping a mile of road in constant repair. They were used on the Bedfont–Bagshot Trust's roads and on the Beaconsfield Road (ibid. pp. 77-9).

[263] Ibid. p. 78.

and 1s 6d in 1825 and in 1829.[264] In Bedfordshire (1822),[265] Worcestershire (1818–21),[266] and Warwickshire (1829)[267] 1s 8d was paid, while in Lincolnshire, between 1825 and 1829, wages were from 1s 8d to 2s.[268] In 1824 James McAdam estimated that in the South-east wages varied from 9s to 14s per week, being generally 10s or 11s.[269] In London, where he claimed some trusts were paying 'extravagant prices', wages ranged from 15s to 18s.[270] In the first report of the Metropolis Trust, in 1826–7, McAdam stated that he had settled a standard wage of 14s per week.[271] The regional wage differences of this period can be ascribed to the increasing demands for labour in the rapidly industrializing North and the availability and use of pauper labour in the southern counties.

Although wages fell in the post-war period, they remained higher than they had been before the 1790s. The popularity of McAdam's system may have been due, in part, to the fact that it relied on the use of inefficient labour (i.e. women, children and old labourers) which was both abundant and inexpensive. It may also be significant that his techniques were more widely employed in the southern areas of the country where labour was least expensive.[272]

6

Under the parish repair system owners or occupiers of lands valued at £50 per year were obliged to provide a cart, horses, tools and two men for six days' work a year. All others in the parish had to labour for six days on the roads.[273] The turnpike trusts were entitled to a portion of this statute duty from the parishes along their roads. In some cases the number of days which the trusts could demand was prescribed in

[264]Minutes – 21 December 1825 and 29 August 1829, T.P.Ham 1 Mid. CRO.
[265]Hitchin–Bedford Trust, Minutes – 1 January 1821, X46/1a Beds. CRO. (In 1822, the following order was made: 'that the wages of the ordinary Labourers on the Road be reduced to 10s/p Week from Saturday next' (ibid. 1 April 1822).)
[266]Innings Lane Trust, Accounts Journal 1798-1871, 705:585, BA 705/1 Worces. RO.
[267]Evesham–Alcester Trust, Surveyor's Accounts 1829-54, CR 446/26 War. CRO.
[268]Lincoln Heath Trust (South East District), Surveyor's Accounts 1825-38, Smith 6/2/4-/6 Lincs. AO.
[269]B.P.P. 1824 (392) vi. 401, p. 11.
[270]Ibid. p. 14.
[271]B.P.P. 1826-1827 (309) vii. 23, p. 21. In 1825 J. L. McAdam reported that road labourers in London were receiving 15s per week (B.P.P. 1825 (355) v. 167, p. 71).
[272]Spiro, 'John Loudon McAdam', pp. 479-83. Of the 25 trusts supervised by the Mc-Adams in 1819, none were north of Birmingham. Of the 137 trusts employing a member of his family on his system in 1825, 42 were north of Birmingham.
[273]Webbs, King's Highway, p. 15.

the local acts,[274] in others the justices in special sessions decided the proportion of statute duty due to the trusts.[275]

The practice of commuting statute duty for money was fairly common during the seventeenth and eighteenth centuries.[276] Persons not wanting to perform their duty simply paid the prescribed fine to the surveyor. In 1712 the Shoreditch–Enfield Trust was authorized to accept £100 a year from the parish of Hackney in lieu of statute duty.[277] From the mid-1730s most trusts were empowered to agree with parishes for a lump sum in place of statute work.[278]

Statute labour was notoriously inefficient,[279] and many trusts may therefore have welcomed the opportunity to commute the duty. It may also have proven advantageous for the parishes, for it seems that in some instances the amount of composition was less than what a man could otherwise earn. From 1746 to 1800 the New Cross Trust received only £2 per year from the parish of Greenwich and other parishes' compositions were similarly low.[280] In 1804 the Greenwich payment rose to £80 a year,[281] and this suggests that it had been extremely low during the preceding period. In 1777 the Sheffield–Wakefield Trust paid its labourers from 1s 3d to 1s 4d per day and its carters from 6s to 7s a day.[282] At the same time, one day's statute labour was commuted at 4d to 8d, and carting at 2s 6d.[283] While some parishes continued to perform statute duty, the practice of commutation became increasingly popular.

In 1835 statute labour was abolished and replaced by a system of parochial rates.[284] Four years later it was estimated that this had cost the trusts about £200,000 a year.[285] However, to many trusts statute duty was of only marginal importance. In 1840, 58·8% of the trusts reported that their securities had not been affected by the abolition of the duty.[286]

274For example, 13 Geo. I c.17, art. 14 (Luton–Westwood Gate Trust).

275This provision was included in most trust acts from the late 1730s. It was also included in the General Act of 1773 (13 Geo. III c.81, art. 63).

276Webbs, *King's Highway*, pp. 33-5.

27712 Anne c.19, art. 22.

27813 Geo. III c.81, art. 63.

279Jackman, *Development of Transportation*, pp. 57-9 and Webbs, *King's Highway*, pp. 28-31.

280Account Books 1739-54, 1765-72, 1788-97, T9/F1/1-/2-/4 Kent AO. In 1718 the parish paid £6 17s 6d. Minutes – 8 July 1718, T9/A1/14 Kent AO.

281Account Book 1798-1813, T9/F1/5.

282See above, p. 162.

283Receipt, T.C. 364-42 Shef. Cent. Lib. Teams were paid 4s 6d per day.

2842 & 3 Vic. c.81.

285*B.P.P. 1839 (295)* ix. *369*, p. iii. This was about 12% of the trusts' yearly income.

286*B.P.P. 1840 (280)* xxvii. *15*, appendix. 639 trusts reported their securities were unaffected by the abolition, while 449 reported the opposite.

7

Throughout the eighteenth century the basic repair techniques employed by the turnpike trusts differed little from those used by the parish surveyors. However, the trusts' more ample financial resources permitted them to apply these traditional methods far more intensively. Salaried surveyors were hired, wage labour replaced inefficient and unwilling statute labour, and unified control was established over long stretches of road formerly repaired by many parishes. Although the trusts were more capable of repairing the roads than the parishes had been, there were many defects in trust repair administration. Most trustees were inexperienced administrators, they were often lax in the performance of their duties, jobbery was widespread and the lack of sound general principles of repair led to much waste and inefficiency. Despite these shortcomings, as has been shown, the repairs undertaken by the trusts proved to be fairly effective and provided benefits for both the road-users and the economy.

In the nineteenth century the trusts' repair techniques and administrative procedures came under increasing criticism. It was during this period, and primarily through the work of Telford and McAdam, that the salient problems of repair and administration were, for the first time, clearly defined and coherent practices postulated to deal with them. The trustees, who had had to rely on an archaic and relatively static body of technical knowledge, could now avail themselves of more effective 'scientific' techniques. The evidence suggests that many did. The rise of the professional surveyor and repair contractor, associated with the growing awareness of the need for greater technical competence, offered the trusts the services of men more capable of successfully undertaking road repair. While faulty administrative practices and ill-considered repair methods continued to be employed, it would seem that generally the trusts were able to keep pace with the demands being made by an ever increasing volume of internal traffic.

In 1840 a parliamentary committee asked the trusts to report on the condition of their roads. While a questionable source, the report does give some idea of the physical state of the turnpike roads. 706 trusts (65·7%) reported that their roads were well-repaired, 233 (21·6%) reported tolerable repair and 135 (12·7%) reported their roads to be in bad condition.[287] These figures lend support to the conclusions reached regarding the beneficial effects of the innovations in repair techniques and administrative procedures.

[287]*B.P.P. 1840 (280) xxvii. 15*, appendix.

8

Movements in the
Cost of Road Transport[1]

A transport improvement is not, from the economic point of view, represented by any physical alteration or addition to the available transport facilities but by a fall in the costs of transport.[2]

The main criterion for assessing the effectiveness of the turnpike trusts is, therefore, whether the facilities which they provided contributed to a reduction in the cost of land transport. Although there is a paucity of data on land carriage rates, the extant material does indicate that these rates tended to decline during the eighteenth century.

The following study is based primarily on the rates for land carriage assessed by the justices of the peace between 1692 and 1827.[3] Referring to these assessments, Professor Willan has concluded that the 'repetition of rates suggests that the justices of the peace were not making an effective assessment, but simply complying with the law in a formal manner'.[4] New material has been uncovered which calls for a reconsideration of this conclusion. By the act of 1748 the justices were to send annually their assessments of the price of land carriage to the clerks of the peace of Westminster, Middlesex and Surrey, and the Lord Mayor of London. These records have survived, and in certain cases provide a fairly continuous series of assessed rates from 1748 to 1827.

---

[1] There are two main reasons why only the cost of land carriage has been dealt with in this book. Firstly, although passenger transport was very important, goods carriage was of greater economic significance. Secondly, the cost of freight transport is a neglected aspect of transport history, while there is a voluminous literature on coaching (for example, Jackman, *Development of Transportation*, pp. 310-45, J. Copeland, *Roads and Their Traffic, 1750-1850* (Newton Abbot, 1968), chps. 4-8) to which little new information can, at this time, be usefully added.

[2] A. M. Milne and J. C. Laight, *Economics of Inland Transport*, p. 18.

[3] The justices were empowered to assess rates by two acts: 3 Wm. & Mary c.12 (1692) and 21 Geo. II c.28 (1748).

[4] T. S. Willan, 'The Justices of the Peace and the Rates of Land Carriage, 1692-1827', *The Journal of Transport History*, v, no. 4 (1962) p. 202.

1

The increasing amount of legislation devoted to the roads, rivers and harbours in the second half of the seventeenth century was the beginning of a concerted attempt to mitigate the limitations imposed on economic expansion by the unimproved transport system. It was within this framework of improvement legislation that the carriage of goods by land first came to the attention of Parliament. The first two acts dealing with parish road repair included clauses limiting carriers' draft power,[5] on the grounds that by restricting their use the roads would be kept in better repair. In 1691, when a further act to strengthen the parish system was being considered, a clause was added giving the justices power to assess the prices charged for land carriage.[6] This power complemented the restrictions laid down in previous acts by granting the justices control over prices in the event of carriers using the restrictions as an excuse for higher charges. This was an extension of the established powers of the justices as administrators of price control, and a development of an earlier precedent. In 1606 the Lord Mayor of London in response to complaints of merchants that the carters were charging excessive rates, fixed the prices that the carmen could take.[7] When in 1672 the carters were apparently charging more than the legal rate the justices of the peace made and advertised a new scheme of charges.[8] The act of 1692 must be viewed, therefore, both within the framework of transport legislation, and against the background of attempts to control prices by justice assessment.

In 1692 the justices of the peace in quarter-sessions were empowered to 'assess and rate the prices of all Land Carriage of Goods whatsoever to be brought into any place or places within their respective Limitts or Jurisdictions by any common Waggoner or Carrier'. They were to assess these rates at each Easter Sessions and communicate the rates fixed to the various market towns within their jurisdiction. The act states the reason for the imposition of this control was that the carriers had combined to raise the price of carriage. Although evidence of their combination is lacking, the possibility that they did cannot be overlooked. The nature of the carrying business with its depots at various London inns gave the carriers ample opportunity to meet and fix rates.[9] Another

[5] 14 Car. II c.6 (1662) and 22 Car. II c.12 (1670).
[6] *J. H. of C.* x, p. 550, 11 Nov. 1691.
[7] Jackman, *Development of Transportation*, p. 131.
[8] *Ibid.* p. 132.
[9] Combination among carriers was not uncommon in the eighteenth century. The carriers of Manchester and those of Birmingham agreed to increase their rates in the 1760s and the West Riding carriers did the same in the last decades of the century. See below, pp. 182, 185.

factor which may have brought about a rise in carriage prices and a need for their control was the increased demands on land transport caused by the war's disruption of coastal trade.

In 1748 another act was passed respecting the justices' power to assess rates of carriage.[10] By this act the justices' assessments, which under the first act were only to apply to goods carried into their jurisdictions, now applied to goods carried both to and from the areas of their control. The magistrates were further required to send their assessments annually to the clerks of the peace in the London area and the Lord Mayor of London. Why in 1748 was the justices' authority reviewed and strengthened? The reasons are to be found both in the conditions of the period and the parliamentary activity prior to the act's passage.

Between 1692 and 1748 the roads had received increasing legislative attention. The growing demands for improvement were reflected both in the enactment of turnpike trusts and in acts restricting the use of the roads. Because these acts sought to limit road users, tension was created between them and the supporters of this legislation. This conflict of interests was a major theme underlying the road improvement legislation of the eighteenth century.

Although there were those who opposed specific turnpike trusts, a more concerted opposition was directed against stipulations in the general acts for 'Preservation of the Highways'. There were four such acts passed between 1695 and 1715, all of which sought to limit the draft powers of wagons.[11] In 1719 an act was passed which further curtailed draft power and made it mandatory for wagons to have wheels bound with streaks of two and a half inches when worn.[12] It was this last provision which gave rise to strong protest from both the carriers and those who used their services. The carriers of Leicester, Derby, and Nottingham presented petitions in 1719 complaining that the act hindered them in their business.[13] In 1721 a petition was presented by the 'Carriers and Waggoners who carry Goods for Hire' which said that although they had tried to conform to the letter of the law,

many vagrant and idle Persons take Advantage of the Petitioners, if the Streaks of their Wheels are worn ever so little within the Bredth of Two Inches and a Half, by taking off one or more of their Horses, and detaining them until they have extorted considerable Sums from the Petitioners, and make it their Business to follow and meet the Petitioners, for that Purpose.[14]

The evidence presented to the committee showed that in certain areas

[10]21 Geo. II c.28.
[11]7 Wm. III c.29 (1695/6); 6 Anne c.29 (1707); 9 Anne c.18 (1711); 1 Geo. I c.11 (1715).
[12]5 Geo. I c.12.
[13] *J. H. of C.* xix, pp. 211, 233.
[14]*J. H. of C.* xix, p. 680.

informers were systematically harassing the carriers.[15] Although it was resolved to bring in a bill to amend the act, it was dropped after the first reading. More petitions came in against the act in 1729; this time from those who made use of the carriers' services. A petition from the gentlemen, farmers and traders of Dudley stated

for that before the making thereof (5 Geo. I) many Farmers, who had not constant employ for their Teams, would at leisure times carry Goods from *London*, and other Places for Hire, whereby they kept down the exorbitant Demands of common Carriers, and now the Farmers do not think it worth while to be at the Expense of altering their Wheels

and the price of carriage had consequently increased by one third.[16] Similar petitions were presented from Leicester, Birmingham, the City of London and the Cutlers of Sheffield.[17] Committee witnesses claimed that the act had created a shortage of carriers, driven up prices and forced goods to be shipped by circuitous sea routes.[18] Again it was resolved to repeal the act, and again it was defeated.[19] It was not until 1740, in another act for 'Preservation of the Highways', that the clause dealing with the breadth of wheels was repealed.[20]

In 1744 the laws respecting the highways were again brought up for review. A committee was ordered at the end of January to bring in a bill to render more effectual the laws for the 'Preservation of the Highways'.[21] In February the committee was instructed to include a clause dealing with the justices' assessment of the rates of carriage.[22] There was, however, strong opposition from many parts of the country and the bill was dropped.[23] The opposition claimed that the restrictions imposed on carriers would greatly raise the price of land carriage. No mention is made of the clause for rate assessment, and it is assumed that they were either unaware of it, or being aware did not find it contrary to their interests. The bill was revived in 1747 and passed in 1748 without opposition.[24] Seen against the background of road legislation the inclusion of the clause increasing the justices' power

---

[15]*Ibid.* pp. 685, 689. Witnesses claimed that they had been forced to pay off professional informers on certain roads to ensure against seizure of their horses.
[16]*J. H. of C.* xxi, pp. 463-4.
[17]*Ibid.* pp. 463-4, 472.
[18]*J. H. of C.* xxli, p. 486.
[19]*Ibid.* p. 584.
[20]14 Geo. II c.42. The wheel breadth restriction was only repealed in the summer months. A weight limit of 6,000 lb was added, and turnpike trusts were authorized to erect weighing engines and take 20s for every hundredweight over the prescribed limit.
[21]*J. H. of C.* xxiv, p. 730.
[22]*Ibid.* p. 757.
[23]*Ibid.* pp. 783, 787-8, 795, 801, 803, 806, 808-10, 812, 814-17, 824-5, 839, 846, 851.
[24]21 Geo. II c.28.

emerges as a conciliatory measure. It would seem that it was intended to placate those concerned with raising carriage prices, while not compromising those wanting further restrictions. The clause was a successful compromise in that the strong opposition to the first act in 1744 was not renewed against its successor in 1748. There were also other factors which may have made it necessary to strengthen the justices' power in this period.

The clause was first introduced during the war years when the greater demands being made on land transport may have meant increasing prices. A petition from Wakefield against the proposed bill in 1744 mentioned that it would have been wrong to impose limits on carriers at a time when it was impossible to send goods by sea.[25] Another reason for the inclusion of the clause is cited in the act: 'whereas no Rates for the Carriage of Goods from distant Parts of the Kingdom to the City of London and Places adjacent have yet been settled; and several Common Waggoners and Carriers have from then taken the Occasion to Enhance the Price'.[26] The act of 1692 gave the justices power to fix rates for the carriage of goods into their jurisdictions; and although the Middlesex Justices thought of doing so they never did assess rates.[27] The problems created by the consequent one-way assessment are well illustrated in a letter from Bath to the Deputy Recorder of London in 1727:

When you was here last season I had the honour of talking w'th you a'bt the impositions of our Comon Carriage for want of a rate on the Bath carriage of Goods from this place to London, in asking all people pay 9s4d p. hundred, when the Carrage downe is but 7s (and that to much by a shilling) that on such talke you farther favored me w'th your promise that a rate persuant to the Act should be made at the next Easter quarter Sessions for the Carriage of Goods from Bath to London and Midde.... and humbly begg that a Rate for the prices of Carrage may be made at 6s p. hundred. It being a shilling more than from Bristole ... it being a general Complaint here by all Strangers What prices you settle from this hall.[28]

The difficulty of fixing rates to so many different areas may have been why the justices never settled the charges. The provision of 21 Geo. I was a solution to this problem.

2

Before discussing the trends of assessed prices something needs to be said about the different types of assessments and to whom they

[25]*J. H. of C.* xxiv, p. 810.
[26]21 Geo. I c.28.
[27]Willan, 'Justices of the Peace', p. 198.
[28]Ra. Car. 1825-7 and Misc. Mid. CRO.

applied. The returns varied from county to county, both in their detail and the manner in which the rates were prescribed. Some justices settled the rates at so much per hundredweight per mile, while others fixed the price for carriage between certain towns. The most common type of assessment was that made for goods carried to and from London. Over the entire period, of the forty-six areas from which returns were submitted, thirty-nine set London rates. Besides the London rates, in sixteen of the thirty-nine areas rates were settled between provincial towns. Seventeen areas had assessments in hundredweight per mile ratios and of these, eleven were made in conjunction with London rates. Clearly, the justices' major concern was setting the price for carriage to and from the metropolis.[29] Over time, however, this bias decreased. At the end of the eighteenth century rates for carriage between provincial towns became more common, as did assessments in hundredweight per mile ratios. Of the eleven areas submitting returns for the first time after 1800, four were in hundredweight per mile, five had both London and inter-provincial rates, and only two gave solely London rates. While London remained most important, the greater diversity of justice assessments denotes a concern with expanding inland markets. This is especially the case in the North, with assessments made between many towns in Lancashire, Yorkshire, and Northumberland.

Besides returning their assessments to London, the justices in the North also sent assessments to other towns. The Newcastle returns (1768) were ordered to be sent to Doncaster, York, Leeds, Pontefract and Edinburgh, and the Leeds returns (1766) were sent to York, Newcastle-upon-Tyne, Rochdale and Manchester. The charges were thereby made known in areas in which they were relevant. This was done on the justices' initiative, for by the Act of 1748 they were only liable to send returns to London and the market towns within their respective jurisdictions.

Although there were no outstanding regional price variations over the period, the returns show that it was generally cheaper to carry goods along the main routes. In 1750 it cost 6.3d–8.3d per ton-mile for carriage from London along the Western Road to Bristol.[30] In the same period the carriage to Devon or Cornwall was 16d per ton-mile.[31] From

29All mention of *returns* refer to the returns made to Middlesex and Westminster, Ra.Car. 1748-1827 Mid. CRO. A few returns were also found at the Corporation of London Record Office (Misc. MSS. 30.1).

30Ra.Car. 1750 Mid. CRO. For the carriage of 'heavy goods' by wagon: 5s per cwt from March to September and 6s per cwt from September to March. The distance from London to Bristol is taken as 116 miles.

31Ra.Car. Mid. CRO. Cornwall 1765-6 (8d per cwt for every 10 miles). Devon 1758-68 (8d per cwt for every 10 miles).

York to London was 12*d* per ton–mile, while from York to Bridlington or Scarborough cost 16*d* per ton–mile.[32] In 1827 the West Riding justices allowed one-half less for goods brought via the London road. Cheaper carriage prices on the main routes point to the beneficial effects of turnpike trusts, employed to the greatest extent on these roads. The greater volume of goods carried on the arterial roads, by assuring the carriers of full loads, may have also contributed to the lower prices.

While the justices' primary concern was assessing the prices for wagon carriage, they fixed rates for other types of conveyance as well. In some early returns rates were given for carriage by horse although in later years this assessment was usually not included.[33] The disappearance of this assessment denotes the changeover from the more expensive and less efficient pack-horse to the wagon.[34] The justices' attention was given solely to carriage by wagon until the 1800s when rates began to be included for parcel carriage by coach and van, or 'flying wagon'.[35] Carriage by coach or van was generally from 30% to 100% more expensive than by wagon,[36] although, as with the wagon, cheaper on the main routes. In 1826 from Newcastle-upon-Tyne to London it was 2*s* 9*d* per stone by wagon and 4*s* 1*d* per stone by coach. The coach rates from Newcastle to eleven other towns were double or more than double the wagon rates.[37] Cheaper coach carriage on the main routes supports the conclusion reached with regard to lower wagon prices along these routes. Also the returns mirror the development of carrier services, and show that by the early nineteenth century goods' carriage could be obtained at a price to speed ratio.[38] The diversified demands of commerce

---

[32]Ra.Car. Mid. CRO. 1751. York–London 15*d* per stone (200 miles). York–Scarborough 4*d* per stone (40 miles). York–Bridlington 4*d* per stone (40 miles).

[33]Shropshire and Cheshire in 1692 and 1693 respectively, assessed rates for horse carriage (Willan, 'Justices of the Peace', p. 199), but by 1750 neither area returned such assessments. Bristol (1750), Devonshire (1758–82), Cumberland (1772) and the West Riding assessed pack-horse rates. However, except for the West Riding no other area made these rates after 1782. (Ra.Car. Mid. CRO.)

[34]Pack-horse carriage was from 1*s*–2*s* more than by wagon in Devon (1771), and about the same in Bristol (1750). (Ra.Car. Mid. CRO.)

[35]The only exceptions to this are returns from the City of Lincoln (from 1764) and from Kesteven, Lincs. (from 1768), in which rates were assessed for carriage by stage coach.

[36]There is difficulty in comparing the rates because they varied with distance, and did not always maintain a constant ratio. For example, from Chester coach carriage was six times more expensive than by wagon for 10 miles, but only twice as expensive for 90 miles.

[37]From Newcastle to: (selected rates)		*Wagon*	*Coach*
	York	10*d*/stone	1*s* 6*d*/stone
	Lancaster	1*s*/stone	2*s*/stone
	Leeds	10*d*/stone	2*s*/stone
	Darlington	4½*d*/stone	1*s*/stone

[38]This is not to say that 'fly wagons' and coach carriage were new in the nineteenth century, but only that the returns show their increased use and importance in the later period.

were therefore reflected and accommodated by the variety of services offered.

The returns show not only the prices assessed for land carriage, but also the characteristics of the charges. The Bristol return of 1750 listed higher prices for the carriage of light and bulky goods such as deal boxes and chairs, than for 'heavy goods as Linnen, Grocery, and Saltery'. The Chester carriers were allowed to take one-half more for the carriage of light or hazardous goods,[39] and the Boston justices granted extra charges, not to exceed one-fourth, for parcels of a disproportionate bulk.[40] The cost of carriage was therefore not only a function of weight, but also of volume. Many returns, expecially in the early years, gave higher rates for goods' carriage in the winter than the summer. The Leicester assessments were 6d per cwt more in the winter months (1750–99), and in Boston the winter rates were 2s per cwt higher than the summer rates from 1749–57, and 1s per cwt higher from 1758 to 1780. This meant that the bad roads and high feed costs more than offset the greater number of farmers available as carriers in the winter months. By the beginning of the nineteenth century most returns ceased making a distinction between winter and summer rates. While the exact reasons for this are unclear, it may have been due to improved roads, and a more regularized and competitive carrying trade.[41] Indeed, Willan's recent study of Abraham Dent suggests that road transport services were both regular and well organized, and that at least from the 1770s there was little difficulty sending goods in the winter months.[42]

Since the majority of the assessments were for carriage to and from London and between the provincial centres, they were most relevant to the carriers travelling these routes. Although an oversimplification, for the present study two main types of carriers may be distinguished: the professional and the part-time carrier. The former regularly travelled a prescribed route and was often listed in the local directory. He may have been a long-distance carrier, as Pickford's or Jackson's, or a local carrier of the type employed by Peter Stubs.[43] The professionals, especially those carrying to and from the metropolis, plied their trade on the main routes, and were therefore directly affected by the justices' assessments. Indeed it was the 'London Carriers' who petitioned the

[39]Ra. Car. 1826, Mid. CRO.

[40]Ra. Car. 1814, Mid. CRO.

[41]Jackman, *Development of Transportation*, p. 340, notes the same occurrence with coaches which ceased making seasonal rates in the second half of the eighteenth century.

[42]T. S. Willan, *An Eighteenth-century Shopkeeper Abraham Dent of Kirkby Stephen* (Manchester, 1970), pp. 80, 109-10.

[43]T. S. Ashton, *An Eighteenth Century Industrialist: Peter Stubs of Warrington 1756-1806* (Manchester, 1961), pp. 87-92.

West Riding Quarter-Sessions for increases in the assessed rates.[44] The part-time carrier, usually a farmer hired to haul agricultural goods or the product of local industry, carried for short distances and sold his services on a day-to-day basis.[45] Although he may have carried between the provincial centres or to London, he was mainly concerned with carriage in a limited area and therefore not directly bound by the official rates. However, while the justices' assessments seem to refer mainly to the professional carriers, the factors affecting the assessed rates, such as feed costs, the cost of wagons and horses and depreciation, would also have influenced the prices taken by the part-time carriers. In this sense the assessed rates give an overall picture of the movements in the price of land carriage.

3[46]

Were the rates assessed by the justices valid, and were they adjusted relative to changing conditions? Professor Willan poses these questions and concludes that the justices did not conscientiously settle the prices for land carriage.[47] Indeed, the scarcity of evidence about the rates fixed under the first act makes it difficult to arrive at a definite conclusion as to the act's effectiveness. This is not, however, the case after 1748. The returns sent to London provided an excellent picture of assessed rates in certain areas to 1827. The question of whether these official rates were similar to those taken by the carriers can be answered, in part, by a comparison with actual prices charged for goods' carriage, and by looking at the method by which the justices assessed the rates.

In 1716 the Middlesex justices appointed a committee to set the rates of carriage.[48] They were to have 'regard and making difference of the prices in respect of the number of miles which Comon waggoners or Carriers doe brung such goods ... and in carrying the same in the sumer or winter Season'.[49] Charles Midlyrot, a justice on the committee, directed Thomas Wilkinson, the assistant to the Deputy Clerk, to find out the rates charged for goods' carriage. Wilkinson proceeded with

---

[44]*Leeds Intelligencer*, 17 April 1781, p. 3; 14 April 1794, p. 1; 13 April 1795, p. 1; 13 January 1800, p. 3.

[45]The distinction between 'professional' and 'part-time' carrier is artificial in that the two groups overlapped and there were many types of carriers within each category. R. A. Lewis, 'Transport for Eighteenth-Century Ironworks', *Economica* (N.S.) XVIII, No. 7 (1951), describes organization of part-time carriers including farmers, husbandmen or tenants who did hauling as part of their leases. See also: Alfred Fell, *The Early Iron Industry of Furness and District* (Ulverston, 1908), p. 302.

[46]The assessed rates are given in Appendix H.

[47]Willan, 'Justices of the Peace', p. 202.

[48]Quarter-Sessions Papers Middlesex QS, MSP-AP/72 Mid. CRO.

[49]*Ibid.*

the investigation and sent Midlyrot a letter detailing what he had found:[50]

I have endeavored to find out the prices w'th are taken by waggoners & Carriers for the carriage of goods to this Towne, but have not obtained soe full acc't thereof as I was in Hopes I should, the acc't w'th I have obtained is as fol: Goods bro't by waggon between 40 & 50 miles pay 3s 6d in the sumer time and 4s p. ⊕ in the winter time
60 miles 5s p. ⊕ both in sumer and winter time
70 miles the like prices
90 miles 1d p. po.d both in sumer and winter time
100 miles 3/4 p. po.d by some waggoners & 1d p. po.d by others in the sumer time & 1d p. po.d in the winter time
150 miles 8s p. ⊕ and when under ⊕ then 1d p.pd. both in sumer and winter time.[51]

However, the justices made no use of Wilkinson's list and never settled the rates for carriage. It would seem by this account that, at least at the initial stages, the justices enquired into the prices charged for goods' carriage. If this was true in other counties, the rates assessed in 1692 may may have been a fairly accurate reflection of the actual prices being demanded. It is possible, however, that justices may have attempted to bring down prices by making low assessments.

Once the initial rates had been settled, how and why were they adjusted? Two cases have been found which indicate that the carriers were responsible for initiating increased assessments. In 1780 the West Riding justices lowered the assessed rates for goods carried to and from London.[52] The following year the London Carriers advertised their intention to petition the Pontefract Sessions for higher rates,[53] which they were successful in obtaining.[54] In 1794, 1795, 1800 and again in 1809 the carriers followed the same procedure and were granted permission to take higher rates.[55] The same method was used in 1794 by the Fellowship of Carters, who petitioned the City of London for an increase in the rates they might demand.[56] While the solicitation for

[50]*Ibid.* MSP-AP/73.
[51]*Ibid.* Wilkinson also listed prices for carriage by packhorse which were from 50% to 100% more expensive than by wagon.
[52]*Leeds Intelligencer*, 25 April 1780, p. 1—the justices advertised the reduction of London rates (reduced by 1d/stone). Also Ra.Car. 1780 Mid. CRO.
[53]*Leeds Intelligencer*, 17 April 1781, p. 3.
[54]Ra.Car. 1782 Mid. CRO.
[55]*Leeds Intelligencer*, 14 April 1794, p. 1; 13 April 1795, p. 1; 13 January 1800, p. 3. Also, Mid.CRO, 1794, 1795, 1800 and 1809.
[56]Misc.MSS.30.1 (Corporation of London Record Office). An account sheet of the costs of petitioning the City for higher rates. They petitioned and were ordered to advertise their demands, which they did. When they again presented the petition they were met by opposition from the merchants, but, after a counter-memorial from the carters, the rates were raised one tenth. The total cost of these proceedings was £50 17s 4d.

increased assessments came from the carriers, the justices were responsible for downward adjustment. If the West Riding is indicative, once the alleged reason for higher charges had lapsed the justices lowered the rates. The carriers cited the high price of grain as the reason they wanted increased rates.[57] The West Riding assessments from 1794 to 1809 closely parallel the movement in grain prices, indicating that the justices were exercising their authority by lowering the rates as corn prices decreased. The justice–carrier relationship is clearly shown by the following note appended to the rate schedule in 1809: 'The above rates may be taken until the next Pontefract Sessions unless the Price of Corn shall in the mean time be materially lower in which case the Carriers have undertaken to reduce the Rates in such Proportion as the Justices shall think reasonable' The West Riding evidence not only demonstrates the process by which assessed rates were adjusted, but also supports the validity of the area's assessments from 1780 to 1809.

Although information on the actual prices taken by carriers is fragmentary, a few documents have been found which generally support the validity of the justices' assessments. The only series of vouchers found for the early period was for Sir George Savile's estate at Rufford, Notts.[58] While the prices paid by Savile were higher than those fixed by the East Retford Quarter-Sessions, they moved in close sympathy with the official rates.[59] The assessed rates were lowered in 1754, 1757, and again in 1761; the price dropping by 1s 6d per cwt over the period. Savile paid 9s 4d per cwt (Rufford to London) from 1748 to 1759, and in 1760 the price decreased by 1s 4d, to 8s per cwt.[60] Although the vouchers do not show an exact price correlation, they do point to the justice rates as being an accurate reflection of the trends in land transport charges, and also lend validity to the downward movement of assessed rates in this period. In 1766 a committee was ordered by the House of Commons to enquire into the prices charged for goods' carriage and the weights drawn by carriers.[61] On finding that eighteen counties had not submitted returns the committee resolved that the law was not being implemented.[62] However, it was contended by

---

57See below, p. 185.

58Savile Papers: DDSR 206/2, 206/4-16 and DDSR 210/20-23, Notts. CRO.

59It is not clear whether the East Retford assessment applied to Rufford. The return gives the rates as covering carriage to London from Harworth, Worksop, Blyth, Barnby Moor, Retford, Tuxford, and places adjacent. While Rufford is close, it is outside the area bounded by these towns. Also Rufford is in the Hatfield Division of the county; and, although certain of the towns mentioned in the return are in this division, East Retford itself is in the North Clay Division.

60Savile used the services of five London Carriers, and that their rates decreased simultaneously shows that these lower rates were taken generally.

61*J. H. of C.* xxx, p. 526.

62*J. H. of C.* xxx, p. 608.

witnesses that 'in those Places where the Price of Carriage has been settled by the Quarter Sessions they usually take the full price from Gentlemen, and somewhat less from tradesmen, as Tradesmen's Goods are, in general, much heavier in Proportion to the space they occupy'.[63] While these two examples are not sufficient to verify the validity of the assessed rates in the period, after 1794 there is good evidence of correlation between assessed and actual charges.

By 1799 Peter Stubs paid 1s 9d per cwt for goods carried from Sheffield to Macclesfield, and by March of the following year the price had risen to 2s 6d.[64] The rates he paid for carriage from Rotherham to Manchester also increased from 2s in 1799 to 3s – 2s 9d in 1800.[65] While these rates were lower than those assessed by the West Riding justices, they moved in conjunction with the assessed rates. The prices charged between Warrington and Manchester rose in 1792, increased sharply in 1800 and then declined from the end of 1801 to 1804.[66] The rates from Leeds to London show a similar movement, doubling between 1793 and 1800.[67] These charges also follow the trends of assessed rates. In November 1799, the New Cross Trust allowed their gravel contractors an extra $\frac{1}{2}d$ per load per mile, due to the 'very great advance in the prices of keeping horses'.[68] Clearly, the rising charges in 1800 were not confined to the professional carriers. The limited material discovered on actual prices and the method of assessment shows that the justices' rates in this period were close to those taken, and that the direction of change of the assessed rates was mirrored by the movement of actual prices. Nevertheless, the evidence of actual charges is for the most part thin, and it is therefore necessary to scrutinize the movement of assessed prices in order to ascertain whether or not these official rates could have been a valid reflection of the actual charges.

4

The continued validity of the rates assessed under the act of 1692 is questionable; however, as has been suggested, the rates set in 1692 may reflect fairly accurately the prices prevailing in that year.[69] These rates can, therefore, be used in conjuction with the rates assessed in

---

63 *Ibid.*
64 Ashton, *Peter Stubs*, pp. 89-90.
65 *Ibid.* p. 90.
66 *Ibid.*
67 Jackman, *Development of Transportation*, pp. 720-1.
68 Minutes – 30 November 1799, T9/A1/3 Kent AO.
69 'It is doubtful whether the assessment of carriage rates was effective, except perhaps during the first few years after passing the Act of 1692' (Willan, 'Justices of the Peace', p. 202).

the 1750s, to indicate the long-term movement of land carriage rates.

The Northamptonshire justices set the rates of carriage from Northampton to London at 4s per cwt in 1710,[70] and reduced their assessment to 3s 6d per cwt in 1743. Charles Duke charged 4s per cwt for goods carried from London to Northampton in 1806.[71] Taking into account the considerable rise in the general price level over the period, this indicates a dramatic fall in land transport charges. The North Riding assessment (to London) was 18s 4d per cwt in 1692, 16s per cwt in 1727 and 10s per cwt in 1758. The receipts for goods carriage from London to York, found by Thorold Rogers,[72] show a similar trend (16s per cwt – 1705, 12s per cwt – 1743, 10s 8d per cwt – 1753).[73] The Buckinghamshire assessment fell from 1s 2d/cwt/mile in 1692 to 6d/cwt/mile in 1756, and the West Riding assessment (to London) 9s 4d per cwt in 1692 was lowered to 8s per cwt in 1750. In Lincolnshire, Cheshire and Shropshire, assessments were higher in the 1750s than they had been in the seventeenth century;[74] however, these rates began to decline in the late fifties and early sixties.

While this evidence is not conclusive, it does suggest that land transport charges had been lowered by the middle of the eighteenth century. In the 1720s, Defoe commented:[75]

The benefit of these turnpikes appear now to be so great, and the people in all places begin to be so sensible of it, that it is incredible what effect it has already had upon trade in the countries where it is more completely finish'd; even the carriage of goods is abated in some places, *6d.* per hundred weight, in some places *12d.* per hundred, which is abundantly more advantageous to commerce than the charge paid amounts to, and yet at the same time the expense is paid by the carriers too, who make the abatement; so that the benefit in abating the rate of carriage is wholly and simply the tradesmens, not the carriers.

An observer in 1752 claimed 'carriage in general is now thirty *per Cent* cheaper than before the Roads were amended by Turnpikes'.[76] He ascribed this change to the fact that the improved roads had made travel easier and faster, and by allowing carriers to draw greater weights

[70]Rates were also assessed to many other towns in the county. These rates also declined in 1743. (D(CA) 96 Northam. RO.)
[71]Receipt 30 April 1806, YZ. 7073 Northam. RO.
[72]J. E. T. Rogers, *A History of Agriculture and Prices in England*, Vol. VII (Oxford, 1902), p. 533.
[73]The 1753 charge approximates the 1751 York assessment of 10s/cwt.
[74]Willan notes that both the Cheshire and Shropshire rates were inordinately low (Willan, 'Justices of the Peace', p. 199).
[75]Defoe, *A Tour*, Vol. II, p. 129.
[76]*The Farmers and Traders Apprehensions of a Rise upon Carriage* (London, 1752), p. 5.

with the same number of horses, had reduced costs.[77] The general highway acts suggest that, in fact, the weights drawn by the carriers were increasing. In 1662 the maximum weight which wagons could draw was set at twenty cwt in winter and thirty cwt in summer.[78] Presumably these were considered to be fairly heavy loads. By 1741 the limit had been raised to sixty cwt,[79] and twenty-four years later stood at six tons.[80] Furthermore, in 1662 waggoners were permitted to have seven horses in draft, and by 1751[81] they were allowed but five.[82] Greater weights carried by fewer draft animals denotes a rise in the efficiency of road transport and an increase in the productivity of capital invested in its facilities. In light of this, the turnpike trusts established during the first half of the eighteenth century represent an important transport improvement in the economic sense. This lends support to the view that the significance of trust development before the 'Turnpike Mania' has been seriously underestimated.[83]

From 1754 to 1767 assessed rates[84] continued to fall even though the conditions of the period were such as to make increased charges more likely. Wages and prices were rising from 1754 and the improvement in both internal commerce and exports meant a greater demand for carriers' services. During this period carriers' costs were also increasing. From 1754 wagons were required to have nine-inch wheels, and a heavy penalty was taken from those who did not comply.[85] This increased expenses by forcing carriers to re-equip or at least modify their wagons. The factor central to all demands for advanced rates, the price of horse-feed, was also high in these years. Why then did the justices lower the assessments? Better roads and a series of concessions granted to carriers from 1753 to 1765 provides a partial answer.

Were the advantages offered by improved roads offset by the toll charges? Even if we accept for argument that they were, from 1754 to 1765 the General Highway Acts by offering preferential treatment to the users of broad wheeled wagons largely negated any adverse effects of toll charges on the carriers. The first 'Broad Wheel Act' was passed

[77]Ibid. pp. 8-9.
[78]14 Car. II c.6.
[79]14 Geo. II c.42.
[80]5 Geo. III c.28. These weights were the minimum allowed, for wagons with larger wheels were permitted to carry greater weights. See below, p. 182.
[81]24 Geo. II c.43.
[82]In 1767 (7 Geo. III c.40) wagons with less than 9-inch wheels were allowed only four horses. As with weights, wagons having wide wheels were permitted to be drawn by more animals. See below, p. 182.
[83]See above, p. 56.
[84]The rates discussed in the following section will be those to and from London by wagon.
[85]26 Geo. II c.30. The penalty was to be £5 or one horse. Coaches were exempted, as were wagons with fewer than five horses and two-wheeled carts with fewer than four.

G

in 1753,[86] by which wagons (drawn by more than five horses) with wheels less than nine inches wide, were prohibited on the turnpike roads. The carrot to this stick was that wagons with nine-inch wheels could be drawn by up to eight horses, carry unlimited weight, and in certain instances be granted lower tolls. This was a great incentive for carriers to change to nine-inch wheels, for by former acts they had been limited to six horses and a maximum weight of sixty cwt.[87] Further, in 1755, to encourage the use of broad wheels, wagons which adopted them were allowed to pass all turnpikes toll-free for three years.[88] This blanket exemption was dropped in 1757, and in its place half-tolls were granted on broad wheel wagons at gates within 100 miles of London.[89] In 1765, because of protests that the unlimited weights allowed were ruining the roads, all preference was withdrawn and a six ton weight limit imposed.[90] This prompted an immediate reaction from the Manchester carriers:

The undermentioned persons take this method of acquainting their friends and customers, the People in trade, that they are under an unavoidable necessity of raising the price of Carriage of Goods to and from London etc., owing to the great advance in toll on Broad Wheel Waggons and the reduction of Weight they have heretofore been allowed to carry, as well as the additional Expense at the Inns through the scarcity of Hay and the bad crops and Oats and Beans, the said advance will take place at Michaelmas next, and they humbly hope no person will take umbradge at it.—James Pickford, Hulse, Widdens and Higginson, Catherine Mille, Wilham Bass, John Swaine, Richard Overall, John Farrow, Thomas Pyott, Thomas Washington, William Stubbs.[91]

While the price of horse feed had been high since 1763, it was not until the broad wheeled wagon no longer received special consideration that the Manchester carriers found it necessary to advance their prices. It seems that the carriers had not overlooked the advantage of the nine-inch wheel.[92] Improved roads on which carriers could draw unlimited weights at low tolls may therefore have offset the effects of both high

---

[86] 26 Geo. II c.30.

[87] 5 Geo. I c.12, six horse limit and 2½-inch wheels. 14 Geo. II c.42 rescinded wheel provision for the summer months, kept horse limit, added 60 cwt limit, and gave turnpike trusts the authority to erect weighing engines.

[88] 28 Geo. II c.17.

[89] 30 Geo. II c.28.

[90] 5 Geo. III c.38. If wagons had axle trees of different lengths so that the nine-inch wheels rolled a sixteen-inch path they were granted half-tolls, and unlimited weight. The nine-inch wheel still was allowed to draw more weight than the narrow wheel; six tons as against 60 cwt.

[91] *Manchester Mercury*, 21 Sept. 1765 (found in Pickford's Records, Pic. 4-14). British Railways Board; Historical Records Dept.

[92] A petition from the farmers and traders of Worcester in 1760 complained that with all the advantages given to the broad wheeled wagon few used them, except stage wagons (*J. H. of C.* xxviii, p. 790). Also see Jackman, *Development of Transportation*, pp. 306-7.

feed prices and the cost of re-equipment. Especially from 1755 to 1758, when oat prices increased sharply, the toll-free carriers had a cost advantage that lessened the effects of high-price horse-feed.[93] This factor may have been reinforced by some fall in the volume of inland trade during the sixties as a result of bad harvests, less exports and a sluggish home market.[94] This being the case, the justice rates in the period to 1765 may indeed have been an accurate reflection of the movement in actual prices.

From 1765 to 1775 assessments remained stable or continued to decrease in spite of generally unfavourable conditions. The carriers were not only faced with the loss of toll concessions on nine-inch wheels,[95] but also with higher feed costs – the price of oats being generally higher in these years than in the 1750s. In Birmingham in 1763[96] and Manchester in 1765, carriage charges rose because of the high price of horse-keep, and it is likely that carriage rates in other parts of the country were also affected. If, as it seems, the price of 'Horse Corn' was in the short-run the major factor determining carriage charges, the movement in assessed rates prior to 1795 is puzzling. Before 1775 only two areas returned higher assessments. In 1775 and 1776 six more areas increased their rates, perhaps as a late recognition of the high feed prices. From 1776 to 1782, however, oat prices were lower than in the preceding six years, and by 1782 of the eight areas that had earlier advanced their rates four had again lowered them. The decline of foreign and inland trade during much of the American War of Independence may again have exerted its effect. Because of the few returns it is difficult to tell whether the assessments were adjusted from the middle 80s to the early 90s, but they do not seem to have been.[97] Either the justices had lost touch with actual price movements, or there were factors which stabilized carriage charges.

[93] Only one example of carriers' costs has been found. This is for the Pickford's wagons between Sheffield and Manchester in 1835. It shows of a total cost for two wagons, of £2,455 8s 0d (not including feed), the toll charges were £1,123 4s 0d or about 40% of the total. Even allowing for a reduction because of fewer turnpikes in 1750, it still represents a large cost factor. (Pickford's Records, Pic. 4/7 – pp. 82-3.)

[94] A. H. John, 'Miles Nightingale-Drysalter', Econ. Hist. Rev. XVIII, no. 1 (1965), 161-3.

[95] The nine-inch wheel was still allowed more favoured treatment (see p. 182) than the narrow wheel, although the toll concession was not granted. By 7 Geo. III c.40 (1767) the wagons rolling a sixteen-inch path were allowed half-tolls at gates within 100 miles of London. If the carriers employed these wagons they would have had lower tolls until 1773 when 13 Geo. III c.84 repealed this provision.

[96] A. H. John, 'Agricultural Productivity', p. 28.

[97] From 1783 to 1794 there were but few returns found in London. This does not mean that assessments were not made. For Lindsey (Lincs.), assessments were found for 1785, 87, 89 and 90 – (Lincs. Archive Office) As W10/81 2-5, 16 & 19. The Leeds QS were still making assessments in 1795, though no returns were found (Leeds Intelligencer, 29 April 1795, p. 1). The Durham assessment of 1801 was also not returned to London (Newcastle Advertizer, 6 June 1801, p. 1).

While grain prices, especially from 1770–5 and 1783–94, created an upward pressure on carriage rates, long-run factors were probably tending to lower carriers' charges. By improving roads, the extension of turnpikes afforded greater speed of transport. This is suggested by the increased speed of coach travel.[98] The coach trip between London and Edinburgh took ten days in 1754 but only four in 1776.[99] The travelling time between London and Shrewsbury was reduced from three and a half days in 1753 to one and a half days in 1772, and similar savings were realized on other routes.[100] If, as seems likely, the carriers too were able to travel faster this would have meant lower costs and also enabled them to get a higher return on their capital – wagons and horses. Another factor which may have contributed to lower charges was the increasing competition in the carrying trade. 'If, in other branches of trade, evidence has been found of partial monopoly, in road transport there is little sign of anything but pure competition; and rivalry, indeed, was so keen that carriers sometimes overstepped the bonds of honesty in their scramble for business.'[101] Although improved roads and active competition may have offset the effects of high grain prices, it is difficult to quantify the extent of their influence.

One further observation may be made on the pre-war period. It is improbable that the prices fixed by the justices were taken *per se* by the carriers. It seems they were rather a ceiling under which the prices charged were allowed to fluctuate. The rate from London to Leeds in 1791–2 was 6s per cwt,[102] while the assessment was 7s 4d per cwt.[103] In 1793 Wormold & Co. paid approximately 2s 7d per cwt for the carriage of machinery from Manchester to Leeds.[104] In 1782 the Leeds–Manchester rate was assessed at 3s 4d per cwt. The prices paid by Peter Stubs were also below those fixed by the justices. Given that they served as a maximum upper limit and not a fixed price this may in part explain the ambiguity in the justices' assessments before the war years. If the limits set were high enough there would have been no need for advanced assessments before 1794. Hick, Peech & Co. charged 4s per cwt for carriage from Newcastle-upon-Tyne to Leeds in 1791,[105] and the assessment set in 1768 was also *4s per cwt.*[106]

---

[98]No comparative data for carriers has been found.
[99]Jackman, *Development of Transportation*, p. 335.
[100]*Ibid.* pp. 335–9.
[101]Ashton, *Peter Stubs*, p. 88. Combination to increase charges was not, however, unknown. See above, p. 182.
[102]*Leeds Intelligencer*, 4 October 1791, p. 4.
[103]West Riding assessment 1793, Ra.Car. 1793 Mid. CRO. This assessment was the same as that made in 1782.
[104]W. B. Crump (ed.), *The Leeds Woollen Industry 1780–1820* (Leeds, 1931), p. 21n.
[105]*Leeds Intelligencer*, 27 December 1791, p. 4.
[106]Newcastle-upon-Tyne assessment 1768, Ra.Car. 1768 Mid. CRO.

William and Isaac Frewer, the proprietors of the weekly stage wagon between London and Ipswich, from 1774 to 1796, charged 5s per cwt for carriage from London to Saxmondham.[107] While it is impossible to argue from these few examples, they show that it was not unlikely that there was relative price stability during this period. However, more supporting evidence is needed before a satisfactory appraisal can be made of the justice assessments in this period.

After 1794 there is more evidence available, and the reasons for and relevance of the justice rates can be seen more clearly. As has been said, the increased assessments in the West Riding were called for by the carriers. In 1794 and again in 1795 the 'London Carriers' were given permission by the quarter-sessions to take higher rates.[108] The reason given for the increased charges was the high prices of horses and horse provisions and, indeed, grain prices were high from 1794 to 1796. Though returns from other areas are sparse, the assessed rates for the cities of York and Lincoln were higher in 1795. With the fall in grain prices after 1796 the justices decreased the rates, for in 1799 both the West Riding and the City of York had lower assessments. From 1799 to 1801 the price of grain rose sharply, and in 1800 the following notice appears in the Leeds' paper:

We the undersigned Magistrates acting for the West Riding of the County of York, having been applied to by the Carriers in the said Riding to make further Advance, upon Land Carriage, on Account of the very High Price of Hay and Corn, and it being our opinion that an Advance is reasonable & proper do hereby signify our Approbation... to an ADVANCE of THREE-HALF-PENCE per STONE on LAND CARRIAGE... and do strongly recommend it to all Persons to allow the same.[109]

The assessed rates for the West Riding were doubled in 1800, but the carriers agreed with the justices to take lower rates in the following year.[110] There were no other returns for 1800; however, in 1801 assessments advanced in Southampton, York, the North Riding,

107 Receipts for Carriage, 1774–96, Rous Family Archives, Hall/c7/1/1-36 Ips. and E.Suf. RO. Frewer's charges were about 10½d/ton/mile, and the Suffolk assessment for 1809 was 14d/ton/mile. This correlates with the percentage increases in other parts of the country.

108 Leeds Intelligencer, 19 May 1794, p. 1 and 20 April 1795, p. 2. Both are notices by carriers to merchants, tradesmen, and gentlemen of the increased rates allowed by the quarter-sessions; the first by Jackson & Co. to merchants, etc., and the second by Jackson, Willan & Co., Jackson & Heaton, and Thomas Hadfield to the merchants, etc., of Leeds, Wakefield, Bradford, Huddersfield and Halifax. The advertisement of rates shows that those who used the carriers were made aware of the official rates. Rates were also advertised in Leicester, Leicester and Nottingham Journal, April and May 1760 to 1775.

109 Leeds Intelligencer, 20 January 1800, p. 3.

110 Note appended to West Riding assessment in 1801, Ra. Car. 1801 Mid. CRO.

Shrewsbury, Louth, and Newcastle-upon-Tyne. The Leicestershire assessment, unchanged since 1750, was higher in 1799, and the Durham justices, who had not previously made a return to London, in 1801 advertised a schedule of rates.[111] It is not surprising, in a period of general price increase, that the carriers' charges rose. The greater demand for carriers' services generated by rapid agricultural and industrial development was in part responsible, but undoubtedly the major factor was the increased price of horse-keep. Hay and oat prices rose by 16% and 23% respectively from 1793 to 1799, and from 1799 to 1800 increased by one-third.[112] When in 1801 the prices of grain began to decrease the assessed rates soon followed.

Assessments in York, Southampton, and the West Riding were lower by 1802. Although other areas did not show the same movement, for the North Riding the assessed rates were stable for the next seven years. In 1808 grain prices began to rise, and in 1809 four areas returned increased assessments. As indicated in the West Riding return, feed costs were again the excuse for taking higher rates.[113] In 1812 grain prices began decreasing, and, although two areas increased their assessments in 1814, by 1816 many had lowered their official rates. For the next ten years the movement in assessed prices is mixed, but the trend is generally upward, the six areas showing higher assessments by 1826.

5

There are many problems in using the justice assessments as an indication of the movement in actual prices, but a few tentative conclusions may be drawn from the information they provide. Firstly, while recognizing the need for more supporting evidence especially for the years 1700–48 and 1765–94, it would seem that the justice rates provide an overall picture of land transport charges and their level. In light of this the price of land carriage tended to be lower in the 1750s than at the beginning of the century, and this underlines the significance of turnpike development during the first half of the century. In the late fifties and early sixties charges tended to be stable and relatively lower than in the early 1750s, at a time when prices were rising and increased economic activity was making greater demands on road services. Therefore, apart from the effect of canals, the turnpiking of roads and the increased number of carriers had a beneficial effect and contributed to the expansion after 1765. Thirdly, although wartime

[111]See above, p. 183n.
[112]J. E. T. Rogers, *History of Agriculture*, Vols. VI and VII.
[113]West Riding assessment 1809, note appended to return, Ra. Car. 1809 Mid. CRO.

grain shortages made a marked impression on the cost of land carriage, the percentage rise in these costs was generally lower than the percentage rise in prices. This is in fact, a continuation of the trends established between 1765 and 1794. Finally, transport costs were higher on many routes after 1815 than before the war, the fall in 1816 being, for the most part, temporary. This supports, in view of contemporary falling prices and the distress of many small farmers, the belief that the volume of internal trade was rising. The higher charges of this period also provide the background for railway development.

Summary and Conclusions

1

The first turnpike authority, formed in 1663, was designed to provide temporary financial assistance for the parishes responsible for repairing a portion of the heavily travelled Great North Road. This was not, however, an attempt on the part of Parliament to foster a new road repair system. The legislators, aware that many parishes were finding it increasingly difficult to maintain their roads in the face of the growing demands being made by the steady increase in the volume of traffic, sought instead to strengthen the existing parochial system. It was only after 1691, when the power to levy rates to supplement statute duty was made permanent, that Parliament turned once again to the toll device in order to meet the demands of those parishes which under the new law still could not properly maintain their roads.

The use of the new turnpike device spread slowly at first, for besides a generally unsettled political situation, there was also much hostility both locally and at Westminister toward what must have been seen as a vexatious new tax. This particular objection may have lost some of its force from the early eighteenth century when the administration of the turnpikes was taken from the official authority of the justices of the peace in quarter-sessions and given to independent groups of locally appointed commissioners. It was in this form that the turnpike trusts gradually became accepted as the method of dealing with the problem of increasingly costly road maintenance. Originally conceived as a temporary device they became virtually permanent through repeated renewal acts; and the tolls, initially envisaged as supplementary to statute duty became, in effect, a replacement for that duty and the means by which all major road improvement was to be financed during the eighteenth and early nineteenth centuries.

The pattern of early trust development underlined the importance of London in both society and the economy,[1] for it was the roads near the metropolis and the main London trunk routes, the most heavily travelled

[1] For an interesting discussion of this question see E. A. Wrigley, 'A simple model of London's Importance in Changing English Society and Economy 1650-1750', *Past and Present*, no. 37 (1967), pp. 44-70.

and therefore the most costly to repair, which were the first to be turnpiked. By 1750 most of the main roads between London and the provincial centres, as well as a number of important inter-provincial routes, had been almost completely turnpiked, and by the mid-1770s an interconnected and fairly comprehensive network of improved roads had been formed. Furthermore, it is apparent that trust development in these years was highly integrated and not as the Webbs have alleged scattered and unconnected. The following years saw short bursts of trust creations which extended the turnpike network, especially in the rapidly industrializing North. By the mid-1830s the country had an extensive turnpike road system consisting of over one thousand trusts, controlling over 20,000 miles of main road and disposing of about one and a half million pounds of toll receipts each year.

In 1839 a select committee report was presented on 'how far the formation of Railroads may affect the interests of Turnpike Trusts'. The committee concluded that the railways had materially affected the turnpike trusts, and they also claimed that the decrease in some trusts' revenues could be explained by the greater number of 'Steam vessels plying on Rivers and as coasting traders'.[2] Generalizing further from their findings they observed:[3]

Whenever mechanical power has been substituted for animal power, the result has hitherto been, that the labour is performed at a cheaper rate; it must, therefore, appear very doubtful whether any circumstance will ever restore the transit trade to its former channel, the course of science, and its concomitant, improved mechanical power, being found seldom to be retrograde, but generally advance.

These views proved to be substantially correct. Where railways provided alternative services coaches and wagons could not compete, and this in turn led to a reduction in toll receipts on the roads affected. For example, a coaching proprietor claimed that the opening of the London–Birmingham Railway had forced him to reduce the number of coaches on this route from nine to two.[4] The passengers using these remaining coaches were, he said, 'mostly people who are timid people, and do not like to go by railroad', and he feared that the number of 'timid people' was rapidly declining.[5] Not surprisingly the toll receipts of the trusts along the road showed a substantial drop: from £29,525 in 1836, before the railway, to £15,789 in 1839 three years after it had opened.[6] This

[2] B.P.P. 1839 (295) ix. 369, p. iii.
[3] Ibid. p. iii.
[4] Ibid. p. 8.
[5] Ibid. p. 10.
[6] Ibid. p. 66.

story was repeated, with some variation, throughout the country, and by 1848 total national toll receipts had decreased by almost 25% from their 1837 level.[7] The railroads did give rise to some increased traffic on feeder roads but their overall effect was sharply to decrease the demand for long and medium distance road transport, and thereby reduce the use and usefulness of the turnpike trusts. This change in the trusts' fortunes was aptly summed up in the introduction to the 1851 Report on turnpike trusts in Kent:

In 1833 Turnpike Roads were the chief means of communication throughout the kingdom for the transit of goods and passengers; much expense and skill had been bestowed in adapting the roads to the increased traffic of goods, and the more speedy passage of the mails and stage coaches. From this period railways have gradually superseded the use of Turnpike Roads for the conveyance of goods and passengers, except for short distances and local convenience, and the Turnpike Roads in a large majority of the counties are assuming more the character of ordinary highways. From the reduction of income, the Trustees have been compelled, in numerous instances, either to abandon the repair of the roads to the parishes, or to discontinue the payment of interest of the debt.[8]

It is reasonably clear that from the 1840s the turnpike trusts were becoming increasingly redundant. But how important had they been in the years before the advent of the railways? What, if anything, had they contributed towards economic development? On the most general level it can be said that the improved road system by contributing towards the lowering of carriage costs enhanced the opportunity for investment both through widening the market and because the more reliable year-round services freed industrialists from having to hold capital in the form of large raw material or finished goods inventories. The landed interests also benefited, for improved roads tended to enhance an area's competitive position and thereby contributed towards higher rents.[9] Furthermore, better roads made travel easier and in this way helped to break down parochial and regional isolation and this was important in promoting economic and social change. However these factors in themselves provide neither an adequate analysis of the relationship between improved transport and economic development nor a method for assessing the relative success or failure of the turnpike trusts. As a guide to these questions it is instructive to consider some work that has lately been done on the growth of the railways in the United States.

---

[7]*B.P.P. 1851 (18) xlviii.* Toll receipts were £1,509,985 in 1837 and £1,140,918 in 1848.
[8]*B.P.P. 1851 (18) xlviii*, p. 3.
[9]See below, p. 195.

2

In recent years attempts have been made to test some of the long-standing qualitative generalizations made about the effects of specific transport innovations on economic growth. Probably the two best known of these studies are those by A. Fishlow and R. W. Fogel on United States railway development.[10] No attempt will be made either to summarize or evaluate these works for the many complex problems which they raise defy a simple précis. It is rather their general approach, their rigorous definition of the problems and their general conclusions which are of relevance to this study. In trying to gauge the significance of railway development for the United States economy it was necessary for both Fishlow and Fogel to calculate the direct and indirect benefits (social savings) accruing from the railways, the social rate of return and the derived demand from railway construction (Rostow's backward linkages). For the roads the latter factor is of little importance as the material demands made for road construction were relatively negligible,[11] but the questions of social savings and social rate of return are of central importance.

Fishlow begins his study by clearly defining the possible effects of innovation in transport:[12]

First, there is the direct consequence of lower cost of carriage of goods and persons. The ability of the railroad to produce transport services at a lower cost has an analogue in lessened resource requirements. Thus overland transport rates of fifteen cents a ton–mile imply the consumption of fifteen cents of labor, capital, and entrepreneurial inputs for the unit output. A railroad rate of three cents, say, means that twelve cents of inputs formerly needed can be applied to other tasks. The difference in costs of transportation due to the introduction of the railroad therefore provides one measure of the increased production it made possible.

He also distinguishes the related effect of the increase in the size of the market stemming from the lower transport costs:[13]

A larger market meant both a more specialized one and one in which expansion might be more profitable. The greater the specialization at the moment in time, the higher the real income of all through concentration upon activities they perform especially well . . . The greater the incentives for expansion, the

10Albert Fishlow, *American Railroads and the Transformation of the Ante-Bellum Economy* (Cambridge, Mass. 1965). Robert William Fogel, *Railroads and American Economic Growth: Essays in Econometric History* (Baltimore, 1964).
11This is not to suggest that the turnpike trusts' demands for paving-stones, gravel, bricks for bridges and drains, etc. were not important locally.
12Fishlow, *American Railroads*, p. 14.
13*Ibid.* p. 15.

greater is the potentiality of capital formation and technological progress, and thus the higher the rate of growth over time.

The first effect gives rise to direct benefits which can be measured, while the more indirect benefits accruing from a larger market area are more difficult to quantify, although by no means of lesser importance.

In order to calculate the direct benefits Fishlow compares the total cost of transport by rail in a given year with the cost of the most efficient alternative route. 'The difference between the costs incurred under the two regimes then is the measure of direct benefits.'[14] Although the relevant calculations are rather complex and give rise to numerous procedural difficulties, the availability of data relating to the volume of goods carried, the distances of journeys and the costs of transport make it possible for Fishlow to arrive at a fairly meaningful estimate. To the direct benefits he adds net railway earnings, and the total of these two amounts over time as a percentage of railway capital provides a figure for the internal rate of return.[15] By 1859 Fishlow estimates that the railways were realizing an internal rate of return of about 15%.[16] Despite this highly favourable rate he concludes that the indirect effects of the railways were probably of greater importance for the United States economy in the ante-bellum period, and that therefore the internal rate of return understates the social rate of return.[17]

The indirect effects of transport innovation can be distinguished as the net increase in incomes generated by the demands of the project itself, i.e. steel for the railways, and/or by the production possibilities brought into view by the reduction in transport costs. The latter case is directly related to the observations made above as to the effects of an increase in the size of the market. Paul David lays particular stress on 'the importance of more subtle indirect influences transmitted via backward-linkages from the railroad sector – indirect effects involving scale economies, or learning effects dependent upon the volume of production of goods specifically needed by railroads'.[18] However, as Fishlow points out, 'Although we can identify induced development sequences, whether arising from derived demand or forward linkages, it is a herculean task to assign values to them because the alternative path of growth is largely unknown.'[19] There is, in fact, considerable

[14]*Ibid*. p. 32.

[15]*Ibid*. pp. 18–95. This is to be distinguished from the normal meaning of an internal rate of return, which would generally only include private earnings.

[16]Fishlow, *American Railroads*, p. 54.

[17]*Ibid*. p. 305.

[18]Paul David, 'Transport Innovation and Economic Growth: Professor Fogel on and off the Rails', *Econ.Hist.Rev.* XXII, No. 3 (1969), 519.

[19]Fishlow, *American Railroads*, p. 304.

debate as to what significance should be attached to these secondary benefits in modern cost–benefit analysis.[20] McKean has shown how the inclusion of these benefits can often lead to double-counting. For example:

Over-counting . . . occurs whenever both the value of the increased agricultural output and the increased value of the land are counted as benefits. . . . The increase in the land valuation reflects the market's capitalization of the value of the new output stream, and both increases in value can not be realized at the same time.[21]

He also argues that there are no secondary benefits created when there is full employment, and that even if there are unemployed or under-employed resources the practical difficulties of measurement and fore-casting should generally preclude attempts at calculating secondary benefits in cost–benefit analyses.[22] However, for our purposes these problems are relatively unimportant. Our period was not one of full employment, and while the danger of double-counting must be kept in mind, we need only a very rough idea as to the importance of the turnpike trusts' indirect effects, not a figure upon which to base an investment decision.

The lack of even the most basic statistical data for the period of this study precludes any attempt at quantification similar to that undertaken by Fishlow. Nonetheless, the concept of a social rate of return does provide a useful framework within which the contribution of the turn-pikes can be discussed and assessed. As Paul David has observed,[23] the social rate of return is important for it indicates 'whether this particular innovation afforded opportunities for utilizing resources in a manner that yielded higher rates of return than those obtainable in other direc-tions'. It is clear that if the relevant data were available we would want to derive figures for private earnings, direct and indirect benefits, the capital value of the turnpike trusts and from this to calculate the social rate of return.

The turnpike trusts were formed to administer sections of the King's Highway and were therefore, unlike the railways and canals, not essentially profit-making ventures.[24] However, the interest payments made to the trusts' creditors can be considered as the private earnings of the turnpike trusts. Although non-payment of interest modifies the

20 A. R. Prest and R. Turvey, 'Cost-Benefit Analysis: A Survey', in *Surveys of Economic Theory*, Vol. III (London, 1966), pp. 160-2.
21 R. N. McKean, *Efficiency in Government Through Systems Analysis* (New York, 1958), p. 152.
22 *Ibid.* pp. 154-67.
23 David, 'Transport Innovation', p. 521.
24 See above, p. 93.

picture to some extent, in the years for which we have data the average rate of return was above the prevailing long-term market rate.[25] For example, in 1829 the average rate of return, as measured by the interest payments actually made, was 3·74%,[26] while the market rate stood at 3·3%. Subsequently the rate of return rose to 4·07% in 1834 and 4·16% in 1837, compared with a market rate of 3·3% in both years.[27] While this return seems fairly reasonable when seen against the market rate, it is difficult to judge whether the difference between the two rates was sufficient to account for relatively greater risk involved in trust investment. The trusts' return also compares rather unfavourably with the dividends paid by some canals. For example, in 1829 the Loughborough Navigation was paying yearly dividends of 140%, while the Birmingham and Erewash canals paid about 70%.[28] These were, however, unusually high returns for in 1825 it was reported that of eighty canals investigated the average return was 5·75%.[29] Many canals paid no dividends at all, and in the southern counties the average return on capital invested in canals and river navigations was about 2·5% in 1842,[30] while the turnpike trusts in these counties paid on average 4·5% in 1834 and 4·1% in 1837.[31]

The direct and indirect benefits to which the turnpike trusts gave rise are virtually impossible to measure, and even if it were possible it would be difficult to derive a meaningful figure for the amount of capital embodied in the trusts.[32] But if does seem clear that the trusts were instrumental in lowering carriage costs. Although fragmentary, the evidence presented above does suggest quite substantial cost reductions by the mid-eighteenth century and a continued fall in the following years. While the effects of competition probably contributed to these lower costs, evidence of faster rates of travel and heavier loads being drawn by fewer animals suggests that the improved roads were also an important, if not the central factor in explaining lower charges. Despite inexperienced and often inefficient administration by trustees as well as incompetence on the part of surveyors, the fact that toll charges did not result in higher carriage charges indicates that the levy imposed was on average more than compensated for by the better facilities

[25]As indicated by the yield on Consuls.
[26]B.P.P. 1833 (703) xv. 409, p. 174.
[27]B.P.P. 1836 (2) xlvii. 297 and B.P.P. 1839 (447) xliv. 299.
[28]Jackman, Development of Transportation, p. 426.
[29]Ibid. p. 419.
[30]C. Hadfield, The Canals of Southern England (London, 1955), pp. 333-4.
[31]The counties were Cornwall, Devon, Dorset, Gloucester, Hampshire, Kent, Somerset, Surrey, Sussex, and Wiltshire.
[32]Current research being undertaken by a group led by Professor S. Pollard into capital formation during the Industrial Revolution should help clarify this aspect of the problem.

provided. On these grounds it can be argued that the trusts gave rise to positive direct benefits.

It was expressly to derive these direct benefits that a good deal of trust investment, as well as other transport investments, was undertaken. The landed interests and the industrialists gained considerably from improved roads, and the reasons given for supporting road schemes were often couched in terms which suggested to the investor not so much the direct return he would earn in the form of interest but rather the benefits he would derive from better transport facilities.[33] Fishlow notes a similar phenomenon in the case of early railroad development in the United States:[34]

Although many of the indirect effects of railroads inevitably were external to the enterprise, they could accrue to the *owners* of that enterprise. Thus land owners invested in railroads not for the private return the projects earned, but for the indirect transport advantages that ultimately raised his land value. The manufacturer contributed, not only for the dividends he received, but for the additional profits he could subsequently earn. Appeals were always phrased in such terms, and the long rolls of investors proximate to the line testify to their success. This method of internalization enabled the private market response nonetheless to reflect external economies.

It is only possible to guess at the importance of the indirect benefits stemming from the turnpike trusts. But if, as it would seem, lower transport costs helped to extend the market and thereby brought new production possibilities into view, it could be argued that in any final reckoning indirect benefits would tend to increase the social rate of return.

The inability to quantify, even to a limited degree, the direct and indirect benefits makes it impossible to estimate the social rate of return with any degree of accuracy. However, the private rate of return does provide the lower limit of the social rate of return,[35] and it can therefore be claimed that the turnpike trusts gave rise to a social rate of return of at least 4% and most probably more. This return must have varied quite considerably over time. In the first half of the eighteenth century and during the 'Turnpike Mania' the roads and road transport were probably of greater relative importance for the economy than after the canals became widespread.[36] Also the greatest percentage fall

---

[33]See above, pp. 102-3.

[34]Fishlow, *American Railroads*, pp. 309-10.

[35]It must be remembered, however, that the private rate of return is calculated on the amount of the trust's mortgage debt — whereas the social rate of return is calculated on the value of the capital embodied in the trusts, and presumably the capital value of the trusts was greater than their mortgage debt.

[36]Flinn, *Origins of the Industrial Revolution*, pp. 96-7.

in carriage charges seems to have taken place by the 1760s. The social rate of return may therefore have been considerably higher in this period than in the early decades of the nineteenth century. As Flinn has observed:[37]

The role of turnpike roads in economic development is often underestimated . . . Inland industrial towns such as Manchester, Birmingham, Sheffield and Leeds could hardly have existed without the extensive use of roads for their industrial traffic . . . the development of turnpike roads (before 1760) was preparatory to subsequent industrial advance.

However, as industry expanded in the late eighteenth and nineteenth centuries the increased scale of its transport requirements progressively reduced the utility of road transport. While roads may have been a major channel for industrial traffic throughout much of the eighteenth century, the changing character of this traffic during the Industrial Revolution increased the importance of other forms of transport.

The canal's contribution to economic growth overshadowed that of the turnpike trusts. On average private returns were higher, the savings in carriage costs (direct benefits) more dramatic[38] and the indirect benefits probably more extensive. However, despite cases of canal–road rivalry,[39] by and large these sectors complemented one another. The canals and rivers excelled in the carriage of bulky low-value goods over long distances, while the roads were more important in the transport of passengers, the mails and goods for which speed or security of delivery were essential. The fact that carriers, such as Pickford's,[40] combined land and water services underlines this complementarity. Although canals may have been generally more profitable with regard to both private and social rates of return the improved road system afforded by the turnpike trusts was also necessary, and their lower rate of return does not indicate that the funds invested in the trusts were misallocated.[41]

From the seventeenth century the improvement of roads, rivers and harbours and canal building had proceeded side by side fulfilling the demands made by an expanding economy and creating in the process a transport system characterized by a high degree of complementarity. The railways effectively put an end to this for they offered severe competition to all the other transport sectors. The roads were the first and hardest hit victim. As the economy moved into the new age of

[37] *Ibid.*
[38] Jackman, *Development of Transportation*, pp. 724–9.
[39] Hadfield, *Canals of Southern England*, pp. 19, 81.
[40] C. Hadfield, *The Canals of the East Midlands* (Newton Abbot, 1966), p. 130.
[41] This is not to deny that funds were misallocated with regard to individual trusts or canals, a good number of which proved both unnecessary and unprofitable.

Victorian prosperity the railways made the turnpikes increasingly obsolete, and in most cases the trusts soon became nothing more than relics of the early Industrial Revolution. But this should not obscure the fact that by the 1840s the much maligned turnpike trust, an important part of English life for over 150 years, had made a most significant contribution to economic development before and during the Industrial Revolution.

Appendices

APPENDIX A

New Acts for the Improvement of Harbours and Rivers, 1662-1750[1]

Year	River or Harbour	Act
1662	Rivers Salwerp and Stower	14 Car. II c.14 Pr.
—	Rivers Wye and Lugg	— c.15 Pr.
—	Dover Harbour	— c.27
1663	Wells Harbour	15 Car. II c.5 Pr.
1664/5	Bristowe Causey (Surrey) to Thames	16 & 17 Car. II c.6 Pr.
—	River Avon (Christchurch–New Sarum)	— c.11 Pr.
—	River Medway	— c.12 Pr.
—	'divers Rivers'	— c.13 Pr.
1670	Great Yarmouth Harbour	22 Car. II c.2
—	Rivers Brandon and Wavney	— c.16 Pr.
1670/1	River Trent	22 & 23 Car. II c.25 Pr.
—	River Wey	— c.26 Pr.
1678	River Vale (Cornwall)	30 Car. II c.20 Pr.
1696/7	Bridlington Harbour	8 & 9 Wm. III c.29
1697/8	Bridgwater Harbour	9 Wm. III c.12
—	River Colne (Wivenhoe–Colchester)	— c.19
1698	River Tone	10 Wm. III c.8
—	Rivers Aire and Calder	— c.25
—	River Trent	— c.26
1698/9	River Larke	11 Wm. III c.22
—	Rivers Avon and Frome	— c.23
—	River Dee	— c.24
1700/1	Minehead Harbour	12 & 13 Wm. III c.9
1702	Whitby Harbour	1 Anne c.13
—	River Derwent	— c.14
—	River Cam	1 Anne Stat. 2 c.11
1705	River Stour	4 & 5 Anne c.2
1707	Watchett Harbour	6 Anne c.69
1708	Whitehaven Harbour	7 Anne c.9
1709	Plymouth Harbour	8 Anne c.4
—	Liverpool Harbour	— c.8
1711	River Avon (Bristol)	10 Anne c.2
1713	River Nen	13 Anne c.19
1715	River Kennet	1 Geo. I c.24 Pr.
1717	River Wear and Sunderland Harbour	3 Geo. I c.3 Pr.
1720	River Derwent	6 Geo. I c.27
—	River Ouse (Great)	— c.29
—	River Douglas	— c.28

[1]This table does not include renewal acts.

Year	River or Harbour	Act
1720	River Idle	6 Geo. I c.30
1721	River Weaver	7 Geo. I c.10
—	Rivers Mersey and Irwell	— c.15
—	River Dane	— c.17
1722	Bridport Harbour	8 Geo. I c.11
—	River Eden	— c.14
1723	Rivers leading into Great Yarmouth	9 Geo. I c.10
—	Rye Harbour	— c.30
1725	Margate Harbour	11 Geo. I c.3
—	Patton Harbour	— c.16
1726	River Don (Doncaster–Tinsley)	12 Geo. I c.38
1727	Beverly Beck	13 Geo. I c.4
—	River Don (Doncaster–Bramley Dun)	— c.30
—	River Ouse (Yorkshire)	— c.33
1730	River Stroudwater	3 Geo. II c.11
1731	Newhaven Harbour	4 Geo. II c.17
—	Ilfracombe Harbour	— c.19
1732	Scarborough Harbour	5 Geo. II c.11
1733	Littlehampton Harbour	6 Geo. II c.12
1734	River Weaver	7 Geo. II c.28
1737	Worsley Brook	10 Geo. II c.11
—	River Roding	— c.33
1739	River Lea	12 Geo. II c.32
1740	River Don	13 Geo. II c.11
1747	Southwold Harbour	20 Geo. II c.14
1749	Ellenfoot Harbour	22 Geo. II c.6
—	Ramsgate and Sandwich Harbours	— c.40
1750	River Lune	23 Geo. II c.12

APPENDIX B

The Turnpike Acts 1663-1836

The acts in this appendix are, with a few exceptions, new acts which initiated trusts on previously un-turnpiked roads. Renewal acts, consolidation acts and amending acts have not been included. Only the terminal points of the main roads turnpiked have been recorded.

The 'Areas' are as follows:

(1) Middlesex (Middx.), Buckinghamshire (Bucks.), Essex, Hertfordshire (Herts.) and Berkshire (Berks.).
(2) Surrey (Surr.), Sussex (Suss.), Hampshire (Hants.) and Kent.
(3) Norfolk (Norf.), Suffolk (Suff.), Lincolnshire (Lincs.) and eastern Cambridgeshire (Cambs.).
(4) Wiltshire (Wilts.), Gloucestershire (Glos.), Herefordshire (Heref.) and northern Somerset (Somer.).
(5) Devon, Dorset, Cornwall (Corn.) and southern Somerset (Somer.).
(6) Cambridgeshire (Cambs.), Bedfordshire (Beds.), Northamptonshire (Northants.) and Huntingdonshire (Hunts.).
(7) The area south of Birmingham to the borders of the other areas.
(8) The area north of Birmingham to the borders of the other areas.
(9) Derbyshire (Derbys.), Leicestershire (Leices.), Nottinghamshire (Notts.).
(10) Yorkshire (Yorks.) and Lancashire (Lancs.).
(11) Cumberland (Cumber.), Westmorland (Westmor.), Durham, and Northumberland (Northum.).

New Turnpike Acts

Year	Road	County	Area	Act
1663	Wadesmill–Stilton	Herts., Hunts., Cambs.	(6)	(15 Car. II c.1)
1695	Shenfield–Harwich	Essex	(1)	(7 & 8 Wm. III c.9)
—	Wymondham–Attleborough	Norf.	(3)	(— c.26)
1696/7	Reigate–Crawley	Suss. & Surr.	(2)	(8 & 9 Wm. III c.15)
1697/8	Gloucester–Birdlip Hill	Glos.	(4)	(9 Wm. III c.18)
1702	Thornwood–Woodford	Essex	(1)	(1 Anne c.10)
1705	Barnhill–Hutton	Ches.	(8)	(4 & 5 Anne c.26)
1706	Fornhill–Stony Stratford	Beds. & Bucks.	(6)	(6 Anne c.4)
—	Hockliffe–Woburn	Beds.	(6)	(— c.13)
—	Shepherds' Shore–Devizes	Wilts.	(4)	(— c.26)
1707	Roads leading into Bath[1]	Somer.	(4)	(— c.42)
—	Cherhill–Calne	Wilts.	(4)	(— c.76)
—	Old Stratford–Dunchurch	War. & Northants.	(7)	(— c.77)
1709	Stoke Golding–Northampton	Bucks. & Northants.	(6)	(8 Anne c.9)
—	Sevenoaks–Tunbridge Wells	Kent	(2)	(— c.20)
1710	Royston–Wansford Bridge	Herts., Cambs., Hunts.	(6)	(9 Anne c.14)
—	Portsmouth–Petersfield	Hants.	(2)	(— c.33)
—	Dunstable–Hockliffe	Beds.	(6)	(— c.34)
1711	Kilburn Bridge–Sparrow's Herne	Middx. & Herts.	(1)	(10 Anne c.3)
—	Highgate–Barnet	Middx. & Herts.	(1)	(— c.4)
—	Northfleet–Rochester	Kent	(2)	(— c.16)
—	Ipswich–Clayton, etc.[2]	Suff.	(3)	(— c.42)
1713	Shoreditch–Enfield	Middx. & Herts.	(1)	(12 Anne c.19)
1714	Shepherds' Shore–Horsley	Wilts.	(4)	(13 Anne c.17)
—	Worcester–Droitwich	Worces.	(7)	(— c.27)
—	Reading–Puntfield	Berks.	(1)	(— c.28)
—	Tittensor–Lawton	Staffs.	(8)	(— c.31)
1715	St Albans–South Mimms	Middx. & Herts.	(1)	(1 Geo. I c.12)
—	Tyburn–Uxbridge	Middx.	(1)	(— c.25)
1717	Islington, etc.–Highgate	Middx.	(1)	(3 Geo. I c.4)
—	Kensington–Cranford Bridge	Middx.	(1)	(— c.14)
1718	Southwark–Kingston & Sutton	Suss. & Surr.	(2)	(4 Geo. I c.4)
—	Southwark–Lewisham, etc.	Kent & Surr.	(2)	(— c.5)
—	Maidenhead Bridge, Twyford and Henley	Berks.	(1)	(— c.6)
—	Reading–Basingstoke	Berks., Wilts., & Hants.	(1)	(— c.7)
1719	Beaconsfield–Stokenchurch	Bucks.	(1)	(5 Geo. I c.1)
—	Stokenchurch–Oxford–Woodstock	Bucks. & Oxon.	(7)	(— c.2)
1720	Stevenage–Biggleswade	Beds. & Herts.	(1)	(6 Geo. I c.25)
1721	Roads leading into Ledbury	Heref.	(4)	(7 Geo. I c.23)
—	Buckingham–Wendover	Bucks.	(1)	(— c.24)
—	St Giles Bridge–Kilburn Bridge	Middx.	(1)	(— c.26)
1722	Market Harborough–Pitsford Bridge	Northants. & Leices.	(6)	(8 Geo. I c.13)

[1]'Roads leading into . . . ', denotes a town-centred trust.
[2]'Etc.' denotes that only one of a number of roads has been listed.

Year	Road	County	Area	Act
1722	Whitechapel–Shenfield	Middx. & Essex	(1)	(8 Geo. I c.30)
1723	St Albans–Dunstable	Beds. & Herts.	(1)	(9 Geo. I c.11)
—	Gloucester–Birdlip and Crickley Hills[3]	Glos.	(4)	(— c.31)
1724	Thornwood–Woodford	Essex	(1)	(10 Geo. I c.9)
—	Newmarket–Chesterford	Essex & Cambs.	(6)	(— c.12)
—	Dunchurch–Meriden Hill	War.	(7)	(— c.15)
1725	Enfield–Ware	Middx. & Herts.	(1)	(11 Geo. I c.11)
—	Manchester–Buxton, etc.	Derbys. & Lancs.	(9)	(— c.13)
—	Trumpington–Foulmire	Cambs.	(6)	(— c.14)
—	Biggleswade–Alconbury, etc.	Beds. & Hunts.	(6)	(— c.20)
1726	Loughborough–Market Harborough	Leices.	(9)	(12 Geo. I c.5)
—	Birmingham–Stratford-upon-Avon and Warmington	War.	(7)	(— c.6)
—	Newbury–Marlborough	Wilts. & Berks.	(4)	(— c.8)
—	Shrewsbury–Shifnal	Salop	(8)	(— c.9)
—	Lemsford Mill–Hitchin, etc.	Herts. & Beds.	(1)	(— c.10)
—	Chippenham–Box, etc.	Wilts.	(4)	(— c.11)
—	Gloucester–Hereford, etc.	Heref. & Glos.	(4)	(— c.13)
—	Roads leading into Worcester	Worces.	(7)	(— c.14)
—	Grantham–Little Drayton	Lincs.	(3)	(— c.16)
—	Roads leading into Tewkesbury	Glos.	(4)	(— c.18)
—	Liverpool–Prescot	Lancs.	(10)	(— c.21)
—	Shenfield–Harwich, etc.[4]	Essex	(1)	(— c.23)
—	Gloucester–Stone, etc.	Glos.	(4)	(— c.24)
—	Kensington, Fulham and Chelsea Roads	Middx.	(1)	(— c.37)
1727	Wigan–Preston	Lancs.	(10)	(13 Geo. I c.9)
—	Wigan–Warrington	Lancs.	(10)	(— c.10)
—	Cirencester–Lechlade	Glos.	(4)	(— c.11)
—	Roads leading into Bristol	Somer. & Glos.	(4)	(— c.12)
—	Chippenham–Toghill, etc.	Wilts. & Glos.	(4)	(— c.13)
—	Birmingham–Stourbridge, etc.	War., Staffs. & Worces.	(8)	(— c.14)
—	Bromsgrove–Birmingham, etc.	War. & Worces.	(7)	(— c.15)
—	Roads leading into Warminster	Wilts.	(4)	(— c.16)
—	Luton–Westwood Gate	Beds.	(6)	(— c.17)
—	Maidenhead Bridge–Cranford Bridge	Middx. & Bucks.	(1)	(— c.31)
1728	Ely–Chatteris Ferry, etc.	Hunts.	(6)	(1 Geo. II c.4)
—	Powder Mills–Bagshot, etc.	Middx. & Surr.	(1)	(— c.8)
—	Hockliffe–Newport Pagnell[5]	Beds. & Bucks.	(1)	(— c.10)
—	Evesham–Worcester, etc.	Worces.	(7)	(— c.11)
—	Rochester–Maidstone, etc.	Kent	(2)	(— c.12)
1729	Lichfield–Stone, etc.	Staffs. & Derbys.	(8)	(2 Geo. II c.5)
—	Roads leading into Leominster	Heref.	(4)	(— c.13)

[3] The justice-trust formed in 1697-8 had expired and was replaced by this trust which included new roads.

[4] The justice-trust formed in 1695 had expired and was replaced by this trust, which included many new roads.

[5] This trust superseded the Hockliffe–Woburn Trust, a justice-trust formed in 1706.

Year	Road	Country	Area	Act
1730	Stratford-upon-Avon–Long Compton	War.	(7)	(3 Geo. II c.9)
—	Gally Corner–Lemsford Mill	Herts. & Middx.	(1)	(— c.10)
—	Rochester–Canterbury, etc.	Kent	(2)	(— c.15)
—	Roads leading into Hereford	Heref.	(3)	(— c.18)
—	Woodstock–Roll Right, etc.	Oxon.	(7)	(— c.21)
—	Wisbech–March, etc.	Cambs.	(6)	(— c.24)
—	Roads leading into Bridgwater	Somer.	(4)	(— c.34)
1731	Lawton–Cranage	Ches.	(8)	(4 Geo. II c.3)
—	Chappel-on-the-Hill–Bourton-on-the-Hill	Oxon. & Glos.	(4)	(— c.23)
—	Fulham–Hammersmith	Middx.	(1)	(— c.34)
1732	Manchester–Saltersbrook	Lancs. & Ches.	(10)	(5 Geo. II c.10)
1733	Lechlade–Fyfield	Berks.	(1)	(6 Geo. II c.16)
1735	Manchester–Oldham–Austerland	Lancs. & Yorks.	(10)	(8 Geo. II c.3)
—	Rochdale–Halifax, etc.	Lancs. & Yorks.	(10)	(— c.7)
1736	Canterbury–Whitstable	Kent	(2)	(9 Geo. II c.10)
—	Henley-on-Thames–Oxford, etc.	Oxon.	(7)	(— c.14)
—	Twyford–Reading	Berks.	(1)	(— c.21)
1737	Basingstoke–Odiham, etc.	Hants.	(2)	(10 Geo. II c.12)
1738	Nottingham–Cotes Bridge, etc.	Notts. & Leices.	(9)	(11 Geo. II c.3)
—	Shoreditch–Mile End, etc.	Middx.	(1)	(— c.29)
—	Loughborough–Hartington, etc.	Leices. & Derbys.	(9)	(— c.33)
1739	Stamford–Grantham	Lincs.	(3)	(12 Geo. II c.8)
—	Lincoln–The Wolds, etc.	Lincs.	(3)	(— c.10)
—	Chesterfield–Worksop, etc.	Notts. & Derbys.	(9)	(— c.12)
—	Dunchurch–Duston, etc.	War. & Northants.	(7)	(— c.18)
1740	Hockliffe–Stony Stratford	Bucks. & Beds.	(1)	(13 Geo. II c.9)
1741	Doncaster–Wakefield, etc.	Yorks.	(10)	(14 Geo. II c.19)
—	Wakefield–Pontefract, etc.	Yorks.	(10)	(— c.23)
—	Elland–Leeds	Yorks.	(10)	(— c.25)
—	Doncaster–Boroughbridge, etc.	Yorks.	(10)	(— c.28)
—	Doncaster–Saltersbrook, etc.	Ches. & Yorks.	(10)	(— c.31)
—	Selby–Leeds–Halifax, etc.	Yorks.	(10)	(— c.32)
1743	Bowes–Brough-under-Stainmore	Yorks. & Westmor.	(11)	(16 Geo. II c.3)
—	Boroughbridge–Piercebridge	Yorks.	(10)	(— c.7)
—	Marlborough–Cherhill, etc.	Wilts.	(4)	(— c.10)
—	Cirencester–Monument-upon-Landsdown	Glos.	(4)	(— c.22)
1744	Harlow–Great Chesterford	Essex	(1)	(17 Geo. II c.9)
—	Middleton Tyas–Bowes	Yorks.	(10)	(— c.22)
—	Kingston-upon-Hull–Beverley	Yorks.	(10)	(— c.25)
—	Buckingham–Warmington	Bucks. & War.	(7)	(— c.43)
—	Kingston-upon-Hull–Kirk Ella	Yorks.	(10)	(18 Geo. II c.4)
1745	Kingston-upon-Hull–Hedon	Yorks.	(10)	(— c.6)
—	Boroughbridge–Durham	Durham & Yorks.	(11)	(— c.8)
—	Tadcaster Bridge–York	Yorks.	(10)	(— c.16)
—	Birmingham–Stone Bridge	War.	(7)	(— c.19)
—	Godmanchester–Newmarket Heath	Cambs. & Hunts.	(6)	(— c.23)
1747	Newcastle–Buckton Burn	Northum.	(11)	(20 Geo. II c.9)
—	Durham–Newcastle	Durham & Northum.	(11)	(— c.12)

Year	Road	County	Area	Act
1747	Durham–Sunderland	Durham	(11)	(20 Geo. II c.13)
—	Cirencester–Birdlip Hill	Glos.	(4)	(— c.23)
—	Stockton–Barnard Castle	Durham	(11)	(— c.25)
—	Catterick–Stockton–Durham	Yorks. & Durham	(11)	(— c.28)
1748	Bowes–Barnard Castle– Bishop Auckland, etc.	Yorks. & Durham	(11)	(21 Geo. II c.5)
—	Sutton Coldfield–Walsall, etc.	Staffs.	(8)	(— c.25)
—	Piercebridge–Kirkmerrington, etc.	Durham	(11)	(— c.27)
1749	Farnborough–Sevenoaks	Kent	(2)	(22 Geo. II c.4)
—	Newcastle–River Wanspeck	Northum.	(11)	(— c.7)
—	Newcastle–North Shields	Northum.	(11)	(— c.9)
—	Wansford Bridge–Stamford	Lincs. & Northants.	(3)	(— c.17)
—	Roads leading into Ross	Heref.	(4)	(— c.26)
—	Southwark, Rotherhithe, etc.	Surr.	(2)	(— c.31)
—	Kingston-upon-Thames– Petersfield, etc.	Surr., Suss. & Hants.	(2)	(— c.35)
1750	York–Boroughbridge	Yorks.	(10)	(23 Geo. II c.38)
—	Egremont–Salthouse	Cumber.	(11)	(— c.40)
1751	West Lavington–Seend	Wilts.	(4)	(24 Geo. II c.9)
—	Stretford–Manchester	Lancs.	(10)	(— c.13)
—	Richmond–Lancaster	Lancs. & Yorks.	(10)	(— c.17)
—	Preston–Lancaster– Hyning Syke	Lancs.	(10)	(— c.20)
—	Tadcaster–Halton Dyal	Yorks.	(10)	(— c.22)
—	Carlisle–Newcastle	Cumber. & Northum.	(11)	(— c.25)
—	Crickley Hill–Oxford, etc.	Glos. & Oxon.	(4)	(— c.28)
—	Ludlow–Orleton, etc.	Salop & Heref.	(7)	(— c.29)
—	Darlington–West Auckland, etc.	Durham	(11)	(— c.30)
—	Lewisham–Southwark, etc.	Kent & Surr.	(2)	(— c.58)
1752	Wrotham Heath–Foot's Cray	Kent	(2)	(25 Geo. II c.8)
—	Warminster–Bath, etc.	Wilts. & Somer.	(4)	(— c.12)
—	Cirencester–Stroud, etc.	Glos.	(4)	(— c.13)
—	Seend–Trowbridge	Somer.	(4)	(— c.17)
—	Morpeth–Weldon Bridge, etc.	Northum.	(11)	(— c.18)
—	Wallingford–Wantage– Farringdon	Berks.	(1)	(— c.21)
—	Shrewsbury–Wrexham	Salop & Denbigh	(8)	(— c.22)
—	Trowbridge–Edington, etc.	Wilts.	(4)	(— c.24)
—	Morpeth–Elsdon	Northum.	(11)	(— c.33)
—	Alnmouth–Rothbury, etc.	Northum.	(11)	(— c.46)
—	York–Scarborough, etc.	Yorks.	(10)	(— c.47)
—	Glenwilt–Shildon Common	Northum.	(11)	(— c.48)
—	Shrewsbury–Bridgnorth	Salop	(8)	(— c.49)
—	Lewes–Witch Cross, etc.	Suss.	(2)	(— c.50)
—	Combe Bridge–Bradford	Wilts. & Somer.	(4)	(— c.52)
—	Knaresborough–Green Hammerton	Yorks.	(10)	(— c.53)
—	Roads leading into Taunton	Somer.	(5)	(— c.54)
—	Bromyard–Sapey Wood, etc.	Heref. & Worces.	(7)	(— c.56)
—	Market Harborough– Brampton, etc.	Leices., Hunts., Northants.	(6)	(— c.57)
—	Leeds–Harrogate, etc.	Yorks.	(10)	(— c.58)
—	Chippenham–Toghill, etc.	Wilts. & Glos.	(4)	(— c.59)

Year	Road	County	Area	Act
1752	Upton Bridge–Tirley, etc.	Worces., Heref. & Glos.	(7)	(25 Geo. II c.60)
1753	Penrith–Chalk Beck, etc.	Cumber.	(11)	(26 Geo. II c.1)
—	Roads leading into Bewdley	Salop & Worces.	(7)	(— c.3)
—	Carlisle–Penrith–Eamont Bridge	Cumber.	(11)	(— c.4)
—	Seend–Box	Wilts.	(4)	(— c.6)
—	Leicester–Ashby-de-la-Zouch	Leices.	(9)	(— c.10)
—	Roads leading into Stourbridge	Worces., War., Salop & Staffs.	(7)	(— c.11)
—	Carlisle–Workington	Cumber.	(11)	(— c.13)
—	Redstone Ferry–Tenbury	Worces.	(7)	(— c.14)
—	Basingstoke–Winchester	Surr. & Hants.	(2)	(— c.15)
—	Hyning Syke–Kirby-in-Kendal–Eamont Bridge	Westmor. & Lancs.	(11)	(— c.16)
—	Ticehurst–Hastings	Suss.	(2)	(— c.18)
—	Burton-upon-Trent–Derby	Staffs. & Derbys.	(9)	(— c.23)
—	Roads near Sherborne and Shaftesbury	Wilts. & Dorset	(5)	(— c.24)
—	Cranage Green–Altrincham, etc.	Ches.	(8)	(— c.26)
—	Salford–Wigan, etc.	Lancs.	(10)	(— c.27)
—	Tadcaster–Otley	Yorks.	(10)	(— c.28)
—	Winterslow–Harnham Bridge, etc.	Wilts. & Hants.	(4)	(— c.30)
—	Brough–Eamont Bridge	Westmor.	(11)	(— c.31)
—	Dover–Barham Downs	Kent	(2)	(— c.32)
—	Roads near Yeovil	Dorset & Devon	(5)	(— c.33)
—	Burford–Preston	Oxon. & Glos.	(4)	(— c.34)
—	Roads leading into Shepton Malet and Ilvelchester	Somer.	(5)	(— c.35)
—	Roads leading into Exeter	Devon	(5)	(— c.38)
—	Northallerton–Thirsk–York, etc.	Yorks.	(10)	(— c.39)
—	Ashcott–Glastonbury	Somer.	(5)	(— c.40)
—	Banbury–Edge Hill	Oxon. & War.	(7)	(— c.42)
—	Buckton Burn–Berwick, etc.	Northum.	(11)	(— c.46)
—	Elton–Middlewich, etc.	Ches.	(8)	(— c.48)
—	Ashby-de-la-Zouch–Burton-upon-Trent, etc.	Leices. & Staffs.	(9)	(— c.49)
—	Keighley–Kirby-in-Kendal	Westmor. & Yorks.	(11)	(— c.50)
—	Shoreditch–Goswell St	Middx.	(1)	(— c.51)
—	Oundle–Alconbury, etc.	Northants. & Hunts.	(6)	(— c.52)
—	Fivehead–Langport, etc.	Somer.	(5)	(— c.56)
1754	Peterborough–Oundle–Wellingborough	Northamp.	(6)	(27 Geo. II c.3)
—	Uckfield–Westham	Suss.	(2)	(— c.4)
—	Leicester–Wansford–Peterborough	Leices., Rut. & Northants.	(9)	(— c.10)
—	Kettering–Wellingborough–Olney–Newport Pagnell	Northants. & Bucks.	(6)	(— c.11)
—	Bridport–Beaminster, etc.	Dorset & Devon	(5)	(— c.12)
—	Knotting–Barton–Seagrave	Northants. & Beds.	(6)	(— c.13)

Year	Road	County	Area	Act
1754	Bedford–[Olney–Newport P. Road] etc.	Beds.	(6)	(27 Geo. II c.14)
—	Stratford-upon-Avon–Alcester, etc.	Worces. & War.	(7)	(— c.16)
—	Nottingham–Kettering	Notts., Leices., Rut. & Northants.	(9)	(— c.19)
—	Cannon St, Brook St, etc.	Middx.	(1)	(— c.20)
—	Roads leading into Truro	Corn.	(5)	(— c.21)
—	Leicester–Coventry, etc.	Leices. & War.	(9)	(— c.22)
1755	Ramsey–Huntingdon	Hunts.	(6)	(28 Geo. II c.26)
—	Sutton–Reigate, etc.	Surr.	(2)	(— c.28)
—	Roads leading into Monmouth	Heref. & Mon.	(4)	(— c.31)
—	Great Stoughton–Wellingborough, etc.	Hunts. & Northants.	(6)	(— c.33)
—	Bury–Stratton	Hunts., Cambs. & Beds.	(6)	(— c.35)
—	Market Harborough–Lutterworth–Coventry	Leices. & War.	(9)	(— c.40)
—	Basingstoke–Winterslow	Hants. & Wilts.	(2)	(— c.44)
—	Horsham–Ebbisham, etc.	Suss. & Surr.	(2)	(— c.45)
—	Southam–Banbury, etc.	War. & Oxon.	(7)	(— c.46)
—	Dowdeswell–Stow-on-the-Wold	Glouces. & War.	(4)	(— c.47)
—	Roads leading into Droitwich	Worces.	(7)	(— c.48)
—	Hannock–South Brent	Devon	(5)	(— c.49)
—	Bradford–Colne, etc.	Yorks.	(10)	(— c.50)
—	Thirsk–Masham	Yorks.	(10)	(— c.51)
—	Rochdale–Burnley	Lancs.	(10)	(— c.53)
—	Epsom–Ewell–Kingston-upon-Thames	Surr.	(2)	(— c.57)
—	Manchester–Rochdale and Bury, etc.	Lancs.	(10)	(— c.58)
—	Addingham–Kildwick, etc.	Lancs.	(10)	(— c.59)
—	Leeds–Walton and Skipton–Preston	Lancs. & Yorks.	(10)	(— c.60)
1756	Bethnal Green–Church Street, etc.	Middx.	(1)	(29 Geo. II c.43)
—	Whiteparish–Southampton	Wilts. & Hants.	(2)	(— c.45)
—	Basingstoke–Lobcomb Corner	Hants. & Wilts.	(2)	(— c.46)
—	Wincanton–Sherborne, etc.	Somer. & Wilts.	(5)	(— c.49)
—	Roads leading into Brewton	Somer.	(5)	(— c.50)
—	Roads leading from Tewkesbury	Glos.	(4)	(— c.51)
—	Roads leading into Poole	Dorset & Wilts.	(5)	(— c.52)
—	New Sarum–Dorchester, etc.	Wilts. & Dorset	(5)	(— c.54)
—	Mead Brook–Christian Malford Bridge	Glos. & Wilts.	(4)	(— c.56)
—	Gloucester toward Cheltenham and Tewkesbury	Glos.	(4)	(— c.58)
—	Roads leading into Ludlow	Salop	(7)	(— c.59)
—	Roads leading into Much Wenlock	Salop	(8)	(— c.60)
—	Shrewsbury–Church Stretton, etc.	Salop	(8)	(— c.61)
—	Shrewsbury–Shawbury, etc.	Salop	(8)	(— c.64)

Year	Road	County	Area	Act
1756	Roads leading from Kington	Heref.	(4)	(29 Geo. II c.65)
—	Farringdon–Malmesbury, etc.	Berks., Glos. & Wilts.	(4)	(— c.77)
—	Chilton Pond to road near Farrington	Berks.	(1)	(— c.81)
—	Derby–Sheffield; Duffield–Wirksworth	Derbys. & Yorks.	(9)	(— c.82)
—	Ripon–Pateley Bridge	Yorks.	(10)	(— c.83)
—	Bracebridge–Lincoln, etc.	Lincs.	(3)	(— c.84)
—	Lincoln Heath–Peterborough, etc.	Lincs. & Northants.	(3)	(— c.85)
—	Yarpole–Presteigne, etc.	Heref. & Radnor.	(4)	(— c.94)
1757	Roads leading into Tenbury	Salop, Worces. & Heref.	(7)	(30 Geo. II c.38)
—	Roads leading into Frome	Somer.	(4)	(— c.39)
—	Melksham–Castlecombe	Wilts.	(4)	(— c.41)
—	Hitchin–St Albans' Turnpike, etc.	Beds. & Herts.	(1)	(— c.43)
—	Loughborough–Ashby-de-la-Zouch	Leices.	(9)	(— c.44)
—	Hertford–Broadwater, etc.	Herts.	(1)	(— c.45)
—	Corsham–Bath–Easton Bridge	Wilts. & Somer.	(4)	(— c.46)
—	Towcester–Weston-on-the-Green	Northants. & Oxon.	(6)	(— c.48)
—	Markfield Turnpike–Snape Gate on Loughborough Turnpike	Leices.	(9)	(— c.49)
—	Milford–Peckworth–Stopham Bridge	Surr. & Suss.	(2)	(— c.50)
—	Jeremy's Ferry–Snaresbrook	Essex & Middx.	(1)	(— c.59)
—	Stoke–Guildford–Arundel	Suss. & Surr.	(2)	(— c.60)
—	Bagshot–Hertfordbridge Hill	Suss. & Hants.	(2)	(— c.61)
—	Spalding High Bridge–Maxey Outgang	Lincs. & Northants.	(3)	(— c.68)
1758	Roads leading into Lyme Regis	Devon & Dorset	(5)	(31 Geo. II c.43)
—	Magor–Chepstow, etc.	Mon. & Glos.	(4)	(— c.44)
—	Roads leading into Tiverton	Devon	(5)	(— c.49)
—	Donington High Bridge–Wigtoft, etc.	Lincs.	(3)	(— c.50)
—	Cirencester–Cricklade	Glos. & Wilts.	(4)	(— c.61)
—	Little Sheffield–Sparrow Pit Gate, etc.	Derbys. & Yorks.	(10)	(— c.62)
—	Leeds–Sheffield	Yorks.	(10)	(— c.63)
—	Roads leading into Tetbury	Glos.	(4)	(— c.65)
—	Christian Malford Bridge–Shillingford Gate	Wilts. & Berks.	(4)	(— c.66)
—	Roads leading from Welch Gate and Cotton Hill in Shrewsbury	Salop	(8)	(— c.67)
—	Westbury–Market Lavington, etc.	Wilts.	(4)	(— c.68)
—	Chawton–Gosport, etc.	Hants.	(2)	(— c.73)
—	Bishops Waltham–Alresford–Odiham	Hants.	(2)	(— c.74)

Year	Road	County	Area	Act
1758	Stockbridge–Winchester–Southampton	Hants.	(2)	(31 Geo. II c.75)
—	Leatherhead–Stoke near Guildford	Surr.	(2)	(— c.77)
—	Guildford–Farnham	Surr.	(2)	(— c.78)
1759	Mansfield–Hasland (Chesterfield–Derby Road)	Notts.	(9)	(32 Geo. II c.37)
—	Nottingham–New Haven, etc.	Notts. & Derbys.	(9)	(— c.38)
—	Chard–West Moor, Yeovil Turnpike–Kenny Gate, etc.	Somer.	(5)	(— c.39)
—	Roads leading into Bridgwater	Somer.	(5)	(— c.40)
—	Macclesfield–Buxton	Ches. & Derbys.	(9)	(— c.41)
—	Chesterfield to Turnpike at Hernston Lane, etc.	Derbys.	(9)	(— c.43)
—	Roads leading into South Molton	Devon	(5)	(— c.45)
—	Sunning–Virginia Water	Berks.	(1)	(— c.46)
—	Wakefield–Austerlands	Yorks.	(10)	(— c.48)
—	Oxdown Gate–Winchester, etc.	Hants. & Dorset	(2)	(— c.50)
—	End of Exeter Turnpike–Bideford	Devon	(5)	(— c.52)
—	Grantham–Nottingham–Derby, etc.	Lincs., Derbys. & Notts.	(9)	(— c.53)
—	Dewsbury–Elland	Yorks.	(10)	(— c.54)
—	Littlegate–Newark-upon-Trent, etc.	Lincs. & Notts.	(9)	(— c.57)
—	Newcastle-under-Lyme–Derby	Staffs. & Derbys.	(9)	(— c.60)
—	Stretford Bridge, Winstanstow, etc.	Heref. & Salop	(8)	(— c.66)
—	South Malling–Alfriston	Suss.	(2)	(— c.67)
—	Modbury–Plympton, etc.	Devon	(5)	(— c.68)
—	Netherbridge–Dixes; Miltrop–Hangbridge	Westmor.	(11)	(— c.69)
—	Barnsley Common–Grange Moor–Whitecross	Yorks.	(10)	(— c.70)
—	Wetherby–Grassington	Yorks.	(10)	(— c.71)
1760	Roads leading into Oakhampton	Devon	(5)	(33 Geo. II c.36)
—	Chesterfield–Matlock Bridge, etc.	Derbys.	(9)	(— c.39)
—	Tamworth–Ashby-de-la-Zouch, etc.	Leices.	(9)	(— c.41)
—	Halworthy–Mitchell	Corn.	(5)	(— c.42)
—	Hinckley–Woefull Bridge, etc.	Leices. & Derbys.	(9)	(— c.46)
—	Several roads in Leices., Derbys. & War.	Leices., Derbys. & War.	(9)	(— c.47)
—	Halifax–Littleborough	Yorks. & Lancs.	(10)	(— c.48)
—	Roads leading into Kidderminster	Worces.	(7)	(— c.50)
—	Chester–Whitchurch–Newport, etc.	Salop, Ches. & War.	(8)	(— c.51)
—	Bridge over Avon into Bristol	Somer.	(4)	(— c.52)
—	Bawtry–Sheffield–Wortley	Yorks.	(10)	(— c.55)
—	Deanburn Bridge–Berwick–Cornhill	Northum. & Durham	(11)	(— c.56)
—	Maidstone–Cranbrooke	Kent	(2)	(— c.57)

Year	Road	County	Area	Act
1760	Brecon–Whitney Passage	Heref.	(4)	(33 Geo. II c.58)
—	Roads leading into Launceston	Corn.	(5)	(— c.59)
1761	Weymouth–Malcombe Regis–Dorchester	Dorset	(5)	(1 Geo. III c.24)
—	West Taphouse Lane–Liskeard, etc.	Devon & Corn.	(5)	(— c.25)
—	Islington–Old Street–Chriswell Street	Middx.	(1)	(— c.26)
—	Grampound–St Austell–Lostwithiel–West Taphouse Lane	Corn.	(5)	(— c.27)
—	Dyed Way–Somerton, etc.	Somer.	(5)	(— c.29)
—	Falmouth–Helston, etc.	Corn.	(5)	(— c.32)
—	Ashburton–Highweek	Devon	(5)	(— c.34)
—	Thorngumbold–Pattrington Haven, etc.	Yorks.	(10)	(— c.35)
—	Fisherton Bridge–West Knoyle, etc.	Wilts.	(4)	(— c.37)
—	Stone–Wordsley Green; Wolverhampton–Dudley; Dudley–Birmingham, etc.	Staffs., Worces. & War.	(8)	(— c.39)
—	Gatherby Moor–Staindrop	Yorks. & Durham	(11)	(— c.41)
—	Leven-in-Holderness–Beverley	Yorks.	(10)	(— c.42)
—	Appleby–Kirby-in-Kendal, etc.	Westmor.	(11)	(— c.43)
1762	Amesbury–Anstlow Hill, etc.	Hants. & Wilts.	(4)	(2 Geo. III c.39)
—	Sandon–Bullock Smithy, etc.	Staffs. & Ches.	(8)	(— c.42)
—	St Germans–Saltash–Plymouth, etc.	Devon & Corn.	(5)	(— c.43)
—	Bolton–Leigh, etc.	Lancs.	(10)	(— c.44)
—	(TR)⁶ Creed–Roundanhorne, etc.	Corn.	(5)	(— c.46)
—	(TR) Swindon–Marlborough–Everley	Wilts.	(4)	(— c.49)
—	Roads leading into Tavistock	Devon	(5)	(— c.50)
—	Kelsall–Whiston Cross, etc.	Salop & Staffs.	(8)	(— c.53)
—	Hinckley–Lutterworth, etc.	Leices. & Northants.	(9)	(— c.54)
—	(TR) Bradford–Laycock	Wilts.	(4)	(— c.59)
—	(TR) Weyhill–(TR) Lyde Way	Hants. & Wilts.	(4)	(— c.60)
—	Winchester–Whitchurch; Worthy Cow Down–(TR) Andover	Hants.	(2)	(— c.61)
—	Ryecroft Gate–Congleton, Blyth Marsh–Blore (TR), etc.	Ches., Derbys. & Staffs.	(8)	(— c.62)
—	Sparrows Herne–Walton (TR)	Bucks. & Herts.	(1)	(— c.63)
—	Bridge Town Pomeroy–Waton Gate, etc.	Devon	(5)	(— c.64)
—	Cranbrook–Appledore Heath, etc.	Kent	(2)	(— . c.65)

⁶'(TR)' denotes that the act explicitly stated the road was to be turnpiked to an existing trust.

Year	Road	County	Area	Act
1762	(TR) Whitesheet Hill–Harnham Hill (TR), etc.	Wilts.	(4)	(2 Geo. III c.66)
—	Flimwell Vent–Rye, etc.	Kent & Suss.	(2)	(— c.72)
—	Stamford–Morcot, etc.	Lincs. & Rut.	(3)	(— c.73)
—	Sudbury–Bury St Edmunds	Suff.	(3)	(— c.75)
—	Faversham–Hythe, etc.	Kent	(2)	(— c.76)
—	Stourbridge–Cradley, etc.	Worces., Staffs. & Salop	(7)	(— c.78)
—	Roads from Bridgnorth and Cleobury Mortimer	Salop & Worces.	(7)	(— c.79)
—	Atherstone–Over Whitacre, etc.	Leices. & War.	(9)	(— c.80)
—	Hasket–Cockermouth–Keswick–Kirby-in-Kendal	Westmor. & Cumber.	(11)	(— c.81)
—	Kirby-in-Kendal–Sedbergh, etc.	Westmor., Lancs. & Yorks.	(11)	(— c.83)
—	Cosham–Chichester	Hants. & Suss.	(2)	(— c.84)
1763	Heath Charnock–Bolton	Lancs.	(10)	(3 Geo. III c.31)
—	Newmarket–(TR) leading to Stump Cross	Cambs. & Suff.	(3)	(— c.32)
—	Kirby-in-Kendal–Kirby Ireleth	Lancs. & Westmor.	(11)	(— c.33)
—	Roads leading into Barnstaple	Devon	(5)	(— c.35)
—	Cambridge–Ely, etc.	Cambs.	(3)	(— c.36)
—	Totnes–Staverton Bridge, etc.	Devon	(5)	(— c.38)
—	Lawton–Burslem–Newcastle-under-Lyme	Ches. & Salop	(8)	(— c.45)
—	Penryn–Redruth	Corn.	(5)	(— c.52)
—	Stafford–Sandon, etc.	Salop & Staffs.	(8)	(— c.59)
1764	Shillingford–Reading, etc.	Oxon. & Berks.	(1)	(4 Geo. III c.42)
—	Horsham–Breeding	Suss.	(2)	(— c.44)
—	Romsey–Middle Wallop, etc.	Hants.	(2)	(— c.47)
—	Roads leading into Collington	Corn.	(5)	(— c.48)
—	Worksop–Attercliffe (TR)	Notts. & Yorks.	(9)	(— c.52)
—	Spalding–Sutton Wash	Lincs.	(3)	(— c.53)
—	Derby–Mansfield, etc.	Derbys. & Notts.	(9)	(— c.61)
—	Milford–Portsmouth Road (TR)	Surr., Suss. & Hants.	(2)	(— c.63)
—	Tinsley–Doncaster	Yorks.	(10)	(— c.64)
—	Rotherham–Pleasley (TR)	Yorks.	(10)	(— c 65)
—	Alfreton–Mansfield, etc.	Derbys. & Notts.	(9)	(— c.67)
—	Whitby–Middleton	Yorks.	(10)	(— c.69)
—	Beverley–Kexby Bridge	Yorks.	(10)	(— c.76)
—	Spalding–Donington	Lincs.	(3)	(— c.80)
—	Sutton–Beckby, etc.	Salop	(8)	(— c.81)
—	Ashbourne–Openwood Gate (TR)	Derbys.	(9)	(— c.82)
—	Trowell–Nottingham, etc.	Notts. & Derbys.	(9)	(— c.83)
—	Melton Mowbray–Leicester, etc.	Leices.	(9)	(— c.84)
—	Roads leading into Bideford	Devon	(5)	(— c.87)
1765	Wadhurst–Pullins Hill, etc.	Kent & Suss.	(2)	(5 Geo. III c.52)
—	Dunham Ferry–Great Markham Common	Notts.	(9)	(— c.54)
—	Roads leading into Great Torrington	Devon	(5)	(— c.58)

Year	Road	County	Area	Act
1765	Lymington–Buckland, etc.	Hants.	(2)	(5 Geo. III c.59)
—	Roads leading into Crewkerne	Somer.	(5)	(— c.61)
—	(TR) Kippings Cross– Cranbrooke (TR)	Kent	(2)	(— c.63)
—	Etchingham–Burwash	Suss.	(2)	(— c.64)
—	Balby–Worksop	Yorks. & Notts.	(9)	(— c.67)
—	(TR) Wrotham Heath– Oxted (TR)	Kent & Suss.	(2)	(— c.68)
—	Newton Abbot–Kinswear, etc.	Devon	(5)	(— c.69)
—	Woolborough– Combintinhead, etc.	Devon	(5)	(— c.70)
—	Tonbridge–Maidstone, etc.	Kent	(2)	(— c.71)
—	Birsall–Nunbrook (TR)	Yorks.	(10)	(— c.72)
—	Grimsby–Wold Newton, etc.	Lincs.	(3)	(— c.73)
—	Welford Bridge–Keighton, etc.	Leices. & Northants.	(9)	(— c.78)
—	Charteris Ferry–March, etc.	Norf. & Cambs.	(3)	(— c.82)
—	Newcastle-under-Lyme– Hassop, etc.	Derbys. & Staffs.	(8)	(— c.83)
—	Bawtry Bridge–Hainton, etc.	Notts. & Lincs.	(3)	(— c.85)
—	Brigg–Clixby and Caistor Road, etc.	Lincs.	(3)	(— c.88)
—	(TR) Mansfield–Tansley (TR), etc.	Notts. & Derbys.	(9)	(— c.90)
—	Roads leading from Minehead and Watchet	Devon & Somer.	(5)	(— c.93)
—	Romsey–Swathling, etc.	Hants.	(2)	(— c.95)
—	Alford–Boston, etc.	Lincs.	(3)	(— c.96)
—	York–Kexby Bridge, etc.	Yorks.	(10)	(— c.99)
—	Stockport–Awdenshaw (TR)	Lancs. & Ches.	(10)	(— c.100)
—	Wisbech–Walsoken, etc.	Lincs.	(3)	(— c.101)
—	Blandford–Marnhull, etc.	Devon & Dorset	(5)	(— c.102)
—	(TR) Banbury–Lutterworth, etc.	Oxon. & Leices.	(7)	(— c.105)
—	Warwick–Northampton	War. & Northants.	(7)	(— c.107)
—	New Malton–Pickering	Yorks.	(10)	(— c.108)
1766	Tunbridge Wells–Maresfield Street	Kent & Suss.	(2)	(6 Geo. III c.56)
—	Beverley–Molescroft	Yorks.	(10)	(— c.59)
—	Bawtry–East Markham, etc.	Notts. & Yorks.	(9)	(— c.67)
—	Wimborne Minster– Blandford Forum	Dorset	(5)	(— c.68)
—	Cromford Bridge–Langley Mill (TR)	Derbys.	(9)	(— c.69)
—	Ashbourne–Sudbury, etc.	Derbys. & Staffs.	(8)	(— c.79)
—	(TR) Brimington– Chesterfield–Sheffield Road (TR)	Derbys.	(9)	(— c.80)
—	(TR) Haverhill–Shelford	Suff. & Cambs.	(3)	(— c.84)
—	(TR) Tunbridge Wells– Uckfield	Suss. & Kent	(2)	(— c.85)
—	(TR) Hursley–Newbury, etc.	Berks. & Hants.	(2)	(— c.86)
—	(TR) 9 miles Stone (near Mansfield)–Ashover	Derbys.	(9)	(— c.87)
—	High Bridges–Uttoxeter, etc.	Staffs.	(8)	(— c.88)

Year	Road	County	Area	Act
1766	Newcastle-under-Lyme– Nantwich (TR)	Ches. & Staffs.	(8)	(6 Geo. III c.89)
—	Wareham–Ulwell, etc.	Dorset	(5)	(— c.92)
—	Biddenden–Boundgate (TR)	Kent	(2)	(— c.93)
—	Wednesbury–Bilston, etc.	Staffs.	(8)	(— c.95)
—	Dartford–Sevenoaks	Kent	(2)	(— c.98)
—	Walsall–Wolverhampton, etc.	Staffs.	(8)	(— c.99)
1767	Oxford–near Fyfield (TR)	Oxon. & Berks.	(4)	(7 Geo. III c.66)
—	Presteigne–Knighton, etc.	Heref. & Radnor.	(4)	(— c.67)
—	Northfield–Wootton (TR)	Worces. & War.	(7)	(— c.68)
—	Spernal Ash–Birmingham	War.	(7)	(— c.77)
—	(TR) Hatton–Bromsgrove, etc.	War. & Worces.	(7)	(— c.81)
—	Carlisle–Skillbeck (TR)	Cumber.	(11)	(— c.83)
—	Tunbridge Wells– Etchingham, etc.	Kent & Suss.	(2)	(— c.84)
—	Bromley–Farnborough, etc.	Kent	(2)	(— c.86)
—	Whitecross–Bridlington	Yorks.	(10)	(— c.89)
—	East Malling Heath– Pembury Green (TR)	Kent	(2)	(— c.91)
—	Whitchurch–Nantwich and Newcastle Road (TR)	Ches. & Salop	(8)	(— c.92)
—	Tenterden–Ashford, etc.	Kent	(2)	(— c.103)
—	Marchwiail–Bangor– Whitchurch	Denbigh, Flint., Salop, & Ches.	(8)	(— c.104)
1768	Roads leading into Goudhurst	Kent	(2)	(8 Geo. III c.35)
—	Huddersfield–Entreclough Bridge, etc.	Derbys. Yorks. & Ches.	(8)	(— c.47)
—	Reading–Hatfield, etc.	Herts., Bucks., Oxon. & Berks.	(1)	(— c.50)
—	Roads leading into Bishop's Castle	Salop, Mont. & Radnor.	(8)	(— c.51)
—	Hardingston–Old Stratford	Northants.	(6)	(— c.52)
—	Buckland Dinham– Timsbury, etc.	Somer.	(4)	(— c.53)
—	York–Craike, etc.	Yorks.	(10)	(— c.54)
—	Thetford–Newmarket Heath	Suff. & Cambs.	(3)	(— c.55)
—	Abingdon–Swinford	Berks.	(1)	(— c.61)
1769	(TR) Cranbrooke–Sandhurst (TR), etc.	Kent	(2)	(9 Geo. III c.43)
—	Dorchester–Stafford, etc.	Dorset	(5)	(— c.47)
—	West Peckham–Hadlow (TR)	Kent	(2)	(— c.49)
—	(TR) Shawbury–Newcastle- under-Lyme, etc.	Salop & Staffs.	(8)	(— c.55)
—	Cirencester–Tetbury, etc.	Glos.	(4)	(— c.58)
—	Macclesfield–Nether Tabley (TR)	Ches.	(8)	(— c.65)
—	Norwich–Scole	Norf.	(3)	(— c.66)
—	Scole–Bury St Edmunds	Norf. & Suff.	(3)	(— c.67)
—	Norwich–2½ miles from Yarmouth	Norf.	(3)	(— c.68)
—	Roads leading into Bodmin	Corn.	(5)	(— c.69)
—	Maidstone–Bobbing	Kent	(2)	(— c.78)
—	Beverley–Hessle, etc.	Yorks.	(10)	(— c.79)
—	Cheadle–Butterton Moor, etc.	Staffs.	(8)	(— c.80)
—	Darley Moor–Ellstone, etc.	Derbys. & Staffs.	(8)	(9 Geo. III c.81)

H

Year	Road	County	Area	Act
1769	(TR) Tring–Bourn Bridge (TR)	Herts., Bucks., Beds. & Cambs.	(1)	(9 Geo. III c.86)
—	Stony Stratford–Woodstock	Bucks. & Oxon.	(7)	(— c.88)
—	Blackfriars Bridge–Newington Butts	Surr.	(2)	(— c.89)
1770	Norwich–Trowse, etc.	Norf.	(3)	(10 Geo. III c.54)
—	Aylesbury–Little Molton (TR), etc.	Bucks. & Oxon.	(1)	(— c.58)
—	(TR) Westerham–Titsey (TR)	Kent & Surr.	(2)	(— c.62)
—	Ratley–Wellesbourne Hastings, etc.	War.	(7)	(— c.63)
—	Lewes–Brighthelmston	Suss.	(2)	(— c.64)
—	Barton–Brandon Bridge	Suff.	(3)	(— c.65)
—	Tunstall–Bosley, etc.	Staffs. & Ches.	(8)	(— c.66)
—	Norwich–Swaffham, etc.	Norf.	(3)	(— c.67)
—	Bicester–Aylesbury	Oxon. & Bucks.	(1)	(— c.72)
—	New Chapel–Ditchling	Surr. & Suss.	(2)	(— c.76)
—	Norwich–Watton	Norf.	(3)	(— c.77)
—	Stoke Ferry–Barton, etc.	Norf.	(3)	(— c.78)
—	King's Lynn–Stoke Ferry, etc.	Norf.	(3)	(— c.85)
—	King's Lynn–Hillington	Norf.	(3)	(— c.86)
—	Whitchurch–Aldermaston (TR)	Berks. & Hants.	(2)	(— c.88)
—	Worksop–Kelham (TR), etc.	Notts.	(9)	(— c.92)
—	Wellesbourne–Mountfort–Stratford-upon-Avon	War.	(7)	(— c.94)
—	Brighthelmston–Lowell Heath	Suss.	(2)	(— c.95)
—	Bury St Edmunds–Newmarket, etc.	Cambs. & Suff.	(3)	(— c.96)
—	Macclesfield–Fernilee (TR)	Ches. & Derbys.	(9)	(— c.98)
—	Tamworth–Lichfield, etc.	Staffs., War. & Derbys.	(9)	(— c.99)
—	Burford–Banbury, etc.	Oxon., Glos. & Northants.	(7)	(— c.101)
—	Saltfleet–Louth, etc.	Lincs.	(3)	(— c.109)
—	Onecute–Buxton and Ashbourne Road (TR)	Derbys. & Staffs.	(9)	(— c.113)
1771	Collingham–York	Yorks.	(10)	(11 Geo. III c.68)
—	Elloughton–Coney Clappers	Yorks.	(10)	(— c.71)
—	Witney–Clanfield	Oxon.	(4)	(— c.73)
—	Peniston Bridge–Grindleford Bridge	Derbys. & Yorks.	(9)	(— c.76)
—	Great Farringdon–Burford	Berks. & Oxon.	(4)	(— c.84)
—	Stone–Blyth Bridge	Staffs.	(8)	(— c.86)
—	Shelton Road between Cheadle and Leek	Staffs.	(8)	(— c.87)
—	Liverpool–Preston	Lancs.	(10)	(— c.93)
—	(TR) Mountfield–Beckley (TR)	Suss.	(2)	(— c.94)
—	Wem–Bron-y-Garth, etc.	Denbigh & Salop	(8)	(— c.95)
—	Wantage–Marlborough, etc.	Wilts. & Berks.	(4)	(— c.97)
—	Burwash–Ticehurst, etc.	Suss.	(2)	(— c.98)
—	Slaugham–West Grinstead, etc.	Suss.	(2)	(— c.99)
1772	Aldermaston–Basingstoke, etc.	Hants.	(2)	(12 Geo. III c.78)
—	(TR) Hungerfield Road–Leckford	Berks. & Wilts.	(4)	(— c.85)
—	St Neots–Cambridge	Hunts. & Cambs.	(6)	(— c.90)

Year	Road	County	Area	Act
1772	Solihull–Kenilworth, etc.	War.	(7)	(12 Geo. III c.91)
—	(TR) Dunsford–Cherry Brook	Devon	(5)	(— c.93)
—	Norwich–New Buckenham	Norf.	(3)	(— c.95)
—	Burlton–Knockin, etc.	Salop	(8)	(— c.96)
—	Downham Market–towards Swaffham	Norf.	(3)	(— c.98)
—	Spalding–Peakirk, etc.[7]	Lincs. & Northants.	(3)	(— c.103)
—	Crickhowel–New Inn (TR)	Brecon. & Heref.	(4)	(— c.105)
—	(TR) Cardington–Temsford Bridge	Beds.	(6)	(— c.107)
—	Sheetbridge–Portsmouth	Hants.	(2)	(— c.108)
—	Bewdley–Coalbrookdale (towing path along the Severn)	Staffs.	(8)	(— c.109)
1773	Newark-upon-Trent–Bingham (TR)	Lincs. & Notts.	(3)	(13 Geo. III c.90)
—	Wrotham Heath–Maidstone, etc.	Kent	(2)	(— c.98)
—	Hampton–Staines	Middx.	(1)	(— c.105)
—	Stamford–Oakham, etc.	Rut. & Lincs.	(3)	(— c.108)
1774	Averham Park–Kirklington, etc.	Notts.	(9)	(14 Geo. III c.101)
1775	Yarmouth Bridge–South Town	Suff.	(3)	(15 Geo. III c.67)
1776	Doncaster–Bawtry and Retford Road (TR)	Yorks. & Notts.	(10)	(16 Geo. III c.71)
—	Clitheroe–Blackburn	Lancs.	(10)	(— c.75)
1777	Henfield–Ditchling	Suss.	(2)	(17 Geo. III c.73)
—	Henfield–Brighthelmston, etc.	Suss.	(2)	(— c.90)
—	Bedford–Ampthill, etc.	Beds.	(6)	(— c.93)
—	Combe Bridge–Bradford	Wilts.	(4)	(— c.97)
—	Warminster–Beckington, etc.	Wilts. & Somer.	(4)	(— c.98)
—	Skipton–Harrogate (TR), etc.	Yorks.	(10)	(— c.101)
—	Crickrell–Bridport Road (TR), etc.	Dorset	(5)	(— c.102)
—	(TR) Asthall–Buckland (TR)	Oxon. & Berks.	(7)	(— c.104)
—	Halifax–Sheffield	Yorks.	(10)	(— c.105)
—	Loughborough–Cavendish Bridge	Leices.	(9)	(— c.107)
—	Ovingham–Bywell St Peter, etc.	Durham	(11)	(— c.109)
1778	Birches Brook–Tern Bridge (TR)	Salop	(8)	(18 Geo. III c.88)
—	Barwick–Charminster, etc.	Somer. & Dorset	(5)	(— c.95)
—	Gloucester–Stroud	Glos.	(4)	(— c.98)
—	Hesham–Alston	Northum. & Cumber.	(11)	(— c.116)
1779	Maidenhead–towards Cookham[8]	Berks.	(1)	(19 Geo. III c.84)
—	Sheffield–Handsworth	Yorks. & Derbys.	(10)	(— c.99)
1780	Horsley–Rodborough (TR)	Glos.	(4)	(20 Geo. III c.84)
—	Melton Mowbray–Grantham	Lincs. & Leices.	(9)	(— c.95)

[7] This act was for repairing the Welland River bank.
[8] Although a new trust, this was added to an existing trust.

Year	Road	County	Area	Act
1781	Wilmslow–Church Lawton	Ches.	(8)	(21 Geo. III c.82)
—	Norton–Hathersage	Derbys.	(9)	(— c.83)
—	(TR) Weston-on-the-Green–Kidlington (TR)	Oxon.	(7)	(— c.87)
1782	(TR) Parton–Monkland Hill, etc.	Heref. & Worces.	(7)	(22 Geo. III c.100)
—	Wrexham–Barnhill	Denbigh & Ches.	(8)	(— c.105)
—	Tarporley–Acton Bridge	Ches.	(8)	(— c.106)
—	Clifford–Dewchurch, etc.	Heref.	(4)	(— c.112)
1783	Wetherby–Knaresborough	Yorks.	(10)	(23 Geo. III c.103)
—	Newnham–Little Dean	Glos.	(4)	(— c.104)
1785	Churchover–Bilton (TR)	War.	(7)	(25 Geo. III c.115)
—	Ipswich–South Town	Suff.	(3)	(— c.116)
1786	Roads leading into Wilvescombe	Somer.	(5)	(26 Geo. III c.135)
—	Newton–Appleton, etc.	Ches.	(8)	(— c.139)
—	Alfreton–Tibshelf, etc.	Derbys.	(9)	(— c.151)
1787	Gainsborough–Saundby	Lincs. & Notts.	(3)	(27 Geo. III c.71)
—	Nottingham–Mansfield	Notts.	(9)	(— c.76)
—	Chester–Birkenhead, etc.	Ches.	(8)	(— c.93)
1788	Hurdcot–Barford (TR), etc.	Wilts.	(4)	(28 Geo. III c.86)
—	Walsall–Sutton Coldfield, etc.	Staffs.	(8)	(— c.98)
—	(TR) Blidworth–South Normanton	Notts. & Derbys.	(9)	(— c.99)
—	(TR) Foston Lane–Borleston (TR)	Leices.	(9)	(— c.100)
—	Elton–Talke	Ches. & Staffs.	(8)	(— c.104)
—	Kingsham–Kington and Radnor Road (TR), etc.	Heref.	(4)	(— c.105)
1789	Bishop Wearmouth–Norton	Durham	(11)	(29 Geo. III c.81)
—	Wakefield–Abberford	Yorks.	(10)	(— c.86)
—	Odiham–Farnham	Surr.	(2)	(— c.89)
—	Congleton–Prestbury, etc.	Ches.	(8)	(— c.91)
—	Overbury–London Road (TR)	Worces.	(7)	(— c.102)
—	Bury–Haslingden–Blackburn	Lancs.	(10)	(— c.107)
—	Heywood–Heaton	Lancs.	(10)	(— c.110)
1790	Dudley–Sedgley, etc.	Worces., Salop & Staffs.	(8)	(30 Geo. III c.102)
—	Fosbrook–Cheadleton (TR)	Staffs.	(8)	(— c.100)
—	Bromham–Olney (TR), etc.	Bucks. & Beds.	(6)	(— c.114)
1791	Canterbury–Barham (TR)	Kent	(2)	(31 Geo. III c.94)
—	Bicester–Aynho (TR)	Oxon. & Northants.	(6)	(— c.103)
—	Swindon–Christian Malford, etc.	Wilts.	(4)	(— c.121)
—	Buckingham–Banbury	Northants. & Bucks.	(6)	(— c.133)
—	Great Marlow–Stokenchurch	Bucks. & Oxon.	(1)	(— c.135)
1792	West Auckland–Elishaw	Durham & Northum.	(11)	(32 Geo. III c.113)
—	Folkestone–Barham (TR)	Kent	(2)	(— c.117)
—	Yoxford–Aldeburgh, etc.	Suff.	(3)	(— c.126)
—	Middleton-on-Tees–Staindrop, etc.	Durham	(11)	(— c.127)
—	Chapel-en-le-Frith–Entreclough Bridge, etc.	Yorks., Ches. & Durham	(9)	(— c.128)

Year	Road	County	Area	Act
1792	Peterborough–Thorney	Cambs.	(6)	(32 Geo. III c.129)
—	Bradford–Bathford Bridge (TR)	Wilts. & Somer.	(4)	(— c.137)
—	Saddleworth–Oldham, etc.	Yorks. & Lancs.	(10)	(— c.139)
—	Belford–Ford Bridge, etc.	Northum. & Durham	(11)	(— c.145)
—	Lower Swell–Alderton (TR)	Glos. & Worces.	(4)	(— c.146)
—	Bury St Edmunds–Cranwich (TR)	Norf. & Suff.	(3)	(— c.148)
—	(TR) Burford–Lechlade (TR), etc.	Berks., Oxon., Glos. & Wilts.	(4)	(— c.153)
1793	Uttoxeter–Stoke	Staffs.	(8)	(33 Geo. III c.131)
—	Saddleworth–Thornset, etc.	Derbys., Yorks. & Ches.	(8)	(— c.140)
—	Little Bowden–Rockingham (TR)	Northants.	(6)	(— c.143)
—	Cockerton Bridge–Staindrop	Durham	(11)	(— c.146)
—	(TR) Whickham–Stanhope, etc.	Durham & Northum.	(11)	(— c.147)
—	(TR) Thundersly–Hornden, etc.	Essex	(1)	(— c.149)
—	New Sleaford–Tattershall Ferry	Lincs.	(3)	(— c.150)
—	Wirksworth–Hulland Ward (TR)	Derbys.	(9)	(— c.152)
—	Stafford–Church Bridge, etc.	Staffs. & Salop	(8)	(— c.153)
—	Hemingborough–Market Weighton	Yorks.	(10)	(— c.159)
—	Ashford–Orlestone	Kent	(2)	(— c.162)
—	West Harptree–Marksbury, etc.	Somer.	(4)	(— c.165)
—	Bawtry–Selby	Yorks.	(10)	(— c.166)
—	Wombourne–Sedgley, etc.	Staffs.	(8)	(— c.167)
—	Maidstone–Ashford	Kent	(2)	(— c.173)
—	Hedge–Duffield	Derbys.	(9)	(— c.177)
—	(TR) Clay Hill–Bicester, etc.	Oxon.	(7)	(— c.180)
—	Odiham–Alton	Hants.	(2)	(— c.182)
—	Kelso–Cornhill, etc.	Durham & Northum.	(11)	(— c.185)
1794	Norwich–Aylsham	Norf.	(3)	(34 Geo. III c.114)
—	Ticknall–Castle Gresley, etc.	Derbys. & Leices.	(9)	(— c.120)
—	Rochdale–Edenfield	Lancs.	(10)	(— c.124)
—	Bartry Ford–Burnstones	Durham, Northum. & Cumber.	(11)	(— c.125)
—	Oundle–Middleton, etc.	Northants.	(6)	(— c.126)
—	Dunchurch–Southam	War.	(7)	(— c.128)
—	Rawreth–Chelmsford	Essex	(1)	(— c.137)
—	Lyne Bridge–Scotch Dyke	Cumber.	(11)	(— c.143)
1795	Odiham–Ripponden, etc.	Yorks. & Lancs.	(10)	(35 Geo. III c.137)
—	Preston Condover–Alton	Hants.	(2)	(— c.138)
—	Burnley–Tottington (TR)	Lancs.	(10)	(— c.146)
—	Bedford–Kimbolton	Beds.	(6)	(— c.148)
—	(TR) Ellesborough–West Wycombe	Bucks.	(1)	(— c.149)
—	Stamford–Greetham, etc.	Lincs. & Rut.	(3)	(— c.152)
—	Towcaster–Hardingstone	Northants.	(6)	(— c.153)
1796	Roads in the Forest of Dean	Glos.	(4)	(36 Geo. III c.131)
—	Monk Wearmouth–South Shields	Durham & Northum.	(11)	(— c.136)

Year	Road	County	Area	Act
1796	(TR) Little Yarmouth–Blythburgh (TR)	Suff.	(3)	(36 Geo. III c.142)
—	Macclesfield–Congleton	Ches.	(8)	(— c.148)
—	Old Trent Bridge–Nottingham	Notts.	(9)	(— c.152)
1797	Rochdale–Middleton–Bury	Lancs.	(10)	(37 Geo. III c.145)
—	Castleton–Bury	Lancs.	(10)	(— c.146)
—	Norwich–North Walsham	Norf.	(3)	(— c.147)
—	Cambridge–Arrington Bridge	Cambs.	(6)	(— c.152)
—	Dover–Deal–Sandwich	Kent	(2)	(— c.156)
—	(TR) Holmes Chapel–Chelford	Ches.	(8)	(— c.157)
—	Milnthorpe–Kirkby Lonsdale	Westmor.	(11)	(— c.165)
—	Wellingborough–Northampton	Northants.	(6)	(— c.167)
—	Atcham–Dorrington (TR)	Salop	(8)	(— c.172)
—	Little Bolton–Blackburn	Lancs.	(10)	(— c.173)
—	Tottington–Little Bolton–Bury	Lancs.	(10)	(— c.174)
1799	Cheadle–Rochester, etc.	Staffs.	(8)	(39 Geo. III c.75)
1800	(TR) Witney–Tew (TR), etc.	Oxon.	(4)	(39 & 40 Geo. III c.16)
—	Ince in Makerfield–Ashton in Makerfield	Lancs.	(10)	(— c.73)
—	Great Bolton–Westhoughton Chapel (TR)	Lancs.	(10)	(— c.74)
1801	(TR) Curdridge Common–Corhampton	Hants.	(2)	(41 Geo. III c.8)
—	Dover–Sandwich	Kent	(2)	(— c.11)
—	New Windsor–Datchet	Berks. & Bucks.	(1)	(— c.37)
—	Ewhurst–Northiam, etc.	Suss.	(2)	(— c.50)
—	Rugby–Kilworth	War.	(7)	(— c.83)
—	Stockport–Marple Bridge, etc.	Ches. & Derbys.	(8)	(— c.98)
—	Bolton–Blackburn	Lancs.	(10)	(— c.123)
—	Paddington–Harrow-on-the-Hill	Middx.	(1)	(— c.129)
1802	Canterbury–Sandwich	Kent	(2)	(42 Geo. III c.6)
—	Woodbridge–Eye	Suff.	(3)	(— c.8)
—	Banbury–Barcheston	Oxon. & War.	(7)	(— c.38)
—	Newant–Gloucester–Hereford Road (TR)	Heref. & Glos.	(4)	(— c.45)
—	Broadwater–Steyning (TR)	Suss.	(2)	(— c.62)
—	Great Staughton–Lavendon	Hunts., Beds. & Bucks.	(6)	(— c.64)
—	Alfreton–Derby	Derbys.	(9)	(— c.83)
—	East India Docks Roads	Middx.	(1)	(— c.101)
1803	Thirsk–Yarm	Yorks.	(10)	(43 Geo. III c.2)
—	(TR) Maidstone–Sutton Valence	Kent	(2)	(— c.13)
—	Glossop–Marple Bridge, etc.	Derbys.	(9)	(— c.18)
—	Arundel–Petworth	Suss.	(2)	(— c.67)
—	Marsden–Long Preston	Yorks. & Lancs.	(10)	(— c.69)
—	(TR) Harwell–Streatley (TR)	Berks.	(1)	(— c.92)
—	Scartho–Louth	Lincs.	(3)	(— c.133)
1804	Eccles–Farnworth (TR)	Lancs.	(10)	(44 Geo. III c.26)
—	(TR) West Bromwich–Sutton Coldfield	Staffs. & War.	(8)	(— c.40)

Year	Road	County	Area	Act
1804	Grantham–Swanton, etc.	Lincs.	(3)	(44 Geo. III c.50)
—	Cromford–Hopton Moor	Derbys.	(9)	(— c.67)
1805	Chadderton–Huddersfield, etc.	Yorks. & Lancs.	(10)	(45 Geo. III c.7)
—	(TR) Wadsley–Langsett (TR)	Yorks.	(10)	(— c.107)
1806	Manchester–Eccles, etc.	Lancs.	(10)	(46 Geo. III c.2)
—	Huddersfield–New Hay	Lancs. & Yorks.	(10)	(— c.13)
—	(TR) Leversage–Cleckheaton	Yorks.	(10)	(— c.17)
—	Carlisle–Westleton	Cumber.	(11)	(— c.53)
1807	Upottery–Ilminster (TR)	Somer.	(5)	(47 Geo. III c.6)
—	Sandwich–Margate and Ramsgate	Kent	(2)	(— c.22)
—	Croydon–Reigate	Surr.	(2)	(— c.25)
—	Birmingham–Shenstone, etc.	War.	(8)	(47 Geo. III 2nd Sess. c.10)
—	Percy's Cross–Millfield, etc.	Northum.	(11)	(— c.13)
—	Brampton–Longtown	Cumber.	(11)	(— c.15)
1808	Leeds–Roundhay	Yorks.	(10)	(48 Geo. III c.15)
—	Ideridge–Duffield	Derbys.	(9)	(— c.31)
—	(TR) West Ham–Tilbury Fort	Essex	(1)	(— c.92)
—	(TR) Pyecombe–Stapleford Common (TR)	Suss.	(2)	(— c.101)
1809	Rotherham–Swinton	Yorks.	(10)	(49 Geo. III c.5)
—	(TR) Horsham–Warnham (TR)	Suss. & Surr.	(2)	(— c.12)
—	Churchdown–Cheltenham	Glos.	(4)	(— c.29)
—	Rickmansworth–Pinner, etc.	Herts.	(1)	(— c.51)
—	Malmsbury–Sutton Benger, etc.	Wilts.	(4)	(— c.89)
—	Wootton Basset–Swindon and Marlborough Road (TR)	Wilts.	(4)	(— c.90)
—	Tonbridge–Ightham	Kent	(2)	(— c.91)
—	Stockershead–Chilham (TR)	Kent	(2)	(— c.92)
—	Horley Common–Cuckfield (TR)	Suss.	(2)	(— c.94)
—	Coalbrookdale–Welsh Bridge (towing path on Severn)	Salop	(8)	(— c.121)
—	Burton-upon-Trent–Bagots Bromley	Staffs.	(8)	(— c.145)
—	Soho Hill–Hamstead Bridge	Staffs.	(8)	(— c.147)
—	Southwark–Kent Street	Surr.	(2)	(— c.186)
1810	Cheltenham–Bishop's Cleeve (TR)	Glos. & Worces.	(4)	(50 Geo. III c.2)
—	Durham–Shotley Bridge	Durham	(11)	(— c.3)
—	Titchfield–Cosham	Hants.	(2)	(— c.14)
—	Shoreham–Chelsfield, etc.	Kent	(2)	(— c.18)
—	Titchfield–Twyford, etc.	Hants.	(2)	(— c.22)
—	Pulborough–Steyning	Suss.	(2)	(— c.55)
—	(TR) Clown–Budby (TR)	Derbys. & Notts.	(9)	(— c.59)
—	Wisbech–Thorney	Cambs.	(6)	(— c.74)
—	Aylesbury–Hockliffe	Bucks. & Beds.	(1)	(— c.94)
—	Bury–Elton–Blackburn, etc.	Lancs.	(10)	(— c.137)
—	Ashford–Buxton	Derbys.	(9)	(— c.171)
—	Cirencester–Wootton Bassett	Wilts. & Glos.	(4)	(— c.174)
1811	Barton Bridge–Stretford	Lancs.	(10)	(51 Geo. III c.31)
—	(TR) Wem–Sandford (TR)	Salop	(8)	(— c.44)
—	(TR) Bakewell–Bentley (TR)	Derbys.	(9)	(— c.74)
—	Billinghurst–Broadbridge Heath	Suss.	(2)	(— c.80)

Year	Road	County	Area	Act
1811	Kingston-upon-Thames–Leatherhead	Surr.	(2)	(51 Geo. III c.109)
—	Long Preston–Sawley	Yorks.	(10)	(— c.111)
—	Kentish Town–Holloway Road	Middx.	(1)	(— c.156)
—	Ightham–Wrotham	Kent	(2)	(— c.157)
—	Kent Road–Deptford (TR)	Surr.	(2)	(— c.220)
1812	Buckland–Lidford–Dartmoor Prison	Devon	(5)	(52 Geo. III c.4)
—	Ipswich–Helmingham, etc.	Suff.	(3)	(— c.23)
—	Ipswich–Stratford St Mary	Suff.	(3)	(— c.24)
—	(TR) Ockley–Warnham (TR)	Suss. & Surr.	(2)	(— c.26)
—	Roads in Coventry	War.	(7)	(— c.57)
—	Rugby–Hinckley	War. & Leices.	(9)	(— c.82)
—	Storrington–Walberton	Suss.	(2)	(— c.92)
—	Offham–Ditchling	Suss.	(2)	(— c.115)
—	Eccleshall–Dore, etc.	Yorks. & Derbys.	(9)	(— c.116)
—	Tideswell–Blackwell, etc.	Derbys.	(9)	(— c.121)
—	Broughton–Penrith, etc.	Westmor. & Cumber.	(11)	(— c.122)
—	Tower Hill–Smithfield	Middx.	(1)	(— c.149)
—	Highbury–Shoreditch	Middx.	(1)	(— c.154)
1813	Coventry–Wolvey	War.	(7)	(53 Geo. III c.6)
—	Battle–Dallington, etc.	Suss.	(2)	(— c.22)
—	Cullompton–Broad Cliff	Devon	(5)	(— c.65)
1814	(TR) Burbage–Narborough (TR)	Leices.	(9)	(54 Geo. III c.24)
—	Tynemouth–Morpeth	Northum. & Durham	(11)	(— c.29)
—	Swindon–Ramsbury	Wilts.	(4)	(— c.50)
—	Sturry–Herne	Kent	(2)	(— c.51)
—	Balderstone–Burscough Bridge	Lancs.	(10)	(— c.54)
—	Bingley–Halifax	Yorks.	(10)	(— c.62)
—	Stroud–Sapperton	Glos.	(4)	(— c.80)
—	Alcester–Upton Wawen	War.	(7)	(— c.84)
—	Bedford–Sherrington (TR)	Bucks. & Beds.	(6)	(— c.124)
—	(TR) Potton–Eynesbury (TR)	Cambs., Beds. & Hunts.	(6)	(— c.180)
1815	Stanhope–Shotley	Northum. & Durham	(11)	(55 Geo. III c.10)
—	Halifax–Dewsbury	Yorks.	(10)	(— c.13)
—	(TR) Mytholmroyd Bridge–Calderbrook	Yorks. & Lancs.	(10)	(— c.32)
—	Buckingham–Old Stratford (TR)	Bucks.	(1)	(— c.75)
1816	Dewsbury–Leeds	Yorks.	(10)	(56 Geo. III c.6)
—	Nantwich–Sandbach	Ches.	(8)	(— c.15)
—	Stourbridge–Worfield and Bridgnorth Road	Worces. & Salop	(8)	(— c.16)
—	Gatton Lodge–Povey Cross	Surr.	(2)	(— c.30)
—	Gittisham–Sidmouth	Devon	(5)	(— c.32)
1817	Broad Compton Hill–Halford Bridge, etc.	Glos., War. & Worces.	(7)	(57 Geo. III c.5)
—	Coalbrookdale–Wellington	Salop	(8)	(— c.12)
—	Cromford–Belper, etc.	Derbys.	(9)	(— c.13)
—	Boughton-under-Stainmore–Ronaldkirk	Westmor. & Yorks.	(10)	(— c.45)

Year	Road	County	Area	Act
1817	Manchester–Newton Chapel, etc.	Lancs.	(10)	(57 Geo. III c.47)
—	Leeds–Holmefield Lane End	Yorks.	(10)	(— c.51)
—	Crowland–Eye	Lincs. & Northants.	(3)	(— c.54)
1818	Stroud–Gloucester	Glos.	(4)	(58 Geo. III c.1)
—	Manchester–Denton– Stockport	Ches. & Lancs.	(10)	(— c.6)
—	Rugby–Warwick	War.	(7)	(— c.32)
—	Sheffield–Glossop, etc.	Yorks. & Derbys.	(10)	(— c.35)
—	Brampton–Mexborough, etc.	Yorks.	(10)	(— c.37)
—	Lockwood–Meltham, etc.	Yorks.	(10)	(— c.41)
—	Bramley–Ridgewick	Surr. & Suss.	(2)	(— c.69)
—	Ulverstone–Heversham	Lancs. & Westmor.	(10)	(— c.70)
—	Chipping Campden–Old Stratford	Glos. & War.	(7)	(— c.72)
—	Greenwich–Woolwich Lower Road	Kent	(2)	(— c.78)
1819	Kettering–Northampton	Northants.	(6)	(59 Geo. III c.41)
—	(TR) Barnsdale–Castleford (TR)	Yorks.	(10)	(— c.81)
—	Marlborough–Liddington	Wilts.	(4)	(— c.83)
—	Runcorn–Northwich	Ches.	(8)	(— c.85)
—	Biddulph–Astbury, etc.	Ches. & Staffs.	(8)	(— c.87)
1820	Cheltenham–Prinknash (TR)	Glos.	(4)	(1 Geo. IV c.16)
—	Stockport–Warrington, etc.	Ches. & Lancs.	(10)	(— c.28)
—	Tenterden–Warehorne, etc.	Kent	(2)	(— c.46)
1821	Bury–Little Bolton	Lancs.	(10)	(1 & 2 Geo. IV c.90)
1822	Brighton–Shoreham	Suss.	(2)	(3 Geo. IV c.13)
—	Mansfield–Worksop	Notts.	(9)	(— c.37)
—	Great Marlow–West Wycombe, etc.	Bucks.	(1)	(— c.92)
1823	Stroud–Bisley	Glos.	(4)	(4 Geo. IV c.14)
—	Leeds–Holmefield Lane End (Wortley)	Yorks.	(10)	(— c.16)
—	Horsham–Crawley	Suss.	(2)	(— c.42)
—	East Teignmouth–Starcross (TR)	Devon	(5)	(— c.44)
—	Wibsey Low Moor– Huddersfield, etc.	Yorks.	(10)	(— c.54)
—	Greenfield–Shepley Lane Head	Yorks.	(10)	(— c.58)
—	Norwich–Fakenham	Norf.	(3)	(— c.80)
1824	Carlisle–Cockermouth	Cumber.	(11)	(5 Geo. IV c.7)
—	Pulborough–Horsham	Suss.	(2)	(— c.16)
—	Broadway–Mickleton (TR)	Worces. & Glos.	(7)	(— c.28)
—	Pedbrook–St Arvans, etc.	Glos. & Mon.	(4)	(— c.29)
—	Roads leading into Cerne Abbas	Dorset	(5)	(— c.30)
—	Dartmouth–Modbury, etc.	Devon	(5)	(— c.31)
—	Colne–Boughton (TR)	Yorks. & Lancs.	(10)	(— c.44)
—	Rugeley–Alrewas	Staffs.	(8)	(— c.45)
—	Blackburn–Preston (TR)	Lancs.	(10)	(— c.55)
—	Clarborough–Littleborough Ferry	Notts.	(9)	(— c.57)
—	Roundhay–Collingham	Yorks.	(10)	(— c.82)
—	Salterhibble–Huddersfield, etc.	Yorks.	(10)	(— c.89)

Year	Road	County	Area	Act
1824	Bradford–Heckmondwicke	Yorks.	(10)	(5 Geo. IV c.90)
—	Brighthelmston–Newhaven	Suss.	(2)	(— c.91)
—	Godley Lane Head–Halifax	Yorks.	(10)	(— c.106)
—	Camden Town–Holloway	Middx.	(1)	(— c.138)
—	Buckingham–Towcester	Bucks.	(1)	(— c.141)
—	Manchester–Bolton	Lancs.	(10)	(— c.143)
—	Shipley–Caisthorne	Yorks.	(1)	(— c.146)
1825	Penworth am Bridge–Little Hanging Bridge	Lancs.	(10)	(6 Geo. IV c.2)
—	(TR) Wellington–Tong Lane End	Yorks.	(10)	(— c.3)
—	Midhurst–near Sheetbridge (TR)	Suss.	(2)	(— c.11)
—	Kirkby Stephen–Gayle	Westmor. & Yorks.	(11)	(— c.12)
—	Winchester–Petersfield	Hants.	(2)	(— c.14)
—	Minchinghampton–Stroud, etc.	Glos.	(4)	(— c.23)
—	(TR) Snodland–Strood	Kent	(2)	(— c.25)
—	Hope (TR)–Bromyard (TR)	Heref.	(4)	(— c.26)
—	Wooler–Adderstone Lane	Northum.	(11)	(— c.28)
—	Wakefield–Denby Dale	Yorks.	(10)	(— c.38)
—	Eccleshill–Bradford	Yorks.	(10)	(— c.42)
—	Brighouse–Denholme Gate	Yorks.	(10)	(— c.44)
—	Barnsley–Cudworth Bridge	Yorks.	(10)	(— c.48)
—	Gravesend–Borough Green	Kent	(2)	(— c.50)
—	Manchester–Ashton-under-Lyne	Lancs.	(10)	(— c.51)
—	Trebarwith Sands–Condolden Bridge	Corn.	(5)	(— c.84)
—	Cockermouth–Wigton	Cumber.	(11)	(— c.85)
—	Bolton–Haslingden, etc.	Lancs.	(10)	(— c.92)
—	(TR) Almondbury–Austonley (TR)	Yorks.	(10)	(— c.103)
—	Birmingham–Pershore	War.	(7)	(— c.142)
—	Kingston-upon-Hull–Ferriby	Yorks.	(10)	(— c.152)
—	Brompton–Fulham Road	Middx.	(1)	(— c.160)
—	Doncaster–Thorne	Yorks.	(10)	(— c.185)
1826	Worthing–Lancing	Suss.	(2)	(7 Geo. IV c.10)
—	Godalming–Pains Hill	Surr.	(2)	(— c.13)
—	South Shields–Vigo Lane	Durham & Northum.	(11)	(— c.17)
—	Little Neston–Hoose	Ches.	(8)	(— c.19)
—	Ashton-under-Lyne–Saddleworth	Yorks. & Lancs.	(10)	(— c.21)
—	Arrow–Pothooks Lane End	Worces. & War.	(7)	(— c.23)
—	Wimpole–Potton	Cambs. & Beds.	(6)	(— c.29)
—	Langport Eastover–Meare	Somer.	(5)	(— c.39)
—	Maltby–Barnby Moor, etc.	Yorks. & Notts.	(10)	(— c.40)
—	Cows Hill–Calton, etc.	Durham & Northum.	(11)	(— c.74)
—	Alwick–Haggerston	Durham & Northum.	(11)	(— c.75)
—	Coxbridge–Ramshill	Hants.	(2)	(— c.80)
—	Manchester–Pilkington (TR)	Lancs.	(10)	(— c.81)
—	Swineshead–Fosdyke	Lincs.	(3)	(— c.83)
—	Marylebone–Finchley Road	Middx.	(1)	(— c.90)

Year	Road	County	Area	Act
1826	Gomersal–Dewsbury	Yorks.	(10)	(7 Geo. IV c.93)
—	Shipley–Bramley	Yorks.	(10)	(— c.129)
1827	Chesterfield–Tibshelf Side Gate (TR)	Derbys.	(9)	(7 & 8 Geo. IV c.4)
—	Ashcott–Rowburrow Hill (TR)	Somer.	(4)	(— c.5)
—	Northampton–Cold Brayfield	Northants. & Bucks.	(6)	(— c.71)
—	Wotton-under-Edge–Wickwar	Glos. & Wilts.	(4)	(— c.100)
1828	Allington–Crewkerne, etc.	Wilts. & Somer.	(4)	(9 Geo. IV c.19)
—	Carlisle–Brampton	Cumber.	(11)	(— c.20)
—	Mildenhall–Littleport, etc.	Norf. & Suff.	(3)	(— c.44)
—	Hunslet–Leeds, etc.	Yorks.	(10)	(— c.67)
—	Earls Court–Hammersmith Bridge	Middx.	(1)	(— c.103)
1829	Barnstaple–Braunton	Devon	(5)	(10 Geo. IV c.17)
—	Tarporley–Whitchurch	Salop & Ches.	(8)	(— c.77)
—	Sheepscar–Leeds	Yorks.	(10)	(— c.87)
1830	Allesley–Canwell	War. & Staffs.	(8)	(11 Geo. IV c.20)
—	Great Yarmouth–Acle	Norf.	(3)	(— c.39)
—	Kingston-upon-Hull–Hedon	Yorks.	(10)	(— c.96)
1831	Coventry–Stoney Stanton (TR)	Leices. & War.	(7)	(1 Wm. IV c.40)
—	Perry Barr–Aston juxta Birmingham	Staffs. & War.	(8)	(— c.47)
—	Darlington–Middleton Tyas	Durham & Yorks.	(11)	(1 & 2 Wm. IV c.13)
—	Thornset–Disley	Derbys. & Ches.	(8)	(— c.17)
—	Kirkgate–Westgate (both in Wakefield)	Yorks.	(10)	(— c.27)
—	Tedburn St Mary–Chudleigh	Devon	(5)	(— c.31)
1832	New Windsor–Hurst	Berks. & Wilts.	(4)	(2 & 3 Wm. IV c.17)
—	Lympstone–Exmouth	Devon	(5)	(— c.52)
—	Cann St Rumbold–Bramshaw	Dorset & Hants.	(5)	(— c.64)
—	Doncaster–Selby	Yorks.	(10)	(— c.86)
1833	Bishop's Waltham–Owslebury	Hants.	(2)	(3 Wm. IV c.17)
—	Winlaton–Shotley Bridge	Durham	(11)	(— c.79)
1834	Ministerly–Churchstoke	Salop & Mont.	(8)	(4 & 5 Wm. IV c.11)
1835	Hurstpierpoint–Cuckfield	Suss.	(2)	(5 & 6 Wm. IV c.24)
—	Nantwich–Congleton	Ches.	(8)	(— c.28)
—	Chester–Sandbach–Congleton	Ches.	(8)	(— c.37)
1836	Radcliffe–Bolton–Bury	Lancs.	(10)	(6 & 7 Wm. IV c.10)
—	Richmond–Reeth	Yorks.	(10)	(— c.17)
—	Ewhurst–Whatlington, etc.	Suss.	(2)	(— c.19)
—	Hollington–Hastings	Suss.	(2)	(— c.46)

APPENDIX C

Main Route Turnpike Trust Development

In the following tables only the towns on the main routes have been noted, although many trusts controlled other roads.

The mileages given are approximate and were derived by measuring distances on the Quarter Inch Series Ordnance Survey Maps, Sheet 12 (1960), Sheets 10, 13, 14, 15, 16, 17 (1962), Sheets 9 and 11 (1964). Reference was also made to *Paterson's Roads* (18th edition, London, 1831-2 ?).

(1) *Great North Road*

Route via Highgate and Barnet

Islington, Holborn etc.–Highgate	4m	1717 (3 Geo. I c.4)
Highgate–Barnet	6m	1711 (10 Anne c.4)
Barnet–Gally Corner	1m	*not turnpiked by 1750*
Gally Corner–Lemsford Mill	9m	1730 (3 Geo. II c.10)
Lemsford Mill–Stevenage	7m	1726 (12 Geo. I c.10)
Stevenage–Biggleswade	12m	1720 (6 Geo. I c.25)
Biggleswade–Alconbury	22m	1725 (11 Geo. I c.20)

Route via Ware and Royston

Shoreditch–Enfield	12m	1712 (12 Anne c.19)
Enfield–Ware	12m	1725 (11 Geo. I c.11)
Ware–Wadesmill[1]	2m	1733 (6 Geo. II c.15)
Wadesmill–Royston[2]	15m	1663 (15 Car. II c.1)
Royston–Wansford Bridge	42m	1710 (9 Anne c.14)

Wansford Bridge–Stamford	6m	1749 (22 Geo. II c.17)
Stamford–Grantham	22m	1739 (12 Geo. II c.8)
Grantham–Little Drayton	28m	1726 (12 Geo. I c.16)
Little Drayton–Doncaster[3]	22m	*not turnpiked by 1750*
Doncaster–Boroughbridge	42m	1741 (14 Geo. II c.28)
Boroughbridge–Darlington–Durham[4]	48m	1745 (18 Geo. II c.8)
Durham–Newcastle-upon-Tyne	14m	1747 (20 Geo. II c.12)
Newcastle-upon-Tyne–Buckton Burn	51m	1747 (20 Geo. II c.9)
Buckton Burn–Berwick-upon-Tweed[5]	10m	*not turnpiked by 1750*

387 miles

by 1730: 169 miles
by 1750: 355 miles

[1] This road was added to Enfield–Ware Trust.

[2] This justice-trust extended to Stilton; however, it seems that only the Hertfordshire portion was ever affected. For the portion of the road north of Royston the act expired in 1674.

[3] The road from Little Drayton to Bawtry was turnpiked in 1766 (6 Geo. III c.67). The Doncaster–Bawtry Road was turnpiked in 1776 (16 Geo. III c.71).

[4] The road from Boroughbridge through Catterick to Piercebridge was turnpiked in 1743 (16 Geo. II c.7).

[5] This road was turnpiked in 1753 (26 Geo. II c.46).

(2) *London–Derby–Manchester Road*

Islington, Holborn etc.–Highgate	4m	1717 (3 Geo. I c.4)
Highgate–Barnet	6m	1711 (10 Anne c.4)
Barnet–South Mimms	3m	*not turnpiked by 1750*
South Mimms–St Albans	6m	1715 (1 Geo. I c.12)
St Albans–Dunstable	13m	1723 (9 Geo. I c.11)
Dunstable–Hockliffe	4m	1710 (9 Anne c.34)
Hockliffe–Woburn	5m	1706 (6 Anne c.13)
Woburn–Newport Pagnell[6]	8m	1728 (1 Geo. II c.10)
Newport Pagnell–Stoke Goldington[7]	4m	1723 (9 Geo. I c.13)
Stoke Goldington–Northampton	10m	1708 (8 Anne c.9)
Northampton–Pitsford Bridge[8]	5m	1750 (23 Geo. II c.8)
Pitsford Bridge–Market Harborough	12m	1722 (8 Geo. I c.13)
Market Harborough–Loughborough	25m	1726 (12 Geo. I c.5)
Loughborough–Hartington	39m	1738 (11 Geo. II c.33)
Hartington–Buxton	10m	*not turnpiked by 1750*
Buxton–Manchester	23m	1725 (11 Geo. I c.13)

177 miles

by 1730: 120 miles
by 1750: 164 miles

(3) *London–Cirencester–Gloucester and Hereford Road*

Kensington–Cranford Bridge	12m	1717 (3 Geo. I c.14)
Cranford Bridge–Maidenhead Bridge	14m	1727 (13 Geo. I c.31)
Maidenhead Bridge–Henley-on-Thames	9m	1718 (4 Geo. I c.6)
Henley-on-Thames–Abingdon	19m	1736 (9 Geo. II c.14)
Abingdon–Fyfield	6m	*not turnpiked by 1750*
Fyfield–St John's Bridge	14m	1733 (6 Geo. II c.16)
St John's Bridge–Cirencester	13m	1727 (13 Geo. I c.11)
Cirencester–Birdlip Hill	10m	1747 (20 Geo. II c.23)
Birdlip Hill–Gloucester	6m	1696/7 (9 Wm. III c.18)
Gloucester–Hereford	29m	1726 (12 Geo. I c.13)

132 miles

by 1730: 83 miles
by 1750: 126 miles

(4) *London–Oxford–Gloucester and Hereford Road*

Tyburn–Uxbridge	15m	1715 (1 Geo. I c.25)
Uxbridge–Beaconsfield[9]	8m	*not turnpiked by 1750*
Beaconsfield–Stokenchurch	12m	1719 (5 Geo. I c.1)
Stokenchurch–Oxford	18m	1719 (5 Geo. I c.2)
Oxford–Crickley Hill[10]	41m	*not turnpiked by 1750*
Crickley Hill–Gloucester	4m	1723 (9 Geo. I c.31)
Gloucester–Hereford	29m	1726 (12 Geo. I c.13)

[6]This road was added to the Hockliffe–Woburn Trust, which by this act was placed under trustee control.
[7]This road was added to the Stoke Goldington–Northampton Trust.
[8]This road was added to the Pitsford Bridge–Market Harborough Trust.
[9]This road, turnpiked in 1751 (24 Geo. II c.32), was added to the Wendover–Buckingham Trust.
[10]This road was turnpiked in 1751 (24 Geo. II c.28).

127 miles

by 1730: 78 miles
by 1750: 78 miles

(5) *London–Bath and Bristol Road*

Kensington–Cranford Bridge	12m	1717 (3 Geo. I c.14)
Cranford Bridge–Maidenhead Bridge	14m	1727 (13 Geo. I c.31)
Maidenhead Bridge–Twyford	8m	1718 (4 Geo. I c.6)
Twyford–Reading	5m	1736 (9 Geo. II c.21)
Reading–Puntfield	6·5m	1714 (13 Anne c.28)
Puntfield–Newbury[11]	11m	1728 (1 Geo. I c.7)
Newbury–Marlborough	17m	1726 (12 Geo. I c.8)
Marlborough–Cherhill	8m	1743 (16 Geo. II c.10)
Cherhill–Studley Bridge	5m	1707 (6 Anne c.76)
Studley Bridge–Toghill	16m	1727 (13 Geo. I c.13)
Toghill–Bristol	8m	1727 (13 Geo. I c.12)
Chippenham–Box[12]	8m	1726 (12 Geo. I c.11)
Box–Bath	7m	1707 (6 Anne c.42)

125·5 miles

by 1730: 97·5 miles
by 1750: 125·5 miles

(6) *London–Oxford–Birmingham and Worcester Road*

Tyburn–Uxbridge	15m	1715 (1 Geo. I c.25)
Uxbridge–Beaconsfield[13]	8m	*not turnpiked by 1750*
Beaconsfield–Stokenchurch	12m	1719 (5 Geo. I c.1)
Stokenchurch–Woodstock	28m	1719 (5 Geo. I c.2)
Woodstock–Roll Right	12m	1730 (3 Geo. II c.21)
Roll Right–Long Compton	2m	*not turnpiked by 1750*
Long Compton–Stratford-upon-Avon	15m	1730 (3 Geo. II c.9)
Stratford-upon-Avon–Birmingham	21m	1726 (12 Geo. I c.6)
Chipping Norton–Bourton-on-the-Hill[14]	15m	1731 (4 Geo. II c.23)
Bourton-on-the-Hill–Broadway Hill	4m	*not turnpiked by 1750*
Broadway Hill–Stonebow Bridge	20m	1728 (1 Geo. II c.11)
Stonebow Bridge–Worcester	3m	1726 (12 Geo. I c.14)

156 miles[15]

by 1730: 126 miles
by 1750: 141 miles

(7) *London–Warwick–Birmingham Road*

Tyburn–Uxbridge	15m	1715 (1 Geo. I c.25)
Uxbridge–Wendover[16]	20m	*not turnpiked by 1750*

[11]This road was added to the Reading–Puntfield Trust.
[12]Chippenham is on the London–Bristol Road.
[13]This road, turnpiked in 1751 (24 Geo. II c.32), was added to the Wendover–Buckingham Trust.
[14]The Woodstock–Roll Right Trust passed within one mile of Chipping Norton.
[15]This total includes the one mile between the Woodstock–Roll Right Trust and Chipping Norton.
[16]This road, turnpiked in 1751 (24 Geo. II c.32), was added to the Wendover–Buckingham Trust.

Wendover–Buckingham	20m	1721 (7 Geo. I (st. 1) c.24)
Buckingham–Warmington	22m	1744 (17 Geo. II c.43)
Warmington–Birmingham	33m	1726 (12 Geo. I c.6)

110 miles

by 1730: 68 miles
by 1750: 90 miles

(8) *London–Birmingham–Shrewsbury Road*

Islington, Holborn etc.—Highgate	4m	1717 (3 Geo. I c.4)
Highgate–Barnet	6m	1711 (10 Anne c.4)
Barnet–South Mimms	3m	*not turnpiked by 1750*
South Mimms–St Albans	6m	1715 (1 Geo. I c.12)
St Albans–Dunstable	13m	1723 (9 Geo. I c.11)
Dunstable–Hockliffe	4m	1710 (9 Anne c.34)
Hockliffe–Stony Stratford	15m	1706 (6 Anne c.4)
Old Stratford–Dunchurch[17]	30m	1707 (6 Anne c.77)
Dunchurch–Meriden	17m	1724 (10 Geo. I c.15)
Meriden–Stone Br.	4m	*not turnpiked by 1750*
Stone Br.–Birmingham	6m	1745 (18 Geo. II c.19)
Birmingham–Wednesbury[18]	10m	1725 (13 Geo. I c.14)
Wednesbury–Shifnal	18m	1748 (21 Geo. II c.25)
Shifnal–Shrewsbury	17m	1726 (12 Geo. I c.9)

153 miles

by 1730: 122 miles
by 1750: 146 miles

(9) *London–Chester Road*

Islington, Holborn etc.-Highgate	4m	1717 (3 Geo. I c.4)
Highgate–Barnet	6m	1711 (10 Anne c.4)
Barnet–South Mimms	3m	*not turnpiked by 1750*
South Mimms–St Albans	6m	1715 (1 Geo. I c.12)
St Albans–Dunstable	13m	1723 (9 Geo. I c.11)
Dunstable–Hockliffe	4m	1710 (9 Anne c.34)
Hockliffe–Stony Stratford	15m	1706 (6 Anne c.4)
Old Stratford–Dunchurch	30m	1707 (6 Anne c.77)
Dunchurch–Meriden	17m	1724 (10 Geo. I c.15)
Meriden–Coleshill	6m	*not turnpiked by 1750*
Coleshill–Lichfield[19]	14m	1744 (17 Geo. II c.24)
Lichfield–Stone–Woore	36m	1729 (2 Geo. II c.5)
Woore–Nantwich–Chester[20]	29m	1744 (17 Geo. II c.24)

183 miles

by 1730: 131 miles
by 1750: 174 miles

[17]Old Stratford adjoins Stony Stratford.
[18]This trust extended to Gibbet Lane, and the adjoining trust, formed in 1748, also extended to Gibbet Lane.
[19]This road may have been turnpiked in 1729. The 1744 Act, which was a renewal of the 1729 Act (2 Geo. II c.5), did not refer to the Lichfield–Coleshill Road as an additional road; however, Coleshill was not mentioned in the 1729 Act.
[20]This road was added to the Lichfield–Woore Trust.

(10) *London–Coventry–Manchester Road*

Islington, Holborn etc.–Highgate	4m	1717 (3 Geo. I c.4)
Highgate–Barnet	6m	1711 (10 Anne c.4)
Barnet–South Mimms	3m	*not turnpiked by 1750*
South Mimms–St Albans	6m	1715 (1 Geo. I c.12)
St Albans–Dunstable	13m	1723 (9 Geo. I c.11)
Dunstable–Hockliffe	4m	1710 (9 Anne c.34)
Hockliffe–Stony Stratford	15m	1706 (6 Anne c.4)
Old Stratford–Dunchurch	30m	1707 (6 Anne c.77)
Dunchurch–Meriden	17m	1724 (10 Geo. I c.15)
Meriden–Coleshill	6m	*not turnpiked by 1750*
Coleshill–Lichfield	14m	1744 (17 Geo. II c.24)
Lichfield–Stone	22m	1729 (2 Geo. II c.5)
Stone–Tittensor	4m	*not turnpiked by 1750*
Tittensor–Lawton	11m	1714 (13 Anne c.31)
Lawton–Cranage	10m	1731 (4 Geo. II c.3)
Cranage–Manchester	24m	*not turnpiked by 1750*

189 miles

by 1730: 142 miles
by 1750: 152 miles

(11) *London–Harwich Road*

Whitechapel–Shenfield	18m	1722 (8 Geo. I c.30)
Shenfield–Harwich	50m	1695 (7 & 8 Wm. III c.9)

68 miles

by 1730: 68 miles

(12) *London–Dover Road*

Southwark–Blackheath	8m	1718 (4 Geo. I c.5)
Blackheath–Dartford[21]	7m	1738 (11 Geo. c.36)
Dartford–Rochester[22]	12m	1738 (11 Geo. II c.37)
Rochester–Canterbury[23]	28m	1730 (3 Geo. II c.15)
Canterbury–Dover[24]	16m	*not turnpiked by 1750*

71 miles

by 1730: 36 miles
by 1750: 55 miles

(13) *London–Portsmouth and Chichester Road*

Southwark–Kingston-upon-Thames	12m	1718 (4 Geo. I c.4)
Kingston-upon-Thames–Petersfield	42m	1749 (22 Geo. II c.35)

[21]This road added to the Southwark–Blackheath Trust.
[22]This road added to the Chalk Trust (10 Anne c.16).
[23]In 1725 (11 Geo. I c.5) the Chalk Trust (a justice-trust) was authorized to spend £100 from the trust's revenue on the road from Chatham to Boughton-under-Blean (the Canterbury Road). This provision was repealed by the act of 1730 (3 Geo. II c.15).
[24]The Rochester–Canterbury Trust was to contribute towards the repair of the road from Dover to Lydden Hill.

Petersfield–Portsmouth	17m	1710 (9 Anne c.33)
Hindhead–Chichester[25]	23m	1749 (22 Geo. II c.35)

94 miles

by 1730: 29 miles
by 1750: 94 miles

---

[25]This road and the road from Kingston to Petersfield were under the same trust.

APPENDIX D

The Financial Condition of the Trusts: County Totals: 1821 and 1837

The data upon which this appendix is based were taken from the following sources:

(1) *B.P.P. 1821 (747) iv. 343*
(2) *B.P.P. 1839 (447) xliv. 299*
(3) *B.P.P. 1840 (280) xxvii. 15* (trusts' mileages)

In judging a trust's financial condition the following criteria were employed: To be considered in a favourable financial condition a trust must have:

(1) spent 20% or less of its income for interest payments.
This figure was calculated as follows:

$$1821:[1] \quad \frac{\text{Mortgage Debt} \times 5\% \text{ (unless another rate was stated)}}{\text{Income}}$$

$$1837:[2] \quad \frac{\text{Total Debt} - \text{Unpaid Interest}[3] \times \text{Rate of Interest}}{\text{Total Income} - \text{Loans}}$$

(2)—had three years or less unpaid interest.

(3)—allocated 55% or more of expenditure for repair. This can be calculated only for the later return.

$$\frac{\text{Total Expenditure} - (\text{Salaries} + \text{Law Charges} + \text{Interest on Debt} + \text{Incidental Expenses} + \text{Debts paid off})}{\text{Total Expenditure}}$$

This tends to understate the amount allocated for repair, as the surveyor's salary can be considered a repair expense. For trusts on the borderline, for which both interest payments and arrears suggest a favourable position, 'Debts paid off' has been deducted from both the divisor and the dividend. This has been done because this expense is more properly amortized over a number of years.

A number of factors make it difficult to compare county figures for the two years. Firstly, the mileages reported in 1821 do not seem to have been as accurate as those given in 1840, the later being quoted in miles, furlongs, poles and yards. Secondly, some trusts were placed in different counties in the two periods, and finally, consolidations tended to reduce the number of trusts. However, on aggregate these factors tend to cancel out.

---

[1] See below, p. 231 for a sample of the form of this return.
[2] See below, pp. 232-3 for a sample of the form of this return. The figure for interest payment given in the return has not been used, as it was frequently less than the full amount due.
[3] Unpaid interest has been deducted because the trusts did not generally pay interest on this.

Form of 1821 Return
B.P.P. *1821* (*747*) *iv.* 343; p. 62.

Name of trust	Length of road	Annual income averaged from the last 3 years	Amount of debt mortgaged
Penrith (2nd District)	9 miles from Penrith to old town Gill Syke	£483	£400

Annual expenditure averaged from the last 3 years	Number of trustees and qualification	Balance of Accounts	Amount of Interest due	Sinking fund
£442	130 land	£177 due to trust	£14	—

Dates and number of Acts, etc.	Observations
1st 26 Geo. II c.40	(not quoted)
last, 48 Geo. III c.4 Acts	

Form of 1837 Return
B.P.P. 1839 (447) xliv. 299, pp. 20–1.

INCOME

Names of trusts	Balance in treasurers' hands 1 January 1837	Balance due to treasurers 1 January 1837	Revenue received from tolls	Parish composition in lieu of statute duty
	£ s d	£ s d	£ s d	£ s d
Whitehaven	324 14 1	— — —	2,189 13 10	— — —

INCOME

Estimated value of statute duty performed	Revenue from fines	Revenue from incidental receipts	Amount of money borrowed on the security of the tolls	Total income
£ s d	£ s d	£ s d	£ s d	£ s d
— — —	2 0 0	2 10 0	— — —	2,194 3 10

EXPENDITURE

Manual labour	Team labour and carriage of materials	Materials for surface repair	Land purchased	Damage done in obtaining materials
£ s d	£ s d	£ s d	£ s d	£ s d
749 16 11	238 11 5	— — —	54 0 0	— — —

EXPENDITURE

SALARIES OF

Tradesmen's bills	Treasurer	Clerk	Surveyor	Law charges	Interest on debt	Improvements
£ s d	£ s d	£ s d	£ s d	£ s d	£ s d	£ s d
16 4 7	10 0 0	30 0 0	150 0 0	6 18 4	428 4 0	142 19 5

EXPENDITURE

Debts paid off	Incidental expenses	Estimated value of statute duty performed	Total expenditure
£ s d	£ s d	£ s d	£ s d
— — —	12 6 11	— — —	1,839 1 7

DEBTS

Floating debts	Unpaid interest	Balance due to treasurers, 31 December 1837	Total debts
£ s d	£ s d	£ s d	£ s d
— — —	— — —	— — —	10,705 0 0

ARREARS OF INCOME

Arrears of other receipts for current year	Arrears of former years	Balance in treasurers' hands, 31 Dec. 1837	Total assets
£ s d	£ s d	£ s d	£ s d
— — —	— — —	679 16 0	670 16 0

DEBTS

Bonded or mortage debts	Rate of Interest per cent
£ s d	
10,705 0 0	4

ARREARS OF INCOME

Arrears of tolls for current year	Arrears of parish composition for current year
£ s d	£ s d
— — —	— — —

Financial Condition of the Turnpike Trusts by County, 1821 and 1837

Financial Condition

	Favourable				Adverse		
	Trusts		Mileage		Trusts		Mileage
Bedfordshire							
1821	6	(40%)[4]	92	(38%)	9	(60%)	150	(62%)
1837	6	(46%)	104	(48%)	7	(54%)	112	(52%)
Berkshire							
1821	7	(35%)	76	(24%)	13	(65%)	243	(76%)
1837	9	(60%)	107	(52%)	6	(40%)	97	(48%)
Buckinghamshire							
1821	8	(66·5%)	115	(64%)	4	(33·5%)	65	(36%)
1837	8	(57%)	124	(60%)	6	(43%)	82	(40%)
Cambridgeshire							
1821	9	(60%)	161	(57%)	6	(40%)	117	(43%)
1837	7	(54%)	131	(63%)	6	(46%)	79	(37%)
Cheshire							
1821	10	(40%)	159	(49·5%)	15	(60%)	162	(50·5%)
1837	13	(33·3%)	198	(37%)	26	(66·6%)	340	(63%)
Cornwall							
1821	3	(25%)	91	(29%)	9	(75%)	218	(71%)
1837	4	(28·5%)	140	(37%)	10	(71·5%)	236	(63%)
Cumberland							
1821	7	(50%)	71	(33%)	7	(50%)	145	(67%)
1837	7	(50%)	157	(42%)	7	(50%)	221	(58%)
Derbyshire							
1821	3	(8%)	53	(10%)	34	(92%)	509	(90%)
1837	9	(22·5%)	165	(27%)	31	(77·5%)	456	(73%)
Devon							
1821	4	(16%)	120	(15%)	21	(84%)	663	(85%)
1837	5	(17%)	151	(17%)	24	(83%)	777	(83%)
Dorset							
1821	5	(38·5%)	128	(37%)	8	(61·5%)	219	(63%)
1837	4	(25%)	157	(32%)	12	(75%)	338	(68%)
Durham							
1821	5	(33·3%)	125	(35%)	10	(66·6%)	236	(65%)
1837	11	(58%)	319	(67%)	8	(42%)	160	(33%)
Essex							
1821	10	(91%)	245	(99%)	1	(9%)	2	(1%)
1837	11	(100%)	277	(100%)	0		0	
Gloucestershire							
1821	28	(58%)	582	(70%)	20	(42%)	246	(30%)
1837	23	(51%)	612	(63%)	22	(49%)	358	(37%)
Hampshire							
1821	12	(40%)	285	(52%)	18	(60%)	263	(48%)
1837	13	(36%)	279	(44%)	23	(64%)	358	(56%)
Herefordshire							
1821	7	(50%)	307	(56%)	7	(50%)	243	(44%)
1837	6	(43%)	336	(66%)	8	(57%)	170	(34%)
Hertfordshire							
1821	8	(89%)	153	(90%)	1	(11%)	17	(10%)
1837	10	(91%)	210	(91%)	1	(9%)	21	(9%)

[4]Percentages have, generally, been carried to the nearest full percentage.

Financial Condition

	Favourable			Adverse		
	Trusts	Mileage		Trusts	Mileage	
Huntingdonshire						
1821	3 (33·3%)	53 (36%)		6 (66·6%)	93 (64%)	
1837	4 (57%)	77 (55%)		3 (43%)	63 (45%)	
Kent						
1821	16 (34%)	249 (41%)		31 (66%)	361 (59%)	
1837	15 (30%)	238 (36%)		35 (70%)	418 (64%)	
Lancashire						
1821	21 (41%)	238 (37%)		30 (59%)	412 (63%)	
1837	19 (29%)	172 (23%)		46 (71%)	574 (77%)	
Leicestershire						
1821	10 (43·5%)	195 (48·5%)		13 (56·5%)	208 (51·5%)	
1837	14 (61%)	210 (57·5%)		9 (39%)	155 (42·5%)	
Lincolnshire						
1821	8 (30%)	148 (28%)		19 (70%)	390 (72%)	
1837	12 (41%)	220 (40%)		17 (59%)	337 (60%)	
Middlesex						
1821	14 (70%)	132 (84%)		6 (30%)	25 (16%)	
1837	3 (50%)	188 (89%)		3 (50%)	24 (11%)	
Monmouthshire						
1821	2 (22%)	25 (8%)		7 (78%)	290 (92%)	
1837	3 (30%)	84 (26%)		7 (70%)	232 (74%)	
Norfolk						
1821	5 (36%)	119 (44%)		9 (64%)	152 (56%)	
1837	9 (60%)	225 (65%)		6 (40%)	124 (35%)	
Northamptonshire						
1821	9 (43%)	158 (44%)		12 (57%)	200 (56%)	
1837	14 (52%)	266 (61%)		13 (48%)	170 (39%)	
Northumberland						
1821	5 (31%)	105 (21%)		11 (69%)	394 (79%)	
1837	5 (38·5%)	151 (38%)		8 (61·5%)	250 (62%)	
Nottinghamshire						
1821	4 (22%)	86 (28%)		14 (78%)	215 (72%)	
1837	6 (28·5%)	78 (26%)		15 (71·5%)	220 (74%)	
Oxfordshire						
1821	5 (28%)	144 (42%)		13 (72%)	198 (58%)	
1837	6 (28·5%)	118 (36%)		15 (71·5%)	208 (64%)	
Rutland						
1821	1 (100%)	18 (100%)		0	0	
1837	3 (75%)	48 (70%)		1 (25%)	21 (30%)	
Shropshire						
1821	17 (40·5%)	361 (39%)		25 (59·5%)	569 (61%)	
1837	17 (44%)	467 (61%)		22 (56%)	295 (39%)	
Somerset						
1821	10 (55·5%)	374 (49%)		8 (44·5%)	382 (51%)	
1837	9 (39%)	419 (46%)		14 (61%)	485 (54%)	
Staffordshire						
1821	14 (37%)	311 (49·5%)		24 (63%)	317 (50·5%)	
1837	19 (40·5%)	358 (45%)		28 (59·5%)	438 (55%)	
Suffolk						
1821	8 (61·5%)	179 (61%)		5 (38·5%)	100 (39%)	
1837	10 (71·5%)	214 (76%)		4 (28·5%)	68 (24%)	
Surrey						
1821	9 (53%)	219 (78%)		8 (47%)	62 (22%)	
1837	9 (43%)	196 (64%)		12 (57%)	112 (36%)	

Financial Condition

	Favourable				Adverse		
	Trusts		Mileage		Trusts		Mileage
Sussex							
1821	12	(29%)	190	(31%)	29	(71%)	426	(69%)
1837	17	(33%)	344	(49%)	34	(67%)	355	(51%)
Warwickshire							
1821	13	(43·5%)	238	(52%)	17	(56·5%)	222	(48%)
1837	17	(50%)	289	(62%)	17	(50%)	179	(38%)
Westmorland							
1821	3	(27%)	98	(35%)	8	(73%)	182	(65%)
1837	3	(30%)	46	(22%)	7	(70%)	165	(78%)
Wiltshire							
1821	14	(35%)	276	(35%)	26	(65%)	513	(65%)
1837	13	(41%)	318	(47%)	19	(59%)	365	(53%)
Worcestershire							
1821	11	(50%)	365	(63%)	11	(50%)	218	(37%)
1837	10	(45·5%)	305	(61%)	12	(54·5%)	194	(39%)
Yorkshire							
1821	30	(34%)	569	(40%)	58	(66%)	857	(60%)
1837	43	(36%)	759	(44%)	77	(64%)	955	(56%)
Totals							
1821	376	(39·6%)	7,613	(42·5%)	573	(60·4%)	10,289	(57·5%)
1837	426	(40·7%)	9,275	(47·6%)	621	(59·3%)	10,212	(52·4%)

APPENDIX E

Turnpike Trusts' County Totals, 1837

The data for this appendix were taken from the following sources:

(1) *B.P.P. 1839 (447) xliv. 299*

(2) *B.P.P. 1840 (280) xxvii. 15* (trusts' mileages)

(1) 'Interest payments as a percentage of income' has been calculated as Total County Debt — (Unpaid Interest + Total Assets) × 5% / Total County Income — Loans.

This tends to overstate the amount spent on interest payments for many trusts offered less than 5%.[1]

(2) 'Percentage of expenditure for repair' has been calculated as in Appendix D (see above, p. 230).

(3) New acts were those for new trusts passed from 1790 to 1837.

---

[1] It was necessary to use 5% instead of the trusts' individual rates, because at the time the computation was carried out the county aggregates were not analysed with regard to interest payments.

1837 County Totals

County	Trusts	Total mileage	Average mileage per trust	Income-loans per mile	Interest payment as % of income	% of expenditure for repair	Unpaid interest per mile	Number new acts as a % 1837 total
Bedford	13	215·9	16·6	£64·2	14·9%	73·0%	£61·4	(4) 30·8%
Berkshire	15	197·6	13·2	£82·0	15·7%	68·5%	£11·9	(3) 20·0%
Bucks.	14	196·5	14·1	£96·2	09·0%	68·9%	£78·5	(7) 50·0%
Cambridge	13	210·1	16·2	£64·4	15·8%	73·3%	£26·5	(4) 30·8%
Cheshire	39	537·9	13·8	£105·8	25·8%	49·9%	£34·7	(14) 35·9%
Cornwall	14	376·8	26·9	£46·1	33·2%	72·2%	£19·8	(1) 07·2%
Cumberland	14	378·2	27·0	£37·9	37·3%	65·7%	£68·7	(7) 50·0%
Derby	40	621·4	15·5	£63·7	40·7%	47·7%	£140·1	(15) 37·5%
Devon	29	928·1	32·0	£62·8	38·2%	46·6%	£46·6	(8) 27·6%
Dorset	16	495·3	31·0	£41·2	28·4%	63·7%	£11·2	(2) 12·5%
Durham	19	479·4	24·2	£62·2	21·1%	67·7%	£8·6	(11) 57·9%
Essex	11	276·7	25·2	£121·9	03·8%	73·3%	£0·2	(3) 27·3%
Gloucester	45	970·0	21·6	£75·3	23·2%	67·9%	£32·1	(14) 31·2%
Hampshire	36	626·8	17·4	£42·5	20·9%	63·7%	£49·9	(8) 22·2%
Hereford	14	596·6	36·2	£39·3	17·4%	78·4%	£10·2	(1) 07·2%
Hertford	11	230·9	21·0	£125·6	10·1%	77·2%	£27·3	(1) 09·1%
Huntingdon	7	138·6	19·8	£65·9	12·5%	74·2%	£1·8	0
Kent	50	656·7	13·1	£98·9	19·2%	62·8%	£91·7	(18) 36·0%
Lancashire	65	745·8	11·5	£192·6	31·2%	67·5%	£122·1	(31) 47·7%
Leicester	23	364·3	15·8	£69·5	16·3%	73·3%	£27·9	(2) 08·6%
Lincoln	29	557·1	19·2	£55·6	16·9%	66·3%	£25·8	(4) 13·8%
Middlesex	6	211·7	35·3	£444·8	06·5%	77·2%	£77·5	X

County	Trusts	Total mileage	Average mileage per trust	Income-loans per mile	Interest payment as % of income	% of expenditure for repair	Unpaid interest per mile	Number new acts as a % 1837 total
Monmouth	10	315·5	31·6	£46·7	29·2%	66·6%	£16·2	X
Norfolk	15	348·6	23·2	£39·4	19·1%	64·4%	£5·6	(4) 26·7%
Northampton	27	444·2	16·5	£76·2	14·3%	52·9%	£67·8	(8) 29·6%
Northumber.	13	401·4	30·8	£50·6	23·3%	70·4%	£102·2	(6) 46·2%
Nottingham	21	299·0	14·2	£53·3	33·4%	58·6%	£30·9	(4) 12·9%
Oxford	21	325·9	15·5	£72·7	18·2%	65·5%	£32·3	(5) 23·8%
Rutland	4	68·7	17·2	£66·8	11·6%	84·7%	£03·2	(1) 25·0%
Shropshire	39	761·9	19·5	£37·9	19·9%	70·7%	£7·1	(4) 10·5%
Somerset	23	903·4	39·3	£67·9	25·6%	61·9%	£23·0	(5) 21·8%
Stafford	47	794·9	16·9	£72·2	19·3%	62·6%	£77·0	(10) 21·3%
Suffolk	14	281·6	20·1	£39·7	11·5%	70·4%	£29·1	(7) 50·0%
Surrey	21	308·3	14·7	£211·3	12·2%	65·8%	£129·5	(7) 33·3%
Sussex	51	698·1	13·7	£72·5	27·1%	72·3%	£117·1	(20) 39·3%
Warwick	34	468·3	13·8	£61·4	16·3%	65·5%	£20·7	(11) 32·4%
Westmor.	10	210·9	21·1	£31·2	38·7%	48·5%	£12·2	(3) 30·0%
Wiltshire	32	683·0	21·3	£53·3	15·9%	61·4%	£31·9	(6) 18·8%
Worcester	22	493·4	22·4	£76·9	16·5%	75·4%	£25·3	(4) 18·2%
Yorkshire	120	1,714·0	14·3	£109·6	26·4%	66·2%	£83·6	(43) 35·8%

APPENDIX F

Financial Condition of the 'Large' Trusts (those controlling over forty miles of road in 1837)

The data upon which this appendix is based were taken from the following sources:

B.P.P. 1839 (447) xliv. 299

B.P.P. 1840 (280) xxvii. 15 (trusts' mileages)

The criteria used in assessing a trust's financial condition are the same as those employed in Appendix D (see p. 230).

	Mileage	% of expenditure on repair	Arrears of interest/mile	Income-loans /mile	% of income devoted to interest payments	Classification
Bedfordshire						
Biggleswade Trust	45·5m	71·3%	£1·4/m	£10·6/m	15·7%	Favourable
Cheshire						
Manchester–Buxton Trust	45·0m	51·0%	0	£378·1/m	23·7%	Adverse
Cornwall						
Bodmin Trust	57·0m	71·5%	0	£31·3/m	24·4%	Adverse
Launceston Trust	45·5m	82·0%	0	£39·5/m	28·0%	Adverse
Liskeard Trust	42·0m	34·0%	£151·9/m	£55·/m	37·6%	Adverse
Truro Trust	56·1m	68·8%	0	£65·2/m	18·2%	Favourable
Cumberland						
Alston Trust	130·5m	81·3%	£187·4/m	£23·1/m	62·2%	Adverse
Cockermouth–Maryport Trust	42·0m	69·0%	0	£98·1/m	15·1%	Favourable
Keswick Trust	61·7m	51·2%	£5·6/m	£27·7/m	36·6%	Adverse
Derbyshire						
Chesterfield–Hernstone Trust	58·3m	62·2%	£10·1/m	£51·9/m	20·0%	Favourable
Sheffield–Chapel-en-le-Frith Trust	48·0m	55·5%	£93·3/m	£64·0/m	38·0%	Adverse
Devonshire						
Bideford Trust	42·2m	49·6%	£3·0/m	£50·5/m	30·9%	Adverse
Exeter Trust	146·8m	47·5%	£26·2/m	£96·7/m	34·9%	Adverse
Great Torrington Trust	69·3m	38·4%	£5·8/m	£25·2/m	29·6%	Adverse
Honiton Trust	48·9m	50·5%	£8·8/m	£27·2/m	27·8%	Adverse
Kingsbridge–Dartmouth Trust	56·0m	40·9%	£159·3/m	£30·9/m	60·6%	Adverse
Plymouth–Exeter Trust	42·0m	02·4%	£4·5/m	£24·6/m	77·5%	Adverse
South Molton Trust	42·2m	68·3%	£1·7/m	£26·2/m	07·9%	Favourable

	Mileage	% of expenditure on repair	Arrears of interest/mile	Income-loans /mile	% of income devoted to interest payments	Classification
Tavistock Trust	51·0m	63·8%*	£6·9/m	£63·2/m	16·5%	Favourable
Tiverton Trust	87·9m	48·5%	£9·4/m	£52·3/m	41·2%	Adverse
Totnes Trust	43·5m	66·8%	£14·8/m	£64·0/m	49·0%	Adverse
Dorset						
Hornham & Dorchester Trust	48·6m	51·6%	£3·2/m	£47·4/m	17·1%	Adverse
Lyme Regis Trust	47·8m	41·9%	£45·2/m	£24·5/m	34·8%	Adverse
Maiden Newton Trust	46·4m	55·0%	0	£20·6/m	21·0%	Adverse
Poole Trust	47·6m	79·5%	0	£30·4/m	27·1%	Adverse
Sherborne Trust	51·0m	74·6%	£3·1/m	£44·4/m	10·2%	Favourable
Wareham Trust	47·6m	54·0%	0	£26·3/m	24·6%	Adverse
Durham						
Berwick–North Durham Trust	65·0m	60·9%	£9·9/m	£64·2/m	36·9%	Adverse
Boroughbridge–Durham Trust	52·8m	87·3%	0	£51·1/m	14·4%	Favourable
Catterick Bridge–Durham Trust	40·3m	40·4%	£3·3/m	£44·9/m	21·5%	Adverse
Darlington–Cockerton Bridge Trust	48·5m	76·0%	0	£31·1/m	06·0%	Favourable
Lobley Hill Trust	59·6m	73·4%	£6·7/m	£34·3/m	16·9%	Favourable
Essex						
Chelmsford Trust	45·0m	72·6%	0	£122·2/m	00·9%	Favourable
Gloucestershire						
Berkeley, Dursley etc. Trust	85·5m	79·3%	£2·7/m	£51·6/m	09·3%	Favourable
Bristol Trust	172·8m	74·2%	0	£122·7/m	09·4%	Favourable
Cirencester Trust	62·6m	53·9%	0	£69·5/m	27·0%	Adverse

* 'Debts paid off' has been deducted from expenditure total.

	Mileage	% of expenditure on repair	Arrears of interest/mile	Income-loans /mile	% of income devoted to interest payments	Classification
Forest of Dean Trust	69·5m	76·7%	£1·6/m	£30·1/m	31·1%	Adverse
Foss and Cross Trust	44·0m	76·5%	0	£26·8/m	07·8%	Favourable
Tewkesbury Trust	46·2m	86·3%	0	£92·0/m	05·2%	Favourable
Hampshire						
Andover–Basingstoke Trust	47·3m	84·5%	0	£63·6/m	05·2%	Favourable
Andover–Chilton Pond Trust	42·0m	79·9%	£2·8/m	£22·4/m	19·2%	Favourable
Herefordshire						
Hereford Trust	156·4m	88·5%	0	£39·6/m	05·4%	Favourable
Kingston Trust	62·8m	65·7%	£20·0/m	£30·3/m	22·4%	Adverse
Ledbury Trust	45·6m	84·9%	£1·8/m	£38·0/m	12·8%	Favourable
Ross Trust	41·0m	66·8%	0	£65·3/m	25·6%	Adverse
Hertfordshire						
Reading–Hatfield Trust	51·4m	60·9%	£8·5/m	£41·9/m	07·3%	Favourable
Lincolnshire						
Bawtry Bridge–Hainton Trust	41·0m	56·1%	0	£28·2/m	28·9%	Adverse
Lincoln Trust	40·9m	70·2%	£15·1/m	£57·2/m	04·3%	Adverse
Lincoln, Brigg etc. Trust	46·0m	81·4%	£1·2/m	£37·3/m	14·9%	Favourable
Middlesex						
Metropolis Roads Trust	173·0m	77·1%	0	£484·2/m	03·8%	Favourable
Monmouthshire						
Abergavenny and New Roads Trust	78·0m	54·8%	£11·6/m	£51·9/m	24·4%	Adverse
Chepstow Trust	48·5m	77·1%	£1·0/m	£51·4/m	08·2%	Favourable
Monmouth Trust	59·0m	80·2%	£9·0/m	£39·5/m	31·9%	Adverse

	Mileage	% of expenditure on repair	Arrears of interest/mile	Income-loans /mile	% of income devoted to interest payments	Classification
Northumberland						
Alemouth and Hexham Trust	45·6m	87·4%	£467·2/m	£21·1/m	30·2%	Adverse
Cow-Cawsey–Buckton Burn Trust	49·0m	85·0%	0	£88·2/m	03·7%	Favourable
Newcastle–Carlisle Trust	41·0m	79·7%	0	£26·0/m	10·5%	Favourable
Wooler–Breamish Trust	42·3m	39·0%	0	£47·7/m	26·5%	Adverse
Shropshire						
Bishop's Castle Trust	92·8m	74·5%	0	£16·5/m	16·5%	Favourable
Ludlow Trust	97·8m	77·9%	£4·4/m	£39·8/m	11·9%	Favourable
Oswestry Trust	55·8m	85·3%	0	£85·7/m	12·5%	Favourable
Preston–Brockhurst Trust	60·0m	45·9%	0	£16·3/m	23·5%	Adverse
Somerset						
Bath Trust	51·4m	68·4%	0	£224·8/m	18·1%	Favourable
Bridgwater Trust	49·4m	31·7%	£20·1/m	£96·8/m	32·9%	Adverse
Bruton Trust	56·8m	55·0%	£12·9/m	£34·8/m	36·1%	Adverse
Chard Trust	43·6m	51·8%	£1·6/m	£38·1/m	31·0%	Adverse
Frome Trust	41·5m	60·9%	0	£83·5/m	18·2%	Favourable
Ilminster Trust	42·2m	61·4%	£4·4/m	£42·9/m	39·9%	Adverse
Langport Trust	80·8m	67·9%	£6·4/m	£51·0/m	24·5%	Adverse
Minehead and Bampton Trust	59·6m	30·8%	£122·4/m	£29·5/m	56·8%	Adverse
Shepton Mallet Trust	52·8m	76·4%	£7·7/m	£67·8/m	10·0%	Favourable
Taunton Trust	75·0m	76·8%	£5·2/m	£60·0/m	17·9%	Favourable
Wells Trust	44·0m	67·4%	£12·0/m	£87·2/m	14·5%	Favourable
Wincanton Trust	41·5m	75·8%	0	£64·0/m	11·1%	Favourable
Wivelscombe Trust	63·8m	07·4%	£82·3/m	£18·3/m	98·6%	Adverse

	Mileage	% of expenditure on repair	Arrears of interest/mile	Income-loans /mile	% of income devoted to interest payments	Classification
Staffordshire						
Cheadle Trust	51·3m	58·7%	£145·5/m	£40·0/m	37·9%	Adverse
Lichfield Trust	43·9m	59·5%	£6·6/m	£96·2/m	07·2%	Favourable
Tamworth Trust	41·5m	57·8%*	0	£34·3/m	19·5%	Favourable
Suffolk						
Ipswich–Southtown Trust	67·3m	85·5%	0	£38·2/m	00·6%	Favourable
Surrey						
Surrey and Sussex Trust	63·0m	62·6%	0	£420·1/m	09·5%	Favourable
Sussex						
Rye Trust	89·0m	81·1%	£0·1/m	£10·2/m	04·0%	Favourable
Westmorland						
Appleby–Kendal Trust	41·0m	50·0%	£0·4/m	£16·6/m	33·3%	Adverse
Wiltshire						
Amesbury Trust	62·0m	64·6%	£0·5/m	£20·0/m	17·6%	Favourable
Fisherton etc. Trust	49·0m	78·7%	0	£59·5/m	10·3%	Favourable
Malmesbury (2nd) Trust	40·1m	60·4%	0	£32·3/m	35·8%	Adverse
Sarum–Ealing Trust	40·7m	76·6%*	0	£77·5/m	3·1%	Favourable
Whitesheet Hill Trust	60·5m	79·2%	£11·9/m	£8·0/m	21·8%	Adverse
Worcestershire						
Kidderminster Trust	60·5m	77·4%	£1·5/m	£68·4/m	21·4%	Adverse
Worcester Trust	160·2m	87·3%	£0·2/m	£89·7/m	10·7%	Favourable
Yorkshire						
Boroughbridge–Durham Trust	52·8m	68·9%	0	£67·2/m	07·8%	Favourable
Sedbergh Trust	62·0m	61·4%	£0·4/m	£16·2/m	23·8%	Adverse
York–Scarborough Trust	45·3m	80·9%	£1·3/m	£113·2/m	06·3%	Favourable

* 'Debts paid off' has been deducted from expenditure total.

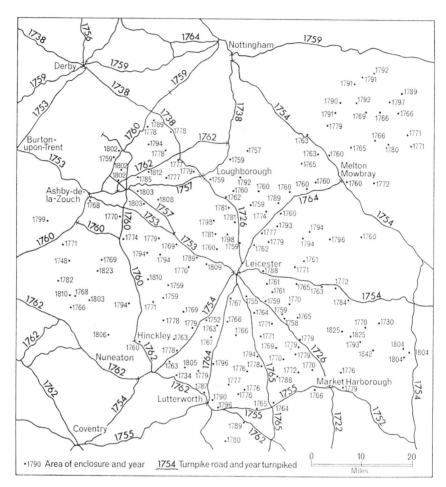

8 Turnpike trusts and parliamentary enclosures in Leicestershire. (The list of enclosures was taken from H. G. Hunt, 'The Parliamentary Enclosure Movement in Leicestershire, 1730-1842', unpublished Ph.D. thesis, University of London, 1955, pp. 306-11.)

APPENDIX H

Rates of interest paid by the turnpike trusts[1]

		to	from
1720s and 30s			
BEDFORDSHIRE[2]			
Woburn–Hockliffe Trust	1728–40	5%	
GLOUCESTERSHIRE[3]			
Gloucester Trust	1701–12	6%	
Stroud Trust	1727	5%	
Gloucester–Hereford Trust	1730	5%	
Chappel-on-the-Hill Trust	1731–53	5%	
HUNTINGDONSHIRE[4]			
Great North Road Trust	1726–36	5%	
KENT[5]			
Chalk Trust	1718/19	6%	
—	1720–35	5%	6%
New Cross Trust	1718 and 1719	5%	
Rochester–Maidstone Trust	1728–37	5%	
LEICESTERSHIRE[6]			
Harborough–Loughborough Trust	1725–36	5%	
LINCOLNSHIRE[7]			
Grantham–Little Drayton Trust	1726–38	5%	
MIDDLESEX[8]			
Kensington, Fulham, Chelsea Trust	1726–33	5%	
Fulham Field Trust	1731–50	5%	
Colnbrook Trust	1727–38	5%	
Bedfont–Bagshot Trust	1728–40/1	5%	
Edgware Trust	1730–36	5%	
Hampstead–Highgate Trust	1733	5%	
WARWICKSHIRE[9]			
Dunchurch–Meriden Hill Trust	1724–38	5%	

---

[1]The dates given in the following tables are those for which it could be confirmed that the stated rates were being offered. The rate changes were either (1) changes of the rate on the entire bonded debt or (2) that the trust was able to borrow at a new rate.

[2]Mortgage 1728 and Letter, 31 March 1740, CH 16/5A Beds. CRO.

[3]Gloucester Trust, Quarter-Sessions Records, Q/SO-3 Glouces. RO; Stroud Trust, Mortgage 1727, 149/T/911 Glouces. RO; Gloucester–Hereford Trust, Minutes – 22 September 1730, D204/2/2 Glouces. RO; Chappel-on-the-Hill Trust, Account Book 1731-67, D671/X4 Glouces. RO.

[4]Minute Book 1725-45 (typed transcript), Hunts. CRO.

[5]Chalk Trust, Quarter-Sessions Records, Q/SB-1718/19 – 1735 Kent AO; New Cross Trust, Mortgages 1718 and 1719, T9/F6 Kent AO; Rochester–Maidstone Trust, Minute Book 1728-41, T12/1 Kent AO.

[6]Abstract of Minutes 1725-77, T/X/1/1 Leices. RO.   [7]*J. H. of C.* xxiii, pp. 283-4.

[8]Kensington, Fulham, Chelsea Trust, Minute Book 1726-34, MS 58/7001 Ken. Pub. Lib.; Fulham Field Trust, Minute Book 1730-50, MS 58/7039 Ken. Pub. Lib.; Colnbrook Trust, Minute Book 1728-84, T.P. Col. 1 Mid. CRO; Bedfont–Bagshot Trust, Minute Book 1728-57, T.P. Bed. 1, Mid. CRO (last 2 trusts near Middx. included here because MSS in Mid. CRO); Edgware Trust, Account Book 1730-1810, LA/HW/TP–21 Mid. CRO; Hampstead–Highgate Trust, *J. H. of C.* xxii, p. 250.

[9]*J. H. of C.* xxiii, p. 445.

		to	from
HUNTINGDONSHIRE[10]			
Great North Road Trust	1736–45	4%	5%
KENT[11]			
Rochester–Maidstone Trust	1737/38	4%	5%
New Cross Trust	1739–44	4%	5%
MIDDLESEX[12]			
Kensington, Fulham, Chelsea Trust	1733–36	4½%	5%
—	1736–71	4%	4½%
Edgware Trust	1737–75	4%	5%
YORKSHIRE[13]			
Blackstone Edge Trust	1735–41	4½%	
1740s			
BEDFORDSHIRE[14]			
Hockliffe–Woburn Trust	1741–74	4%	5%
KENT[15]			
New Cross Trust	1748 and 1749	4½%	
LEICESTERSHIRE[16]			
Harborough–Loughborough Trust	1742–53	5%	
MIDDLESEX[17]			
Bedfont–Bagshot Trust	1740/1–43	4%	5%
—	1743/4–56	4½%	4%
OXFORDSHIRE[18]			
Stokenchurch Trust	1749–55	5%	
WILTSHIRE[19]			
Devizes (Old) Trust	1746–47	4%	
Chippenham Trust	1745	5%	
YORKSHIRE[20]			
Redhouse–Wakefield Trust	1741–57	5% and 4½%	
Doncaster–Tadcaster Trust	1741–83	4½%	
1750s			
BEDFORDSHIRE[21]			
Bedford–Hitchin Trust	1757–1822	4%	
Kimbolton Trust	1755	4½%	

[10]Minute Book 1725-45 (typed transcript, rate changed 30 March 1736), Hunts CRO.

[11]Rochester–Maidstone Trust, Minutes – January 1737/38, T12/1 Kent AO; New Cross Trust, Account Book 1739-54, T9/F1/1 Kent AO.

[12]Kensington, Fulham, Chelsea Trust, Minute Books 1726-34, 1734-40 and 1758-71 (rates changed July 1733 and 6 December 1736), MS58/7001, MS58/7002, MS58/7006, Ken. Pub. Lib.; Edgware Trust, Account Book 1730-1810, LA/HW/TP-21 Mid. CRO.

[13]Register of Mortgages 1735-1872, HAS – 52, Hal. Cent. Lib.

[14]Minute Book 1728-74 (rate changed 6 October 1741), X21/4 Beds. CRO.

[15]Mortgages 1748 and 1749, F9/F6 Kent AO.

[16]Abstract of Minutes 1725-77, T/X/1/1 Leics. RO.

[17]Minute Book 1728-57 (rate changed 23 March 1740/41 and 16 January 1743/44), T.P. Bed. 1 Mid. CRO.

[18]Minute Book 1740-93, Ch. S.1 Oxon. CRO.

[19]Devizes (Old) Trust, Account Book 1746-47, QS:A3/7/4 Wilts. RO. Chippenham Trust, Minutes – 24 June 1745, no. 119 Wilts. RO.

[20]Redhouse (Doncaster)–Wakefield Trust, Account Book 1741-1812, Box 54 West Rid., CRO; Doncaster–Tadcaster Trust, Account Book 1741-1835, box 54 West Rid. CRO.

[21]Bedford–Hitchin Trust, Minute Book 1757-91, K46/1, and Interest Ledger 1792-1822, X46/12; Kimbolton Trust, Mortgages, 1755, WG 894 A-C (documents in Beds. CRO).

		to	from
GLOUCESTERSHIRE[22]			
Chappel-on-the-Hill Trust	1753–65	4%	5%
Cirencester–Monument-upon-Lansdown Trust	1753	4½%	
Burford–Preston Trust	1753–80	4½%	
Chepstow and District Trust	1758–64	4%	
Stone–Clay Pits Trust	1759	4%	
KENT[23]			
New Cross Trust	1750–52	3½%	4½%
LANCASHIRE[24]			
Preston–Lancaster Trust	1751–56	4½%	
Skipton–Colne Trust	1756–60	4%	
Prescot–Liverpool Trust	1759	4½%	
Manchester–Wilmslow Trust	1754–63	4½%	
LEICESTERSHIRE[25]			
Harborough–Loughborough Trust	1753–60	4%	5%
Leicester–Hinckley Trust	1754–64	4%	
LINCOLNSHIRE[26]			
Lincoln Heath–Peterborough Trust	1756–65	4½%	
MIDDLESEX[27]			
Fulham Field Trust	1750–63	4%	5%
Old Street Trust	1753–54	3½%	
—	1754–56	4%	3½%
—	1756–61	4½%	4%
NORTHAMPTONSHIRE[28]			
Market Harborough–Welford Trust	1750	4%	
Market Harborough–Brampton Trust	1752	4%	
Kettering–Newport Pagnell Trust	1754–64	4½%	
NOTTINGHAMSHIRE[29]			
Leadenham Hill–Newark-on-Trent Trust	1759–81	4½%	
OXFORDSHIRE[30]			
Stokenchurch Trust	1755–64	4%	5%

---

[22]Chappel-on-the-Hill Trust, Accounts Book 1731-67, D621/4; Cirencester–Monument-upon-Lansdown Trust, Mortgage 1753, D48 F17; Burford–Preston Trust, Minutes and Accounts 1753-1807, D1070; Chepstow and District Trust, Account Book 1758-65, D428/B1; Stone–Clay Pits Trust, Mortgage 1759, D892/Z7. (All documents in Glouces. RO.)

[23]Mortgages 1750 and 1752, T9/F6 Kent AO.

[24]Preston–Lancaster Trust, Order Book 1751-82, TTD-1 Lancs. RO; Skipton–Colne Trust, Order Book 1756-74, TTI-1 Lancs. RO; Prescot–Liverpool Trust, Baily, 'Minutes of the Trustees of the Turnpike Roads', Part II, Vol. 89, p. 43; Manchester–Wilmslow Trust, Accounts 1753-1805, MSS 7352042/M103 Man. Lib. of Loc. Hist.

[25]Harborough–Loughborough Trust, Abstract of Minutes 1725-77 (rate changed 4 June 1753), T/X/1/1; Leicester–Hinckley Trust, Securities Book 1754-1877, T/X/4/1/. (Both documents in Leices. RO.)

[26]Mortgages 1756 and 1765, ASW 10/51/1-23 Lincs. AO.

[27]Minute Book 1750-65 (rate changed 16 June 1750), MS58/7040 Ken. Pub. Lib. Minute Book 1753-78 (rate changed 1 January 1754, 22 June 1756), Fins. Lib.

[28]Market Harborough–Welford Trust, Accounts 1750-1830, box 1284; Market Harborough–Brampton Trust, Assignment of Mortgage 1752, YZ4641; Kettering–Newport Pagnell Trust, Security Book 1754-1866, ML31. (All documents in Northam. RO.)

[29]Account Book 1759-1809, DDT 27/1 Notts. CRO.

[30]Minute Book 1740-93 (rate changed 21 May 1755), Ch. S.1. Oxon. CRO.

		to	from
SHROPSHIRE[31]			
Ludlow Trust 1st District	1751–77	4%	
Shrewsbury–Wrexham Trust	1752–69	4%	
Ludlow Trust 2nd District	1756–79	4%	
WARWICKSHIRE[32]			
Drayton–Edgehill Trust	1753–54	4%	
Birmingham–Hagley Trust	1754–60	3½%	4½%
Bromsgrove–Stratford Trust	1754–57	4%	
—	1757–74	4½%	4%
WILTSHIRE[33]			
Harnham Bridge–New Sarum Trust	1753	4%	
Seend–Box Trust	1753–58	5%	
Devizes (Old) Trust	1755–81	4%	
WORCESTERSHIRE[34]			
Tenbury Trust	1757–58	4%	
Stourbridge Trust	1753 (July–Dec.)	3%	
—	1753–64	4%	3%
YORKSHIRE[35]			
Doncaster–Saltersbrook Trust	1751–64	4½%	
Leeds–Selby Trust	1751–63	4½%	
Blackstone Edge Trust	1754–59	4%	4½%
—	1759–73	4½%	
Knaresborough–Green Hammerton Trust	1753–55	4%	
—	1755–80	4½%	4%
Harrogate–Boroughbridge Trust	1753–86	4%	
Ripon–Pateley Bridge Trust	1754–94	4%	
Kirkby Hill Moor–Ripon Trust	1752–94	4%	
Harrogate–Hutton Moor Trust	1754–95	4%	
Leeds–Harrogate Trust	1755		
Redhouse–Wakefield Trust	1758–1812	4½%	

---

[31]Ludlow Trust 1st District, Order Book with Accounts 1751–76, SRO 356/23/307; Shrewsbury–Wrexham Trust, Minute Books 1752–67, 1767–83, Giles and Horton 321 box 5; Ludlow Trust 2nd District, Order Book with Accounts 1756–70 and Order Book 1770–1828, SRO 356/23/312 and SRO 356/23/311. (All documents in Salop RO.)

[32]Drayton–Edgehill Trust, Minute Book 1753–1822, CR 580/57; Bromsgrove–Stratford Trust, Minute Books 1754–67, 1767–1806 (rate changed 23 May 1758) CR446/1–/2 (both documents in War. CRO). Birmingham–Hagley Trust, Minute Book 1753–72 (rate changed 30 July 1754), 288223 Birm. Ref. Lib.

[33]Harnham Bridge–New Sarum Trust, Minute Book 1753–95; Seend–Box Trust, Minute Book 1753–90, no. 519; Devizes (Old) Trust, Account Books 1756–83, 3A/7/4 (all documents in Wilts. RO).

[34]Tenbury Trust, Mortgages 1757 and 1758, 705:137 BA 3473/3; Stourbridge Trust, Record Book 1753–1819, 899:31, BA 3762/4(iv) (both documents in Worces. RO).

[35]Leeds–Selby Trust, Mortgage Ledger 1751–1872, box 60; Knaresborough–Green Hammerton Trust, Minute Book 1752–1878 (rate change 11 September 1755), box 27; Harrogate–Boroughbridge Trust, Minute Book 1752–1870, box 27; Ripon–Pateley Bridge Trust, Minute Book 1756–1815, box 27; Kirkby Hill Moor–Ripon Trust, Account Book 1752–1814, box 27; Harrogate–Hutton Moor Trust, Account Book 1752–1814, box 27; Leeds–Harrogate Trust Mortgage 1755, box 57; Redhouse–Wakefield Trust, Account Book 1741–1812, box 54; Toller Lane End–Colne Trust, Minute Book 1755–1823, box 50; Leeds–Wakefield Trust, Account Book 1758–1823, box 45 (all documents in West Rid. CRO). Blackstone Edge Trust, Register of Mortgages 1735–1872, HAS – 52 Hal. Cent. Lib.; Doncaster–Saltersbrook Trust, Abstract from Minutes, Goodchild Collection.

		to	from
Toller Lane–Colne Trust	1755	5%	
Leeds–Wakefield Trust	1758–1823	5%	
1760s			
CAMBRIDGESHIRE[36]			
Newmarket Heath Trust	1763–67	5%	
GLOUCESTERSHIRE[37]			
Chappel-on-the-Hill Trust	1765–91	5%	4%
Gloucester–Hereford Trust	1760–78	4½%	
Gloucester–Birdlip Trust	1761–70	4%	
Maismore Road (section of Glouces.-Heref. Trust)	1769–79	4½%	
Newant New Trust	1769	4½%	
KENT[38]			
Cranbrooke Trust	1762	5%	
Tenterden Trust	1763–66	5%	
—	1766–80	4%	5%
Kipping Cross Trust	1765	5%	
Wadhurst–West Farleigh Trust	1765–70	5%	
Charing Trust	1766–67	5%	
New Cross Trust	1761–65	5%	
—	1765	4%	
—	1766	4½%	
—	1768	4%	
—	1769	4½%	
Wrotham Heath Trust	1768–74	4%	
Chalk Trust	1769–71	4½%	
LANCASHIRE[39]			
Manchester–Wilmslow Trust	1763–1820	5%	4½%
Doffcocker Trust	1765	5%	
Blackburn–Burscough Bridge Trust	1762	4%	
LEICESTERSHIRE[40]			
Harborough–Loughborough Trust	1761–83	4½%	4%
Leicester–Hinckley Trust	1764–79	4½%	4%
Hinckley–Lutterworth Trust	1762–84	5%	

[36]Mortgages 1763-67, T/N/AF/3 & 4 Cambs. RO.

[37]Chappel-on-the-Hill Trust, Deed Poll 1791, D76/13B; Gloucester–Hereford Trust, Minute Book 1769-1812, D204/2/4; Gloucester–Birdlip Trust, Minute Book 1761-75, D204/3/1; Maismore Road, Minute Book 1761-1809, D204/2/3; Newant New Trust, Mortgage 1840, D892/29. (All documents in Glouces. RO.)

[38]Cranbrooke Trust, Mortgage 1762, U106 T2; Tenterden Trust, Accounts 1762-1805, T20/1; Kipping Cross Trust, Register of Securities 1765-1852, T1/2; Wadhurst–West Farleigh Trust, Minutes and Accounts 1765-88, T5/1; Charing Trust, Security Ledger 1766-1869, U442-057; New Cross Trust, Mortgages 1761-66, T9/F6 and Accounts Book 1765-72, T9/F1/2; Wrotham Heath Trust, Account Book 1768-74, U442-058; Chalk Trust Mortgages 1769-1828, T7/F3. (All documents in Kent AO.)

[39]Manchester–Wilmslow Trust, Accounts 1753-1805, MSS 7352 042 M103 Man. Lib. of Loc. His.; Doffcocker Trust, Mortgage 1765, DDPi/10/5 Lancs. RO; Blackburn–Burscough Bridge Trust, Account Book 1755-93, TTE-2 Lancs. RO.

[40]Harborough–Loughborough Trust, Abstract of Minutes 1725-77 (rate changed 2 February 1761), T/X/1/1 and Minute Book 1764-86, T/MB/1/2; Leicester–Hinckley Trust, Securities Book 1754-1877, T/X/4/1; Hinckley–Lutterworth Trust, Minute Book 1762-99, T/MB/2/1. (All documents in Leices. RO.)

		to	from
LINCOLNSHIRE[41]			
Lincoln–Brigg Trust	1765	5%	
Donington Road Trust	1764–84	4½%	
MIDDLESEX[42]			
Colnbrook Trust	1762–75	5%	4%
Bedfont–Bagshot Trust (West)	1763–81	4½%	
Old Street Trust	1761–63	5%	
—	1763–65	4½%	5%
—	1765–78	4%	4½%
OXFORDSHIRE[43]			
Stokenchurch Trust	1764–68	5%	4%
—	1768–1807	4½%	
NORTHAMPTONSHIRE[44]			
Banbury–Lutterworth Trust	1769–97	4½%	
SHROPSHIRE[45]			
Shrewsbury–Wrexham Trust	1769–79	4½%	4%
STAFFORDSHIRE[46]			
Uttoxeter–Newcastle Trust	1761	5%	
Cheadle Trust (Oakmoor Dist.)	1762–84	5%	
Cheadle Trust (Ipstones Dist.)	1769–1803	5%	
WARWICKSHIRE[47]			
Birmingham–Hagley Trust	1760–73	4½%	3½%
WILTSHIRE[48]			
Chippenham Trust	1768	4½%	
WORCESTERSHIRE[49]			
Stourbridge Trust (2nd or Cradley Dist.)	1764–76	5%	
Stourbridge Trust (Wordsley Green, Claygate Dist.)	1765–78	4½%	4%
Worcester Trust	1768	4%	

---

[41] Lincoln–Brigg Trust, Minutes – 7 June 1765, Stubbs 1/1/1/1; Donington Trust, Minute Books 1764-70, 1770-80, 1780-93, Holland 48/1/2/3. (All documents in Lincs. AO.)

[42] Colnbrook Trust, Minute Book 1728-84 (rate changed 7 June 1762), T.P. Col. 1; Bedfont–Bagshot Trust, Minute Book 1763-1804, T.P. Bed. 4 (both documents in Mid. CRO). Minute Book 1753-78 (rate changed 1 January 1761, 3 August 1763, 2 October 1765), Fins. Lib.

[43] Minute Book 1740-93 (rates changed 11 June 1764 and 7 September 1768), CH.S.1 Oxon. CRO.

[44] Account Book 1769-1800, box 1118 Northam. RO.

[45] Minute Book 1767-84 (rate changed 20 June 1769), Giles and Horton 321 box 5, Salop RO.

[46] Uttoxeter–Newcastle Trust, Mortgages 1760-61, D239/M 2427; Cheadle Trust (Oakmoor District), Account Book 1762-84, D239/M box 4; Cheadle Trust (Ipstones District), Mortgages and Assignments 1769-1828, D239/M box 6. (All documents in Staffs. RO.)

[47] Minute Books 1753-72 and 1773-1811 (rate changed 17 June 1760), 288223 and 288224 Birm. Ref. Lib.

[48] Mortgages 1768, 130/44 Wilts. RO.

[49] Stourbridge Trust (2nd or Cradley District), Record Book 1764-1815, 899:31, BA 3762/4 (v); Stourbridge Trust (Wordsley, Claygate District), Record Book 1753-1811, 899:31, BA 3762/4 (v); Worcester Trust, Record of Mortgages and Transfers 1819-67 (one of the transfers gives the 1768 interest rate); 705:583, BA 706/10; Droitwich Trust, Order Book 1754-93 (rate changed 3 September 1764), b705:584, BA 704/1. (All documents in Worces. RO.)

		to	from
Droitwich Trust	1763–64	4½%	
—	1764–78	4%	4½%
YORKSHIRE[50]			
Doncaster–Saltersbrook Trust	1762–1839	5%	4½%
Knaresborough–Pateley Bridge Trust	1764–86	4%	
Doncaster–Tinsley Trust	1766	4½%	
Rotherham–Wortley Trust	1767–1830	4½%	
1770s			
BUCKINGHAMSHIRE[51]			
Bicester–Aylesbury Trust	1770–76	5%	
GLOUCESTERSHIRE[52]			
Gloucester–Birdlip Trust	1771–80	4½%	4%
Maismore Road	1779–87	5%	4½%
Chepstow and District Trust	1776–86	4%	
KENT[53]			
Wrotham–Maidstone Trust	1771	5%	
New Cross Trust	1770–75	4%	4½%
Wadhurst–West Farleigh Trust	1770–74	4½%	5%
—	1774–86	4%	4½%
Kipping Cross Trust	1770	4%	
Chalk Trust	1772–76	4%	4½%
—	1778-(January)	4½%	4%
—	1778-(July) 1802	5%	4½%
LEICESTERSHIRE[54]			
Wanlip Trust	1771–97	4½%	
Leicester–Hinckley Trust	1779–1839	5%	4½%
MIDDLESEX[55]			
Kilburn Trust	1775–79	4½%	
—	1779–1825	5%	4½%
Colnbrook Trust	1775–79	4½%	4%
—	1779	5%	4½%
Old Street Trust	1778	5%	4%

---

[50]Knaresborough–Pateley Bridge Trust, Account Book 1759-1839, box 27; Doncaster–Tinsley Trust, Mortgages 1766, box 33; Rotherham–Wortley Trust, Register of Mortgages 1767-1830, box 19 (all documents in West Rid. CRO); Doncaster–Saltersbrook Trust, Abstract of Minutes, Goodchild Collection.

[51]Mortages 1770-76, T/2/1 Bucks. RO. (These rates provided by Professor A. H. John.)

[52]Gloucester–Birdlip Trust, Minute Books 1761-75 and 1776-1806 (rate changed 5 May 1771), D204/3/1 and D204/3/2; Maismore Road, Minute Book 1761-1809, D204/2/3; Chepstow and District Trust, Account Book 1776-86, D428/B2. (All documents in Glouces. RO.)

[53]Wrotham–Maidstone Trust, Mortgage 1771, U47/38 T33; New Cross Trust, Account Books 1765-72 and 1775-87, T9/F1/2 and T9/F1/3; Wadhurst–West Farleigh Trust, Minutes and Accounts 1765-88 (rate changed 3 October 1770 and March 1774), T5/1; Kipping Cross Trust, Account Book 1765-1811, T1/3; Chalk Trust, Minute Book 1761-1809 (rate changed April 1772, January 1778 and July 1778), T7/A1. (All documents in Kent AO.)

[54]Wanlip Trust, Account Book 1771-1820, T/TA/8/1; Leicester–Hinckley Trust, Abstract of Minutes 1754-1842 (rate changed 7 June 1779), T/X/4/2. (Documents in Leics. RO.)

[55]Kilburn Trust, Minute Book 1775-97, LA/HW/TP 2 and Accounts Ledger 1772-1825, LA/HW/TP 5 (rate changed 12 April 1779); Colnbrook Trust, Minute Book 1728-84 (rate changed 13 March 1775 and 23 August 1779), T.P. Col. 1. (All documents in Mid. CRO.) Minute Book 1753-78 (rate changed 4 February 1778 from 4% to 4½% and 5 August 1778 to 5%), Fins. Lib.

		to	from
NORFOLK[56]			
Norwich–Swaffham Trust	1770–73	4%	
NORTHAMPTONSHIRE[57]			
Stony Stratford Trust	1775–1800	4½%	
NOTTINGHAMSHIRE[58]			
Grantham–Little Drayton Trust	1770	4%	
OXFORDSHIRE[59]			
Oxford–Mileways Trust	1771–75	4%	
SHROPSHIRE[60]			
Wem–Bron-y-Garth Trust	1771–73	4½%	
—	1774–87	5%	4½%
Ludlow Trust 1st Division	1776–1808	5%	4%
Shrewsbury–Wrexham Trust	1779	5%	4½%
STAFFORDSHIRE[61]			
Trentham Trust	1772–1802	5%	
WARWICKSHIRE[62]			
Evesham–Alcester Trust	1778–1825	5%	
Birmingham–Hagley Trust	1773–1811	5%	4½%
WORCESTER[63]			
Innings Lane Trust	1777–1839	5%	
Droitwich Trust	1778–86	5%	4%
Stourbridge Trust (Wordsley Green, Clapgate District)	1773–82	5%	4½%
YORKSHIRE[64]			
Blackstone Edge Trust	1773–1839	5%	4½%
Huddersfield–Peniston Trust	1777–1827	5%	
Knaresborough–Skipton Trust	1777–1813	5%	
Halifax–Huddersfield Trust	1779–1824	5%	
1780s			
BEDFORDSHIRE[65]			
Bedford–Woburn Park Trust	1781	4%	

[56] Entries of Securities 1770-75, Norf. & Norw. RO.
[57] Account Book 1775-1800, box 755 Northam. RO.
[58] Mortgage 1770, PR658 Notts. CRO.
[59] Accounts 1771-75, Misc. Mor. I/I Oxon. CRO.
[60] Wem–Bron-y-Garth Trust, Minute Book 1771-89, Giles and Horton 321 box 5; Ludlow Trust 1st Division, Minute Book 1776-1838 (rate changed 28 June 1776), SRO 356/23/309; Shrewsbury–Wrexham Trust, Minute Book 1767-84 (rate changed 5 July 1779), Giles and Horton 321 box 5. (All documents in Salop RO.)
[61] Account Book 1772-1803, 272/32 Wm. Salt Lib.
[62] Evesham–Alcester Trust, Security Ledger 1778–1825, CR 446/21 War. CRO; Birmingham–Hagley Trust, Minute Book 1773-1811 (rate changed 22 June 1773), 228224 Birm. Ref. Lib.
[63] Innings Lane Trust, Journal 1798-1871, 705:585, BA 706/11; Droitwich Trust, Minute Book 1754-93 (rate changed 4 May 1778), b705:584, BA 704/1; Stourbridge Trust (Wordsley Green, Clapgate District), Record Book 1753-1811, 899:31, BA 3762/4 (iv). (All documents in Worcs. RO.)
[64] Blackstone Edge Trust, Register of Mortgages 1732-1872, HAS – 52 Hal. Cent. Lib.; Huddersfield–Peniston Trust, Accounts Books 1771-1811 and 1811-62, box 72 West Rid. CRO; Knaresborough–Skipton Trust, Account Book 1777-1813, box 27 West Rid. CRO; Halifax–Huddersfield Trust, Mortgages 1779-1824, box 10 West Rid. CRO.
[65] Mortgages 1781, QT 3/4-9 Beds. CRO.

		to	from
CAMBRIDGESHIRE[66]			
Kneesworth–Caxton Trust	1780–81	4%	
—	1781–1829	5%	4%
GLOUCESTERSHIRE[67]			
Gloucester–Birdlip Trust	1780–1806	5%	$4\frac{1}{2}$%
Burford–Preston Trust	1780–1800	5%	$4\frac{1}{2}$%
Stone–Clay Pits Trust			
(Wootton-under-Edge Divsn.)	1784	5%	
Cheltenham–Tewkesbury Trust	1786	5%	
KENT[68]			
Tenterden Trust	1780	5%	4%
Kipping Cross Trust	1780	5%	
New Cross Trust	1781–1824	5%	
LANCASHIRE[69]			
Skipton–Colne Trust	1786	5%	
LEICESTERSHIRE[70]			
Melton Mowbray–Leicester Trust	1783–1839	5%	
Harborough–Loughborough Trust	1783–1803	5%	$4\frac{1}{2}$%
Hinckley–Lutterworth Trust	1784–91	4%	5%
LINCOLNSHIRE[71]			
Donington Trust	1784	5%	$4\frac{1}{2}$%
MIDDLESEX[72]			
Bedfont–Bagshot Trust (West)	1781–89	5%	$4\frac{1}{2}$%
—	1789–96	$4\frac{1}{2}$%	5%
NOTTINGHAMSHIRE[73]			
Leadenham Hill–Newark-on-Trent			
Trust	1781–1801	5%	$4\frac{1}{2}$%
SHROPSHIRE[74]			
Ludlow Trust 2nd District	1782	5%	4%
SUFFOLK[75]			
Ipswich–South Town Trust	1786–1813	5%	

[66]Account Book 1780-1853, T/K/FA Cambs. RO.

[67]Gloucester–Birdlip Trust, Minute Book 1776-1806 (rate changed 3 January 1780), D204/3/2; Burford–Preston Trust, Minutes and Accounts 1753-1807, D1070; Stone–Clay Pits Trust (Wootton-under-Edge Division), Mortgage 1784, D892/Z7; Cheltenham–Tewkesbury Trust, Minute Book and Accounts 1778-98, D204/1/1. (All documents in Glouces. RO.)

[68]Tenterden Trust, Accounts 1762-1805, T20/1; Kipping Cross Trust, Account Book 1765-1811, T1/3; New Cross Trust, Account Books 1775-87, 1788-97, 1798-1813, T9/F1/3–/4–/5 and Abstract of Annual Accounts 1805-35, T9/F2/1. (All documents in Kent AO.)

[69]Order Book 1787-1836 (contains list of creditors 1786), TTI-2 Lancs. RO.

[70]Melton Mowbray–Leicester Trust, Security Book 1812-55 (containing reference to 1783 rate), T/X/3/1; Harborough–Loughborough Trust, Minute Book 1764-86 (rate changed 1 December 1783), T/MB/1/2 and Account Book 1784-1804, T/TA/1/1; Hinckley–Lutterworth Trust, Minute Book 1762-99 (rate changed 24 August 1784), T/MB/2/1. (All documents in Leics. RO.)

[71]Minute Book 1780-93 (rate changed 16 August 1784), Holland 48/3 Lincs. AO.

[72]Minute Book 1763-1804 (rate changed 14 June 1781 and 25 November 1789), T.P. Bed. 4 Mid. CRO.

[73]Account Book 1759-1809, DDT/27/1 and Minute Book 1759-1815 (rate changed 27 September 1781), DDM/11/64 Notts. CRO.

[74]Account Book 1780-87, SRO 356/23/306 Salop RO.

[75]Minute Book 1785-1821, E.H.50/5/2B1. Ips. & E. Suf. RO.

		to	from
WILTSHIRE[76]			
Seend–Box Trust	1781	5%	
Devizes (Old) Trust	1781–83	5%	4%
WORCESTERSHIRE[77]			
Droitwich Trust	1786–91	4½%	5%
YORKSHIRE[78]			
Doncaster–Tadcaster Trust	1784–93	5%	
Harrogate–Boroughbridge Trust	1787	5%	
1790s			
BEDFORDSHIRE[79]			
Luton Trust (Bedford District)	1790 and 1819	5%	
Dunstable–Hockliffe Trust	1794 and 1808	5%	
CAMBRIDGESHIRE[80]			
Cambridge–Ely Trust	1791–1836	5%	
KENT[81]			
Deal–Sandwich Trust	1798–1818	5%	
Canterbury–Barham Trust	1799–1800	5%	
Tonbridge–Maidstone Trust	1799	5%	
LANCASHIRE[82]			
Heywood Trust	1798	5%	
LEICESTERSHIRE[83]			
Hinckley–Lutterworth Trust	1798–1817	4%	
MIDDLESEX[84]			
Bedfont–Bagshot Trust (East)	1794–1816	5%	
NORFOLK[85]			
Norwich–North Walsham Trust	1797–1810	5%	
NORTHAMPTONSHIRE[86]			
Wellingborough–Northampton Trust	1797–1820	5%	
Banbury–Lutterworth Trust	1797–1800	5%	4½%
SUFFOLK[87]			
Little Yarmouth Trust	1797–1832	5%	

---

[76] Seend-Box Trust, Minutes — 20 March 1781, no. 519; Devizes (Old) Trust, Account Books 1755-83 (rate changed November 1781), A3/7/4. (Documents in Wilts. RO.)

[77] Order Book 1754-93 (rate changed 2 May 1786), b705:584, BA 704/1 Worcs. RO.

[78] Doncaster–Tadcaster Trust, Account Book 1741-1835, box 54; Harrogate–Boroughbridge Trust, Minutes — 8 March 1787, box 27. (Documents in West Rid. CRO.)

[79] Luton Trust (Bedford District), Mortgages 1790 and 1819, QTA3/1 and 16; Dunstable–Hockliffe Trust, Mortgages 1794 and 1808, B.592 and B.593-6. (Documents in Beds. CRO.)

[80] Account Book 1791-1837, Cambs. RO.

[81] Deal–Sandwich Trust, Security Ledger 1798-1871, T11/F3; Canterbury–Barham Trust, Account Journal 1799-1802, T6/1; Tonbridge-Maidstone Trust, Account Book 1765-1801, T2/3. (All documents in Kent AO.)

[82] Mortgages 1798, TTH-4-23 Lancs. RO.

[83] Minute Book with Accounts 1798-1817, T/MB/2/2 Leics. RO.

[84] Minute Book 1785-1830, T.P. Bed. 2 Mid. CRO.

[85] Minute Book 1797-1810, Norf. & Norw. RO.

[86] Wellingborough–Northampton Trust, Accounts 1797-1818, box 1023; Banbury–Lutterworth Trust, Account Book 1769-1800, box 1118. (Documents in Northam. RO.)

[87] Minute Book 1796-1832, E.H. 50/5/3B1. Ips. & E. Suf. RO.

		to	from
WARWICKSHIRE[88]			
Bromsgrove–Stratford Trust	1790–94	5%	
Dunchurch–Southam Trust	1797	5%	
WORCESTERSHIRE[89]			
Tenbury Trust	1792	5%	
Droitwich Trust	1791	4%	4½%
Worcester Trust	1793–94	4½%	
—	1794–1818	5%	4½%
YORKSHIRE[90]			
Doncaster–Tadcaster Trust	1793–94	5% and 4½%	5%
Bawtry–Selby Trust	1794–1805	5%	
Harrogate–Hutton Moor Trust	1795–1814	5%	4%
Kirkby Hill Moor–Ripon Trust	1795–1814	5%	4%
Leeds–Harrogate Trust	1798	5%	
1800–1815			
KENT[91]			
Canterbury–Sandwich Trust	1802–03	5%	4½%
Kipping Cross Trust	1802–14	4%	
Stokershead–Chilham Trust	1809–39	5%	
LINCOLNSHIRE[92]			
Lincoln–Brigg Trust	1804–1820	5%	
MIDDLESEX[93]			
Bedfont–Bagshot Trust (West)	1800–03	5%	4½%
—	1807–10	4½%	5%
—	1811–13	5%	4½%
—	1815	4½%	
Harrow Trust	1801 and 1819	5%	
NORFOLK[94]			
Norwich–North Walsham Trust	1811–20	4%	5%
NORTHAMPTONSHIRE[95]			
Kettering–Newport Pagnell Trust	1805–18	5%	
Stony Stratford Trust	1803–16	4½%	

---

[88]Bromsgrove–Stratford Trust, Minute Book 1767-1806, CR446/1; Dunchurch–Southam Trust, Mortgage Ledger 1797-1872, CR580/59. (Documents in War. CRO.)

[89]Tenbury Trust, Mortgages 1792, 705; 137, BA3473/3; Droitwich Trust, Minute Book 1754-93 (rate changed 7 November 1791), b705:584, BA704/1; Worcester Trust, Record of Mortgages and Transfers 1793-1853, b705:583, BA706/11. (All documents in Worcs. RO.)

[90]Doncaster–Tadcaster Trust, Account Book 1741-1835, box 54; Bawtry–Selby Trust, Account Book 1793-1844, box 11; Harrogate–Hutton Moor Trust, Account Book 1752-1814, box 27; Kirkby Hill Moor–Ripon Trust, Account Book 1752-1814, box 27; Leeds–Harrogate Trust, Mortgage 1798, box 57. (All documents in West Rid. CRO.)

[91]Canterbury–Sandwich Trust, Register of Securities and Transfers 1802-68, T4/2; Kipping Cross Trust, Account Book 1765-1811, T1/3; Stokershead–Chilham Trust, Account Book 1809-53, T18/2. (All documents in Kent AO.)

[92]Interest Receipts, 1804-11 and 1813-20, Stubbs 1/1/5/28 and 1/1/6/3-/10 Lincs. AO.

[93]Bedfont–Bagshot Trust, Minute Books 1763-1804 and 1804-15 (rate changed 26 June 1800, 5 December 1807, 13 May 1811, and 26 August 1815), T.P. Bed. 4 and T.P. Bed.5; Harrow Trust, Mortgage Register 1801, LA/HW/TP7 and Minutes – 20 September 1819, LA/HW/TP17. (All documents in Mid. CRO.)

[94]Minute Book 1810-26 (rate changed 13 April 1811), Norf. & Norw. RO.

[95]Kettering–Newport Pagnell Trust, Accounts 1814-18 (contains reference to rates paid in 1805), ML31; Stony Stratford Trust, Accounts 1803-16, ML242. (Documents in Northam. RO.)

		to	from
WARWICKSHIRE[96]			
Banbury–Barcheston Trust	1802–39	5%	
Drayton–Edgehill Trust	1806–22	4%	
Watling Street Trust	1809–33	5%	
Alcester–Wootton Trust	1814–30	5%	
YORKSHIRE[97]			
Rotherham–Swinton Trust	1809	5%	
Bawtry–Selby Trust	1805–16	4½%	5%
1816–1825			
CAMBRIDGESHIRE[98]			
Newmarket Heath Trust	1818	5%	
KENT[99]			
Kipping Cross Trust	1817	5%	
Greenwich–Woolwich Lower Road			
Trust	1818	5%	
—	1824	4%	5%
—	1827	5%	4%
Maidstone–Biddenden Trust	1821	5%	
Biddenden–Boundgate Trust	1823	5%	
New Cross Trust	1824–26	4%	5%
LANCASHIRE[100]			
Clitheroe–Blackburn Trust	1823–39	5%	
Preston–Wigan (north of Yarrow)			
Trust	1823 and 1834	5%–4½%	
MIDDLESEX[101]			
Bedfont–Bagshot Trust (West)	1816–26	5%	4½%
Kilburn Trust	1825	4%	5%
NORFOLK[102]			
Norwich–North Walsham Trust	1820–26	5%	4%
OXFORDSHIRE[103]			
Stokenchurch Trust	1824	4%	
—	1825 and 1827	5%	4%

---

[96]Banbury–Barcheston Trust, Mortgage Ledger 1802-39, CR580/53; Drayton–Edgehill Trust, Minute Book 1753-1822, CR580/57; Watling Street Trust, Minute Book 1809-58, CR 720/1; Alcester–Wootton Trust, Minute Book 1814-50, CR446/4. (All documents in War. CRO.)

[97]Rotherham–Swinton Trust, List of Subscribers 1809, box 80; Bawtry–Selby Trust, Account Book 1793-1844, box 11. (Above documents in West Rid. CRO.)

[98]Mortgages 1818, T/N/AF 3 & 4 Cambs. RO.

[99]Kipping Cross Trust, Minute Book 1765-1827, T1/1; Greenwich–Woolwich Lower Road Trust, Registers of Mortgages and Transfers 1824-49 and 1828-69, T10/F6/1-/2; Maidstone–Biddenden Trust, Mortgage 1821, U24 T431; Biddenden–Boundgate Trust, Mortgage 1823, U78 03; New Cross Trust, Abstract of Annual Accounts 1805-35, T9/F2/1. (All documents in Kent AO.)

[100]Clitheroe–Blackburn Trust, Mortgage Book 1823-71, TTB-2; Preston–Wigan (north of Yarrow) Trust, Mortgages 1823-34, DDL-500-506. (Documents in Lancs. RO.)

[101]Bedfont–Bagshot Trust, Minute Book 1816-29 (rate changed 21 June 1816), T.P. Bed. 6; Kilburn Trust, Minutes – 3 January 1825, LA/HW/TP 4. (Documents in Mid. CRO.)

[102]Minute Book 1810-26 (rate changed 6 October 1820), Norf. & Norw. RO.

[103]Mortgages 1824, 1825 & 1827, CH.S/v/i /5,/8, &/11 Oxon. CRO.

		to	from
WARWICKSHIRE[104]			
Chipping Campden Trust	1824–39	5%	
Evesham–Alcester Trust	1825–26	4½%	5%
WORCESTERSHIRE[105]			
Stourbridge Trust (2nd or Cradley District)	1823–28	5%	
YORKSHIRE[106]			
Tadcaster–Hob Moor Lane Trust	1816–28	5%	
Leeds–Dewsbury Trust	1816–33	5%	
Bawtry–Selby Trust	1816–39	5%	
Balby–Worksop Trust	1816	4%	
Leeds–Holmefield Lane End Trust	1817–39	5%	
Toller Lane End–Colne Trust	1818–23	5%	
Leeds–Barnsdale Trust	1819–39	5%	
Leeds–Elland Trust	1823–25	5%	
Leeds–Selby Trust	1822–39	4½%, 4¾%, 5%	
Knaresborough–Green Hammerton Trust	1823–39	5%	
New Mill District Trust	1823	4%	
Richmond–Lancaster Trust	1825–29	5%	
Leeds–Tong Lane End Trust	1825–29	5%	

---

[104]Chipping Campden Trust, Mortgage Ledger 1824-75, CR446/42; Evesham–Alcester Trust, Order Book 1806-58 (rate changed 28 April 1825), CR446/22. (Documents in War. CRO.)

[105]Minute Book 1821-30, 899:31, BA3762/4 (iv) Worces. RO.

[106]Tadcaster–Hob Moor Lane Trust, Minute Book 1812-33, box 54; Leeds–Dewsbury Trust, Minute Book 1816-33, box 29; Bawtry–Selby Trust, Account Book 1793-1844, box 11; Balby–Worksop Trust, Minutes 1858-74, box 15; Leeds–Holmefield Lane End Trust, Interest Ledger 1817-72, box 52; Toller Lane End–Colne Trust, Minute Book 1755-1823, box 50; Leeds–Barnsdale Trust, Minute Books 1819-27 and 1827-44, box 17; Leeds–Elland Trust, Security Ledger 1823-25, box 48; Leeds–Selby Trust, Mortgage Ledger 1751-1872, box 60; Knaresborough–Green Hammerton Trust, Account Book 1811-78, box 27; New Mill District Trust, Interest Ledger 1823-72, box 1, Richmond–Lancaster Trust, Register of Mortgages 1825-29, box 70; Leeds–Tong Lane End Trust, Minute Book 1825-26 and Security Ledger 1829-68, box 7. (All documents in West Rid. CRO.)

APPENDIX I

Assessed land carriage rates

Note: Unless noted, all the prices are from *Returns to the Clerks of the Peace of Westminster and Middlesex* Ra. Car. 1749-1827 (Middlesex County Record Office). A few prices, mainly for the late 1780s, are from the *Returns to the Lord Mayor of London*, Misc. Mss. 30.1 (Corporation of London Record Office). When only the county is given the rate applies to anywhere within that county, unless a town is noted at the side. Except for Buckinghamshire, when two rates are given for the same year, they are summer and winter rates. Rates assessed to London by wagon from:

BOSTON (LINCS.)
/cwt.
1696:	7s[1]
1749–57:	8s–10s
1758–80:	8s–9s
1814:	8s
1816–26:	6s

BUCKINGHAMSHIRE
1692–1710:	$\begin{cases} 14d/\text{ton/mile (Chilterns)[2]} \\ 20d/\text{ton/mile (sum.)} \\ 25d/\text{ton/mile (win.)} \end{cases}$
1756:	12d/ton/mile
1759–68:	10·6–9·8d/ton/mile

(not seasonal rates)

CHESHIRE
/cwt.
1694:	5s–7s[3]
1757:	8s–9s (Chester)
1760:	7s–8s ,,

DEVONSHIRE (HONITON, TIVERTON or TOPSHAM)
/cwt.
1758:	6s (summer)
1764–71:	6s–8s
1772:	8s
1778–82:	7s 6d

DORSETSHIRE (DORCHESTER or SHERBORNE)
/cwt.
1750–54:	6s
1756:	7s
1757–86:	6s

ESSEX
1749–1809:	12d/ton/mile
1810–27:	16d/ton/mile

KESTEVEN QS (LINCS.)
(Ashwardhurne or Flaxwell)
/cwt.
1758–66:	7s
1767–71:	5s 6d
1773–1827:	6s

KINGSTON-ON-HULL
/cwt.
1749–56:	14s
1759–60:	10s 8d

LEEDS
/cwt.
1766–72:	6s 8d
1775–77:	7s 4d
1779–80:	6s 8d
1782–86:	7s 4d

LEICESTER
/cwt.
1750–81:	5s–5s 6d
1799–1809:	5s 3d–5s 9d
1810:	6s–6s 6d
1814:	7s 3d–7s 9d
1816–24:	5s 3d–5s 9d

CITY OF LINCOLN
/cwt.
1764:	7s
1766–68:	6s
1769–79:	7s

---

[1] *Victoria History of the County of Lincoln*, Vol. II, ed. William Page (London, 1906), p. 340.

[2] *County of Buckingham Calendar of the Sessions Records*, Vol. I, 1678-1694, ed. William Le Hardy (Aylesbury, 1933), pp. 426, 462, 506. *County of Buckingham Calendar of the Sessions Records*, Vol. II, 1694-1705, ed. William Le Hardy and G. Reckett (Aylesbury, 1936), pp. 44, 87, 125, 204, 247, 288, 325, 383, 422. *County of Buckingham Calendar of the Sessions Records*, Vol. III, 1705-1712, ed. William Le Hardy and G. Reckett (Aylesbury, 1939), p. 216.

[3] Willan, 'The Justices of the Peace', p. 199.

1780–81:   6s
1795–1825:   7s

LINDSEY QS (LINCS.)
/cwt.
1751–58:   10s (Louth)
1763–66:   8s 8d   „
1768:   8s   „
1772–95:   7s 6d   „
1799–1801:   9s (Louth QS)
1816:   7s 6d (Louth)
1819–22:   8s   „
1823:   7s 6d   „
1824–27:   8s   „

NEWCASTLE-UPON-TYNE
/cwt.
1759–99:   14s
1801:   20s
1810:   18s
1814:   20s
1816:   18s
1821–26:   22s

NORTHAMPTON
/cwt.
1710:   4s[4]
1743:   3s 6d[5]
1749–58:   3s 6d

NORTH RIDING
/cwt.
1692:   18s 8d
1727:   16s[6]
1751:   16s
1758–99:   10s (Richmond)
1801–03:   12s   „
1805:   10s 8d   „
1807–20:   17s 4d   „
1822:   16s   „
1826:   14s 8d (Northallerton)

NOTTINGHAMSHIRE (East Retford Division)
/cwt.
1752–53:   8s
1754–56:   7s–7s 6d
1757–60:   6s 9d–7s
1761–65:   6s 6d
1769–73:   6s
1775–86:   6s 8d

PORTSMOUTH
1749–74:   16d–20d/ton/mile
1775–86:   13½d–17d/ton/mile

SHREWSBURY
/cwt.
1750–52:   6s 6d
1753–59:   7s–9s
1764–71:   7s–8s
1788–95:   8s–9s
1801–10:   IN. 15d/ton/mile
1822:   10d/ton/mile
1825–27:   20d/ton/mile

SHROPSHIRE
/cwt.
1748–52:   7s
1753–59:   7s–9s
1764–65:   7s–8s 6d
1776–82:   8s–9s
1788:   6s–7s
1795–99:   8s–9s
1801–20:   IN. 15d/ton/mile
1822:   10d/ton/mile
1823:   15d/ton/mile
1825–27:   20d/ton/mile

SKIRKBECK QS (LINCS.)
/cwt.
1814:   8s
1816–28:   6s

SOUTHAMPTON
1795–99:   12d/ton/mile
1801:   16d/ton/mile
1802–25:   14d/ton/mile

SPALDING (LINCS.)
/cwt.
1696:   6s 8d[7]
1749–58:   8s
1759–80:   4s
1803:   5s
1814:   6s
1819–26:   4s 6d

WEST RIDING (DONCASTER, ROTHERHAM, BARNSLEY, PONTE-FRACT, WAKEFIELD, HALIFAX, SHEFFIELD or LEEDS)
/cwt.
1692:   9s 4d[8]
1732:   9s 4d–12s[9]
1750–56:   8s
1757–74:   6s 8d
1775–79:   7s 4d
1780:   6s 8d
1782:   7s 4d

---

[4]Quarter Session Assessment 1710, D(CA)96, Northam. RO.
[5]Willan, 'Justices of the Peace', p. 200.
[6]Ibid. p. 202.
[7]The Victoria History of Lincoln, Vol. II, p. 340.
[8]Quarter Sessions Order Book, p. 182, West Rid. CRO.
[9]Ibid. 18 April 1732.

1794:   8s
1795:   8s 8d–9s
1799:   8s
1800:   16s
1801:   12s
1802–07:   9s 4d
1809–20:   12s
1827:   16d/ton/mile

WORCESTERSHIRE
1804:   15d/ton/mile
1826:   17d/ton/mile

CITY OF YORK
/cwt.
1751–55:   10s
1756–74:   8s
1775–78:   9s 4d
1779–82:   8s
1795:   9s–9s 4d
1799:   8s 8d
1801:   12s
1802:   9s 4d
1809–1810:   10s 8d
1816:   10s
1825–27:   12s

Other areas which made returns
Anglesey: 1822–27
Bristol: 1750
Caernarvon: 1822–27
Cornwall: 1765–66
Cumberland: 1772 and 1774
Derbyshire: 1750–1827 (no change)
Exeter: 1759
Flintshire: 1824–27
Herefordshire: 1749–77 (no change)
Liverpool: 1824
Monmouthshire: 1767
Montgomeryshire: 1816–26
Pembrokeshire: 1803–27
Rutland: 1773–87
Somerset: 1749–69
Suffolk: 1809–10
Surrey: 1748–50
Sussex
    (Lewes QS):   1774 and 1786
Sussex
    (Chichester QS):   1757 and 1806
Warwickshire: 1749–1826 (no change)

Bibliography

PRIMARY SOURCES

BEDFORD COUNTY RECORD OFFICE

Bedford–Ampthill–Woburn Park Trust
Seven mortgages 1781   QT3/4-9
Bedford District of the Luton Trust
Two mortgages 1790 and 1819   QT4A/3/1 and /6
Cardington–Temsford Trust
Five mortgages 1766   QT2/4-8
Notice of Security Auction 1791   X42
Dunstable–Hockliffe Trust
Mortgage 1794   B.592
Four mortgages 1808   B.593-6
Hitchin–Bedford Trust
Minute Book 1757-88   X46/1
Minute Book 1788-1828   X46/1a
Interest Ledger 1792-1822   X46/12
Register of Securities 1757-60   X46/6
Kimbolton Trust
Three mortgages 1755   WG 894A-C
Woburn–Boughton Trust
Minute Book 1774-1821   X21/5/1
Woburn–Hockliffe Trust
Minute Book 1728-74   X21/4
Mortgage 1728 and Letter 31 March 1740
   (re mortgage)   CH.16/5A
Ledger 1830-38   X21/6

BIRMINGHAM REFERENCE LIBRARY

Birmingham–Hagley Trust
Minute Book 1753-72   288223
Minute Book 1773-1811   288224

BRITISH RAILWAYS BOARD: HISTORICAL RECORDS DEPT.

Pickford's Records
Newspaper Cuttings and other documents   Pic. 4/1
List and Accounts of Van and Waggon Stations 1835 Pic. 4/7

CAMBRIDGESHIRE RECORD OFFICE

Cambridge–Ely Trust
Account Book 1791-1837   no reference number
Book of Securities 1828-30   no reference number

Downham Market Trust
Mortgage 1773   L78/157
Mortgage 1776   R.52.12.44
Kneesworth–Caxton Trust
Account Book 1780-1853   T/K/FA
Newmarket Heath Trust
Minute Book 1763-99   T/N/AM-1
Mortgages 1763-67, 1818   T/N/AM-3 and 4

CORPORATION OF LONDON RECORDS OFFICE
Returns of Assessed Rates for land carriage   1773-1816 Misc.
                                                       MSS. 30.1

Receipt re Cost of obtaining higher carriage
rates in the City of London 1794   Misc. MSS. 30.1

FINSBURY LIBRARY
Old Street Trust
Minute Book July 1753-July 1778
Minute Book March 1786-May 1805
Minute Book January 1810-December 1826

GLOUCESTERSHIRE RECORDS OFFICE
Burford–Preston Trust
Minutes and Accounts 1753-1807   D1070
Chappel-on-the-Hill–Bourton-on-the-Water Trust
Accounts 1731-67   D621/X4
Deed Poll 1791   D76/13B
Cheapstow and District Trust
Account Book 1758-65   D428/B1
Account Book 1776-86   D428/B2
Cheltenham and Tewkesbury Trust
Minutes and Accounts 1778-98   D204/1/1
Cirencester–Monument-upon-Lansdown Trust
Mortgage 1753   D48F17
Gloucester–Birdlip and Crickley Hill Trust (Northgate Trust)
Minute Book 1761-75   D204/3/1
Minute Book 1776-1806   D204/3/2
Gloucester–Hereford Trust
Minute Book 1726-69   D204/2/2
Minute Book 1769-1812   D204/2/4
Account Book 1788-1811   D204/2/8
Maismore Road (section of the Gloucester–Hereford Trust)
Minute Book 1761-1809   D204/2/3
Mortgages 1769-1836   D204/2/14
Marshfield Trust
Wage Accounts 1769-70   D1610
Moreton Trust
Deed Poll 1791   D76/13B
Stone–Clay-Pits Trust
Mortgage 1759   D892/Z7

Mortgage 1784 (Wootton-under-Edge Dist.)   D892/Z7
Stroud Trust
Mortgage 1727   149/T/911
Wootton-under-Edge–Aldersley Trust
Mortgage 1763   D892/28
Other Material
Quarter Sessions Records   Q/SO-3

GOODCHILD COLLECTION IN THE CALDER VALLEY MUSEUM (Normanton)[1]
Doncaster–Saltersbrook Trust
Abstracts from draft minutes and accounts (compiled by John F. Goodchild)
Wakefield–Denby Dale Trust
Minute Book 1825-51

HALIFAX CENTRAL LIBRARY
Blackstone Edge Trust
Register of Mortgages 1735-1872   H.A.S. 52
Minute Book 1756-87   H.A.S. 55
Minute Book 1787-1827   H.A.S. 56
Account Book 1825-32   H.A.S. 117
Misc. Documents   H.A.S. 139 and 143
Halifax–Littleborough Trust
Account Book 1763-76   H.A.S. 323
Halifax–Wakefield Trust (Halifax District)
Account of Mortgages 1781-1810   Lister MSS. R & W 15
Book of Subscriptions 1809-23   Lister MSS. R & W 16
Wibsey Low Moor–Huddersfield Trust
Ledger 1823-1835   H.A.S. 45
Orders and Proceedings 1823-30   H.A.S. 36
Orders and Proceedings 1830-38   H.A.S. 37
Misc. Documents   H.A.S. A, 34, 36, 40-42,
                                                 59, 61, 76-79, 82-91, 93,
                                                 97-101, 104, 106.

HOUSE OF LORDS RECORD OFFICE
MSS Committee Minutes 15 May 1663.
MSS Petitions re Brampton Bridge–Market Harborough Road Bill, 19
   December 1721.
MSS Petitions re Counters Bridge–Stains Bridge Road Bill, 12 June 1717.
MSS Petitions re Islington–Paddington Road Bill, 31 March 1756.

HUNTINGDONSHIRE COUNTY RECORD OFFICE
Great North Road Trust
Minute Book 1725-45 (typed transcript)   no reference number

IPSWICH AND EAST SUFFOLK RECORD OFFICE
Ipswich–Helmingham Trust
Mortgages and Bonds 1812, 1862-83   EH: 50/5/1A1
Minute Book 1823-62   EH: 50/5/1B1 (4)
Ipswich–South Town Trust

[1]These documents are not numbered.

Miscellaneous Papers 1822-72	EH: 50/5/2A3
Minute Book 1785-1821	EH: 50/5/2B1
Little Yarmouth Trust	
Minute Book 1796-1832	EH: 50/5/3B1
Minute Book 1832-64	EH: 50/5/3B2
Yoxford–Aldeburgh Trust	
Minute Book 1792-1846	EH: 50/5/4B
Letter from John Garden to Charles Tyrell, M.P.	
re renewal act, 19 January 1832	Tyrell Papers S1/1/82.1
Other Material	
Turnpike Returns 1820-43	B:106/4/5(1)-(3)
Receipts for goods' carriage 1774-96	Rous Family Archives
	HA 11/C7/1/1-36

KENSINGTON PUBLIC LIBRARY

Fulham Field Trust	
Minute Book 1730-50	MS 58/7039
Minute Book 1750-65	MS 58/7040
Minute Book 1765-70	MS 58/7041
Kensington, Fulham, Chelsea Trust	
Minute Book 1726-34	MS 58/7001
Minute Book 1734-40	MS 58/7002
Minute Book 1758-71	MS 58/7006
Labourers' Wage Accounts 1753-57	MS 58/9373
Labourers' Wage Accounts 1771-78	MS 58/9374
Labourers' Wage Accounts 1787-99	MS 58/9375

KENT ARCHIVES OFFICE

Biddenden–Boundgate Trust	
Mortgage 1823	U78 03
Canterbury–Barham Trust	
Account Journal 1799-1802	T6/1
Canterbury–Sandwich Trust	
Ledger 1802	T4/1
Register of Securities and Transfers 1802-68	T4/2
Chalk Trust	
Accounts 1719-44	Q/SB 1719-1744
Minute Book 1761-1809	T7/A1
Mortgages of Tolls 1769-1828	T7/F3
Accounts, Correspondence etc. 1811-41	T7/F1/1
Charing Trust	
Security Ledger 1766-1869	U442-057
Cranbrooke Trust	
Mortgage 1762	U106 T2
Deal–Sandwich Trust	
Accounts 1797-1833	T11/F1
Security Ledger 1798-1871	T11/F3
Greenwich–Woolwich (Lower Road) Trust	
Register of Mortgages 1824-48	T10/F6/1
Register of Mortgages 1828-69	T10/F6/2

Kippings Cross Trust
Minute Book 1765-1827   T1/1
Register of Securities 1765-1852   T1/2
Account Book (First District) 1765-1811   T1/3
Maidstone–Biddenden Trust
Mortgage 1821   U24 T431
New Cross Trust
Minute Book with Accounts, 1718-23   T9/A1/14
Minute Book with Accounts, 1724-38   T9/A1/15
Minute Book 1746-65   T9/A1/1
Minute Book 1765-78   T9/A1/2
Minute Book 1797-1804   T9/A1/3
Committee Minutes 1814-18   T9/A2/1
Committee Minutes 1818-23   T9/A2/2
Account Book 1739-54   T9/F1/1
Account Book 1765-72   T9/F1/2
Account Book 1775-87   T9/F1/3
Account Book 1788-97   T9/F1/4
Account Book 1798-1813   T9/F1/5
Accounts 1813   T9/F1/6
Account Book 1824-35   T9/F1/7
Abstract of Annual Accounts 1805-35   T9/F2/1
Mortgages 1718-66   T9/F6
Rochester–Maidstone Trust
Minute Book 1728-41   T12/1
Stokershead–Chilham Trust
Account Book 1809-53   T18/2
Tenterden Trust
Accounts 1762-1805   T20/1
Tonbridge–Maidstone Trust
Minute Book 1765-1804   T2/1
Minute Book 1804-70   T2/2
Account Book 1765-1801   T2/3
Account Book 1801-56   T2/4
Mortgages 1769   U55 038
Wadhurst–West Farleigh Trust
Minutes and Accounts 1765-88   T5/1
Wrotham Heath Trust
Account Book 1768-74   U442-058
Wrotham–Maidstone Trust
Mortgage 1771   U47/38 T33
Other Material
Misc. papers re turnpike trusts   T21/Z1
Letters, Assignments and Notes re turnpike trusts
    1753-1821 Earl of Guildford Papers   U471 T134
Account Book of Stephen Stevens (toll-farmer)
    1830-38   Q/CI-219
Account Book of John Bryant (toll-farmer)
    1831-33   Q/CI-122

LANCASHIRE RECORD OFFICE

Blackburn–Addingham Trust
Account Book 1822-36 — DDBd 57/1/1
Blackburn–Burscough Bridge Trust
Minute Book 1755-93 — TTE 1
Account Book 1755-93 — TTE 2
Blackburn–Preston Trust
Minute Book 1824-42 — TTJ 7
Bury, Haslingden, Blackburn, Whalley Trust
Minute Book 1789-1875 — TTA 1
Account Book 1820-40 — TTA 6
Clitheroe–Blackburn Trust
Mortgage Book 1823-71 — TTB 2
Doffcocker Trust
Account Book 1781-1818 — DDPi/1/5
Mortgage 1765 — DDPi/10/5
Heywood Trust
Account Book 1790-1820 — TTH 2
Order Book 1800-21 — TTH 26
Mortgages 1798 — TTH 4-23
Preston–Lancaster Trust
Order Book 1751-1782 — TTD 1
Preston–Wigan Trust (North of Yarrow)
Mortgages 1823-34 — DDL 500-506
Skipton–Colne Trust
Order Book 1756-74 — TTI 1
Order Book 1787-1836 — TTI 2
Misc. Documents — TTI 12-18, 33-54
Ulverston–Carnforth Trust
List of Subscribers 1818 — TTK 8
Mortgages — TTK 9
Letters (re interest payments) — TTK 13
Other Material
Annual Trust Accounts submitted to the Clerk of
the County 1822-39 — QDT/1/1-89
Justices' Assessment of Carriage Rates QS
Preston, Easter 1733 — QSP 1361/10

LEICESTER MUSEUM, DEPARTMENT OF ARCHIVES
Loughborough–Ashby-de-la-Zouch Trust
Mortgage 1762 — 5033 412/13

LEICESTERSHIRE RECORD OFFICE
Harborough–Loughborough Trust
Abstract of Minutes 1725-77 — T/X/1/1
Order Book 1726-64 — T/MB/1/1
Minute Book 1764-86 — T/MB/1/2
Account Book 1784-1804 — T/TA/1/1
Hinckley–Leicester Trust
Securities Book 1754-1877 — T/X/4/1

Abstract of Minutes 1754-1842   T/X/4/2
Hinckley–Lutterworth Trust
Minute Book and Accounts 1762-99   T/MB/2/1
Minute Book and Accounts 1798-1823   T/MB/2/2
Melton Mowbray–Leicester Trust
Securities Book 1812-55   T/X/3/1
Tamworth–Sawley Ferry Trust
Register of Mortgages 1809-68   T/X/19/1
Wanlip Trust
Account Book 1771-1820   T/TA/8/1

LINCOLNSHIRE ARCHIVES OFFICE
Donington Trust
Minute Book 1764-70   Holland 48/1
Minute Book 1770-80   Holland 48/2
Minute Book 1780-93   Holland 48/3
Minute Book 1793-1801   Holland 48/4
Minute Book 1801-16   Holland 48/5
Lincoln–Brigg Trust
Minute Book 1765-1810   Stubbs 1/1/1/1
Security Ledger 1767-1865   Stubbs 1/1/5/1
Interest Receipts 1804-11   Stubbs 1/1/5/27-28
Interest Receipts 1812-20   Stubbs 1/1/6/3-10
Lincoln Heath–Peterborough Trust
Subscription List 1755   ASW 10/57/3
Misc. Documents   ASW 10/57/1-23
South-East District of the Lincoln Heath Trust
Minute Book 1756-76   Smith 6/1/1
Minute Book 1776-90   Smith 6/1/3
Minute Book 1803-12   Smith 6/1/5
Minute Book 1812-55   Smith 6/1/6
Account Book 1757-1875   Smith 6/2/9
Lists of Securities 1757-63   Smith 6/4/2
Surveyors' Accounts 1825-38   Smith 6/2/4-6
Other Material
Letters from J. Bourne to Wm. Drake Esq.
   14 September 1766   Tyr. 4/1/48
   1 October 1766   Tyr. 4/1/49
Notices of assessed carriage rates 1785-90   ASW 10/81/2-5, 16, 19

MANCHESTER LIBRARY OF LOCAL HISTORY
Manchester–Wilmslow Trust
Account Book 1753-1805   MSS 7352 042 M103
Deeds, Accounts and etc. 1754-1817   MSS 7352 042 M103
Register of Securities 1812-63   MSS 7352 042 M103
Deeds, Accounts and etc. 1818-58   MSS 7352 042 M103

MIDDLESEX COUNTY RECORD OFFICE
Bedfont–Bagshot Trust
Minute Book 1728-57   TP Bed. 1
K

Minute Book (Eastern District) 1785-1830	TP Bed. 2
Minute Book (Western District) 1763-1804	TP Bed. 4
Minute Book (Western District) 1804-15	TP Bed. 5
Minute Book (Western District) 1816-29	TP Bed. 6
Minute Book (Western District) 1830-50	TP Bed. 7

Colnbrook Trust

Minute Book 1728-84	TP Col. 1
Account Book 1823-1841	TP Col. 3
Mortgages and Assignments 1728-1868	TP Col. 8/1-8

Edgware Trust

Account Book 1730-1810	LA/HW/TP 21

Hampton–Staines Trust

Minute Book 1826-59	TP Ham. 1
Account Book 1825	TP Ham. 2

Harrow Trust

Mortgage Register 1801	LA/HW/TP 14
Account Book 1801-19	LA/HW/TP 15
Minute Book 1801-1819	LA/HW/TP 16
Minute Book 1819-1827	LA/HW/TP 17

Kilburn Trust

Surveyors' Accounts 1743-72	LA/HW/TP 1
Minute Book 1775-97	LA/HW/TP 2
Minute Book 1797-1810	LA/HW/TP 3
Minute Book 1810-26	LA/HW/TP 4
Accounts Ledger 1772-1825	LA/HW/TP 5
Accounts Book 1825-26	LA/HW/TP 6
Clerk's Accounts 1806-07	LA/HW/TP 7

Marylebone–Finchley Road Trust

Minute Book 1826-29	LA/HW/TP 18
Minute Book 1829-34	LA/HW/TP 19

Other Material

Register of Returns 1820	MR/UT
Returns of Assessed Rates for land carriage	1748-1827 Ra. Car.
Quarter Sessions Papers	MSP-AP/72-73

NORFOLK AND NORWICH RECORD OFFICE
Norwich–North Walsham Trust
Minute Book 1797-1810
Minute Book 1810-26
Norwich–Swaffham Trust
Entries of Securities 1770-75
Order Book 1770-90
Minute Book 1785-1810
Minute Book 1811-40
Thetford Trust
Minute Book 1787-1824

none of the documents
from this record office are
numbered.

NORTHAMPTONSHIRE RECORD OFFICE
Banbury–Lutterworth Trust

Account Book 1769-1800   1118
Kettering–Newport Pagnell Trust
Accounts 1814-18   ML31
Security Book 1754-1866   ML31
Market Harborough–Brampton Pound Trust
Assignment of Toll 1752   YZ 4641
Market Harborough–Welford Trust
Accounts 1750-1830   box 1284
Old Stratford–Dunchurch Trust
Account Book 1798-1801   AG112
Stony Stratford Trust
Account Book 1775-1800   box 755
Account Book 1803-16   ML242
Wellingborough–Northampton Trust
Accounts 1797-1818   box 1023
Other Material
Quarter Sessions Assessment of carriage rates
  1710   D(CA)96
Receipt for goods carriage 1806   YZ7073

NOTTINGHAMSHIRE COUNTY RECORD OFFICE
Grantham–Little Drayton Trust
Mortgage 1770   PR 658
Leadenham Hill–Newark-on-Trent Trust
Account Book 1759-1809   DDT 27/1
Minute Book 1759-1815   DDM 111/64
Mansfield–Pleasley, etc. Trust
Mortgages 1760   DDD 17/154-6
Other Material
Receipts for goods carriage 1752-69   DDSR 206/4-16 and
                                             DDSR 210/20-21, 22
Receipts for goods carriage 1746-47   DDSR 206/2
Receipts for goods carriage 1736-37   DDSR A4/45

OXFORDSHIRE COUNTY RECORD OFFICE
Oxford–Mileways Trust
Accounts 1771-75   I/1
Stokenchurch Trust
Minute Book 1740-93   Ch.S.1
Minute Book 1793-1807   Ch.S.2/1/2
Mortgages 1789-1834   Ch.S.v/i/1-14

PROBATE REGISTRY (SOMERSET HOUSE)
Joshua Bower, Probate of Will   October 1855
Lewis Levy, Probate of Will   January 1857

SHROPSHIRE RECORD OFFICE
Ludlow (First) Trust
Order Book and Accounts 1751-76   SRO 356/23/307
Minute Book 1776-1838   SRO 356/23/309

Account Book 1775-1808   SRO 356/23/308
Ludlow (Second) Trust
Order Book and Accounts 1756-70 356/23/312
Order Book 1770-1828   356/23/311
Account Book 1780-87   356/23/313
Shrewsbury–Wrexham Trust
Minute Book 1752-1767   Giles & Horton 321/box 5
Minute Book 1767-1783   Giles & Horton 321/box 5
Wem–Bron-y-Garth Trust
Minute Book 1771-89   Giles & Horton 321/box 5

SHEFFIELD CENTRAL LIBRARY
Chapel-en-le-Frith–Entreclough Bridge Trust
Mortgages 1793-1834   Arundel Castle MSS D58
Dore Road Trust
Wage Accounts 1817-19   MB 362
Repair Contracts 1816   MB 364
Glossop–Marple Bridge Trust
Mortgages 1804-05   Arundel Castle MSS D46
General Accounts 1823-39   Arundel Castle MSS D36
Rotherham–Wentworth Trust
'An Account of the Lab° employed under the
 Direction of Saint. Wroe . . .' 1767-72 WWM A1286
Sheffield–Glossop Trust
List of Subscribers 1818   CPG-8(6)
Mr Hill's Report on the Sheffield–Glossop Trust
 1823   CPG-14(11)
General Accounts 1827-39   CPG-2
Contracting Accounts   CPG-9
Misc. Accounts and Vouchers CPG-8
Treasurer's Accounts 1818 and 1819 Arundel Castle MSS D67
Mortgages and Assignments   SD 420-430
Sheffield–Wakefield Trust
Mortgages 1767   TC 363 and TC 412
List of Subscribers n.d. (1767 ?) TC 364-24
Misc. Vouchers 1759-76   TC 406-TC 411
Misc. Letters 1758-72   TC 404
Misc. Vouchers 1820   Wheat Collection 1255
Vouchers for Labourers' Wages 1759-75 TC 364 and TC 365
Misc. Documents   TC 363
'account of the charge of Repairing the Turnpike
 Road from Sheffield to Wakefield . . . under
 the direction of Saintforth Wroe', 1768-76 TC 363
Wakefield Road
Receipt of Labourers' Wages 1827 Fairbank Collection
            C.P. 15 and 22

Worksop–Attercliffe Trust
Receipts of Labourers' Wages 1827 Fairbank Collection
            C.P. 20

Other Material
Accounts of wages paid labourers, servants, WWM A1502, A1503,
   craftsmen, etc. on Wentworth Estate 1767-84 A1505, A1508, A1511

STAFFORDSHIRE RECORD OFFICE
Alton District Trust[2]
Subscription List 1799   D236M box 8 no. 3
Dilhorne District Trust
Subscription List 1790   D236M box 7 no. 4
Huntley and Wetley Rocks District Trust
Account Book 1762-1830   D239M box 5
Ipstones District Trust
Mortgages 1769 and 1771   D236M box 6 no. 4
Oakmore District Trust
Account Book 1762-84   D239M box 4
Uttoxeter–Newcastle Trust
Mortgages 1760-61   D236M 2427

WARWICKSHIRE COUNTY RECORD OFFICE
Alcester–Wootton Trust
Minute Book 1814-50   CR 446/4
Account Book 1830-50   CR 446/5
Security Ledger 1814   CR 446/9
Arrow–Pothooks End Trust
Security Ledger 1826-59   CR 446/11
Order Book 1826-49   CR 446/13
Banbury–Barcheston Trust
Mortgage Ledger 1802-34   CR 580/53
Bentley Lane Trust
Security Ledger 1827   CR 720/9
Bromsgrove–Stratford Trust
Minute Book 1754-1767   CR 446/1
Minute Book 1767-1806   CR 446/2
Minute Book 1807-1849   CR 446/3a
Chipping Campden Trust
Minute Book 1818-29   CR 446/39
Mortgage Ledger 1824-75   CR 446/42
Drayton–Edgehill Trust
Minute Book 1753-1822   CR 580/57
Dunchurch–Southam Trust
Minute Book 1794-1815   CR 580/58
Mortgage Ledger 1797-1872   CR 580/59
Evesham–Alcester Trust
Security Ledger 1778-1825   CR 446/21
Order Book 1806-58   CR 446/22
Surveyor's Accounts 1829-54   CR 446/26
Warwick–Paddlebrook Trust
Order Book 1816-71   CR 446/34

[2]All 'District' trusts were part of the Cheadle Trust.

Watling Street Trust
Minute Book 1809-58   CR 720/1

WEST RIDING COUNTY RECORD OFFICE[3]
Balby–Worksop Trust
Minute Book 1858-74   box 15
Barnby Moor–Rotherham Trust
List of Mortgages 1828   box 16
Barnsley–Pontefract Trust
Mortgages 1834   box 16
Barnsley–Shepley Lane Head Trust
Subscription List 1823   box 3
Minute Book 1824-1845
Bawtry–Selby Trust
Account Book 1793-1844   box 11
Minute Book 1793-1844
List of Subscribers 1811
Bawtry–Tinsley Trust
Mortgage Ledger 1762-1826   box 35
Minute Book 1807-25
Dewsbury–Gomersal Trust
Minute Book 1826-55   box 49
Doncaster–Tadcaster Trust
Minute Book 1741-1835   box 54
Account Book 1741-1835
Doncaster–Tinsley Trust
Mortgages 1766   box 33
Greenfield–Shepley Lane Head Trust
Subscription List 1822   box 3
Documents re obtaining local act
Halifax–Huddersfield Trust
Mortgages 1779-1824   box 10
Harrogate–Boroughbridge Trust
Minute Book 1752-1870   box 27
Harrogate–Hutton Moor Trust
Minute Book 1752-1814   box 27
Account Book 1752-1814
Homelane End–Heckmondwick Trust
Interest Ledger 1826-39   box 4
Huddersfield–Peniston Trust
Account Book 1771-1811   box 72
Minute Book 1777-88
Account Book 1811-62
Huddersfield–Saltershibble Trust
Minute Book 1824-57   box 6
Keighley–Halifax Trust
Minute Book 1768-88   box 8

[3]None of the documents in this office are numbered individually and, therefore, only the box numbers can be supplied.

Minute Book 1789-1815
Keighley–Kirkby-in-Kendal Trust
Minute Book 1753-1763   box 22
Minute Book 1787-1815
Kirkby Hill–Ripon and Boroughbridge Trust
Minute Book 1752-1814   box 27
Account Book 1752-1814
Knaresborough–Green Hammerton Trust
Minute Book 1752-1878   box 27
Account Book 1811-78
Knaresborough–Pateley Bridge Trust
Minute Book 1759-1851   box 27
Account Book 1759-1839
Annual Returns 1825-73
Knaresborough–Skipton Trust
Account Book 1777-1813   box 27
Minute Book 1783-1842
Knaresborough–Weatherby Trust
Minute Book 1775-1870   box 27
Mortgages 1783
Leeds–Barnsdale Trust
Minute Book 1819-27   box 17
Minute Book 1827-44
Surveyor's Accounts 1833-37
Leeds–Collingham Trust
Minute Book 1823-37   box 56
Account Book 1827-66
Leeds–Dewsbury Trust
Minute Book 1816-1833   box 29
Leeds–Elland Trust
Security Ledger 1823-25   box 48
Leeds–Harrogate Trust
Mortgages 1754, 1755 and 1798   box 57
Surveyor's Accounts 1821-23
Minute Book 1801-19
Leeds–Holmefield Lane End Trust
Mortgage Ledger 1817-72   box 52
Interest Ledger 1817-72
Minute Book 1817-38
Leeds–Otley Trust
Minute Book 1821-74   box 31
Leeds–Selby Trust
Mortgage Ledger 1751-1872   box 60
Lists of Trustees 1767, 1768, and 1833
Leeds–Tong Lane End Trust
Security Ledger 1829-68   box 7
Minute Book 1825-26
Leeds–Wakefield Trust
Minute Book 1758-79   box 45

Minute Book 1779-94
Minute Book 1794-1821
Account Book 1758-1823
Leeds–Whitehall Trust
Record Ledger no. 1 1825   box 23
Road Book 1825-53
Long Preston–Sawley Trust
Minute Book 1811-12   box 16
Marsden–Long Preston Trust
List of Subscribers 1802   box 9
New Mill District of the Wadsley and Langsett Trust
List of Loans and Donations n.d. (1823 ?)   box 1
Interest Ledger 1823-72
Oldham–Ripponden Trust
Mortgage Ledger 1795   box 46
Oldham–Stand Edge Trust
Mortgage Ledger 1797-1839   box 63
Redhouse (Doncaster)–Wakefield Trust
Minute Book 1741-1830   box 54
Account Book 1741-1812
Register of Mortgages 1758
Richmond–Lancaster Trust
Register of Mortgages 1825-29   box 70
Ripon–Pateley Bridge Trust
Minute Book 1756-1815   box 27
Rotherham–Peasley Trust
Receipt Book 1814-1822   box 16
Rotherham–Swinton Trust
Subscription List 1809   box 80
Draft List of Mortgagees 1838
Rotherham–Wortley Trust
Register of Mortgages 1767-1830   box 19
Sedbergh Trust
Register of Mortgages 1765   box 71
Shipley–Bramley Trust
Minute Book 1824-45   box 14
Tadcaster–Hob Moor Lane End Trust
Minute Book 1745-99   box 54
Account Book 1747-65
Minute Book 1812-33
Tadcaster–Otley Trust
Minute Book 1790-1878   box 54
Toller Lane End–Colne Trust
Minute Book 1755-1823   box 50
Wakefield–Halifax Trust
Minute Book 1762-1822   box 32
Minute Book 1823-44
Mortgage Ledger 1758-81

Wakefield–Weeland Trust
Minute Book 1741-1826   box 54
Worksop–Attercliffe Trust
Mortgage Ledger 1767   box 24
Minute Book 1782-1824
Minute Book 1824-41
Other Material
Quarter Sessions Records   Order Books 1692-1802

WILLIAM SALT LIBRARY
Burslem, Lawton, Cobridge and Newcastle Trust
Minute Book 1776-83   88/1/41
Minute Book 1828-59   88/2/41
Drayton–Newcastle Trust (Second District)
Mortgages 1770 and 1778   D1798/B191
Ipstones Trust
Treasurers' Accounts 1770-1806   52/31
Lawton–Burslem Trust
Mortgage 1778   D1798/B191
Lichfield–Stone Trust (Second District)
Mortgage 1814   D1798/B191
Newcastle–Blyth March Trust
General Statements of Accounts 1823-49   53/31
Newcastle–Eccleshall Trust
General Statements of Accounts 1823-45   53/31
Newcastle–Hassop Trust
Mortgage 1773   D1798/B191
Trentham Trust
Account Book 1772-1803   272/32

WILTSHIRE RECORD OFFICE
Chippenham Trust
Minute Book 1727-68   no. 119
Mortgages 1768   no. 130/44
Devizes (Old) Trust
Wage Accounts 1707-08   Quarter Sessions Records
                                              A3/7/4
Account Books 1746-83   Quarter Sessions Records
                                              A3/7/4
New Sarum–Ealing Trust
Minute Book 1753-95   no. 339
Mortgage 1754   no. 339
Seend–Box Trust
Minute Book 1753-90   no. 519

WORCESTERSHIRE RECORD OFFICE
Droitwich Trust
Order Book 1754-93   b705:584, BA 704/1
Evesham Trust
Minute Book 1789-1808   640, BA 2295

Innings Lane Trust
Journals (2 vols.) 1798-1871   705:585, BA 705/1
Mortgages 1777 and 1778   705:585, BA 705/2
Minute Book   705:585, BA 705/3
Stourbridge Trust (Second or Cradley District)
Minute Book 1762-79   899:31, BA 3762/4 (iv)
Record Book 1764-1815   899:31, BA 3762/4 (iv)
Minute Book 1821-30   899:31, BA 3762/4 (iv)
Stourbridge Trust (Wordsley Green, Clapgate District)
Record Book 1753-1811   899:31, BA 3762/4 (iv)
Tenbury Trust
Mortgages 1757, 1758 and 1792   705:137, BA 3473/3
Worcester Trust
Mortgage Ledger 1793-1853   b705:583, BA 706/10
Mortgage Ledger 1819-67   b705:583, BA 706/11

PRIMARY PUBLISHED AND PRINTED SOURCES

Andrews, C. Bruyn (ed.) *The Torrington Diaries* (London, 1935).

Anon. *The Farmers and Traders Apprehensions of a Rise upon Carriage, from the Act passed last Sessions,*... (London, 1752).

'Reasons why the Bill for amending the Highways from Brampton Bridge, ... should not pass into Law, as it now stands . . .', n.d. *B.M. Collection 516 m17.*

'Petition from the parish of Pershore', n.d. *B.M. Collection 816 m16 no. 43.*

Bateman, J. *The General Turnpike Road Act*... (London, 1822).

Bourn, Daniel, *A Treatise upon Wheel Carriages:*... (London, 1763).

Coote, R. H. *A Treatise on the Law of Mortgage* (London, 1821).

Defoe, Daniel, *An Essay upon Projects* (London, 1697).

A Tour through the Whole Island of Great Britain, Vols. I and II (London, 1962).

Edgeworth, Richard L. *An Essay on the Construction of Roads and Carriages* (London, 1813).

Gentlemen's Magazine, 1749.

Hardy, W. J. (ed.) *Hertford County Records, Notes and Extracts from the Sessions Rolls, 1581-1698,* Vol. I (Hertford, 1905).

Hardy, William Le (ed.) *Hertford County Records. Calendar to the Sessions Books, Sessions Minute Book and other Sessions Records, 1619-1657,* Vol. V (Hertford, 1928).

Hertford County Records, Calendar to the Sessions Books, Sessions Minute Book and other Sessions Records, 1658-1700, Vol. VI (Hertford, 1930).

Hertford County Records. Calendar of the Sessions Books, Sessions Minute Books and other Sessions Records, 1700–1752, Vol. II (Hertford, 1931).

County of Buckingham Calendar of the Sessions Records, Vol. I, 1678-1694 (Aylesbury, 1933).

Hardy, William Le and Reckett, G. (eds.) *County of Buckingham Calendar of the Sessions Records,* Vol. II, 1694-1705 (Aylesbury, 1936).

County of Buckingham Calendar of the Sessions Records, Vol. III, 1705-1712 (Aylesbury, 1939).

Homer, Rev. Henry, *An Enquiry into the Means of Preserving and Improving the Public Roads of this Kingdom* (London, 1767).

James, John, *The History and Topography of Bradford . . .* (London, 1841).

Latimer, John, *The Annals of Bristol in the Eighteenth Century* (Bristol, 1893).

Littleton, E. *Proposal for Maintenance and Repair of the Highways* (London, 1692).

McAdam, J. L. *A Practical Essay on the Scientific Repair and Preservation of Public Roads* (London, 1819).

Remarks on the Present System of Roadmaking . . . (7th ed. London, 1823).

Observations on the Management of Trusts for the care of Turnpike Roads, as regards the Repair of the Road, the expenditure of the Revenue, and the appointment and Quality of Executive Officers, . . . (London, 1825).

Mace, Thomas, *Profit, Conveniency and Pleasure to the Whole Nation . . .* (London, 1675).

Marshall, J. D. (ed.) *The Autobiography of William Stout of Lancaster 1665-1752* (Manchester, 1967).

Mather, William, *Of Repairing and Mending the Highways* (London, 1696).

Metcalf, John, *The Life of John Metcalf, commonly called Blind Jack of Knaresborough . . .* (York, 1795).

Mogg, Edward, *Paterson's Roads; . . .* (18th edition, London, 1831-2?).

Morris, Christopher (ed.) *The Journeys of Celia Fiennes* (London, 1947).

Parnell, Sir Henry, *A Treatise on Roads* (2nd ed. London, 1838).

Philip, R. K. *The Progress of Carriages, Roads and Water Conveyances . . .* (London, n.d.).

Phillips, R. *A Dissertation concerning the Present State of the High Roads of England . . .* (London, 1736/7).

Procter, Thomas, *A Profitable Worke to this Whole Kingdom, concerning the mending of all Highways . . .* (London, 1607).

Radcliffe, S. C. and Johnson, H. C. (eds.) *Warwick County Records Quarter Sessions Order Book Easter, 1650 to Epiphany, 1657,* Vol. III (Warwick, 1937).

Rusticum et Commerciale, Vol. II (London, 1766).

Scott, John, *Digests of the General Highway and Turnpike Laws . . .* (London, 1778).

Smith, Adam, *An Inquiry into the Nature and Causes of the Wealth of Nations,* ed. E. Cannon (New York, 1937).

Taylor, Rev. R. V. *The Biographia Leodiensis: or, Biographical Sketches of the Worthies of Leeds and Neighbourhood . . .* (London, 1865-67).

Telford, Thomas, *Life of Thomas Telford, Civil Engineer, written by himself . . . ,* ed. John Rickman (London, 1838).

Young, Arthur, *A Six Weeks Tour through the Southern Counties of England and Wales* (London, 1768).

General View of the Agriculture of the County of Norfolk (London, 1804).

General View of the Agriculture of Hertfordshire (London, 1804).

PARLIAMENTARY PAPERS

Journals of the House of Commons vols. i-l.

Journals of the House of Lords vol. xi.

Statutes of the Realm vols. 4-9.

Acts of Parliament 1713-1839

REPORTS AND ACCOUNTS (B.P.P.)

Report from the Committee appointed to inquire into the Management and Application of money collected within the last twelve years by virtue of any Act of Parliament for repairing any particular Highway. *1765 F.S. ii. 465.*

Report from the Committee on the General Turnpike Acts, 13th and 14th of his present Majesty. *1796 (April) F.S. x. 748.*

Further Report from the Committee on the General Turnpike Acts ... *1796 (May) F.S. x. 749.*

Report from the Committee on the General Turnpike Acts ... *1798 (April) F.S. x. 757.*

Further Report from the Committee on the General Turnpike Acts ... *1798 F.S. x. 758.*

Report from the Committee on the General Turnpike Acts ... *1800 F.S. x. 759.*

First Report from the Committee on Acts regarding the use of Broad Wheels, and other matters relating to the Preservation of the Turnpike Roads and Highways of the Kingdom. *1806 (212) ii. 241.*

Second Report from the Committee on Acts regarding the use of Broad Wheels ... *1806 (321) ii. 249.*

Report from the Select Committee appointed to take into consideration the Standing Orders of the House respecting Turnpike Bills ... *1807 (41) iii. 131.*

First Report of the Select Committee appointed to take into Consideration the Acts now in force regarding the use of Broad Wheels, and to examine what shape is best calculated for ease of draught and the preservation of the Roads, also to suggest such additional regulations as may contribute to the preservation of the Turnpike Roads and Highways of the United Kingdom *1808 (225) ii. 333.*

Second Report ... *1808 (275) ii. 459.*

Third Report ... *1808 (315) ii. 527.*

Report from the Select Committee on Mail-Coach Exemptions. *1810-11 (212) iii. 707.*

Report of the Committee appointed to take into Consideration the Acts now in force, regarding the Highways and Turnpike Roads in England and Wales; and the Expediency of additional regulations as to the better repair and preservation thereof ... *1810-11 (240) iii. 855.*

Report from the Select Committee on the Highways of the Kingdom ... *1819 (509) v. 339.*

Report from the Select Committee on the Turnpike Roads and Highways in England and Wales. *1820 (301) ii. 301.*

Report from the Select Committee appointed to consider the Acts now in force regarding Turnpike Roads and Highways in England and Wales. *1821 (747) iv. 343.*

Report from the Select Committee appointed to take into Consideration the Petition of Mr. McAdam ... *1823 (476) v. 53.*

Report from the Select Committee appointed to inquire into the practice which prevails in some parts of the Country, of paying the Wages of Labour out of the Poor Rates, ... *1824 (392) vi. 401.*

First Report of the Commissioners appointed under the Act of 4 Geo. IV c.74 for ... the further improvement of the Road from London to Holyhead. *1824 (305) ix. 293.*

Second Report ... *1825 (492) xv. 63.*

Third Report ... *1826 (129) xi. 47.*

Fourth Report ... *1826-27 (412) vii. 81.*

Fifth Report ... *1828 (476) ix. 227.*

Sixth Report ... *1829 (316) v. 103.*

Report from the Select Committee appointed to inquire into the Receipts, Expenditure and Management of the several Turnpike Trusts within ten miles of London, and to report their opinion and Observations thereupon to the House ... *1825 (355) v. 167.*

First Report of the Commissioners of the Metropolis Turnpike Roads north of the Thames appointed under the Act 7 Geo. IV. c.142; prepared in obedience to the 138th section of that Act. *1826-1827 (339) vii. 23.*

Report from the Select Committee on Turnpike Trusts Renewal Bills. *1826-1827 (383) vi. 1.*

Second Report of the Commissioners of the Metropolis Turnpike Roads north of the Thames. *1828 (311) ix. 23.*

Report from the Select Committee appointed to inquire into the State of the Roads under the Care of the Whetstone and St Albans Trustees, and to report their Observations thereupon to the House ... *1828 (546) iv. 255.*

Second Report from the Select Committee of the House of Lords appointed to Examine the Turnpike Returns ... *1833 (703) xv. 409.*

Report from the Select Committee appointed to consider the present system of Turnpike Tolls and Trusts, and matters relating to the Roads ... *1826-27 (383) vi. 1.*

Abstract of the Statements of the Income and Expenditure of the Turnpike Trusts in England and Wales, pursuant to Act 3 & 4 Wm. IV c.80 from 1 January 1834 to 31 December 1834. *1836 (2) xlvii. 297.*

Abstract of the Statements of the Income ... from 1 January 1835 to 31 December 1835. *1837 (328) li. 291.*

Abstract of the Statements of the Income ... from 1 January 1836 to 31 December 1836. *1838 (529) xlvi. 97.*

Abstract of the Statements of the Income ... from 1 January 1837 to 31 December 1837. *1839 (447) xliv. 299.*

Abstract of the Statements of the Income ... from 1 January 1838 to 31 December 1838. *1840 (289) xlv. 391.*

Report from the Select Committee appointed for the purpose of ascertaining how far the formation of Railroads may affect the interest of Turnpike Trusts, and the Creditors of such Trusts ... *1839 (295) ix. 369.*

Report of the Commissioners for inquiring into the State of the Roads in England and Wales. *1840 (256) xxvii. 1.*

Appendix to the Report of the Commissioners for inquiring into the State of the Roads in England and Wales. *1840 (280) xxvii. 15.*

General Report of the Secretary of State under Act 3 & 4 Wm. IV c.80. *1851 (18) xlviii.*

County Reports of the Secretary of State under the Act 3 & 4 Wm. IV. c.80. *1851 (18) xlviii.*

Twenty-first General Report made by Direction of the Secretary of State under 3 & 4 Wm. IV. c.80. *1872 xviii. (5).*

MAPS

Smith's New Map of England . . . (London, 1806).

Ordnance Survey Maps, Quarter Inch Series, Sheet 12 (1960), Sheets 10, 13, 14, 15, 16, 17 (1962), Sheets 9, 11 (1964).

THESES

Clarke, C. A. A. 'The Turnpike Trusts of Islington and Marylebone from 1700 to 1825' (unpublished M.A. thesis, University of London, 1955).

Hunt, H. G. 'The Parliamentary Enclosure Movement in Leicestershire, 1730-1842' (unpublished Ph.D. thesis, University of London, 1955).

Martin, J. M. 'Some Social and Economic Changes in Rural Worcestershire, Staffordshire and Warwickshire 1785-1825' (unpublished Master of Commerce thesis, University of Birmingham, 1959).

Spiro, Robert H. Jr. 'John Loudon McAdam, Colossus of Roads' (unpublished Ph.D. thesis, University of Edinburgh, 1950).

Ward, J. R. 'Investment in Canals and House Building in England, 1760-1815' (unpublished D.Phil. thesis, Oxford, 1970).

SECONDARY SOURCES

Ashton, T. S. *The Industrial Revolution* (London, 1948).
  Economic Fluctuations in England 1700-1800 (Oxford 1959).
  An 18th Century Industrialist, Peter Stubs of Warrington, 1756-1806 (Manchester, 1961).
  An Economic History of England: the 18th Century (London, 1964).

Baily, F. A. 'The Minutes of the Trustees of the Turnpike Roads from Liverpool to Prescot, St Helens, Warrington and Ashton in Makerfield 1725-1789', *Transactions of the Historical Society of Lancashire and Cheshire,* Vols. 88 and 89.

Barker, T. C. 'The Beginnings of the Canal Age in the British Isles', in *Studies in the Industrial Revolution,* ed. L. S. Pressnell (London, 1960).

Barker, T. C. and Robbins, M. *A History of London Transport, Passenger Travel and the Development of the Metropolis* (London, 1963), Vol. I.

Cameron, R. 'Some Lessons of History for Developing Nations', *The American Economic Review,* LVII, no. 2 (1967).

Chambers, J. D. 'The Vale of Trent 1670-1800', *Economic History Review Supplement no. 3.*

Chambers, J. D. and Mingay, G. E. *The Agricultural Revolution, 1750-1880* (London, 1966).

Crofts, J. *Packhorse, Waggon and Post, Land Carriage and Communications under the Tudors and Stuarts* (London, 1967).

Crump, W. B. (ed.) *The Leeds Woollen Industry 1780-1820* (Leeds, 1931).

David, Paul, 'Transport Innovation and Economic Growth: Professor Fogel on and off the Rails', *Ec. Hist. Rev.*, XXII, no. 3 (1969).

Dickson, P. G. M. *The Financial Revolution in England. A Study in the Development of Public Credit 1688-1756* (London, 1967).

DuBois, A. B. *The English Business Company after the Bubble Act, 1720-1800* (New York, 1938).

Emmison, F. G. 'The Earliest Turnpike Bill (Biggleswade to Baldock Road), 1622, *Bulletin of the Institute of Historical Research*, Vol. XII (1934-5).

Enke, Stephen, *Economics for Development* (New Jersey, 1963).

Evans, G. H. *British Corporation Finance, 1775-1850, A Study of Preference Shares* (Baltimore, 1936).

Fell, Alfred, *The Early Iron Industry of Furness and District . . .* (Ulverston, 1908).

Finer, S. E. *The Life and Times of Edwin Chadwick* (London, 1952).

Fishlow, A. *American Railroads and the Transformation of the Ante-Bellum Economy* (Cambridge, Mass., 1965).

Flinn, M. W. 'The Poor Employment Act of 1817', *Econ. Hist. Rev.* 2nd Series, Vol. XIV, no. 1 (1961).

The Origins of the Industrial Revolution (London, 1966).

Fogel, R. W. *Railroads and American Economic Growth: Essays in Econometric History* (Baltimore, 1964).

Gay, Edwin, 'Arthur Young on English Roads', *The Quarterly Journal of Economics*, Vol. XLI (1927).

Gayer, A. D., Rostow, W. W., Schwartz, A. J. *The Growth and Fluctuations of the British Economy 1790-1850*, Vol. I (Oxford, 1953).

Gibb, Alexander, *The Story of Telford: the Rise of Civil Engineering* (London, 1935).

Gilboy, Elizabeth W. *Wages in Eighteenth Century England* (Cambridge, Mass., 1934).

Grigg, David, *The Agricultural Revolution in South Lincolnshire* (Cambridge, 1966).

Hadfield, Charles, *British Canals, An Illustrated History* (London, 1959).

The Canals of Southern England (London, 1955).

The Canals of the East Midlands (Newton Abbott, 1966).

Hartwell, R. M. 'The Causes of the Industrial Revolution. An Essay in Methodology', *Econ. Hist. Rev.* 2nd series, Vol. XVIII, no. 1 (1965).

Hughes, Mervyn, 'Telford, Parnell, and the Great Irish Road', *Journal of Transport History*, Vol. VI, no. 4 (1964).

Hunt, H. G. 'The Chronology of Parliamentary Enclosure in Leicestershire', *Econ. Hist. Rev.* 2nd series, Vol. X, no. 2 (1957).

Jackman, W. T. *The Development of Transportation in Modern England* (2nd ed. London, 1962).

John, A. H. 'The Course of Agricultural Change 1660–1760', in *Studies in the Industrial Revolution*, ed. L. S. Pressnell (London, 1960).

'Aspects of English Economic Growth in the First Half of the Eighteenth

Century', *Essays in Economic History*, Vol. II, ed. E. M. Carus-Wilson (London, 1962).

'Agricultural Productivity and Economic Growth in England, 1700-1760', *Journal of Economic History*, Vol. XXV, no. 1 (1965).

'Miles Nightingale—Drysalter, A Study in Eighteenth-Century Trade', *Econ. Hist. Rev.* 2nd series, Vol. XVIII, no. 1 (1965).

Johnson, B. C. L. 'The Charcoal Iron Industry in the Early Eighteenth Century', *The Geographical Journal*, Vol. CVXIII, Part 2 (1951).

Jones, E. L. 'The Agricultural Labour Market in England, 1793-1872', *Econ. Hist. Rev.* 2nd series, Vol. XVII, no. 2 (1964).

Lansberry, H. C. F. 'James McAdam and the St Albans Turnpike Trust', *Journal of Transport History*, Vol. VII, no. 2 (1965).

Lewis, R. A. 'Transport for Eighteenth Century Ironworks', *Economica* (n.s.), Vol. XVIII (1951).

MacMahon, K. A. 'Roads and Turnpike Trusts in Eastern Yorkshire', *East Yorkshire Local History Series*, no. 18 (1964).

Mathias, P. *The First Industrial Nation* (London, 1969).

McKean, R. N. *Efficiency in Government through Systems Analysis* (New York, 1958).

McKendrick, N. 'Josiah Wedgwood: An Eighteenth Century Entrepreneur in Salesmanship and Marketing Techniques', in *Essays in Economic History*, Vol. III, ed. E. M. Carus-Wilson (London, 1962).

Milne, A. M. and Laight, J. C. *The Economics of Inland Transport*, 2nd ed. (London, 1965).

Mingay, G. E. 'The Agricultural Depression, 1730-1750', in *Essays in Economic History*, Vol. II, ed. E. M. Carus-Wilson (London, 1962).

English Landed Society in the Eighteenth Century (London, 1963).

Owen, W. 'Transportation and Economic Development', *The American Economic Review*, XLIX, no. 2 (1959).

Page, William (ed.) *The Victoria History of the County of Lincoln*, Vol. II (London, 1906).

Payne, Peter L. 'The Bermondsey, Rotherhithe and Deptford Turnpike 1776-1810', *Journal of Transport History*, Vol. II, no. 3 (1956).

Pollard, Sidney, 'Investment, Consumption and the Industrial Revolution', *Econ. Hist. Rev.* 2nd series, Vol. XI, no. 2 (1958).

The Genesis of Modern Management. A Study of the Industrial Revolution in Great Britain (London, 1965).

Poston, M. M. 'Recent Trends in the Accumulation of Capital', *Econ Hist. Rev.* Vol. VI, no. 1 (1935).

Pressnell, L. S. *Country Banking in the Industrial Revolution* (Oxford, 1956).

'The Rate of Interest in the Eighteenth Century', in *Studies in the Industrial Revolution*, ed. L. S. Pressnell (London, 1960).

Prest, A. R. *Transport Economics in Developing Countries, Pricing and Financing Aspects* (London, 1969).

Prest, A. R. and Turvey, R. 'Cost-Benefit Analysis: A Survey', *Surveys of Economic Theory*, III (1966).

Rogers, J. E. T. *A History of Agriculture and Prices in England*, Vols. VI and VII (Oxford, 1902).

Rostow, W. W. *The Stages of Economic Growth* (Cambridge, 1967).

Rostow, W. W. (ed.) *The Economics of Take-off into Sustained Growth* (London, 1963).

Searle, Mark, *Turnpike and Tollbars* (London, 1930).

Shannon, H. A. 'Bricks—a Trade Index, 1785-1849', in *Essays in Economic History*, Vol. III, ed. E. M. Carus-Wilson (London, 1962).

Spiro, Robert H. Jr. 'John Loudon McAdam in Somerset and Dorset', *Notes and Queries for Somerset and Dorset*, Vol. XXVII, Part CCLXII, no. 64 (1956).

Supple, B. 'Has the Early History of Developed Countries any Current Relevance?', *The American Economic Review*, LV, no. 2 (1965).

'Economic History and Economic Underdevelopment', *Canadian Journal of Economic and Political Science* (1961).

Unwin, George, *Samuel Oldknow and the Arkwrights . . .* (Manchester, 1924).

Unwin, R. W. 'The Aire and Calder Navigation, Part I: The Beginning of the Navigation', *Bradford Antiquary*, N.S. XLII (1964).

'The Aire and Calder Navigation, Part II: The Navigation in the pre-canal age', *Bradford Antiquary*, N.S. XLIII (1967).

Wadsworth, A. P. and J. de L. Mann, *The Cotton Trade and Industrial Lancashire, 1600-1780* (Manchester, 1931).

Webb, Sidney and Beatrice, *English Local Government: The Story of the King's Highway* (London, 1913).

English Local Government: Statutory Authorities for Special Purposes (London, 1922).

Westerfield, R. B. 'Middlemen in English Business, particularly between 1660 and 1760', *Transactions of the Connecticut Academy of Arts and Sciences*, Vol. XIX (1915).

Williams, O. C. *The Historical Development of Private Bill Procedure and Standing Orders in the House of Commons* (London, 1948).

Williams, David, *The Rebecca Riots, A Study in Agrarian Discontent* (Cardiff 1955).

Willan, T. S. *An Eighteenth-century Shopkeeper Abraham Dent of Kirkby Stephen* (Manchester, 1970).

River Navigation in England, 1600-1750 (London, 1936).

'The River Navigation and Trade of the Severn Valley, 1600-1750', *Econ. Hist. Rev.*, Vol. VIII, no. 1 (1937-8).

English Coasting Trade, 1600-1750 (Manchester, 1938).

'The Justices of the Peace and the Rates of Land Carriage, 1692-1827', *Journal of Transport History*, Vol. V, no. 4 (1962).

Wilson, R. G. 'Transport Dues as Indices of Economic Growth, 1775-1820', *Econ. Hist. Rev.* 2nd Series, Vol. XIX, no. 1 (1966).

Gentlemen Merchants. The merchant community in Leeds, 1700-1830 (Manchester, 1971).

Wood, A. C. 'The History of Trade and Transport on the River Trent', *Thoroton Society Transactions*, Vol. LIV (1950).

Youngson, A. J. *Overhead Capital. A Study in Development Economics* (Edinburgh, 1967).

General Index

accounts: of all trusts, made to Parliament (1821), 89; (1837), 89
administration of trusts, 59–92
agriculture: importance of transport improvement for, 9–10; investment in, 116; improving conditions in, 51–125; *see also* enclosure; landowners
Aire and Calder navigation, 12, 48; opposition to turnpikes by, 25
Alconbury, 33, 137
American War, conditions during, 129, 131
'Angular Road', 138
Argyll, Duchess of, trust loan by, 105
Arkwright and Co. (bank), 77
Ashby-de-la-Zouch, 115
Asheton, Sir Ralph, trust loans by, 99–100, 111, 128
Ashton, T. S., 4, 10, 30, 120–1, 130
assessments of rates of land carriage, 168–87
Austerlands, road to Manchester, 47
Avon, river, 11

backward linkages, 191–2
Bailey, Charles, 80
bakers, as trust investors, 101–2, 111
Bakewell, *see* Chesterfield
Baldock, road to Biggleswade, 17
bankers: as trust investors, 107–80; as trust treasurers, 75–7
banks, growth of county banks, 130
Barlow, Robert (banker), 77
Barnet, 33; road to South Mimms, 36
Barnet Hill, 147
Barnsley, 47
Barret, Richard (surveyor), 80
Barrowstowness Canal, provision in act regarding loan repayment, 95
Bartholomew, Leonard, trust loan by, 99
Basingstoke, 44
Bath: early trust (1707) in, 44; letter (1727) on land carriage rates, 173; road to Chippenham, 37
Bawtry, *see* Doncaster; road to Little Drayton, 34
Beaconsfield, road to Uxbridge, 36–7
Beard, Thomas (landowner), 106
Beauchamp, Lord, trust loans by, 105, 109
Beckett, Blayds and Co. (bankers), 75–6; trust loans by, 107
Bedfordshire: trust surveyor in, 80; wages

(labourers') paid in 1822, 165; financial condition of trusts in, 234, 238
Berkeley, *see* Gloucester
Berkshire, financial condition of trusts in, 234, 238
Berwick-upon-Tweed, 33
Beverley, banks in, 76
Bewdley, 106; *see also* Coalbrookdale
Bexley Heath, 155
Biggleswade, 33; 1609, bill to repair highways in, 17; *see also* Baldock
Billinghay, 103
bills of credit, issued by trusts, 99, 128; *see also* 'turnpike bills'
Bilston, 47
Birdlip Hill, *see* Gloucester; road to Cirencester, 36
Birmingham, 37, 40, 103, 107, 171, 196; roads to Warwick, Warmington, London, 39; roads to Wednesbury, Meriden, 38; rates of interest paid by trusts in, 129; rising price of land carriage from, 183; *see also* Bromsgrove, Buckingham, Warrington, Warwick
Birmingham canal, dividends paid by, 194
Bishop's Stortford, 19
Blackburn, 54
Blackheath: Dartford Road, 41; *see also* Southwark
Blackstone Edge, *see* Rochdale
Blandford, Aaron (surveyor), 80
Blayds, John (banker), 107; trust loans by, 75–6, 107
Blayds, Thomas (banker), 75
Board of Agriculture, 142, 144–5
Bobart, Tillman (repair contractor), 154
Bolton, 54; bankers in, 77
bonds, issued by trusts, 93–4, 109
Boorman, John (banker), trust loan by, 108
Boroughbridge: roads to Piercebridge, Durham, 34; *see also* Doncaster, York
borrowing, reasons for, 93
Boston, 103; special land carriage rate assessments, 175
Boughton-under-Blean, *see* Chatham
Bourn, Daniel, 8
Bourne, John (land agent), 102–3
Bousher, William (surveyor), 154
Bower, Joshua (toll lessee), 86
Bowes, Hutton and Co. (bank), 76

INDEX OF TRUSTS